MW01001541

Demanding the Cherokee Nation

Indians of the Southeast

ANDREW DENSON

Demanding the Cherokee Nation

Indian Autonomy and American Culture 1830–1900

University of Nebraska Press

Lincoln and London

Portions of chapter 4 originally appeared in "'Unite with Us to Rescue the Kiowas': The Five Civilized Tribes and Warfare on the Southern Plains," *Chronicles of Oklahoma* 81: 458–79. Copyright by Oklahoma Historical Society. Reprinted by permission.

An earlier version of chapter 5 appeared as "Muskogee's Indian International Fairs: Tribal Autonomy and the Indian Image," *Western Historical Quarterly* 34 (Autumn 2003): 325–45. Copyright by Western History Association. Reprinted by permission.

Set in Adobe Minion by Kim Essman. Designed by Richard Eckersley. Printed by Thomson-Shore, Inc.

Library of Congress Cataloging-in-Publication Data
Denson, Andrew.
Demanding the Cherokee Nation : Indian autonomy and American culture, 1830–1900 / Andrew Denson
p. cm. (Indians of the Southeast)
Includes bibliographical references and index.
ISBN 0-8032-1726-9 (cloth : alkaline paper)   1. Cherokee Nation – History – 19th century.   2. Cherokee Indians – Government relations.   3. Cherokee Indians – Politics and government.   4. Self-determination, National – United States.   5. United States – Social conditions –19th century.   6. United States – Politics and government – 19th century.   I. Title.   II. Series.
E99.C5D46 2004   323.1197'557–DC22   2004014196

For my mother and father. Thanks.

CONTENTS

SERIES EDITORS' PREFACE

Andrew Denson's study, based largely on Cherokee memorials to Congress, presents the Cherokee Nation's conception of United States Indian policy in the nineteenth century. The Cherokees recognized that while their sovereignty predated the United States, it also depended on United States policy, so they devised a plan whereby the Cherokees could retain political sovereignty while furthering the pacification and acculturation goals of U.S. policy makers. We do not normally think of "intellectual history" encompassing Indians, but Denson has taken Cherokee arguments seriously, interpreted them as a systematic philosophy of government, and presented them as a viable alternative to the destructive policy of allotment and de-tribalization that the United States ultimately adopted. As he notes in his introduction, he is the first scholar to pay serious attention to the Cherokee position on Reconstruction, economic development, territorialization, and allotment, except as resistance, and in the process he reveals a level of political sophistication that no other scholar has attributed to Native peoples, not even the Cherokees. He admirably contextualizes Cherokee political philosophy, placing it in the broader history of an industrializing America obsessed with political corruption. And he examines its expression in two very different but ultimately connected events, the Okmulgee Council and the International Indian Fairs. Carefully argued and beautifully written, this study is a welcome addition to "Indians of the Southeast."

Theda Perdue
Michael Green

ACKNOWLEDGMENTS

Many people helped with this project. First and foremost, I want to thank R. David Edmunds for guiding the dissertation and for advice and help throughout my graduate school years and after (and for all those letters of recommendation). Raymond J. DeMallie, Jeffrey Gould, and Steven Stowe offered useful criticism as members of my dissertation committee. Frederick Hoxie, Loretta Fowler, John Mack Faragher, and Mary Young read and commented on portions of this book in the context of conference panels. Frederick Hoxie also commented on several chapters independently. Theda Perdue kept urging me to submit the manuscript, and when I finally did she gave it a fine reading and offered many useful suggestions. The anonymous reader for the press likewise suggested valuable improvements. Thanks to the good people at the *Western Historical Quarterly* and *Chronicles of Oklahoma* for publishing bits and pieces of this book before it was a book (and then letting me use the bits and pieces again).

Several archivists provided invaluable assistance. Sarah Erwin at the Gilcrease Museum spent a great deal of time helping me troll through the Hargrett Collection and made the Indian International Fair chapter possible by leading me to Grant Foreman's file on the event. William Welge at the Oklahoma Historical Society guided me through the sometimes confusing Indian Archives and always found a microfilm reader for me, even when the basement of the Wiley Post Building was four-deep in genealogists. Thanks also to the staff of the Western History Collection at the University of Oklahoma, Norman; Thomas Mooney of the Cherokee Heritage Center, Tahlequah, Oklahoma; and the staff of the Indiana University government documents division.

Kelly Larson and the girls gave much-needed encouragement and support as I tried to put together some kind of academic career. My students in Indianapolis gave me reasons to keep trying.

Demanding the Cherokee Nation

A Cherokee Literature of Indian Nationhood

The future had looked grim for the Cherokees in early 1870 as Congress began a new session. That, at least, was the recollection of William Penn Adair, Cherokee lawyer, politician, and diplomat. Adair spent much of 1870 in Washington working as a tribal delegate, one of five official representatives sent east that year from the Indian Territory (what is today eastern Oklahoma) by the Cherokee government.[1] In September he wrote a detailed account of his activities in the form of an open letter, printed as a pamphlet, to the Cherokee people. He recalled that when he and his fellow delegates had arrived in Washington in January, they had found the Cherokees' interests – and Indian affairs generally – in a terrible state. "Not only were the rights of the Cherokees and other Indians in great uncertainty," he explained, "but the Indian race itself was seriously threatened."

Members of Congress wanted to abolish the practice of making treaties with Indian tribes, this at a time when the Cherokees were trying to win approval for a new agreement. Some insisted that the Fourteenth Amendment, ratified a year and a half earlier, had given the Indians citizenship in the United States and that the tribes fell within state and federal jurisdiction rather than that of their own laws as a result. Railroad corporations building lines through the Indian Territory pushed Congress to grant them vast tracts of tribal land in obvious violation of the treaties. And most dangerous from the Cherokees' point of view, there was a developing campaign to reorganize the Indian Territory to make it a full possession of the United States. That action would involve the dismantling of the tribal governments, the extension of American law, and the opening of the territory to American settlement. All told, the advocates of these various measures amounted to what Adair called "the most formidable opposition to the Indians ever heretofore arrayed."[2]

Yet all was not lost, Adair explained. He and the other representatives found that many in Washington were in fact sympathetic to the Indians and wanted to behave properly toward them. American authorities were simply misinformed about the treaties and the Indians' needs and desires. That was a situation that the delegates could rectify. As Adair reported in his letter: "In order to enlighten this friendly influence on the Indian question, so that we might secure its valuable aid in our behalf, (which I am happy to say we did,) our delegation spread broadcast before all branches of the Government and before the people, memorials and documents, which in turn were taken up by the press. We also visited the cities of New York and Baltimore, and delivered addresses before the people, which were kindly noticed by the press."[3] The delegates, in other words, lobbied Congress and the president and mounted a public-relations campaign in favor of maintaining the existing state of Indian affairs. They corrected the opinions of well-meaning whites and by doing so "defeated the many schemes used by our opponents to destroy our existence" – at least for the time being. "The storm that threatened the Indians [during the] last session of Congress has been diverted," Adair concluded, "yet it may probably return again at the next session with increased fury."[4]

This is a study of the "memorials and documents" broadcast by Cherokees like Adair in the nineteenth century, an analysis of the public statements that tribal spokesmen produced in their efforts to persuade the "friendly influence" in America. I take up a series of political issues, beginning with the removal crisis of the 1820s and 1830s but emphasizing the period after the Trail of Tears. For each case, I describe the formal messages that tribal leaders directed at the American government and public, explaining what chiefs and delegates said to non-Indians about the Cherokee Nation, Indian people, and American

Indian affairs. Cherokee leaders produced a great number of these messages over the course of the century. Each year they presented formal appeals and petitions to Congress and the president. They circulated pamphlets among their allies in the United States and made speeches in American cities. They published letters and editorials in Indian and American newspapers. Some of these documents were little more than brief statements responding to a particular American policy initiative, but others were detailed discussions of Cherokee history and the tribe's dealings with the United States. Still others were extended and often quite cogent analyses not only of Cherokee affairs but of Indian relations in general. Taken together, these statements amount to a Native American political literature, a decades-long Cherokee commentary on the "Indian question."

The purpose of this literature was the defense of Indian nationhood. Cherokees produced the writings I examine as part of the long struggle to preserve their independent tribal government and the barriers between themselves and non-Indian America. Between 1810 and 1830, in one of the more famous episodes in Native American history, the Cherokees remade themselves politically, founding a constitutional republic fashioned after the United States. For the rest of the century, they defended that status against consistent and intensifying attacks by American authorities and an expanding non-Indian population. Beginning with the removal policy, which eventually sent most of the tribe to the Indian Territory, a long series of American actions undermined and finally nullified Cherokee political autonomy. There were efforts to divide the Cherokee Nation in the 1840s; hostile policies connected to the Civil War and Reconstruction; the arrival of American corporations; the campaign to make Oklahoma a United States territory; and finally the formulation and triumph of the allotment policy at the close of the century. In working against these dangers, tribal leaders consistently claimed sovereign nationhood. Even as the United States government disregarded or openly assaulted Cherokee sovereignty, and as the Cherokee country became encapsulated by non-Indian settlement and colonized by American corporations, Cherokee leaders produced formal arguments insisting that their people were citizens of a separate nation and that this was a status that Americans were bound to respect.

Historians of the Cherokees have amply recounted the struggle for sovereignty; however, they have made poor use of the Cherokees' petitions and appeals.[5] Most cite a handful of these documents, with scholars drawing from the memorials examples of tribal leaders' eloquence and evidence of Cherokee opposition to federal initiatives. But few pause to study them in any detail, and the exceptions to the rule focus on a limited period of time, namely the removal era.[6] That neglect is understandable. The memorials did not stop removal in the 1830s or prevent the dismantling of the Cherokee Nation at century's end. Too few Americans paid attention to Cherokee leaders for the writings to have had their intended effect. If one's goal is to examine how and why the nineteenth-century Cherokee Nation fell, the public messages are not terribly helpful. By the same token, the writings offer little in the way of reliable social and cultural information about the Cherokees. Tribal leaders frequently described their people in the memorials, but they created selective, idealized, and at times simply inaccurate pictures designed to support their political positions. The writings are quite barren when it comes to social history.

Yet if the memorials say little about the Cherokees, they deserve attention as a record of what certain Cherokees said. The petitions and appeals represent a Native American contribution to the nineteenth-century debates over Indian affairs. Cherokee leaders closely followed those debates and entered them, forming their own ideas of what constituted proper relations. While their arguments ultimately went unheeded, they belong in our histories of the Indian question no less than do the positions of federal officials and eastern philanthropists (many of whom, after all, knew much less about Indian affairs than did tribal leaders). The historical literature on Indian policy and on Americans' long conversation about the nature and fate of Indian people focuses almost exclusively on what whites had to say. But Cherokees (and members of other tribes, I suspect) analyzed Indian policy for themselves and participated in that conversation. Their petitions and appeals provide an opportunity to return one set of Indian voices to its rightful place.

In addition, the Cherokee memorials, since they deal with nationhood, invite one to explore an important paradox in Native American history – the contradiction between the sovereignty of Indian nations and the political weakness of Indian peoples. This is one of the central issues in the history of American Indian affairs.[7] The United States both recognized Native American peoples as autonomous communities enjoying an existence that predated the republic and identified them as dependent subjects of the federal government. The continent, by right, belonged to the United States, but Native Americans possessed rights as its original occupants. The Indian question in the nineteenth century often amounted to the problem of how to resolve that contradiction. To put it more accurately, how was the United States to gain possession of the continent without resorting to naked conquest and fraud? By the 1890s the answer that American policy makers and "friends of the Indian" had formulated was to eliminate the sovereignty side of the paradox. According to this view, Indian people were not citizens of separate nations but wards of the federal government. The United States's duty toward them was to break up the tribes and draw their members as individuals into the American population. The rights of Native Americans were reduced to the right to be protected and educated by non-Indian guardians until they were ready to merge with the broader populace. This was the solution enshrined in the allotment policy and assimilation campaign.[8]

Cherokee leaders understood their people's contradictory position. They recognized that the survival of the Cherokee Nation required the cooperation of the United States – a situation that can hardly be said to have represented full sovereignty. But they rejected for their people the role of government wards. Even as American policy reduced them to the status of federal stepchildren, Cherokee leaders labored to convince white Americans that there could be a better answer to the Indian question. Their writings on nationhood document an effort to find an alternative to wardship as the basis for Indian-American relations.

Finally, the memorials are fascinating as the product of a Cherokee analysis of non-Indian America. In demanding the nation, Cherokees not only reminded their neighbors of tribal rights and treaty promises but tried to explain to them that the Indian nation was compatible with an expanding modern United States. Most of their audience assumed that American development and progress necessitated the end of tribal autonomy. At best, the Indian nation was a transitional state, a stopover for Native people on the way to assimilation. Tribal leaders, however, found a variety of ways in which Indian autonomy, as they defined it, belonged in the world that Americans were creating. In particular, they found new reasons for Indian nationhood in the industrialization of the American economy. While many in the United States saw the Indian nation as a doomed relic, Cherokee leaders were able to imagine a modern future for it. Some, in fact, suggested that the nation was the *key* to modernity for Native people, the thing that would allow Indians to reap the benefits of the late nineteenth century's tumultuous change while protecting them from its perils. Anything but an anachronism, the nation would make it possible for Cherokees and other Native people to participate in modern life, because it would give them the power to choose the terms of their participation.

One way to read this book is as a study of resistance, one of the central topics of the literature on the Native American past. The memorials, after all, were meant to keep the government and people of the United States at bay. They reflect a century of opposition to federal policy and American expansion. But the writings also form a record of Cherokee *engagement* with non-Indian America, and this, I think, is their more interesting and vital aspect. As a matter of political survival, tribal leaders continually observed and listened to Americans. They scrutinized their powerful neighbors' politics and culture for arguments in favor of Indian nationhood. They not only opposed American initiatives but attempted to make policy, to imagine a more acceptable version of American Indian affairs. Resistance, in this case, involved an ongoing process of interpretation of the people and forces opposed. It is that process, and not simply resistance in and of itself, that I want to examine.

I begin with a review of Cherokee removal. Historians have explained the policy and the Cherokees' response many times, so I do not attempt an exhaustive account here. In fighting removal, however, tribal leaders adopted some of the basic themes that, in one form or another, would recur in Cherokee writings throughout the rest of the century. In the first chapter I identify those themes and then discuss continuity and change in Cherokee political language between the 1830s and the years immediately following the Trail of Tears. The study then jumps forward to examine several issues in the post – Civil War period: the Reconstruction process in the Indian Territory, in which Cherokee leaders worked to reestablish their people as a sovereign nation; the rise and fall of the "peace policy," now a mostly forgotten initiative, but a policy that loomed large in the thinking of Cherokee leaders; and the penetration of the Indian Territory by American railroads, a source of much anxiety in the 1870s and 1880s and a topic that inspired some of the most interesting Cherokee writing. Along the way, there are chapters on the General Council of the Indian Territory and the Indian International Fair, institutions through which (as I argue) Cherokees and other Native people acted out their conceptions of proper Indian relations. The book concludes with a chapter on allotment – its rise to become the dominant Indian policy, and the Cherokees' effort to find an alternative to it. Together, these cases allow me to describe Cherokee messages to America over a long period of time and in a number of different contexts.

At various points in these chapters, my focus shifts from the Cherokee Nation to developments in the United States that were not directly related to Indian affairs. I use elements of American studies literature on modernization to draw connections between Cherokee political language and broader issues in nineteenth-century American culture. In particular, these sections show the influence of scholars like Alan Trachtenberg, who explores the cultural rifts and anxieties brought by the rise of the modern corporation.[9] To some, these shifts may seem like digressions. My intent, however, is to examine the ways in which Cherokees' political discourse responded to the changes occurring within the culture of their audience. Moreover, making these connections allows

7

me to bring a set of Native American subjects and stories into several of the larger narratives of nineteenth-century United States history.

In addition to the American studies scholarship, the essays of several literary critics have influenced my analysis of the Cherokee writings. The work of Arnold Krupat encouraged me to look closely at the memorials in the first place. Krupat's "rhetorical reading" of several Cherokee documents from the removal era is one of the few works to examine tribal leaders' statements in depth. Krupat treats the Cherokee memorials as narratives amenable to the kind of analysis one might apply to a work of literature. He does the same, meanwhile, with pro-removal documents, including the Indian Removal Act of 1830. His descriptions establish a comparison of the stories told on either side of the debate. The pro-removal statements, he argues, displayed a tragic narrative of Indian decline, one similar to the tales told in popular antebellum novels about Indians. For the tragedy to be complete, however, the Indians themselves had to accept their fate and agree to move beyond the frontier. In the Cherokee memorials, tribal leaders refused to embrace the inevitability of their decline and migration and in so doing created what Krupat labels an "ironic counternarrative" in which Indians were the victims of white oppression rather than sufferers of a tragic but unavoidable doom.[10] My first chapter echoes Krupat's argument at several points. More important, the study as a whole reflects the idea that one may examine Cherokee memorials as a kind of literature. This is a work of history rather than literary criticism, but like Krupat's essay it concerns the stories told in Cherokee political writings.

Another influence from literary criticism requires a somewhat more detailed explanation. In thinking about the Cherokee memorials, I have found the essays of Homi K. Bhabha, the critic and theorist working within the field of postcolonial studies, quite useful.[11] Bhabha writes about British India rather than the Indians of America, so the specific events and texts he cites are well outside the scope of my research. His broader concern, however, is the "discourse of colonialism," the language with which Europeans theorized and explained their power over colonized peoples. In exploring that more general topic, Bhabha

8

offers a model applicable to the history of colonialism and conquest in the United States.

The central idea of much of Bhabha's work is what he calls the "ambivalence of colonial discourse."[12] Bhabha identifies a crucial contradiction in the language and literature of European colonialism. As I read his work, this is fundamentally a contradiction between universality and differentiation. Bhabha notes that in creating colonies, Europeans simultaneously claimed an affinity with the "natives" and defined them as different and inferior. On the one hand, colonial powers invoked universal concepts in legitimizing their rule – concepts such as civilization, enlightenment, and true religion. Colonizers explained their authority in terms of a mission to bring progress and the knowledge of God to the natives, a mission that implied a basic commonality between the colonizer and the colonized. The natives may have been "primitive," but they were joined with the colonizer in a single evolutionary process, at the end of which was a common civilization. Not surprisingly, Bhabha argues that by grounding their authority in those universals, Europeans effaced the disruption, violence, and sheer messiness of their intrusion into other people's worlds. He refers to this phenomenon as colonialism's "strategy of disavowal."[13]

On the other hand, colonial rule – the exercise of colonial power – demanded not the recognition of commonality but an insistence on difference. Colonialism by nature involved discrimination between Europeans and non-Europeans. Colonizers defined natives as subjects and Europeans as masters, and part of that mastery was the power to make the definitions. That impulse to differentiate between natives and newcomers was fundamentally at odds with the universal principles with which Europeans explained their colonial presence. Bhabha suggests that while ideas like the civilization mission served to mute awareness of this basic contradiction, they could never truly resolve it. Colonialism, then, was at its source ambivalent.

Bhabha identifies a number of consequences of this ambivalence, but for my purposes his most useful insight is that the contradictory nature of colonial discourse rendered efforts to obscure the violence

and chaos of European conquest impossible. The necessity of differ-
entiating between Europeans and natives in colonial power relations
meant that a strategy of disavowal could never fully succeed. The appeal to universal ideas of civilization and enlightenment could never
completely hide or explain away colonial oppression. As Bhabha sees
it, the exercise of colonial *power* contradicted the terms by which Europeans claimed colonial *authority*. It left that authority – at least on
the level of discourse – permanently incomplete and unstable.[14]

Cherokee representatives in the nineteenth century found themselves in a situation that corresponded to Bhabha's general model. As
numerous historians have noted, European Americans identified the
"civilization" of Indians as one of the purposes of their relations with
Native peoples. The absorption of Indians into the broader American
society and culture remained at least an official goal of policy makers throughout the century, whether one is speaking of Jeffersonian
philanthropists, peace-policy advocates after the Civil War, or the reformers who championed the assimilation campaign at the end of
the century. At the same time, that commitment to the civilization
process coexisted with the goal of gaining possession of Indian lands
free of Indians. That goal involved a willingness to define people like
the Cherokees as Others. Indians were inferior people who could be
managed and dispossessed if such actions would further the development of non-Indian America. White authorities imagined ways of
resolving that contradiction – by arguing, for example, that as Indians
progressed they would need less territory, or that freeing tribes of "excess" land would help them improve. They could not, however, efface
the violence of expansion when they forced (or contemplated forcing)
policies like removal or allotment on the Cherokees. In the writings I
examine, Cherokees continually called attention to the contradictory
nature of American Indian policy. They picked apart American efforts
to disavow racism and oppression and insisted that if the Cherokees
were to be dispossessed of their government and property it would be
a crime and not the working out of some universal principle.

Strictly speaking, one does not need postcolonial theory to come to
that last point. Bhabha's model, however, has helped me understand the

ideas and arguments to which Cherokees responded in the memorials, and that in turn has aided my analysis of the Cherokees' own discourse. Bhabha's general idea of colonial ambivalence informs much of what I write in this study.

I have one last introductory task. Since delegates operating in Washington produced many of the writings that I examine, a brief description of the practice of sending those representatives is in order. The Cherokee National Council began to appoint official emissaries to the United States in the 1820s, as pressure mounted for the tribe to move west. These were Cherokee leaders, often members of the National Council itself, whose duty it was to watch over the federal government and to convey to American authorities Cherokee opposition to removal. While in the past, leaders had met with federal officials only when called, the growing threat of forced migration inspired them to send representatives to the capital whether they were invited or not.[15] Cherokees maintained the practice after the Trail of Tears, and by the post – Civil War era, appointing delegates had become a standard part of each year's business in the tribal government. In the council's late-autumn session, members would prepare a bill appointing two to five representatives and approving the funds necessary to support them in Washington. Once the legislation passed, council members would draft a second bill instructing the delegates. This act would contain a long list of issues that the representatives were expected to address. Bearing those instructions and council permission to draw upon the tribe's treaty money, the delegates would travel east, usually in late December.[16]

Delegates' activities varied, but in essence their job was to monitor the activities of the United States government. When Congress or the Interior Department acted in ways that the Cherokee government considered dangerous, the delegates interceded, composing the statements I examine in the chapters to follow. They were also expected to keep the principal chief and the tribal government apprised of conditions in the American capital. Reports back to the Cherokee Nation from Washington form a rich documentary resource in their own right. By the late nineteenth century, this business sometimes kept delegates in the East as long as an entire year, although generally they would return to the Indian Territory in the summer, when Congress recessed.

I should note that the delegates' formal statements often did not end up in the files upon which historians of nineteenth-century Native Americans most often rely – the records of the Indian Bureau. Some of the best collections of memorials are in the records of the House and Senate committees on Indian affairs and territories. The published federal serials also contain quite a few Cherokee petitions and appeals, particularly from the removal and Civil War eras. The Cherokee Nation papers housed at Oklahoma University's Western History Collection and the Oklahoma Historical Society contain memorials, as does the Gilcrease Museum's pamphlet collection. Finally, the Cherokees' national newspaper, the *Cherokee Advocate*, reprinted a great many of the delegations' formal statements, particularly in the latter part of the century. I have drawn heavily from all these collections, but less so from the traditional sources in the files of the Bureau of Indian Affairs.

When examining the delegates' writings, one should bear several things in mind. It is important, first of all, to remember that the views expressed in the documents were not necessarily those of the general Cherokee population. Since delegates received specific instructions from the elected tribal legislature, one may assume that their basic positions and goals were in accordance with the desires of the Cherokee majority. Specifically, when they asserted the right of the Cherokees to remain a nation, tribal leaders expressed a dominant view. But the ways in which they defined and defended the nation – the ideas and language that they employed – should not be taken to reflect all Cherokees' understandings of themselves and the United States. These writings were meant to persuade non-Indians. They appealed to European American ideas of politics and Indian affairs.

Moreover, the authors generally belonged to a Cherokee elite. Many were literate in English, formally educated, and members of the tribe's comparatively wealthy class of commercial farmers and businessmen. The quintessential example was John Ross, the Cherokees' principal chief from 1827 to 1866. The son and grandson of European American men, Ross spoke English as his first language, was educated by whites, and before entering politics gained experience with antebellum American commerce. Before removal he owned twenty slaves, who worked a landholding of several hundred acres, and he ran a ferry across the Coosa River.[17] William Penn Adair, whose report opened this introduction, had a university education and a successful law practice. In the 1850s he grew wealthy enough from his law work and farming to own at least ten slaves. He spoke Cherokee, but English was his primary language.[18] Their education and experience made Cherokees like Ross and Adair ideal representatives to non-Indian America, but they may have been isolated from some elements of Cherokee culture. Precontact religion, for example, would have informed many Cherokees' conceptions of the nation, but it seems not to have influenced most of the arguments that delegates presented in their memorials, addresses, and petitions. The writings I study represent tribal leaders' inventive effort to make Indian nationhood compatible with a modernizing United States. As I suggested earlier, however, they do not offer a particularly clear picture of nineteenth-century Cherokee culture or identity.

Finally, one should note that non-Cherokees participated in the writing of some of the memorials and petitions. The tribe sometimes hired European American lawyers to help the delegates with certain tasks. In particular, lawyers were employed to secure money that Cherokee leaders believed the United States owed the tribe under the treaties and to help the delegates negotiate sales of tribal land. These lawyers certainly influenced some of the delegates' writings. In addition, by the 1870s Cherokee representatives regularly combined their efforts in the capital with those of other tribal delegations. The Five Tribes (or Five Civilized Tribes) issued joint statements on matters concerning the Indian Territory as a whole.[19] Multi-tribal documents appear in this study only when they broadcast positions that Cherokee leaders also took independently. Those positions, however, were not purely of Cherokee design.

1

The Long and Intimate Connection

The story of Cherokee removal is well known, the tribe's losing battle to preserve its homeland having become one of the few Native American events now thought indispensable in recounting a broader American history.[1] To understand Cherokee political writing over the course of the nineteenth century, however, it is necessary to describe again the struggles of the Jacksonian era. The removal crisis was an education for Cherokees in American politics and in white America's "Indian question," and it set many of the basic terms for the Cherokees' relations the United States over the rest of the century. It was during the removal struggle that the Cherokees adopted the practice of sending frequent delegations to Washington to keep a watchful eye on federal authorities.[2] Along the same lines, the crisis forced Cherokee leaders to cultivate skills in lobbying and public relations. It compelled them to hire lawyers and to learn how to address government officials, newspaper editors, and "friends of the Indian." It showed them the necessity of constantly informing non-Indians of the Cherokees' rights and desires.[3] Finally, and most important for my purposes, in writing against removal Cherokees developed arguments and adopted language that would appear in varying forms in their communications to white America in the decades to come. While most historical writing on the Cherokees ends with the Trail of Tears, this era was only the beginning of the tribe's long conversation with the United States about the Indian nation.

When Cherokee leaders argued against removal, they insisted that their people had always formed a distinct autonomous community. Their nationhood predated the arrival of Europeans, a fact the newcomers had recognized. At the same time, Cherokees defined their nation in the early nineteenth century as the product of a partnership with white Americans. In the words of one memorial, it was the happy result of a "long and intimate conexion" between the Cherokees and their American neighbors.[4] This contrast captures well the challenge of preserving the Indian nation in the removal era and beyond. Cherokees had to defend their autonomy as an entitlement, while trying to convince Americans that maintaining the nation was in everyone's best interests. Fighting removal became an effort to persuade Americans not only that the Cherokees possessed the rights of a distinct political community but that the preservation of Cherokee autonomy was a necessity for whites and Indians alike.

The removal campaign developed as an alternative to the Indian policies established by George Washington and his secretary of war Henry Knox in the early years of the republic. The historian Robert Berkhofer has called this approach "expansion with honor," a phrase that suggests its essential optimism. The goal was to allow for the growth of the United States while maintaining peace on the frontier and preventing the abuse of Indian people at the hands of whites. Knox believed that Indian tribes enjoyed a status equivalent to that of independent nations, and, more important, he understood that treating them as such was the best way to avoid continual warfare. There were still groups in the East, after all, who could pose a significant military threat to America's borders. Following this principle, the United States ceased to define as conquered peoples tribes that had sided with the British in the Revolution. Federal authorities instead recognized Indian ownership of tribal land and negotiated with tribes on a nation-to-nation basis. Knox and his lieutenants insisted, however, that as the United States grew, the Indians would have to give up land to accommodate settlers. Like most Americans, Knox believed that the necessity of progress granted "civilized" whites a legitimate claim on Indian land. When civilized people needed the land, Indians would have to yield.

Some extended this line of reasoning to argue that Indians possessed a form of property ownership inferior to that of European Americans – "occupancy" titles that could be replaced with absolute ownership by white farmers. While early American policy recognized tribal nationhood and rights, it also anticipated the transfer of a great deal of Indian property to American hands.[5]

For Knox and other early policy makers, this equation could be made to balance if peace were maintained and if the Indians were allowed to become civilized. Many believed that, in the presence of the American republic, Indian people would naturally give up their tribal cultures and adopt the ways of their white neighbors. They would become Christians, learn to speak and read English, and take up European American styles of farming. Eventually they would give up their tribal identities altogether and become citizens of the United States. As that process occurred, Indians would need less land, since they would no longer rely upon hunting broad expanses of territory. They would willingly sell much of their country to allow for expanding American settlement. With Indian civilization, that is, the growth of the new republic would not require conquest. In the 1790s, Congress and the Washington administration translated that logic into legislative form in the first of the Trade and Intercourse Acts. These laws attempted to control interaction between frontier whites and Indian people, and they allowed the president to encourage Indian civilization by providing tribes with domestic animals and tools. With peace and some gentle prodding, it was hoped, the Indians within the borders of the United States would quickly be ready for full participation in American life.[6]

Relations between the United States and the Cherokees followed the "expansion with honor" model. In treaties signed between the War of Independence and the end of the century, the Cherokees ceded a large portion of their homeland. They also promised to maintain relations only with the United States, a standard American demand during this period. In return they received annual payments and at least a qualified affirmation of tribal sovereignty. The treaties declared national boundaries between the United States and the Cherokee country and established an obligation on the part of the federal government to prevent United States citizens from encroaching on tribal territory. Meanwhile, the tribe became one of the first targets of the civilization effort. Missionaries sought permission to work in the Cherokee country, beginning with Moravians at the turn of the nineteenth century. The United States provided farm animals and tools and allocated funds to establish a school to teach Cherokee women spinning and other domestic skills. Later, the government used money from the "Civilization Fund," an annual appropriation begun in 1819, to support the ongoing work of the missionaries. By that time, the Protestant presence in the Cherokee country had grown to include Presbyterians and Congregationalists from the New England-based American Board of Commissioners for Foreign Missions (known simply as the American Board), along with several Baptist representatives. Within a few years, the Methodists had arrived as well.[7]

Overall, the Cherokees proved receptive to the Washington-era programs. With the exception of several early outbreaks of violence, they remained at peace with the United States. While the arrival of missionaries caused conflict within the tribe, many Cherokees welcomed their work, especially when proselytizing was accompanied by secular education. Most members of the tribe did not embrace the ultimate goal of the civilizing mission, the complete remaking of the Cherokees in the European American image, but many took specific attractive elements of their neighbors' culture (in particular economic activities) and adapted them to Cherokee life. Cherokee men raised domestic animals. Cherokee women wove cloth. Some in the tribe converted to Christianity or adopted elements of the new religion. An important Cherokee minority, meanwhile, committed itself to a more thorough transformation. Emulating white Southerners, a small number of Cherokees became commercial farmers, merchants, and entrepreneurs. They purchased black slaves and built plantations, or they opened stores and taverns. In time, they became an economic elite, wealthier than most of their people. These individuals and families were more likely than other Cherokees to accept the missionaries' idea of civilization, seeking to adopt the overall cultural style of white

Southerners as well as their economy. More than anything else, it was the development of this population that won for the Cherokees their reputation as a "civilized tribe."[8]

Many of the most "civilized" Cherokee families were of mixed racial ancestry, the products of marriages between Cherokee women and British traders or Revolution-era loyalists. Because the tribe's kinship system was matrilineal, Cherokees considered the children of these marriages to be fully Cherokee. The presence of a white father, however, often meant that these individuals experienced and understood Euro-pean American ways in greater depth than did the rest of the tribe. That expertise allowed them to move more easily into the American market economy. It also made them useful as diplomats and political leaders, and mixed-lineage Cherokees assumed increasingly important roles in tribal politics in the late eighteenth and early nineteenth centuries. John Ross, the son of a Scottish merchant and a mixed-race Cherokee mother, was the most famous example. His formal education and in-formal experience with non-Indians made him an ideal representative of the tribe in its dealings with the United States, while his maternal kin provided him with a Cherokee identity and a network of potential political allies. From this advantageous position, Ross became one of the tribe's wealthiest members and its most prominent political leader. It is important, however, to emphasize two points. First, not all mem-bers of this segment of the tribe were "mixed-bloods." The "full-blood" Cherokee political leader Major Ridge, and his brother Oo-watie, for example, played significant roles in the tribe's adoption of elements of European American culture. Second, many of the "mixed-bloods" seem never to have thought of themselves as anything but Cherokee. White "blood" did not wash away Cherokee identity, nor did formal education inevitably erode it. As the historian Theda Perdue suggests, the best way to define this new segment of the tribe is as bicultural – Cherokees with special experience and knowledge.[9]

As the bicultural Cherokees gained influence, they transformed tribal politics by leading in the creation of a Cherokee central gov-ernment and the adoption of written law. At the time of European contact, Cherokee law and political life had been the business of matrilineal clans and the councils of the tribe's individual towns. Larger councils could be held, but they wielded very little direct authority. There was no national political structure as such. Dealing with colonial Europeans, who looked for paramount leaders with whom to conduct trade and diplomacy, encouraged the Cherokees to take some steps toward centralization in the eighteenth century, but it was only in the removal era that the trend culminated. Beginning in 1808, tribal leaders drafted national laws regulating matters such as labor contracts, money lending, and the inheritance of property. Other statutes assigned national officials the responsibility for punishing crimes like murder, a step that shifted the burden of law enforcement away from the clans. In the same years, the Cherokees began to put together a formal government structure that concentrated authority at the national level. They drafted articles establishing rules regarding representation on a permanent National Council, defined an executive branch, and created the beginnings of a formal judicial system. Later these features were incorporated into the Cherokee Constitution of 1827, which established a government modeled on that of the United States. The creation of new Indian governments was hardly what Knox had in mind when he made Indian civilization a goal of federal policy. For the Cherokees who led the fight against removal, however, the tribe's written laws and political system were among the highest expressions of Cherokee progress.[10]

The principles of Knox and Washington held for a generation, but by the 1810s many involved in Indian affairs had begun to suspect that the early policies had failed. For one thing, frontier Americans' hunger for new land far outstripped the eastern tribes' willingness to part with their territory. This was particularly true in the South, where a growing population and the rise of the cotton economy created an almost limitless demand for new country suitable for plantation agriculture. For southern whites caught up in this boom, Indian tribes like the Cherokees and Creeks were impediments to economic progress. They represented a waste of valuable land, since in the minds of many whites Indians merely wandered their territory hunting. The tribes during this period gave up a great deal to the United States, but southern citizens and their state governments continually demanded more. Some Americans simply ignored federal law and squatted on tribal property. The more law-abiding pressured federal authorities for a comprehensive solution to the problem.[11]

Questions of states' rights made matters worse. In 1802 Georgia ceded to the United States lands to the west of its modern border, territory originally included in its colonial charter. In return the federal government promised to purchase for Georgia all remaining tribal property in the state. Under the assumptions guiding early American Indian policy, this was a reasonable action. As the Cherokees and Creeks living within the state's borders became civilized, they would yield their land. As time went on, however, the Cherokees proved increasingly unwilling to give up further territory; the Creeks did eventually cede their Georgia possessions and made their stand in Alabama. This placed the federal government in the position of having either to renege on its promise to Georgia or break its treaty pledges to protect the Cherokees. Georgians, for their part, insisted that the Cherokee country was already a portion of their state and urged the government to dispossess the tribe. They held that the Cherokees did not truly own their land but were merely "tenants at will," upon whom a solution to the controversy could be imposed. Federal officials vacillated, but it was clear that the issue could not be held at bay forever.[12]

Strictly speaking, treaties should have held greater legal weight than did the 1802 agreement with Georgia, yet by the late 1810s some involved in Indian affairs were dismissing adherence to the treaties as needless, even foolish. With the War of 1812 the military power of tribes east of the Mississippi had been broken, eliminating the threat that had encouraged earlier policy makers to deal with the tribes as sovereign nations. Some Americans suggested that this new political reality made the treaties unnecessary. Andrew Jackson, the War of 1812's great hero, argued that it was now proper simply to dictate the terms of future relations. According to this way of thinking, increasingly popular in the South, the idea of tribal sovereignty had been little more than a convenient fiction, useful at a time when the new republic was weak.

It could be dispensed with now that America had become a dominant power.[13]

Along with respect for treaties, the optimism that early American policy makers had displayed in the Indians' potential for civilization had begun to fade. The Cherokee elite notwithstanding, few Indian people proved willing to undergo the cultural revolution expected by missionaries and government agents. They ignored the efforts of philanthropic whites or adopted only particular elements of European American culture. Moreover, to many observers, contact between Indians and frontier whites seemed to result in Indian degeneration – disease, intemperance, and violence – rather than improvement. Although Indian civilization remained a stated goal of American policy, some involved in Indian affairs responded to the perceived failure of the civilizing program by questioning whether Indians were capable of progress – or at least capable of progress when surrounded by whites. In the removal debates, that line of reasoning provided a humanitarian argument for pushing the tribes west (albeit one that the Cherokees considered insincere). Migration would give the Indians more time to progress while isolating them from the bad influence of frontier whites.[14]

Removal, discussed for some time as a potential policy, gradually replaced the Washington-era initiatives. Thomas Jefferson had raised the idea in 1803 as a possible dividend of the Louisiana Purchase, and during his administration agents to the southeastern tribes had begun to discuss with Indian leaders proposals for migration that would include an exchange of lands. A true removal campaign then emerged in the years following the end of the War of 1812. James Monroe and his secretary of war, John C. Calhoun, embraced migration as the most logical solution to America's Indian problems, and by the end of the 1810s federal commissioners had begun to make increasingly generous offers of land in the West to the more troublesome tribes. Yet for the time being, authorities restricted themselves to persuasion. Preferring that the Indians depart voluntarily, President Monroe (and later President John Quincy Adams) hesitated to dictate the new policy. They sought to achieve removal within the established treaty process, and they withheld the threat of force, anticipating that the Indians would soon recognize the logic of migration.[15]

During this time the Cherokees faced two significant efforts to effect their removal. In 1808 the federal Indian agent Return J. Meigs proposed that the tribe exchange its homes for new lands in what is now Arkansas. Individuals and families who wanted to stay in the East could do so, but they would have to become state citizens. While the tribe rejected this offer, the leaders of a group of about one thousand Cherokees made a separate removal agreement and migrated in 1809. A decade later, a very similar situation developed. In 1817, federal commissioners, led by Andrew Jackson, again offered the tribe a removal treaty. When the National Council refused to negotiate, the commissioners made an agreement with a group of dissident chiefs. The treaty ceded territory in Tennessee and Georgia and stipulated that Cherokees living on these lands who wanted to stay would have to accept American citizenship and individual land allotments. The National Council condemned this treaty and demanded its repeal, but in the end tribal leaders could secure only a revision of some of its terms in a new pact signed in 1819. In the meantime, another one thousand Cherokees had moved west.[16]

Events like these may have demonstrated to Americans that removal was inevitable, but if anything, the struggles left the Cherokees more determined to preserve the lands they still possessed. After the second crisis, tribal leaders announced that they would surrender no further territory, and a few years later the National Council passed a resolution refusing even to meet with future treaty commissions. Meanwhile, the council produced several new laws to clarify the question of who owned and controlled tribal land. One stated that Cherokees who sold land without the council's permission would be executed. Another declared the nation to be the owner of all tribal land, a principle later written into the 1827 Cherokee Constitution. Individuals and families had the right to use and cultivate available land, but ownership was in common, with the National Council alone having the authority to sell. These laws were meant to help the tribe ward off property-hungry Southerners, but they also preserved a very old conception of the land as a shared resource, the foundation of the people's collective existence. Cherokees came to define common landholding as essential to the nation's survival, a principle to which they adhered long after removal.[17]

Other developments strengthened the tribe's position. The emergence of the bicultural Cherokees meant that the tribe possessed leaders who could effectively communicate the anti-removal position to non-Indians while supporting the arguments of those whites who already opposed the policy. The bicultural Cherokees' very presence as delegates in Washington could disrupt removal advocates' picture of Indians, with its emphasis on Indian decline and the failure of the civilizing mission. Moreover, the Cherokees' progressive image won allies outside the South, especially among members of religious organizations with missionary ties to the tribe. The American Board, in particular, played an essential role in rallying Northeasterners to the Cherokees' cause. For some Americans, the attractive idea of the civilized tribe, combined with the Cherokees' treaties, more than counterbalanced Georgia's state's-rights case.[18]

Cherokee leaders understood the value of courting American opinion, and as Georgia pressed its claims with increasing fervor in the 1820s, the Cherokees mounted their own lobbying and public-relations efforts. Delegates traveled to Washington, and memorials appeared with greater frequency. Christian Cherokees appealed to church organizations for help and sympathy. In 1826 the National Council sent Elias Boudinot, the son of Oo-watie and one of the most talented and best educated of the bicultural Cherokees, on a speaking tour of American cities. In Philadelphia, Boston, and elsewhere, Boudinot eloquently described his people's progress and enlightenment while soliciting donations for the purchase of a printing press. Once secured, the press was used to produce the *Cherokee Phoenix* newspaper, which Boudinot edited. Tribal leaders intended the *Phoenix* to reach both Cherokee and non-Indian readers, and soon it circulated widely outside the Southeast. Under Boudinot's direction, it became a powerful medium through which the tribe broadcast its opposition to removal.[19]

As long as the president hesitated to impose the removal policy, the Cherokees and Georgia seemed evenly matched. That changed, of course, in 1828, when one of America's staunchest removal advocates gained the White House. Andrew Jackson's election did not hinge upon Indian affairs, but many in the South assumed that his success would bring the triumph of the removal policy. With that expectation, Georgia began to force its claim to the Cherokee territory. Soon after the election, the state legislature redrew the boundaries of several counties to include Cherokee land. A year later, it extended state laws over the Cherokees, declaring in effect that the tribe as a political and legal entity no longer existed. The state then completed its legal absorption of the Cherokee country in 1830 by establishing a process to parcel out the tribal lands to Georgia citizens. The Cherokees responded by calling on the federal government to protect the tribe. Led by John Ross, who had been elected principal chief under the 1827 constitution, they reminded Congress and the new president of the treaties, in which the United States had promised repeatedly to defend the Cherokees against American citizens. They continued their public-relations efforts, as well, aided by their missionary allies. Jeremiah Evarts, the leader of the American Board, published a widely circulated series of essays under the name William Penn, in which he systematically reviewed the history of American relations with the Cherokees and demolished the legal doctrines on which Georgia based its claim to tribal lands. To all this, however, the new administration simply insisted that there was nothing it could do. Jackson would not interfere with Georgia's sovereignty.[20]

The Cherokees and their allies next sought to compel federal action through the American judicial system. The tribe and its lawyers (William Wirt and John Sergeant) sought out opportunities to bring a test of Georgia's laws to the Supreme Court, their efforts leading to two of the most famous cases in Native American legal history. First, in *Cherokee Nation v. Georgia* (1831), Wirt and Sergeant asked the Court to grant an injunction halting the enforcement of the state laws on the grounds that they violated international treaties. The Court had the power to do this, they argued, under the Constitution's Article III, which allowed the justices to hear cases between states and foreign nations. The Court's majority, however, refused on the grounds that the Cherokees were not, in fact, a foreign nation. Chief Justice John Marshall wrote that Indian tribes represented "domestic dependent nations" (a term he more or less invented on the spot) and declined to address the question of whether Georgia had violated the treaties or the Constitution.[21]

In response to that ruling, the tribe and its lawyers looked for cases that would undeniably fall within the Court's jurisdiction and found one thanks to a particularly mean-spirited Georgia law. In 1830 the state legislature passed an act requiring whites living in the Cherokee country to swear an oath of allegiance to Georgia and to apply for a permit from the state government. The idea was to root out the tribe's American allies, in particular the missionaries. When a group of American Board ministers defied the law, they were arrested, convicted in a state court, and sentenced to four years of hard labor. The state offered to pardon the missionaries, but two of the group, Samuel Worcester and Elizur Butler, refused, in hopes of testing the law and by extension Georgia's claim to the Cherokee territory. When their case (*Worcester v. Georgia*) made it to the Supreme Court in early 1832, the ruling went against the state, and this time Marshall's majority opinion included a much stronger endorsement of Indian nationhood. He still declined to describe the Cherokees as a foreign nation, but he recognized the tribe's right of self-government and acknowledged that the treaties obliged federal authorities to protect Cherokee land and sovereignty. Marshall did not view the Cherokee Nation as an equal to the United States, but it was still a nation, the rights of which Georgia could not arbitrarily dissolve.[22]

This was the kind of victory the Cherokees had hoped for, but it proved to be of little benefit. Georgia refused to release the ministers, and Jackson declined to enforce the decision.[23] The administration stuck to its position that it could not interfere in the state's business. By this point, Congress had joined the fray and made the Cherokees' situation even worse by passing a comprehensive removal bill. The Removal Act of 1830 empowered the president to seek the expulsion of the eastern Indians and established the process whereby the goal

could be accomplished. Commissioners were to be appointed to negotiate removal agreements with the various tribes, with the federal
government providing the migrants with lands in the West and funds
to defray the cost of moving. Individual Indians could stay in the East,
but only if they accepted state citizenship and laws. Although the act
did not threaten coercion, it was clear by this time that force would
be used if necessary. The passage of the bill at a time when Jackson
was refusing to intervene in Georgia indicated that federal authorities
were content to allow the states to bully the Indians into accepting migration. The states would apply pressure to the tribes, and the federal
government would offer the means of escape. Thus, while the Removal
Act provided for tribal consent, it acted as an ultimatum to groups like
the Cherokees. It was meant to convince them that emigration was
now their only choice.[24]

In this context of state coercion and federal neglect, Cherokee leaders
adopted a style of address and language that would provide the foundation for their political writings for the rest of the century. In messages
from this period, they generally attacked removal from two directions.
They insisted, first of all, that Georgia's actions and Jackson's abandonment were illegal, being violations of America's many treaties with
the Cherokees. The treaties, they reminded non-Indians, recognized
the tribe as a distinct political community, and several of them declared explicitly that the Cherokees did not fall within the jurisdiction
of any state. "This Guarantee," one message pointed out, "is pledged
by the United States *to be continued forever*."[25] Moreover, the treaties
obliged the federal government to protect the Cherokee territory from
an invasion of precisely the sort carried out by Georgia. As long as the
Cherokees remained in the East, those provisions would continue to
operate and federal authorities would be duty-bound to help the tribe
hold Georgia and its citizens at bay. As for removal, it could not be
forced upon them without an even greater violation of American law.
Past agreements had made provisions for the emigration of Cherokees,
but the consent of those who moved had always been required. As John
Ross pointed out, it was "well known that the disposition of the nation

is adverse to a removal, and that no proposition could be made to change their disposition."[26] That being the case, there was nothing that the United States could legitimately do to carry out its policy. It was futile, they insisted, even to discuss the matter. They contended that Americans' own laws defined the Cherokees as a nation, and they should be treated as such regardless of Georgia's demands.[27]

Beyond establishing that legal position, Cherokee representatives depicted the removal campaign as a threat to a valued relationship with the United States. They frequently wrote of the past, recalling times when white America had treated them with kindness and humanity. They recounted a moral history of Cherokee-American relations and suggested that removal would destroy a mutually beneficial friendship between the two peoples. This had begun in the last decade of the eighteenth century, when, as Cherokee leaders explained, the administration of George Washington came to the tribe and offered the Indians a bargain on behalf of the American people. In return for peace, the Americans promised to protect the Cherokees and their land and to help them become civilized. In agreeing, the Cherokees embarked on a long and happy association with the United States that resulted in the Indians' progressing rapidly and winning their reputation as a civilized tribe. "With a commendable zeal the first Chief magistrate of the United States undertook to bring the Cherokees into the pale of civilization," Elias Boudinot recalled in the *Phoenix*. "They placed confidence in what he said, and well they might, for he was true to his promises. Of course the foundation for the improvement which the Cherokees have since made was laid under the patronage of that illustrious man."[28] Washington's heirs, however, had not remained true. Although the Cherokees had done everything they could to keep their side of the agreement, removal advocates were now abandoning the old friendship. For the sake of gaining tribal lands, they were breaking with a proven policy, dismantling the Cherokee Nation, and in the process destroying Cherokee civilization.[29]

A memorial submitted to Congress in February 1829 offers specific examples of these positions. It was the product of a tribal delegation consisting of John Ross and three others: Richard Taylor, Edward

Gunter, and William Shorey Coodey. These were all members of the Cherokees' bicultural families, men whose experience bridged Cherokee and American ways. All had white fathers, and at least two of them had received significant non-Indian education, Coodey from home tutors, and Ross from tutors and at several boarding schools.[30] All had taken part two years earlier in the convention that had produced the Cherokee Constitution, and all remained active in Cherokee politics for years to come as opponents of removal and advocates of Cherokee nationhood. Taylor, for example, was a frequent delegate during the removal struggle, and in 1838 led one of the Cherokees' emigrant parties to the Indian Territory. He and Gunter remained important political allies of Ross in the West. Coodey, a nephew and protégé of the chief, was also frequently selected to go to Washington, and after removal he became the principal author of the tribe's new constitution.[31] It is worth noting that the February 1829 memorial gained broad distribution. Congress had it printed, Boudinot republished it in the *Phoenix*, and a year later it appeared in the important American magazine *Niles Weekly Register*.[32]

The delegates had come to the capital to fight the first of the Georgia laws extending state jurisdiction over the Cherokee territory. By the time they addressed Congress, they had been in Washington for over a month but had little to show for their efforts. They had appealed to the commissioner of Indian affairs for the removal of their agent, whom they suspected of being an ally of the state, but nothing was done. They had asked for help from the War Department against the state government, but again there was no response. They hoped the House and Senate would prove more open to persuasion.[33]

They began by identifying the immediate issue and attempting to convey to their audience the seriousness of its implications. Georgia had redrawn the boundaries of five of its counties to include the Cherokee Nation. The Cherokees' own laws were to be nullified. "This act involves a question of great magnitude and of serious import. . . . It is a question upon which the salvation and happiness or the misery and destruction of *a nation* depends." The Cherokees were well aware, the delegates explained, that Georgians wanted Indian land. The tribe, in fact, had done its best to accommodate that desire by ceding territory repeatedly to its white neighbors "until no more [could] be reasonably spared." They never imagined, however, that Georgians would stoop so low as to seize Indian property. "It was not conceived, much less believed, that *a State*, proud of *Liberty*, and tenacious of the *rights of man*, would condescend to have placed herself before the world, in the imposing attitude of a usurper of the most sacred rights and privileges of a weak, defenceless, and innocent nation." Events having reached that dire point, the Cherokees were forced to beg the United States for help. In all the Cherokees' treaties, the government had "solemnly pledged to protect and defend them against the encroachments of their citizens." The tribe was now calling upon America to make good on those promises.[34]

This was a typical opening. It cited the treaties, reminded readers of the tribe's rights, and emphasized that the Cherokees were a nation and had long been regarded as one by the United States. The tribe wanted nothing extraordinary, only adherence to the established agreements. The moral terms were also typical. The statement combined republican language (liberty, the rights of man) with the implication that Georgia's actions were sinful, as the state sought to deny the Cherokees "salvation" and drive them into "misery and destruction."

Turning to the broader question of removal, the delegates acknowledged that emigration had become a central goal of American policy toward Indians. The delegates had observed that development "with pain and deep regret," finding removal advocates' insistence that the policy would "promote our [the Cherokees'] interest and permanent happiness, and save [them] from the impending fate that [had] swept others into oblivion" particularly unfortunate. The delegates admitted that those who made such claims probably meant well, but held that the Cherokee leaders were themselves better able to judge the matter. "We, as descendants of the Indian race, and possessing both the feelings of the Indian and the white man cannot but believe that this system to perpetuate our happiness is visionary, and that the anticipated blessings can never be realized."[35]

Here the delegates claimed an interesting species of authority. When addressing the United States government, Cherokee leaders often took the role of supplicants – representatives of a powerless people seeking the aid of a guardian. At the same time, they presented themselves as the best possible experts on Indian affairs. They were Cherokees who knew both their own people and the white community that they addressed. They were also their nation's elected representatives, a status they pointedly compared to that of the legislators to whom they directed the memorial.[36] Bicultural leaders could determine more readily than most what was good for the tribe, and they were certain that emigration could never improve Cherokee life.

In explaining that conviction, they turned to the past – the moral history that they shared with Americans – and the image of the "civilized tribe."

The history of the prosperous and improving condition of our people in the arts of civilized life and christianization, is before the world, and not unknown to you. The causes which have produced this great change and state of things, are to be traced from the virtue, honor, and wisdom in the policy of the Administration of the Great Washington – the Congress of the United States and the American People; the relationship and intercourse established by treaties, and our location in the immediate neighborhood of a civilized community. . . . If, under all these advantages, the permanent prosperity and happiness of the Cherokee People cannot be realized, they never can be realized under any other location within the limits of the United States.[37]

Again the language was republican. The delegates lauded Washington's principled and farsighted leadership and implied that those promoting removal were betraying the first president's legacy. They tied the memory of Washington's republican virtue to their own people's rebirth as a civilized tribe. The father of the United States had been a founder of the Cherokee Nation as well.

Later in the document, the delegates again invoked Washington and embellished the memory by listing the elements of civilized life that the Cherokees had embraced under his "kind and generous policy." "Agriculture is every where pursued, and the interests of our citizens are permanent in the soil. We have enjoyed the blessings of Christian instruction; the advantages of education and merit are justly appreciated, a Government of regular law has been adopted." Such lists, often quite long and elaborate, became an almost ubiquitous device in Cherokee appeals. These same attributes – Christianity, agriculture, education, and government – would appear in Cherokee messages for the rest of the century.[38]

Finally, the delegates speculated that most Americans, perhaps even citizens of Georgia, did not want to see the Cherokees assaulted and dispossessed. "We would be wanting in liberal and charitable feelings were we to doubt the virtue and magnanimity of the People of Georgia, and we do believe there are men in that State whose moral and religious worth stands forth inferior to none within the United States." This expression of faith that Americans were essentially good and amenable to reason, that they still knew right from wrong, also became a common feature in Cherokee writing. Whites were often misguided, and apparently they could be deluded with almost ridiculous ease by the few truly despicable among them. But most could still be called back to the better principles of their heritage.[39]

The Cherokee representatives, then, insisted that the Indian policy of the early republic had been successful and that it provided the only legitimate model for relations in the present. They offered antebellum Americans a narrative of productive Indian-white cooperation and claimed Americans' own founding fathers as symbolic allies. They defined removal, moreover, as a moral question. Georgia had allowed itself to be seduced by greed, while federal authorities had failed to observe their duty. Yet the Cherokees' goal was moderate, the way out of this trouble straight. They asked only that their old friendship, the long and intimate connection, be continued.

The legal position taken by the Cherokees in this memorial and in others from this period originated in a fruitful partnership among tribal leaders, their hired attorneys, and their missionary allies. From the latter two groups, William Wirt and Jeremiah Evarts were particularly significant. In preparing to test Georgia's laws in the Supreme Court, Cherokee leaders conducted a detailed correspondence with

Wirt on American law applicable to their situation. This, along with the leaders' own examinations of the treaties, provided the Cherokees with a legal education at a time when the tribe had yet to produce trained attorneys of its own. Evarts, for his part, had practiced law before devoting his life to religious work. His William Penn essays included a treaty-by-treaty discussion of Cherokee-American relations, which significantly influenced the arguments adopted by the tribe and its lawyers. It is worth noting, however, that tribal leaders displayed a solid grasp of the treaties before Wirt's appointment or the appearance of Evarts's essays; the memorial just described, for example, predated both. The development of the Cherokee legal position was a collaborative effort that included tribal leaders as full participants.[40]

The Cherokees' moral arguments invite a more detailed discussion. While the memory of happier relations in the days of Washington accurately recalled that period's more generous policies, it expressed more than tribal leaders' awareness that times had changed. For one thing, the image of Cherokee-American friendship echoed a very old indigenous concept of diplomacy. As the legal scholar Robert A. Williams argues, eastern Native Americans in the contact period shared a view of treaty making as a sacred activity, with negotiations operating within a spiritual as well political realm. Diplomacy involved calling upon and directing divine power in order to establish "good thoughts" among different peoples. The overarching purpose was to create a spiritual or psychological state in which potentially conflicting groups recognized one another's common humanity and became capable of mutual trust.[41] When Cherokees recalled earlier American relations, they wrote in terms of trust and emotional attachment. They described Washington's sympathy for the Indians and their own people's confidence in him. They wrote of the Cherokees' loyalty to the United States and their feelings of kinship with Americans, "our ancient allies, our friends, our brethren." They did not employ the precise language of the contact period, but "good thoughts" still underpinned successful relations.[42] Williams notes, moreover, that stories, narratives of clashing peoples finding peace, formed a crucial element of Native American diplomacy. Storytelling was a way of creating the necessary feelings of trust, with the narratives allowing the parties to imagine themselves free of conflict. The Cherokees' moral history perhaps served such a function. In recalling earlier relations, tribal leaders sought to remind Americans of the possibility of their peaceful coexistence with the Indian nation. I do not know whether antebellum Cherokees thought of old treaty-making traditions when they wrote the memorials. But like the indigenous diplomats that Williams describes, Cherokees invited their potential enemies to imagine themselves connected to the tribe in a relationship of mutual faith.[43]

More directly, the moral terms adopted by Cherokee leaders drew upon another kind of sacred authority, this one provided by the tribe's missionary allies. Ministers like Jeremiah Evarts and Samuel Worcester brought to Indian affairs the outlook of the antebellum era's Christian reformers – the outlook of temperance crusaders and Sabbatarians, abolitionists and proponents of women's rights. While this was a diverse group pursuing a multiplicity of causes, many of the reformers shared a conviction that their work carried both cosmic and social significance. Inspired in equal measures by the American Revolution and the revivals of the Second Great Awakening, they believed that the United States had a special role to play in sacred history. If Americans adhered to their republican principles, remained virtuous, and used their liberty for good, they might witness the dawning of the Kingdom of God in their own place and time. If freedom led them to grow selfish and immoral, however, they would call divine punishment down upon the nation. Most of these reformers were postmillennialists, which is to say that they believed that the Kingdom would begin as human progress toward perfection. Although they differed among themselves as to what form progress would take, they agreed that their Christian duty was to keep Americans on this upward path and to guard against sin. As the historian Robert Abzug observes, to be a reformer in this era was to place oneself in a "sacred drama" of American history.[44]

In the William Penn essays, Evarts attacked removal from this perspective. In explaining the treaties, he sought to prove that the United States had always regarded the Cherokees as a separate nation and thus that removal could not be forced without the betrayal of a half century of promises. His purpose was to reduce the issue to a clear ethical question. Would Americans keep their word, or would they break their promises because they had the power to do so and because they stood to gain from the result? For Evarts, removal represented a test of America's national character, a trial unfolding before the eyes of the world. If the United States drove away the eastern Indians with this "narrow and selfish policy," Evarts prophesied, then would "the sentence of an indignant world . . . be uttered in thunders," which would "roll and reverberate for ages after the present actors in human affairs passed away."[45] And as the rolling-thunder passage implies, American perfidy would make a much higher power angry as well. "The Great Arbiter of Nations never fails to take cognizance of national delinquencies," Evarts warned, "and he has at his disposal most abundant means of executing his decisions."[46] For Evarts, removal threatened more than Indian property and rights; it threatened America's identity as a Christian republic and its place in the world.[47]

The idea of the Cherokee Nation as a test of American virtue clearly appealed to tribal leaders, and they adopted this element of the reformers' worldview. Cherokee writings continually reminded non-Indians that God and the rest of the world were watching, as when John Ross assured an American ally that the Cherokees' friends would be remembered. "To those Gentlemen who have so honorably and ably vindicated the rights of the poor Indians in Congress at the last session, this Nation owes a debt of gratitude which the pages of history will bear record of until time shall be no more – and for which they will receive a just reward in the Courts of Heaven."[48] Elias Boudinot wrote in similar terms in the *Phoenix* when he learned of the passage of the Indian Removal Act. "Let both Houses of Congress decide as they may," the editor declared, "We confidently think justice will be done, even if the Cherokees are not in the land of the living to receive it – posterity will give a correct verdict."[49] God and future generations would see through removal advocates' cant to find the policy's source in greed and the arrogance of power. While Americans might do with the tribe as they pleased, they were courting infamy.

The use of the Washington memory intensified this sense of removal as a test. Jackson and the Georgians were not only trying to rob the Cherokees, they were betraying the ideals of the founders, failing to live up to their own American heritage. In this respect, the Cherokee memorials can be placed in what the literary scholar Sacvan Bercovitch sees as the tradition of the American jeremiad. Bercovitch holds that the jeremiad, the Puritans' recriminatory sermon, survived the Puritans themselves to become a crucial American ritual. In its original form, New England divines reproached their people for forgetting their godly errand in the New World. In the antebellum version, politicians, writers, and reformers employed a sanctified memory of the Revolution and the founders to criticize Americans in the present and often to urge them toward a particular social reform or political course. Many of these later jeremiads represented responses to the anxieties produced by the era's rapid economic expansion. They invoked the revolutionary generation as an example of selflessness in hopes of curbing American materialism.[50] The Cherokee stories of Washington fit this model in most respects. They described an era of progress thrown into doubt by contemporary Americans' decline into greed and corruption. They were efforts to awaken Americans to their collective failure and to call them back to the morally upright ways of the past. Among the virtues of this way of defining removal was that it made the solution to the crisis an easy one – or a straightforward one, at least. Americans simply had to remember who they were: Christians, citizens of a republic, and heirs to the founders.

One more element of the Cherokees' position should be emphasized here. When tribal leaders insisted that the policies of the early republic had been successful, they appealed to the ideas of humanity that had informed those policies. The Washington-era approach had proceeded from the expectation that Indians, when confronted with a civilized nation and aided by philanthropy, would quickly remake themselves, progressing from savagery. There was thought to exist a natural civilizing process through which Indian people could pass if they so chose, an idea rooted in the Christian affirmation of mankind's unity.[51] Cherokee writings embraced that idea, with tribal leaders suggesting that their people proved its essential correctness. In another missionary echo, Cherokees often assumed a millennial tone when writing of their people's progress. They described Cherokee advancement as a near-miraculous conversion, indicating God's hand at work in American Indian affairs.[52]

The other side of the equation, however, was a belief that if Indians did not advance rapidly, they would wither and disappear. By the 1820s and 1830s, many in the United States were convinced that Indians were destined for this second path. As noted earlier, removal advocates asserted that that the civilizing mission had failed and that most eastern Indians remained in a primitive state. That argument could easily become a suggestion that Indians were incapable of progress in the first place. Supporters of the policy tended to vacillate between the position that removal would give the tribes more time to become civilized and the suspicion that they would soon fade away through some natural process.[53] One could find similar ideas expressed (and expressed less ambiguously) elsewhere in the culture. This period, for example, saw the rise of early versions of scientific racism, schools of thought that rejected the idea of human unity and identified innate differences among races. Researchers like Samuel Morton suggested that Indians were biologically (and thus permanently) inferior to whites, and speculated that they would disappear in the presence of an expanding white population.[54] These years also witnessed a vogue for doomed Indians in American literature. James Fenimore Cooper and other popular authors portrayed Indians as capable of heroic good but ultimately incapable of existing with whites. Native people in these works were fading from the presence of white Americans, disappearing because of a fundamental incompatibility with civilization. Americans, it seems, were ridding themselves of Indian neighbors intellectually and culturally, even as Cherokees and others fought to remain in the East.[55]

In their narrative of Indian-white cooperation, Cherokees rejected the idea of the disappearing Indian and the suggestion that nature had already decided their fate. Cherokee leaders acknowledged that many tribes had been "swept . . . into oblivion," but they maintained that their own people stood as "living testimony, that all Indian nations are not doomed."[56] The Cherokees, they insisted, disproved the theory that Indians declined when placed in close proximity to whites. On the contrary, as John Ross explained to Andrew Jackson in 1834, the Cherokees' rapid improvement had come through "good neighborhood between the Cherokees and the citizens of bordering states . . . thereby exhibiting clearly by practical demonstration the force and effects of surrounding circumstances."[57] Or as Elias Boudinot wrote in an 1829 issue of the *Phoenix*, "the causes which have operated to exterminate the Indian tribes . . . did not exist in the Indians themselves, nor in the will of heaven, nor simply in the intercourse of Indians with civilized man, but they were precisely such causes as are now attempted by the state of Georgia – by infringing upon their rights – by disorganizing them, and circumscribing their limits."[58] The tribe's future was still open and would remain so as long as Americans kept faith with the old policies and with the Indian nation.

Cherokee resistance to removal began to break down in the early 1830s – or, rather, Cherokees' unanimous opposition to removal collapsed, setting in motion a chain of events that caused most of the tribe to be finally expelled from the Southeast. As Georgia continued its assault upon Cherokee land and treaty rights, and as federal intervention in defense of the tribe appeared ever less likely, a number of prominent Cherokees broke with the tribal government and began to push for migration. Elias Boudinot was among the leaders of this group. Boudinot had fought as hard as anyone against removal, but after the Cherokees' Supreme Court victory failed to help the tribe's cause, he concluded that continued opposition was pointless. He and the other dissidents argued that the only remaining option was to negotiate the best removal treaty possible. Some also hoped to use the removal crisis to replace John Ross and his closest allies as the tribe's dominant leaders. They charged Ross with deluding the Cherokees for his own political advantage by offering them hope that the eastern homeland might still be saved.[59] Ross, for his part, also wavered during this time, but in a different manner. As the tribe's situation grew worse, the chief indicated that the Cherokees might give up their political autonomy to preserve a remnant of their lands in the East. They would accept state citizenship if the possession of their homes could be made secure. American authorities rejected this idea, and in the future Ross would insist that his people could find happiness only within their own nation.[60]

When the "Treaty Party" began to push for the negotiation of a removal agreement, Ross and the majority of the tribe condemned the dissidents as traitors. They purged their leaders from the tribal government and removed Boudinot as editor of the *Phoenix*. Those actions, however, made the internal conflict only more dangerous. Unable to convince their countrymen that their position was correct, Treaty Party leaders proceeded to negotiate with the United States anyway. In 1835 they signed the Treaty of New Echota, which provided for the complete cession of all Cherokee territory in return for lands in the Indian Territory, transportation to the West, subsistence aid for a year, and a payment of five million dollars. Although the men who had made the agreement were clearly not the Cherokees' recognized leaders, the Senate ratified the treaty in early 1836.[61]

In contesting the New Echota agreement, Ross and his remaining allies employed most of their established arguments and language. They continued to invoke the founding fathers, imploring Americans in the 1830s to remember the old friendship between the Cherokees and the United States. Keeping the jeremiad form, they contrasted the fraudulent treaty with "the affectionate feelings, the pure virtue, the justice which have been exhibited towards our people by Washington [and] by Jefferson."[62] They drew up new lists of their people's civilized achievements under the magnanimous policies of the early republic. And, as before, they reminded their American audiences that God was watching, that "the Great and good Being who created all things and directs the destiny of man, knows the whole truth."[63] At the same time, a stronger tone of fear and desperation entered the Cherokees' anti-removal writings. The immorality of removal, its tyrannical violence, became the focus of many appeals, as tribal leaders turned from explaining Cherokee rights to describing the terrible consequences of their violation. An 1836 memorial to Congress described the treaty as having barred the tribe from "membership in the human family" and listed the natural rights denied the Cherokees in Georgia. "We are despoiled of our private possessions. . . . We are stripped of every attribute of freedom and eligibility for legal self-defense. . . . Violence may be committed upon our persons; even our very lives may be taken away."[64] Yet migration to the West offered no better prospect. Removal, leaders insisted, would undermine everything the Cherokees had gained since the Revolution. In fact, it would likely push the Cherokees back into a primitive state, since it would strip them of their property and expel them from the civilized East. As another response to the treaty put it, they were "to be *despoiled by their guardian*, to become strangers and wanderers in the land of their fathers, forced to return to the savage life, and to seek a new home in the wilds of the far west."[65] Worse, removal might drive the Cherokees into extinction; in returning to savagery, they would share the destiny of tribes that did not become civilized. "Unless you avert your arm we are destroyed," a delegation warned Congress. "Unless your feelings of affection and compassion are once more awakened towards your destitute and despairing children our annihilation is complete."[66]

In these messages, removal became a kind of Cherokee apocalypse, the willful violation of treaty bringing destruction to the tribe. The terms that Cherokee leaders employed in describing these dire consequences were not terribly different from those that European Americans used when they wrote of the Indians' inevitable doom. Native people were strangers, wandering lands over which they were once lords. They were desperate, homeless people pushed ever westward by white America's expansion. In Cherokee writings, however, that terrible state was not the result of some natural process of decline, an unavoidable tragedy. It was the consequence of a crime against the tribe committed by the state of Georgia with the permission of an irresponsible federal government. The doomed savage, in this case, was an identity forced upon the Cherokees by corrupt power. Cherokee protests tended to affirm some of European Americans' basic ideas about Indians – that savagery could not long exist in the presence of civilization, that Native people faced a choice between progressing in emulation of white America and fading into extinction. But they placed the burden of deciding whether the race survived upon American authorities. The Cherokees might disappear like Indians in a Cooper novel, but only if Americans, through their own weakness and cupidity, drove them out of existence.[67]

If federal officials heard the strident language of the 1830s, it did not dissuade them from carrying out the terms of the treaty. In early 1838, after a two-year period during which the Cherokees were meant to be preparing for the move, United States troops began to put the New Echota agreement into effect by force. Rounding up Cherokee families, they imprisoned them in camps, where poor conditions and the Georgia heat claimed the first of many lives that would be lost to removal. In response, Ross and the tribal government at last admitted defeat and asked that the Cherokees be allowed to conduct their own migration. In late August, the first of thirteen groups set out for the Indian Territory, a journey that took more than four months. By the time the last detachment arrived in early 1839, at least four thousand Cherokees had died either en route or in the prison camps. This fell short of the complete annihilation predicted in tribal leaders' warnings, but for those who experienced it, migration must indeed have seemed an apocalyptic event.[68]

As one of its last acts before removal, the Cherokee National Council passed a resolution stating that the tribal government was to be transferred intact to the new homeland. That action reflected John Ross's and his allies' paramount political goal following their capitulation to the United States. They sought to ensure that the Cherokee Nation would be recreated in the West and that the government that they led would be the sole legitimate authority over the tribe once migration was complete. Although removal had divided the Cherokee people and nullified tribal laws, Ross hoped that a reunified nation could be built in the new homeland under the same legal and political structure that had guided affairs in the East. In pursuing that goal, however, Ross faced opposition from two sides. Members of the Treaty Party, almost all of whom had migrated before the Trail of Tears, were understandably reluctant to place themselves under a government dominated by their opponents. They wanted a new administration that would allow them some degree of autonomy and protect them from the Ross faction. Joining them in dissent were many "Old Settlers," Cherokees who had moved west before the 1830s. The Old Settlers feared that their interests would be forgotten now that the new emigration had left them a minority. They also chafed at the notion that the political system that they had created in the West should be perfunctorily replaced simply because John Ross and his followers had at last accepted removal.[69]

Ignoring the Treaty Party, Ross tried to win the support of the Old Settlers. Failing at that, he worked to convince them to participate in the creation of a new government. Few were willing to listen, the Westerners still fearing that they would be subsumed in Ross's much larger following. When attempts at true compromise fell short, Ross convinced a small number of Old Settlers to join his people in drafting an "Act of Union" establishing a new constitution and laws based on those of the old eastern nation. This accomplished, the "united" Cherokees elected Ross chief and declared the matter complete. In the midst of that maneuvering, however, any hopes for a true union were shattered when Ross supporters killed three Treaty Party leaders – Elias Boudinot, Major Ridge, and John Ridge – as punishment for their having signed the Treaty of New Echota. With these acts, the animosity between pro- and anti-removal Cherokees flared into violence that was to continue intermittently for years to come. A truce in 1840 averted full-scale war between the Cherokee government and the dissidents, but murders and acts of revenge stemming from the conflict became a regular part of life in the nation. Near – guerilla warfare raged at times as groups of dissidents, such as the band led by the Starr family, traded attacks with Cherokee police companies and Ross Party vigilantes.[70]

The violence threatened to destroy any hope of the Cherokee Nation's reestablishment. In addition to undermining the Act of Union's already questionable legitimacy, the killings led the United States government to intervene in the tribe's internal politics. Following the initial murders, Treaty Party leaders appealed to the United States for help. Charging their old enemies with mounting a campaign to kill all who opposed their rule, they asked for protection and called for

American authorities to free them from the domination of Ross and his followers. Meanwhile, a group of Old Settlers joined the Treaty Party in rejecting the Act of Union and requesting American aid. In response, federal officials considered dissolving the Cherokee government and deposing Ross. For a time, they refused to negotiate with the principal chief, declaring that he had forfeited the right to federal recognition. Even more significant, American authorities considered partitioning the new homeland into two or more distinct Cherokee territories, as demanded by the dissidents, who argued that the only way to ensure peace was to completely separate the factions. Finally, as the conflict continued, some federal agents began to believe that the best way to settle their Cherokee problems would be simply to extend the laws of the United States over the Cherokee territory. That act would have eliminated the Cherokee Nation as a distinct political entity and amounted to a step toward the tribe's incorporation into the United States.[71]

Ross and his allies responded to all this by insisting that their new government was legitimate and would safeguard the rights of all Cherokees, regardless of their politics. "The Government of the Cherokee Nation recognizes *no* party distinctions . . . our constitution and laws are republican . . . they secure equal rights and privileges to each and all free citizens."[72] They portrayed the dissidents as outlaws, a small group of malcontents unworthy of American officials' aid. At times, they suggested that their opponents were part of a conspiracy formulated by non-Indians hoping to seize control of the tribal lands. "Some vile mercenary white demagogue," they hypothesized, was at work among their opponents. "White lawyers and white speculators" sustained the conflict by supporting the dissidents' campaign.[73] The proper course for the federal government, Ross and his allies argued, was to recognize the Act of Union and return relations with the Cherokees to their proper nation-to-nation basis. Toward that end, the Cherokee government asked for the negotiation of a new treaty to replace the fraudulent New Echota agreement. This they hoped would resolve all remaining issues concerning removal, while reasserting that the principal chief and National Council were the only authorities with whom the United States could legitimately deal. Along the way, they hoped to win a better price for the eastern homeland than the five million dollars promised at New Echota, as well as more money to offset the cost of migration.[74]

In broadcasting those positions, representatives of the new government used some of the same rhetoric that they had employed in fighting removal. The American founders, for instance, continued to appear in Cherokee writing, with tribal leaders recalling the cooperation of the early republic in statements urging a resumption of normal relations in the present. "There can be no necessity for going into any detail upon the subject of the relative positions of the United States & the Cherokees," Ross wrote in 1840 to the American secretary of war, John Bell. "You are aware, Sir, of its entire history. You are aware, that, from the moment when our Fathers began to execute the wishes of the founders of your republic, and to change our people from hunters to herdsmen & husbandmen, we were pointedly and invariably recognized as a 'nation.' "[75] While Americans in the 1830s had failed to prove worthy of the "illustrious Washington," they had been given another chance. Recognizing Cherokee nationhood in the Indian Territory, they could go back to the founders' approach, which would in turn bring peace and renewed Cherokee progress.[76]

Removal only underscored the correctness of those earlier policies. As the letter to John Bell pointed out, while under the protection of the early republic, "the Cherokees were rapidly advancing in agriculture; in all the arts of civilized life." Forced migration, however, had thrown their achievements into doubt. "In the midst of this onward march," Ross recalled, "one of the most monstrous political frauds which ever stained the page of history is perpetrated upon the United States and against the Cherokees; and in consequence of it, the Cherokees are told they must depart forever from the land of their fathers to the wilderness!"[77] The Cherokees suffered immensely in consequence of that crime, but they never broke faith with the United States. Remaining peaceful and patient, they continued to honor their side of the bargain with the founders. "To endure is not easy; yet still the Cherokees went through it all, Sir, in the hope that the United States would ultimately be just."[78] Removal had made obvious the need to return to the old co-operative relations, the Cherokees having experienced firsthand what happened when Americans ignored Indian rights.

Cherokee suffering, in fact, became an important theme in the writings of the immediate post-removal years. In demanding that federal officials cease their support for the dissidents, tribal leaders often described the agonies of the Cherokees' capture and forced migration. "Children were abruptly severed from doting parents who never met them more," an 1840 protest recalled, "Vast multitudes of both sexes and all ages, ever until then habituated to domestic comforts, were sickened by the wretchedness and unwholesomeness of being congregated in open fields, . . . and thousands of those nearest and dearest to many of us at length sunk into miserable graves." Yet despite their anguish, the Cherokees continued to believe that American authorities would come to their senses. As they made their way into the wilderness, they looked forward to the day when "the United States would secure to them elsewhere, that national independence, that exemption from intrusive meddlers, from prying and lying tale-bearers, and from military protection of the few, to overawe the many, from which the ill-starred peculiarities of their previous position had for ever debarred them."[79]

In fighting removal, tribal leaders had predicted such torments and had promised that the Cherokees would suffer patiently. They would keep faith with the United States and honor their ancestors' promise to remain at peace.[80] After removal, the ordeal of the Trail of Tears became part of the foundation of the revived Cherokee Nation in the West. Tribal leaders translated their people's agony into a debt that the United States owed the tribe. They reminded federal officials of the pain that Americans had inflicted upon the Cherokees and explicitly tied that memory to the demand for a renewal of Cherokee autonomy under American protection. The United States, tribal leaders implied, could make up for its crimes and begin to regain its place as a Christian republic by accepting the Act of Union, recognizing the new government, and ending its interference in the Cherokees' internal affairs.

If the federal government did not embrace a just policy, a new tragedy akin to removal would inevitably come. After 1839 Ross and his allies continued to insist that federal actions threatened the Cherokees' civilized achievements and perhaps their very survival. The Trail of Tears had not quite destroyed the tribe or driven the Cherokees back into savagery, but the United States might still finish the job in the West if it did not take care. George Lowrey, an important Ross ally, employed this theme in an open letter to the "Christian community of the United States." Lowrey asked pious Americans to pray that Congress would not carry out proposals to extend federal law over the Cherokee territory. He recalled how the Cherokees, with American help, had adopted Christianity and civilized republican government, and he argued that the proposal then under consideration would destroy this good work. The American government no doubt meant well, he wrote, "but with the Nation must fall also, all our churches, schools, and institutions for religious and literary improvement, and all our hopes, and the hopes of the Christian public with regard to our future prosperity."[81] The language here was not so florid as that employed in the late 1830s to describe the anticipated apocalypse of removal, but the idea was the same. Actions that undermined the Cherokees' political rights and autonomy threatened the civilization process as well. If anything, the connection between Cherokee rights and Cherokee civilization had become even clearer in the later writings.

As a final embellishment on the arguments of the 1830s, tribal leaders suggested that if the nation and its new government were preserved, the Cherokees might exert a salutary influence over other Indians in the West. The arrival of the Cherokee majority, they pointed out, had already improved the state of the Old Settlers, whom Ross and his allies portrayed as less civilized than the more recent immigrants. The Old Settlers were the "hunter party," who had left the eastern nation to avoid the changes brought by Cherokee civilization. Had the eastern Cherokees been forced to conform to the Old Settlers' ways, they would have "relapse[d] into a state of comparative barbarism."[82] As it happened, however, when the more advanced community arrived, the Westerners seized the opportunity for progress afforded by a reunion. "The Cherokees of the West echoed the wish of the great eastern majority to

46

intermingle with them and form again one nation," an 1840 statement
explained. "They had long been wishing for a Constitution, which they
had never had; and had long been dissatisfied with the vague manner
in which their laws were administered: all of which were crude, and
but few written."[83] That recollection, of course, provided a justification
for the supplanting of the Old Settlers' political system, but it also suggested that in accepting removal the Cherokees had become emissaries
of Indian civilization in the savage West. A few years later William
Potter Ross, the chief's nephew and political lieutenant, expanded on
that theme, imagining for his people a crucial role in the redemption
of the entire Indian race.

*They [the Cherokees] are already the most important tribe on the western
frontier, and being the eldest brother of the Indians within the limits of the
United States, already exercise an influence over their younger ones that
is great and must continue to increase. In fact, the destiny of the whole
Indian population in the west will be determined by that which awaits
the Cherokees. If they falter before opposition, cower under adversity,
remove their eye from the standard of enlightened civilization, or perish
from discord, or, neglect or unwise treatment by the Government of the
United States, all is lost. The whole Indian race will meet their doom.
On the contrary, if they maintain their position; remain united, defend
their government, support their schools, encourage industry, and imbibe
the precepts of religion, all will be well. Each and every Indian tribe will
ultimately follow them and partake of their glory and renown.*[84]

This idea, that the Cherokees were the "eldest brothers" of the race,
would become an increasingly prominent theme in tribal leaders' writing as the century went on. Cherokees would frequently identify themselves as missionaries to their fellow Indians, as a model civilized tribe
for the "wild" Indians of the West. The Cherokees could serve that
function, however, only if the United States respected their political
rights and autonomy. Cherokee nationhood, in these terms, became
not only inseparable from Cherokee progress but conducive to the
progress of all Indian people.

Ross and his allies, one should note, were not the only ones using

the language of Indian civilization. Their opponents found the idea
of a civilizing process equally helpful in explaining their own political positions. The Old Settlers, for example, offered a version of the
Ross faction's memory of the early republic. They admitted that the
original migrants to the West had separated from their countrymen
in order to remain "hunters," but they argued that since that time the
Westerners had chosen to become civilized and had been progressing
steadily, independent of the eastern nation. "They increased in numbers and intelligence," one memorial recalled of the early nineteenth
century, "advancing from the rudest state of savage life, through the
different grades, to a regular government and written laws; and in
1833 were rapidly approaching the highest stage of civilization."[85] The
treaty Cherokees also claimed to be the genuine party of progress.
They argued, for example, that dividing the nation would help their
people preserve and advance Indian civilization. Their first concern
in their new country, the faction's leaders stated in 1840, would be to
"attend to the education of [their] rising generation." They planned
to form a village and build a college and various primary schools.
This settlement, they explained, would draw "all the wealthy and intelligent of the country" and become the nucleus of a new civilized
society: "a community where good order and good security" might
be found, and where all would be "engaged in feeding the lamp of
science," to enlighten "the entire surrounding Indian community."[86]
Here, the division of the tribe rather than its reunification became the
anticipated catalyst for the revival of the civilizing process. Only by
freeing the dissidents from the savage power of the Ross faction could
the United States ensure Indian improvement. In the debates born of
the Cherokees' internal struggle, factional conflict often took the form
of an argument over who truly represented civilization.

The standoff in the Indian Territory, and the violence it inspired,
continued into the mid-1840s. At different points during this time it
looked as if one or the other side might gain the upper hand through
federal intervention. Investigators sent by John Tyler's administration
in 1844 blamed the Treaty Party and Old Settler dissidents for the
continued upheaval and endorsed the Ross faction's goals. Their report

urged the negotiation of a new treaty, one that would reunite the tribe under the Act of Union government while better indemnifying the Cherokees for the loss of the eastern homeland.[87] James K. Polk, on the other hand, supported the dissidents and urged Democrats in Congress to introduce a bill to divide the Cherokee Nation. As events in Washington shifted back and forth in this manner, the fighting in the Indian Territory grew worse. Violence reached a level even greater than that of 1839, as political killings became an almost weekly occurrence. As one Treaty Party Cherokee noted, "Murders in the country have been so frequent until the people care as little about hearing these things as they would [about] hear[ing] of the death of a common dog."[88]

In the summer of 1846, under conditions that one historian has described as "compulsory arbitration," a federal treaty commission at last brought the Cherokee factions into agreement. To avoid a division of the tribe, Ross accepted the validity of the Treaty of New Echota and ceased his government's efforts to win additional compensation for the eastern homeland. He also agreed that the Old Settlers should share in any disbursement of the funds promised to the Cherokees in 1835 and that a portion of the tribal funds should be used to compensate Treaty Party members for losses experienced during the troubles of the previous seven years. In return, the most important demands of Ross and his allies were met: the Cherokee Nation remained intact and the constitution written following the Act of Union was sustained. Moreover, the United States issued the Cherokee government a patent for the new homeland's seven million acres, held in common, an act that Ross had long demanded as a further assurance that there would be no sequel to removal. Finally, all sides agreed to a general amnesty for crimes committed during the factional warfare. With this treaty, signed in early August 1846, the removal era came to an end.[89]

The manner in which the lingering conflict over removal was put to rest provides an especially clear example of the paradox of Indian nationhood. The treaty of 1846 reaffirmed the tribe's status as a distinct political community. The Act of Union government survived as the sole political authority of a single Cherokee Nation, and that government received a patent declaring it the absolute owner of the new homeland. Yet those results only came about through the intervention of federal officials, who compelled the Cherokee factions to come to terms. The same officials had contemplated breaking up the nation, American authorities apparently believing that they possessed the right to divide or completely dissolve the nation if they saw fit. The Cherokee Nation survived the post-removal crisis but only with the permission of the United States.

Tribal leaders like John Ross understood as well as anyone that the Cherokees relied on the American government to preserve their own nationhood. In the context of the removal struggle, however, they came to define nationhood as indispensable to the tribe, and the protection of the nation as white America's only reasonable choice. At the heart of that definition was the idea of Indian progress. The nation, they suggested, was the only institution through which progress could occur. The civilizing process was not simply a matter of white missionaries and government agents teaching Indians or of Indians individually adopting their white neighbors' ways. The progress that the Cherokees had made in the early republic had required the founding fathers' respect for Cherokee autonomy as well as their benevolence. Likewise, the continuation of Cherokee progress in the 1840s required the preservation of Cherokee nationhood. To paraphrase George Lowrey, without the nation and its independent Cherokee government, there could be no Cherokee farms, schools, or churches. And without the farms, schools, and churches, the Cherokees' very survival was in doubt. Within the culture of American Indian affairs, the absence of progress was not only savagery but a prelude to extinction. When Cherokee leaders identified the nation as the key to the civilizing process, they suggested as well that it was the only institution that could prevent the annihilation of their race.

The tendency of all this language was to reduce America's Indian policy decisions to stark moral choices between life and death, survival and extinction. The United States possessed the power to violate treaties with impunity, but to do so was to drive Native Americans out of existence. Federal officials could undermine Cherokee nationhood, but only if they were willing to destroy the tribe.

Cherokee political writing in the removal era accepted the basic terms with which European Americans identified Indian people. In particular, it embraced as a structuring principle the notion that Native Americans faced a choice between emulating white civilization and disappearing. Cherokee leaders claimed for themselves, however, the authority to decide the path that Indian civilization would take, insisting that there could be no progress without autonomy. It was this definition of the Indian nation – a civilizing institution, a barrier to decline, and a test of American morality – that tribal leaders would carry with them as they met the new crises of the middle and late nineteenth century.

2

The Civil War and Cherokee Nationhood

We have watched and cherished your interests with faithful and devoted hearts. . . . In the war to suppress the late rebellion almost one half of our people have been sacrificed upon the altar of your country. Our land is filled with helpless widows and orphans, and our country and our people, war-ridden, poverty-stricken, and stripped even to nakedness, present such evidences of devotion to your government as defy parallel in history.
—Lewis Downing to the United States Senate, 1869

They scalped for those who paid, fed, and clothed them. As to loyalty, they had none at all.—Albert Pike to the commissioner of Indian Affairs, 1866

Both these quotations refer to a common subject, Cherokee actions in the American Civil War.[1] They reflect the contradictory positions in a crucial postwar debate concerning the nature of Cherokee participation in the conflict. At the close of hostilities, the United States government negotiated new treaties with the tribes of the Indian Territory, a region that became a battleground in the war. The federal officials involved in that process defined Confederate-allied tribes as conquered peoples, groups upon whom the government could act as it saw fit. In the case of the Cherokees, however, it was difficult to determine whether they belonged in that category, since over the course of the war's four years Cherokee citizens and the tribal government had assumed virtually every possible attitude toward the dispute. After an early attempt at neutrality, the nation's elected leaders had signed a treaty with the Confederacy, only to repudiate it soon thereafter and attempt to reestablish relations with the Union. Cherokee citizens, meanwhile, had served in both northern and southern armies and had often fought against one another. For a time there had even been two governments in the Cherokee Nation, one consisting of Union men, the other of Confederates.

That confusion became an important element of treaty talks between federal officials and Indian leaders at the fighting's end, since one's definition of the Cherokee position during the Civil War went a long way toward determining one's idea of proper postwar relations. As always, nationhood and sovereignty were at the heart of the matter. For American negotiators, the conviction that the Cherokees had betrayed the United States came with a willingness to ignore the old treaties and undermine Cherokee nationhood. On the other hand, Cherokees who considered themselves steadfast American allies felt that their service in the Union cause warranted the preservation, if not the strengthening, of Cherokee sovereignty. Sorting through the chaos of the war years became a vital political process as Cherokees and non-Indians alike imagined the future of the Indian Territory.

This chapter describes the argument over the Civil War as a way of exploring the conflict's effect on Cherokee claims to nationhood and sovereignty. Along the way, it places the Cherokee debate in the broader story of Reconstruction. The war and the task of rebuilding and reintegrating the South altered – at least for a time – the power of the federal government and its place in American life. That change had implications for Cherokee and Indian affairs, insofar as the central government already assumed a responsibility for watching over Native Americans. Cherokee leaders in the postwar era often seemed to be searching for the right kind of federal power, a United States government strong enough to live up to its treaty promises but one whose authority would not be used to destroy the Indian nation. Viewed from the perspective of that search, the expansion of federal power in the 1860s was simultaneously attractive and threatening.

Two key terms recur in the argument over the nature of the Cherokees' participation in the Civil War: loyalty and protection. Had the

Cherokees truly shown unparalleled devotion to the United States, as Lewis Downing remembered, or had they behaved like mercenaries? Had the United States adequately protected the Cherokees during the crisis? What did the answers to these questions portend for relations in the postwar decades? These are strange terms to have applied to a people claiming to be a sovereign nation. Presumably, an independent political community requires neither loyalty to another nor another's protection. Understanding the significance of these terms brings one closer to the strange, often contradictory, meaning of Cherokee nationhood in the nineteenth century.

The period immediately preceding the Civil War is sometimes remembered as the Cherokees' "golden age." When the factional violence ended in 1846, the Cherokees at last had the opportunity to rebuild the nation and reestablish the institutions they had begun in the East. By most standards, their efforts were successful. Relative normalcy returned to Cherokee politics, with the factions remaining content to fight most of their battles within the tribe's constitutional system. John Ross was still principal chief, and his supporters continued to dominate the tribal government; however, members of the Treaty Party, along with Old Settlers, won election to political office and exerted a measure of influence over the nation's affairs. Economically, the Cherokees enjoyed a decade of prosperity. The bicultural elite rebuilt their plantations and businesses, while according to missionaries and federal agents the more numerous class of subsistence farmers maintained at least a decent standard of living. Most impressive, the Cherokee government used its treaty funds to create a public education system equal to or better than those of neighboring states. More than one hundred primary schools were operating by the early 1850s, along with the Cherokee Male and Female Seminaries – high schools founded with the intent of training better Cherokee teachers. All this occurred within the context of comparatively settled relations between the Cherokee Nation and the United States. There was talk in the 1850s of extending American territorial law over the Indian country, but for the most part the federal government refrained from mounting assaults on the tribal autonomy such as the Cherokees had faced in the removal era.[2]

In the midst of this renaissance, the sectional crisis over slavery presented the tribe with a cruel dilemma. The fracture of the Union threatened to alter completely the conditions in which Cherokees labored to maintain their homeland, their political rights, and their hard-won peace and prosperity. It left them with the choice of either clinging to the established relations or attempting to move with the changes at work among their powerful neighbors. Both options involved terrible risks. The Cherokee Nation was bound to the government of the United States by treaties that Indian leaders described time and again as the sacred foundation of the tribe's progress. At the heart of those treaties was a Cherokee promise to maintain political relations only with Washington, in effect to trust in the goodwill and power of the federal government. But Washington was far away and the authority of the federal government under attack. Meanwhile, several important factors tied the tribe to the South. With Arkansas on the Cherokees' eastern border and Texas close by, geography seemed to place the Cherokee Nation in the southern camp. Most of the tribe's American agents over the years had been Southerners. And of course the tribe participated in the practice over which their neighbors were coming to blows: at least some of the Cherokees were slaveholders. America's sectional hostility came to the Cherokees as a conflict between an all-important but distant ally and the tribe's immediate neighbors.

In later years, Cherokee leaders liked to depict the Civil War as strictly a white man's affair that tragically overflowed into the Indian Territory, but in fact some Cherokees began choosing sides as early as the mid-1850s. Inspired most likely by events in "bleeding Kansas," pro-slavery Cherokees around 1855 founded societies dedicated to defending the "peculiar institution" in the Indian Territory. In particular, these "Blue Lodges" aimed to expel abolitionist missionaries from the nation, an effort assisted by the Indian Bureau officers assigned to the tribe. Although it is impossible to determine their membership exactly, the lodges were thought to be organs of the old Treaty Party or Ridge faction. Led by Stand Watie, who had signed the 1835 removal agreement and narrowly escaped death in 1839, the treaty Cherokees were generally slaveholders. Many had close business and personal ties to white residents of Arkansas and were strongly sympathetic to the southern position in the growing crisis. The formation of the Blue Lodges was a sign that if the Union were to break apart, the South would have immediate allies among the former dissidents.[3]

The identification of the Treaty Party with the South worried and angered John Ross and his supporters. Some Ross faction leaders, the principal chief included, were themselves slaveholders, but they feared that Cherokee support for the South would invite renewed American efforts to undermine Cherokee sovereignty and landholding. Moreover, many still considered the treaty Cherokees traitors and assumed that their involvement in the slavery issue was a play for political power. In response to the creation of the Blue Lodges, Ross Party men, aided by the antislavery Baptist missionaries Evan and John B. Jones, organized a brotherhood of their own, the Keetoowahs – also known as the "Pins" for some members' habit of wearing crossed pins as an identifying badge. Taking their name from a Cherokee-language term for the tribe (*ani-kituwah*) and from a precolonial organization, the Keetoowahs dedicated themselves to preserving the unity of the Cherokee people and the sovereignty of the nation. In the short term those goals translated into limiting the pro-southern faction's power by electing Keetoowah members and other proven Cherokee patriots to tribal political office. In the longer term, however, the goal of Cherokee unity and strength would be achieved by winning control of the nation for the "full-bloods," by which the Keetoowahs meant people of mostly Cherokee descent who spoke their native language and who preserved some of their people's cultural traditions. The Keetoowahs limited their membership to such full-bloods, kept their records in Cherokee, and often combined their political organizing with traditional activities such as dances and the ball game. Thus, several years before the fall of Fort Sumter, America's sectional crisis had found its way into the Cherokee Nation and had been translated into the terms of the Cherokees' internal politics.[4]

When southern states began to secede in the winter of 1860–61, leaders in Arkansas and Texas demanded to know with whom the Cherokees stood. John Ross answered by insisting that the Cherokee Nation was neutral; the Cherokees were sympathetic toward their southern neighbors, but since their treaties were with Washington they intended to take no part in the developing conflict.[5] Stand Watie and the other "Southern Party" leaders, however, made it clear that they supported secession and would work to ally the Cherokee Nation with an independent South. When a Confederate treaty delegation traveled to the Indian Territory in May 1861, the southern Cherokees asked for and received guarantees of protection were they to decide to fight in the Confederate cause. Two months later, against the express wishes of Ross, Confederate general Ben McCulloch commissioned Watie as a colonel and issued arms to three hundred of his followers who gathered at Fort Smith, Arkansas, to enlist in the rebel army. Compounding the trouble, by this time there remained no significant federal presence to answer the Southern Party's move. The government agents had returned to their home states to join the Confederacy, and the federal army had withdrawn every garrison in the Indian Territory in preparation for war. There were federal officers over the northern border in Kansas, but these men declined to offer any concrete aid to the Cherokee leaders. As Union and Confederate armies met in northern Virginia in their first major battle, Cherokee neutrality was already crumbling, and Ross faced the real possibility that his bitter rivals, possessing Confederate arms and support, would move to seize control of the tribal government.[6]

Ross and his immediate allies abandoned neutrality in the weeks following the formation of Watie's Confederate regiment. In late August 1861, the principal chief called a general council, a meeting open to the entire nation, and announced that he now felt it was necessary for the Cherokees to seek an alliance with the Confederacy. It seemed likely, he noted, that the United States would henceforth be two separate nations (the war, of course, was not going well for the Union at this time). Since the Cherokees were geographically situated in the South, the logical course would be to transfer political relations to the Confederacy. Moreover, it was crucial that in a period of change and upheaval the

Cherokees should maintain their national unity. "Union is strength," Ross told the assembly, "dissention is weakness, misery, ruin! . . . As Brothers live; as Brothers die!" And unity, he reasoned, could now only be served by a Confederate alliance. Cherokees had already sided with the South, as had many members of the other Indian Territory tribes. Under those conditions, continued official neutrality might result in Cherokees fighting Cherokees, or Cherokees fighting other Indians, tragedies to be avoided at all costs. If the Cherokees could not avoid involvement in the American conflict, they should participate as one people.[7]

Following the address, the assembled Cherokees passed by acclamation a series of resolutions that granted the principal chief the authority to negotiate a Confederate treaty. This Ross and his lieutenants did several months later, with their efforts securing an agreement that preserved Cherokee national sovereignty, transferred annuity payments from the federal to the Confederate government, and stipulated that Cherokees would not be required to fight for the Confederacy outside the Indian Territory. Meanwhile, Ross and his allies raised a new Confederate regiment, one consisting of Keetoowahs and other Ross supporters and led by John Drew, an ally of the chief. By taking control of relations with the Confederacy and raising an armed force loyal to Ross, the Cherokee leadership nullified the possibility of a Watie-led coup d'état. They did so, of course, at the expense of their treaties with Washington, but in the summer and autumn of 1861, when a Union defeat seemed likely, they may not have considered this too great a sacrifice.[8]

Ross reportedly called the Confederate agreement the best they had ever signed, and indeed the treaty contained several provisions that could have strengthened the nation, had the South won the war.[9] The Confederacy promised, for example, never to enter into negotiations with Cherokees not authorized by the tribal government. The treaty also stipulated that the Confederate government would consult the Cherokees when appointing agents to the tribe, while it set up procedures for removing and replacing agents when the Cherokees desired it. The Cherokee government was given the authority to remove intruders in the nation, something that would have proven increasingly useful later in the nineteenth century. And the South offered the tribe the option of electing a delegate to the Confederate Congress, an officer who would possess the same status as did delegates from Confederate territories. The Treaty of New Echota had contained a similar provision, allowing a Cherokee delegate in the U.S. House of Representatives. The idea's reappearance in 1861 may indicate that Cherokee leaders envisioned the tribe's eventually becoming a full-fledged member of the Confederacy, a tribe but also a state.[10]

While the Confederate treaty was a relatively good one from an Indian standpoint, the Confederacy itself soon proved to be a rather poor Cherokee ally. In November 1861 the Confederate command ordered Cherokee soldiers to participate in the pursuit of Opothleyoholo, a pro-Union Creek leader fleeing with a band of refugees toward Kansas. That is, they ordered Indians to fight Indians, precisely the situation that Ross had hoped to avoid. When the Confederates caught up with Opothleyoholo, much of Drew's regiment deserted and joined the Creeks. Now Cherokees fought Cherokees. Although the deserters later returned, the episode created new animosity between Watie's faction, committed as they were to the Confederate cause, and the more mercurial Ross men.[11] The following spring there arose even greater trouble. The Confederates broke the treaty by sending Cherokee soldiers into Arkansas to participate in the campaign that culminated in the Battle of Pea Ridge. Then, when federal troops won that battle, almost all the rebel forces withdrew to the southern border of the Indian Territory, leaving the Cherokee Nation completely exposed to invasion. Clearly, the Confederate alliance had secured neither harmony among the Cherokees nor safety for the Cherokee homeland.[12]

In late June 1862 an army of ten thousand federal soldiers, pro-Union Indian refugees among them, entered the Cherokee Nation from Kansas. There they encountered and defeated a Confederate force that included the two Cherokee regiments. Again, large numbers of Ross Party soldiers deserted and joined the pro-Union Indians; this time there were enough to form a new federal regiment. Watie's men, meanwhile, fled to the South. Ross used this development to change course once again. Waiting for the federal troops to reach his home at Park Hill, he allowed himself to be put under arrest and then taken, along with much of his family, to Kansas. Once on Union soil, he received a parole from his captors and promptly set out for the East, where he spent the remainder of the war trying to reestablish relations with the federal government and secure military and financial aid for the Cherokees.[13]

As the chief departed the nation, full-scale civil war arrived. In August the Confederate Cherokees took control of Tahlequah and declared a new government, with Watie as principal chief and his lieutenants and allies as the National Council. Several months later, refugees serving in the Union Army in Kansas crossed back into the Indian Territory, held a council, and formed a government of their own. Calling themselves "Loyal Cherokees," they reelected Ross in absentia and filled the various other posts with Cherokee Union Army officers. Neither of these governments, however, succeeded in controlling much of the nation for any length of time. Instead, for the next two years power shifted back and forth between the Loyal and the Southern factions, dominance often being determined by how much aid the Loyal Cherokees' Union allies could spare and for how long. When federal troops and supplies were plentiful, the Loyal Cherokees were able to hold much of the nation. When support dwindled, Watie and his allies returned. In these uncertain conditions, the war in the Cherokee Nation became a cycle of irregular raids, assassinations, and reprisals – a bloodier version of the factional violence of the early 1840s. While one substantial battle did take place (at Honey Springs in July 1863), for the most part combatants focused on plundering and destroying their enemies' property and murdering the occasional captive. "Killed a few Pins in Tahlequah," Stand Watie reported to his wife in November 1863. "They had been holding council. I had the old council house set on fire and burnt down, also John Ross's house. Poor Andy Naves was killed. He refused to surrender and was shot by Dick Fields. I felt sorry as he used to be quite friendly towards me before the war, but it could not be helped."[14] This kind of guerilla warfare destroyed much of the nation's agriculture and livestock and emptied the Cherokee countryside as terrified residents fled to refugee camps. Those uprooted suffered horribly from disease and malnutrition. "Sickness made dreadful havoc among them," Loyal Cherokee officers wrote of one refugee group. "The camp ground at Dry Wood is literally a grave yard."[15] By the time the war ended, the worst fears of Cherokee leaders in 1860 had been realized. Cherokees had fought and killed Cherokees. Some four thousand of the nation's citizens had lost their lives, while those who survived faced a homeland in ruins.[16]

When John Ross fled the territory and traveled east, he hoped to convince Washington to restore Cherokee-American relations to their prewar basis. By the end of the fighting, however, federal officials had different ideas. The American delegates who in early September 1865 began multi-tribal treaty negotiations at Fort Smith came prepared to transform the Indian Territory, not merely return it to its antebellum status. Led by D. N. Cooley, the commissioner of Indian Affairs, they presented Indian leaders with a common set of conditions for their return to the good graces of the Union. They demanded that the Indians abolish slavery and admit their former slaves to full tribal citizenship. They declared the American government's intention to buy a portion of the Territory for use in resettling tribes then living in Kansas. And they insisted that the Indians commit themselves to forming a common government for the Territory, a change that they intended to be a step toward making the Indian country a regular federal possession. As negotiations proceeded, Cooley and his lieutenants added to these points a demand that the tribes accept railroad rights-of-way through their nations and make land grants to aid the corporations building the lines. All told, these conditions pointed to an Indian Territory far more integrated into the life of the United States than previously. This was particularly true of the idea of a territorial government. If the Indian country were to be reorganized to match the normal structure of American possessions, the change would likely bring the dismantling of the independent nations and the opening of the Territory to non-Indian settlement under federal law.[17]

Before the Cherokees could begin to address these demands, however, the commissioners made a new one, specific to their tribe. Having learned more about John Ross's dealings with Confederate authorities, Cooley and his lieutenants refused to recognize him as principal chief. Ross had not dealt honestly with the federal government, they concluded, and could not be trusted. For all practical purposes, the commissioners attempted to have Ross deposed. The Confederate Cherokees enthusiastically endorsed that action and added a new condition of their own. They asked that the federal government divide the Cherokee homeland and all its funds between the Loyal and Southern factions. After years of bitter warfare, they insisted, it was impossible for them to live any longer with the Ross Party. Ross and his supporters thus found themselves in a situation almost identical to that of the immediate post-removal years, when federal authorities had tried to oust the chief and had considered dividing the nation. Negotiations ostensibly meant to reestablish Indian relations became, in the Cherokees' case, a process that threatened to completely alter the tribe's government, national status, and connection to the United States.[18]

Under these conditions, not surprisingly, the treaty talks went nowhere. Ross and his allies protested angrily and asserted their devotion to the Union during the war. The Confederates attacked Ross and declared their unwillingness to return to a tribe led by either the old chief or his friends. The federal commissioners insisted on treating the Cherokees as rebels and Ross as beneath contempt.[19] It was at Fort Smith, then, that the debate over the Cherokee Civil War began in earnest. No treaty was signed at the council, only vague articles of peace, and for close to a year after, federal authorities, Ross Party leaders, and the former Confederates continued the arguments begun there. Back and forth they disputed the events of the war years and their meaning for postwar relations. During that time, it was an open question as to whether the remainder of the century would see one Cherokee Nation, two, or any such entity at all.

The most complete rendering of the federal government's position in this argument came in a pamphlet written by Commissioner Cooley and published by the Indian Bureau in June 1866. "The Cherokee Question," as it was titled, consisted of a long letter from Cooley to President

Andrew Johnson, followed by appendices containing wartime correspondence of the Cherokee government and postwar testimony of non-Indian observers. The primary purpose was to discredit Ross and justify the ongoing effort to exclude him from tribal leadership and the treaty negotiations. In the process, Cooley presented a detailed, if not entirely accurate, account of the war and discussed various proposals regarding the reestablishment of Cherokee relations with the United States.[20]

Cooley leveled three charges against Ross. The first and most important was that Ross had been sympathetic to the southern cause from the very beginning and that his initial neutrality had only been a pose meant to fool federal authorities. While he had rejected early requests for a Confederate alliance, Cooley argued, Ross had assured the secessionists that he was with them in spirit, as a fellow Southerner and slaveholder. In making that point, the commissioner referred to the testimony of Confederate officers active in the Indian Territory early in the war, one of whom explained: "[Ross] said it was his intention to maintain the neutrality of his people. . . . But he said all his interests and all his feelings were with us, and he knew that his people must share the fate and fortunes of Arkansas."[21] Cooley also made much of the chief's own writings, in which he had frequently admitted that his nation's geography and "domestic institutions" made it a natural Confederate ally, and emphasized Ross's assertion that the agreement with the Confederacy was "the very best treaty we ever made." Such statements, the commissioner argued, demonstrated that the Cherokees' neutral stance had never been anything more than a holding action, allowing Ross time to see whether the Confederacy might succeed in gaining its independence. When the initial campaigns of the war went against the Union, Ross acted on his true allegiance. "Mr. Ross thought the Union forever dissolved and secession an accomplished fact. He then made haste to join the rebellion."[22] On the whole, Cooley's version of the early months of the war suggested the existence of a Ross-led conspiracy to mislead federal authorities while moving the tribe toward a Confederate alliance.

If the Cherokees' neutrality was a sham, then so too was their later loyalty to the Union. Cooley insisted that Ross and his followers sought to restore their connection to the federal government not for devotion to the Union cause but because the Confederacy proved a poor and neglectful ally. Drawing again on Confederate officers' testimony, the commissioner explained the defection of Ross allies from the rebel army by pointing to losses on the battlefield and the Confederate government's failure to provide adequate support. "'Unpaid, unclothed, uncared for, unthanked even, services unrecognized,' they were easily convinced that they were loyal, and by a slight strain on a lively imagination they could see that they had been loyal to the United States from the first."[23] As for Ross himself, Cooley suggested that the chief had gone north merely to save his own skin, and he depicted Ross's departure from the nation as a flight from honor and duty.

If his zeal were as great as he now pretends it always has been in the Union cause and for the Cherokee people, . . . it seems somewhat strange to me that he should have abandoned the Union cause in its great peril in 1862, and strange beyond belief that he should for more than three years have abandoned the Cherokee people, when ruin, swift and certain, was overwhelming them; when his influence, acknowledged ability and foresight were so much needed among his people; and quietly settled himself down in Philadelphia, 1,600 miles from his people, at the expense of some thirty thousand dollars to the nation, while the people whom he loved so well were half starving for want of these thousands so prodigally spent by him.[24]

The Ross faction's return to loyalty, like all their actions during the war, reflected self-interest rather than principle or dedication.

Finally, the commissioner attacked what he considered Ross's pernicious influence over his people. The chief's own disloyalty and scheming would have been harmful in themselves, but Ross compounded the damage by bringing his dedicated followers with him as he moved from neutrality to rebellion to pretended loyalty. Along the way, he tried to convince true allies of the Union, such as the Creeks' Opothleyoholo, to join the rebellion in the interest of maintaining unanimity among the tribes. And as a final act of contumacy, he led the Loyal Cherokee delegation in opposing the fair and reasonable terms offered by federal officials for reestablishing relations. Cooley suggested, in fact, that if Ross could be removed from the negotiations, a treaty between the government and the Cherokees would quickly follow.[25]

There was truth to the commissioner's charge of disloyalty. The motive behind Ross's wartime peregrinations appeared never to be devotion to the Great Father. Rather, it was the desire to keep the Cherokee government (along with his own leadership) intact and his people unified in the face of the American crisis. That goal dictated that the Cherokees tie themselves to whichever side appeared most likely to be in control of the Southwest when the fighting stopped and whichever side promised to safeguard the Indian nation's autonomy. Loyalty, it seems, was largely irrelevant to Cherokee leaders' immediate problems during the war years. This did not mean that there was a conspiracy at work in the Indian Territory during the first months of the war, but Cooley was surely correct when he questioned the principal chief's devotion to the Union cause.[26]

Cooley's depiction of Ross, meanwhile, invoked several very traditional themes in interpreting the confusing events of the war years. For one thing, Cooley created an image of Cherokee leadership that could have come straight out of the debates over removal. During the 1830s, one of the arguments made by removal advocates was that Cherokee leaders, John Ross among them, deluded their people into resisting migration. The chiefs led average Cherokees to believe that the eastern homeland could be saved, while keeping them in the dark about the true precariousness of their situation and the generosity of the government's offer of lands in the West. The leaders did this, it was usually suggested, out of self-interest: educated commercial farmers like Ross owned valuable plantations that they hoped to preserve. In addition, those making such arguments often pointed out the mixed racial status of many Cherokee leaders, who were "more white than Indian," a state taken to indicate both superiority to and isolation from the general tribal population. What all this amounted to was an image of the Cherokee chief as a scheming "mixed-blood," a man whose power came from his command of the "ignorant full-blood"

Indians but one who had his own interests more than those of his people at heart. The *real* Cherokees, by this way of thinking, would have readily accepted removal, which in its proponents' view was the best course possible for the endangered eastern tribes, had it not been for the unnatural influence of clever, duplicitous chiefs.[27]

John Ross never quite shook off this characterization after the Trail of Tears. It was very much in evidence, for example, when American officials attempted to have him deposed in the wake of the killings of 1839.[28] A quarter century later, Cooley renewed the theme, and Ross and his lieutenants were again identified as self-interested schemers. Throughout, the commissioner's pamphlet showed Ross manipulating both his own followers and the Confederate and Union representatives with whom he dealt. His main purpose, Cooley implied, was to maintain the great power he enjoyed in the Indian Territory. When that was no longer possible, Ross abandoned his people. Cooley called upon an established model of the cunning, unprincipled mixed-blood leader to cut through the tangled events of the war and reach the conclusion that Ross and his fellow Loyal Cherokees had been loyal only to themselves.

Meanwhile, Cooley maintained a consistent paternalism in his writing, a second indication that the commissioner was calling upon older habits in interpreting the war in the Cherokee Nation. The very fact that he and other government officials judged Cherokee actions in terms of loyalty or its absence suggests a fundamentally paternalistic outlook. The Cherokees claimed the status of an autonomous nation. They had treaties with the United States, and at the time of Cooley's writing were in the process of negotiating a new one. Yet the commissioner, like most federal officials, depicted the Cherokees strictly as federal clients. He never mentioned the treaties, even though their repudiation by the Cherokee government would seem to have supported some of his positions. Instead, he characterized the turn to the Confederacy as an act of betrayal. Informing the entire argument was the assumption that the Cherokees' course in 1861 should have been to choose sides: either rebellion or unquestioning service in the Union cause, whatever the consequences.

A further indication of Cooley's paternalism was his analysis of the Cherokees' postwar needs. A proper settlement, he argued, would make at least two fundamental changes in the Cherokee Nation. First, the tribe's land base would be sharply reduced, an action that would both allow the settlement of newly removed tribes in the ceded territory and encourage Cherokee progress. Cooley objected to a Ross Party proposal that would have left the tribe, by the commissioner's calculations, over three hundred acres for every man, woman, and child. This was "an amount ten times larger than is convenient under their present circumstances and twenty times greater than will be advantageous or convenient when (if ever) they become perfectly civilized." The Cherokees, he went on, "cannot use it, and really do not require it, and withhold it from civilization, which does require it, and can and will use it."[29] Following an old line of reasoning, Cooley suggested that too much land was bad for Indians and, what was more, an offense against civilized white people, who needed land and would use it properly. Those with the ability to improve Indian land had a right to possess it, and it was incumbent upon federal authorities to adjust tribal landholding to reflect this wisdom (Cooley's preferred adjustment would have left 177 acres per Cherokee).[30] In addition to paring down the tribe's territory, the commissioner endorsed the idea of dividing the Cherokee Nation in order to give the Southern Party its own homeland. The revival of this tactic came in part from the expectation that the "ancient feud," as Cooley called it, between the Ridge and Ross factions could never be resolved. "The feud still exists," the commissioner wrote, "and that it has always existed since it first arose there can be no doubt." As the Cherokees had proven themselves incapable of living peacefully with one another, the federal government had a duty to step in and settle the dispute for them.[31]

Both these proposals, of course, assumed for the federal government the authority to judge and direct Cherokee internal affairs – to be, as another observer put it, the Cherokees' "umpire and guardian."[32] In a sense, this attitude represented a natural progression from the discrediting of Ross. The treacherous chief having failed both the United States and his own people, the Cherokees would now be led responsibly by Indian Bureau agents. Ultimately, Cooley's message –

and the conviction of government officials generally – was that the Cherokee Civil War proved the need for more direct control over the Indian Territory. The answer to the chaos of the war years was the reassertion of federal power.

That conclusion was in keeping not only with old ideas about Indians but with an important broader trend at work in the immediate postwar era. As most historians of the Civil War and Reconstruction point out, the conflict magnified, at least temporarily, the power of the federal government. Waging a four-year war across a wide section of the continent required an unprecedented level of federal action. Besides recruiting and drafting soldiers and spending the money necessary to equip and support them, the central government adopted policies that strengthened its presence in many areas of American life. It created a national banking system and currency to help it marshal the economy in support of the war. Tariffs were raised and new taxes levied. Congress passed the Homestead and Land Grant College Acts and began to give away large amounts of public land for the promotion of railroad building. And of course it ended slavery and took upon itself the responsibility of drawing the freed people more fully into American society.[33]

While the war empowered the state, it also resulted in its glorification. In the burst of nationalism that accompanied victory, some Northerners, Republicans in particular, came to identify the federal government as a savior, an agent of national redemption. The accomplishments of the war years, especially the destruction of slavery, suggested that government could be a positive actor in American life and a powerful instrument of progress.[34] Interestingly, that new image closely resembled one traditionally ascribed to the federal government in Indian affairs. Long before the war, the government was the Indians' Great Father, the chief agent of their salvation, and their guide in the civilization process. In a sense, what happened in the 1860s was that a portion of the northern public came to accept an ideal of government already at work in Indian relations. When D. N. Cooley tackled the "Cherokee question," he did so as a representative of both the familiar Great Father and the exalted state imagined by the Civil War's victors.[35]

Social-reform movements after the war reflected this assurance that government could be a progressive agent. Whether involved in old causes (such as temperance) or newer ones (like universal education or public health), reformers worked at least partly through the political process, and they showed a willingness to use political power to bring order to their fellow Americans. As was perhaps fitting for men and women energized by a military victory, postwar reformers emphasized discipline as a crucial ingredient of an improved nation. They took from the war the lesson that great leaps of progress could be secured if Americans worked together in a uniform and orderly manner, and they tried to better American society by making it more homogeneous. Thus, education advocates sought not only to make access to schools universal but to standardize schooling as well; temperance crusaders were willing to let government compel citizens to limit or even eliminate their consumption of alcohol. This represented a shift in emphasis from the ways of antebellum activists. Before the war, many abolitionists, for example, had hoped to end slavery through moral suasion, by awakening individual slaveholders to right and wrong; now there was a greater willingness to achieve improvement through command.[36]

The cultural historian Richard Slotkin places this shift within the development of a "managerial ideology" in postwar American life. Slotkin suggests that authorities in government, business, and social institutions increasingly acted on the conviction that continued progress in the United States demanded the regulation of disorderly portions of the populace. This was a lesson not only of the southern rebellion, but also of industrialization, the growth of cities, and new currents of immigration. Those categorized as disorderly included virtually every marginal group in the country: African Americans, Indian people, the Chinese, other immigrants, and especially industrial workers. America could be perfected, in the managerial outlook, but only if discipline were imposed upon the unruly.[37]

D. N. Cooley was concerned with nothing if not bringing discipline to the Indian Territory. His account of the war among the Cherokees, his depiction of Ross, and his prescriptions for postwar Indian relations all operated within not only traditional notions of Indian affairs but also within this postwar managerial outlook. Cooley promised the Cherokees peace and justice; he could speak the language of a reformer. But he proposed to fix the Cherokees' problems by treating them like fractious children. He would rid them of troublesome leaders, separate the mutually belligerent, and divest the Cherokees of the "unnecessary" portion of their detrimentally large homeland. He would bring tranquility to the Cherokee Nation by imposing an order that substantially undermined its ability to act outside federal authority. Future progress would be the state's achievement as much as the tribe's. For the treaty commissioners, as for many postwar reformers, the goal of securing justice and humanity could not be separated from the exercise of power by the disciplined over the disorderly.

If Cooley's version of the war was about renewing the authority of the United States government, then that of the Confederate Cherokees was about escaping the authority of the Ross Party. For the Southern leaders, the war came down to two factors: slavery and the old dispute between the Ross and Ridge factions. They admitted to having sided with the secessionists in the interest of maintaining slavery and out of sympathy for their white neighbors. It was a "course we adopted in all honor and sincerity."[38] The Confederacy having lost the war, however, the Southern Party now consented to the abolition of slavery and agreed to bind themselves again to the United States government. In essence, the Southern Party adopted the same position as did the leaders of seceded states: they had succumbed to superior force and were ready to return to the Union. Reaching a settlement, however, was complicated by strife within the Cherokee population. The war had heightened animosity between the Ross Party and the Southern Cherokees, and by the last years of fighting it had become an open conflict between the two factions. The Southern Party leaders declared themselves prepared to live in peace: "We are willing and ready again to proffer the olive branch." But the followers of John Ross remained hostile, so much so that it was unsafe for the Southern Cherokees to live in the nation as it currently existed. The Southern Party, its leaders claimed, could willingly swear renewed allegiance to the United States, but they could not do the same to a Cherokee government dominated by Ross or his allies.[39]

In making that argument, the Southern representatives emphasized the age and intractability of the factional dispute – much as did Cooley and other federal officers. "The bitter feuds now distracting the Cherokees are of no recent date," one statement read. "They are as old as the treaty of 1835."[40] It was the Ridge Party's embrace of removal that had won for it the hostility of Ross and his followers, and the latter group's animosity had never faded. The Ross faction's latest attack had begun even before the war, with the formation of the Keetoowahs. The secret organization, according to Southern leaders, was a tool used by Ross and his allies to maintain their power and punish their enemies. "Arraying the mass of fullbloods against the halfbloods and white men of the Nation," the Keetoowah society was meant to "inflame and excite the innate prejudices of caste among the Indians and thus enable demagogues, peculators of public funds, and murderers to enjoy in security their ill-gotten gains."[41] With such men still in control of the Cherokee Nation, the Confederates could not hope to be safe when they returned to their homes.

The only answer to the feud was to divide the Cherokee territory and provide the Southern Party with a protected country of its own. The Confederates reminded their readers that federal agents in the 1840s had recommended such a division and that President James K. Polk had even drafted a special message to Congress endorsing the idea. Had his advice been followed, they argued, much of the death and destruction of the war years would have been avoided. Now, with that terrible history added to the original dispute, it was unlikely that the Cherokees could ever be reunited. "After all the blood which has been shed, and the intense bitterness that seems to fill the bosoms of our brethren, we should not be expected to live in an undivided country."[42]

In several important ways, the Confederate Cherokees confirmed the federal government's interpretation of the war in the Indian Territory. They admitted that they were rebels, that they had been disloyal to the United States. Here there were no strained attempts to prove a clandestine devotion to the Union. By their own admission, Stand Watie and his allies had chosen the Confederate side in the dispute, served the southern cause steadfastly, and lost. Moreover, their depiction of Ross matched the image presented by Cooley of the unscrupulous mixed-blood chief manipulating his ignorant Indian masses. If anything, the Southern Party's Ross was even more sinister than the government's. Beyond merely conniving, this Ross was evil, a murderous tyrant. Finally, in all these themes the Confederate Cherokees verified the general picture of the tribe – and one might say of Indians as a whole – that officials like Commissioner Cooley favored. The Cherokees were disorderly and violent, quick to attack one another, and slow to forget a grudge. In short, they wanted for an "umpire and guardian." They needed the sternly paternal hand of the federal government to manage them. Many Confederate leaders still believed that Indian tribes should be nations separate from the United States, but their writing invited precisely the kind of federal oversight and regulation that threatened to destroy Cherokee nationhood in the wake of the Civil War.[43]

John Ross recognized that the Confederate alliance and the tribe's internal conflict placed Cherokee nationhood in jeopardy, and he began making explanations almost immediately after fleeing the Indian Territory. In September 1862 he met with Abraham Lincoln and laid out the position of his rapidly dissolving tribal government. The theme he emphasized was protection – the responsibility of the federal government to provide the Cherokees with it, and the government's failure to do so at the beginning of the war. The treaties that formed the foundation for Cherokee-American relations, he reminded the president, were agreements of "friendship and alliance," and the key to that alliance was the Cherokees' acceptance of American protection. In return for the Cherokees' promise to treat with no other power, the United States agreed to shield them from outside assault. The United States, however, withdrew its protection at the outset of the war, leaving the Cherokees exposed to the secessionists all around them. In that situation, "for the preservation of their Country and their existence," they were forced to make a treaty with the Confederacy. When Union forces returned, however, "the great Mass of the Cherokee People rallied spontaneously around the authorities of the United States."[44] Clearly, then, the Confederate treaty did not signify a real alliance, but only an act of self-defense on the part of the Cherokees. As a later message would put it, "We are not, have not been, *bona fide* rebels."[45] Ross assured the president that if he would now send a strong force into the Cherokee Nation to protect it for the duration of the conflict, the United States would have no further trouble from his people.[46]

This was a straightforward analysis. The war had disrupted relations between the Cherokees and the federal government, but nothing substantial about those relations had changed. With renewed federal protection, all would be well. By the end of the war, however, new conditions elicited a more complex position from Ross and his friends. They continued to argue that they had agreed to the Confederate treaty only under extreme duress and had returned to the Union side as soon as possible. But as efforts were made to depose the chief, and as there emerged proposals to alter the nation fundamentally, the Ross Party elaborated on their version of the war.

For one thing, they quite logically began to emphasize their people's loyalty to the Union while continuing to insist that the Union had failed to protect them. A statement presented to the federal commissioners at Fort Smith in 1865 provides an example. In addition to arguing that the Cherokees had no choice in 1861 but to treat with the Confederacy ("There was not only danger, but a strong probability of annihilation"), the statement suggested that the treaty, in fact, was part of a pro-Union subterfuge mounted by the Loyal majority of the tribe. "The plan was proposed and agreed to that our tribe would seemingly acquiesce in the policy of the Confederate States. . . . But it was clearly, distinctly understood that as soon as the safe opportunity offered, and we could act as free moral agents, act out our true sentiments and feelings, we would fly to our Father's house." The treaty itself, by this account, became almost an act of loyalty. It allowed the pro-Union Cherokees to avoid destruction at the hands of secessionists and thus bought them time to watch and wait for a chance to serve the federal cause.[47] That service, in the form of the enlistment of Cherokees in the Union Army, then became the definitive proof of Cherokee devotion. As the same

1865 message stated: "We have engaged the enemy wherever found. We have endured the toils, privations, and hazards of the war, patiently, courageously; have at all times been obedient to officers, until regularly and honorably discharged. . . . One third of our men are dead. We do not bring up these things in the spirit of boasting, but to show that we are in earnest; that we considered that under the folds of the glorious flag of the Union was our home, and that we, as well as your own people, would lay down our lives to defend it."[48] Another appeal claimed that three-quarters of the Cherokees' adult men had fought in the federal army – a proportion far greater than that of any northern state. "Patriotic Cherokees," Ross Party delegates reminded their audience, "have helped cement the Union."[49]

Ross and his supporters, meanwhile, made much of the fact that the loyal Cherokee council in 1863 had passed a law abolishing slavery. That institution, an 1865 memorial recalled, had been the "one dark spot" on the Cherokees' otherwise ideal antebellum constitution and laws. It had been "introduced into their political system by intercourse with their surrounding white neighbors," the memorial explained. When ending slavery became one of the Union's war aims, however, the Cherokees quickly did away with it. "Be it recorded to the honor of the Cherokees, that they were the first to wipe off that dark spot; and in February, 1863, by their national council, forever abolished slavery within the limits of the Cherokee Nation."[50] As it happened, the law in itself freed no one. It was passed during the period when both a Loyal and a Confederate council claimed to be the nation's government, and neither wielded the power necessary to enforce something like an emancipation edict. One should note, moreover, that the council's act explicitly denied citizenship in the Cherokee Nation to freed slaves. In ending their bondage, it turned them into aliens and intruders.[51] Yet that mattered little to the Ross Party's version of the war. What was important was that the Cherokees had abolished slavery by law before any Confederate state and in so doing had given further proof of their fidelity to the Union.

While providing such evidence of the tribe's loyalty, Ross and his allies made certain that federal authorities understood the depth of

Cherokee suffering during the conflict. Often, they did this by setting up stark comparisons between the nation's antebellum prosperity and its current desolate state. "Before the present war," one statement recalled, "agriculture, stock-raising, and other branches of industry, were successfully and profitably pursued by [the Cherokees]; comforts of life had accumulated, and, in many cases, (comparative) wealth had rewarded the labor and skill of their citizens. . . . But the ravages of war have changed the scene, and spread destitution, bereavement, and desolation, like the shadow of death, over all the land. Not a family has escaped."[52] Particularly intense was the travail of Cherokee refugees. Subjected to "the most brutal outrages" at the hands of rebel soldiers, Loyal Cherokee families, mostly women and children, fled their homes. "The sufferings of these people, both in exile and after their return, have been frightful in privation, sickness, and death."[53] Cherokee leaders argued, in fact, that their people's wartime torments had been worse than those of any white community – a plausible claim, considering the tribe's death toll in proportion to its prewar numbers.[54] One of the Ross Party's goals as the fighting ended was to secure the resumption of treaty funds' normal payment, an aspect of government relations that the war had disrupted. Invoking their people's suffering was part of that effort; they were reminding federal authorities of the Cherokees' great needs. But they also tied suffering in a very direct way to the memory of Cherokee loyalty. As they recalled, it had been the pro-Union sentiment of the Cherokee majority that had drawn Confederate raiders to the nation. Moreover, the rebels had preyed upon the defenseless families left behind by Loyal Cherokee men fighting in the Union Army. Had the Cherokees been less faithful to the United States, the nation would not have become so terrible a battleground. More than an unfortunate by-product of the war, the Cherokees' suffering was a measure of their devotion.

This story of fidelity, abandonment, and suffering resembled nothing so much as the Cherokee memory of removal. By the time treaty negotiations were underway, Ross and the Loyal faction had come to depict the Civil War as a parallel experience to their loss of the eastern homeland. In post-migration Cherokee writings, the events of the 1830s were about the failure of the United States to live up to its obligations, and the hardships inflicted upon the tribe as a result. Although the Cherokees, in their rapid progress, had done everything that American authorities had ever asked of them, the government broke its promises of protection. It caved in to the demands of southern states and abandoned the tribe to the cruelties of its white neighbors. When the Cherokees resisted, federal authorities negotiated a treaty with a group of unauthorized and unrepresentative chiefs and then carried it out, as Cherokees liked to say, "at the point of a bayonet."[55]

That memory proved highly adaptable when it came to relations with the United States after 1839. It could be applied whenever Cherokee representatives wanted to demonstrate that breaches of treaty or challenges to tribal autonomy were ill-advised. In 1845, for example, when President James K. Polk expressed support for the idea of dividing the Cherokee Nation, delegates reminded him of what had happened the last time the United States so violated the treaties. "Torn up by the roots, driven from their humble homes, and confined in camps open to the weather, many sickened and perished; and on the long journey to the distant country allotted to them, many more of the aged and infirm, and of our women and children, sunk from exposure and exhaustion. . . . Is it, then, asking too much to save us from a recurrence of like scenes?"[56] Later, when Kansas's application for statehood included Cherokee territory within its proposed borders, tribal leaders cited removal as an example of why the federal government should take care when considering states' claims to Indian land. "The Cherokee people," they reminded Congress, "are just recovering from their losses brought on them by their forced removal from within the limits of an organized State." Having been "greatly harassed and troubled" by Georgia, they asked that all their land be kept outside state boundaries in the future.[57]

The Ross Party's version of the Civil War duplicated this memory of removal in almost every major feature. A weakness of will on the part of the leaders of the United States left the steadfast and trusting Cherokees to the devices of the unscrupulous whites of the South. The consequence was a repetition of the horrors of the Trail of Tears

– deprivation, sickness, and death on a massive scale. Now federal commissioners were even listening to some of the same Cherokees who had signed the treaty of 1835. The similarities were striking.

Loyal Cherokee messages often invoked removal explicitly. They would remind federal authorities of the provisions in the removal treaties that secured for the tribe independence and federal protection in the new homeland. Or they might begin an appeal regarding a war-related issue with a summary of the tribe's experiences in the removal era. A reply to D. N. Cooley's report, for example, opened by recalling the events of the 1830s, when the United States made an alliance with "a few irresponsible men of [the Cherokee] nation, the better to despoil it; and after inviting [the Cherokees] to form a free republican government like its own endeavored, by arbitrary acts, to disrupt it." Now, American authorities were poised to do it all again, listening to "an irresponsible handful of rebels" rather than the legitimate leaders of the nation.[58] Another appeal linked the memory of the lost Cherokee homeland to the sacrifices of Union soldiers in the war. "But a few years ago," it began, "the Cherokee Nation owned and occupied a country healthful, fruitful and beautiful, eight or nine hundred miles from their present possessions, toward the rising sun." That country had now become the site of American suffering in war. "The memories of Chattanooga, Lookout Mountain, Missionary Ridge, Rossville, Etowah, Spring Place, Red Clay, Creek Path, and other places, made sacred by the graves of our fathers, no less than by the blood of your patriots, will in history be associated with the Cherokee people no less than with yours."[59] In placing allusions to removal alongside their account of the Civil War, Ross and his allies transformed the whole of the tribe's nineteenth century into a story of Cherokee perseverance in the face of white America's weakness and inconstancy. Not only the Cherokees' loyalty in the war but their fidelity through six decades of dealing with a mercurial United States won for the tribe the right to better treatment in the years to come.[60]

If most Cherokees had proven so unwaveringly loyal, how did one explain Stand Watie and his fellow Confederates? The Ross Party interpretation of the war dealt with this in several ways. Often, Ross and his allies simply ignored the conflict within the tribe, implying that the "bona fide rebels" were so few and marginal as not to require consideration. The federal government's threat to divide the homeland, however, made that approach insufficient. Addressing the feud directly, Cherokee leaders depicted the Southern Party as a band of self-interested troublemakers. They admitted that the origin of the conflict was the split over removal but argued that all the difficulties created by the treaty of 1835 had been put to rest by the treaty of 1846. There was little conflict, they insisted, in all the years between the latter agreement and the outbreak of the American war, and as proof they noted that Stand Watie had been elected many times to national office, as had other Cherokees who later joined the Confederacy. True, the feud revived in the 1860s, but only because Watie and his friends chose to defy their government's neutrality and join the secessionists. They were the ones who renewed the dispute, not the Keetoowahs, who were in fact a "loyal league," the equivalent of the pro-Union organizations founded by patriots in the Confederate states during the war.[61]

In light of these facts, the Loyal Cherokee leaders were amazed – or so they wrote – that the United States should take the Southern Party's demands so seriously. Federal officials, it seemed, had been persuaded by the Confederates' claims that their lives would be at risk if they returned to the nation. In fact, the Loyal Cherokees explained, many Southern Party families had already come back and were living peacefully, unmolested by a majority willing to forgive and forget. Watie and his friends said that a division of the Cherokee Nation was necessary to secure peace and safety, but what they truly desired was wealth and power. Having failed during the war to take control of the nation, they were now attempting to use the United States government to seize land and money that rightfully belonged to all Cherokees.[62]

Or perhaps it was the Southern Party itself that was being used. In a pamphlet rebutting D. N. Cooley's "The Cherokee Question," Ross Party delegates suggested that the Confederates were part of a broader conspiracy to defraud or even destroy the Cherokee Nation. "Designing parties," whom the Ross Party identified as "this or that set of contractors, or railroad stock-jobbers," had incited the Confederate leaders to demand the splitting of the tribal land and funds. Otherwise, the delegates implied, Watie and his allies would have accepted a reconciliation with the Loyal majority. Joining in the scheme were Indian Bureau officers. "Our Agent is the enemy of our people," the delegates charged. "[He] misrepresents them, and is in league with corporations and contractors who seek to destroy us."[63]

It is unclear from the pamphlet precisely what the delegates had in mind, but several inferences can be made. During this period, tribal leaders complained of the misuse of tribal funds by businessmen with whom the Indian Bureau had contracted to supply Cherokee refugees. One of the reasons Ross and his allies insisted on an immediate return to normal treaty payments was to end this fraud, which they considered "unparalleled even in the history of the Affairs of the Indians." As other writings from this period confirm, the delegates suspected those contractors of encouraging the division of the nation – perhaps in the hope that the continued disruption of Cherokee affairs would result in the fraudulent supply system remaining in place.[64] "Railroad stock-jobbers," meanwhile, likely referred to the question of how much Indian land would go to the railroads that the federal government insisted the Cherokees allow through the nation. The Southern Party had promised very large grants, while Ross and the Loyal Cherokees had offered only narrow strips along the completed lines. This discrepancy logically placed railroad companies on the side of the Confederates, and from here the delegates apparently concluded that railroad men were in fact driving the effort to empower the Southern Party.[65] Finally, the Loyal Cherokee representatives seem to have believed that the conspiracy's ultimate aim was to denationalize the Cherokees and neighboring tribes. Dividing the nation would perhaps serve as the entering wedge of an effort to turn the Indian country into a full-fledged United States territory – one violation of Indian sovereignty leading to another, more complete assault. If any of these accusations were true, the conceivably just claims of the Southern Party hid a terrible threat.

In a way, the conspiracy theory represented the Ross Party's most strident expression of the theme of Cherokee loyalty. Now, not even the former Confederates were truly disloyal; they were simply being manipulated by very bad white men. While it is doubtful that such a plot existed, at least in the form suggested by the delegates, the charges illustrate well a crucial impulse at work in the Ross Party's version of the Civil War. Cherokee leaders identified nearly all elements of violence and disorder as coming from outside the nation. These were not the unruly Indians of Commissioner Cooley's rhetoric, but an upright and disciplined people who unfortunately became infected with their neighbors' tumults. Even black slavery was defined as something foisted upon them by Americans. The sectional crisis was a white man's scourge that fell undeservedly upon the peaceful, progressive tribe. In their discovery of the conspiracy, Cherokees succeeded in blaming the United States for the persistence of factional conflict among their people. All would have been well had disreputable whites left them alone. All could still be well if the discord bred by white America were held beyond the borders of the Cherokee Nation.

The United States occupied a dual role in the writings of Ross and his supporters. It was the power to which the Cherokees claimed unswerving loyalty but also the source of most of their troubles. In essence, the Cherokees expressed a boundless faith in the United States while depicting it as thoroughly undeserving of their loyalty. That is a strange and ironic image, but it is the key to the war's meaning to Cherokee nationhood. When Cherokees insisted on their devotion to the Union, they accepted a measure of the paternalism of federal officials like Cooley. Although notions of loyalty or betrayal had figured little in tribal leaders' wartime decisions, Ross and his allies acceded to their actions' being judged in precisely those terms. They allowed themselves to be defined not as the leaders of an independent nation but as underlings bearing a duty toward the United States. At the same time, it was white America and the federal government's failure as a guardian that had brought crisis and suffering to the Cherokees in the first place. Indeed, such was the story of most of the Cherokees' recent past, with the Civil War amounting to a reprise of removal. The message of that history was that the United States should ensure that its social and political evils did not again infiltrate Cherokee life. And in the Ross Party's view, that meant the rejection of any measure that further eroded the tribe's national autonomy, be it the ouster of the chief, division of the Cherokee lands, or the political reorganization of the Indian Territory. To be a proper guardian, to be worthy of the Cherokees' devotion, the government of white America had to keep its citizens and itself in check. It had to use its power to keep Indian nationhood viable and real.

That prescription for the future had interesting connotations when placed alongside the broader developments mentioned earlier – the expansion and celebration of federal power and the rise of a "managerial ideology" in many areas of American life. One of the war's lessons for the Cherokees was that their well-being, even their survival, required the presence of a strong United States government. For when the protection of Washington was withdrawn, white America's turmoil and violence contaminated Cherokee life. From that perspective, increased federal power was a positive development, provided that it was applied to guarding the Cherokees. Likewise, when Americans identified the state with justice and humanity, Cherokees could take this as a renewed promise to observe treaty obligations, since adherence to the treaties was in their view the very definition of justice in Indian affairs. The glorification of the central state, then, potentially meant a new commitment to the protection of Indian nationhood.

The willingness of American authorities to pursue progress through the regulation of groups deemed untrustworthy, however, was another matter. As applied to Indian affairs, the managerial ideology promised to dismantle Indian nations in the interest of order and the pursuit of homogeneity. From a Cherokee perspective, this represented the perversion of American power, a misapplication of the lessons of the Civil War. If the new strength of the federal government were used to undermine Indian autonomy, the celebrated state would be transformed from an agent of humanity to an oppressor, its enhanced power made tyrannical rather than redemptive. The Cherokees needed a potent federal government, but a protector who was also a manager became a destroyer.

The Ross Party's version of the war, however, turned the managerial ideology back upon white America. Disorder and trouble, in the Loyal

Cherokees' view, came entirely from the United States. The war in the Cherokee Nation was not a product of Indian unruliness but the tragic result of Americans' own animosities. Cherokee suffering during the war years had indeed demonstrated that management was necessary, but not the management of Cherokees at the hands of federal officers. It was white America itself that required regulation if the people of the Indian Territory were to be spared such undeserved anguish in the future. In the Southwest, the best use of the central government's new power would be to maintain the barriers between the various tribes and the United States and thus ensure that Americans never again exported their conflicts to loyal, peaceful Indians.

Whether federal officials ever accepted the Loyal Cherokees' version of the war is impossible to say. Ross and his allies, however, did succeed in avoiding the most immediate threats to their nation's autonomy and their own leadership in the treaty that finally reestablished relations in July 1866. For one thing, it was the Loyal faction that signed the treaty, not the former Confederates. Federal commissioners had earlier worked out a separate agreement with the Southern Party, but that document never made it to the United States Senate.[66] Instead, it was supplanted by one negotiated by the Loyal delegates and Ross, who although he lay dying in his Washington hotel room signed the document as principal chief and thus remained un-deposed to the very end. That treaty, moreover, did not include the most dangerous government demand – the dividing of the nation and its funds. The former Confederates (along with former slaves) were given the choice of settling in a semiautonomous district, where they would elect their own council representatives, sheriffs, and judges. They would remain, however, subject to the laws of the National Council and would not receive separate treaty money.

In return, the Ross Party acceded to a number of the federal commissioners' points. They agreed to grant citizenship to former Cherokee slaves, thus significantly amending the Loyal council's emancipation law of 1863. They also agreed to sell a portion of the nation along the Kansas border and to allow the future sale of lands in the western part of the nation (known as the Cherokee Outlet) for the resettlement of other Indian tribes. They accepted two railroad rights-of-way through the nation, although land granted to railroad companies would be limited to one hundred feet on either side of the track. Finally, the Loyal delegates approved two changes in the legal and political structure of the Indian Territory. First, the federal government would establish a new district court in the Cherokee Nation, which would handle all cases involving crimes between American and Indian citizens. Second and more controversially, the Cherokees would participate in creating a general council for the territory. This was to be a multi-tribal legislature, and in the federal commissioners' view it represented a definitive step toward bringing the Indian country under ordinary territorial law. The Cherokee treaty, however, specified that no further change would take place without the agreement of all the territory's tribes, and the Loyal delegates made it clear that they did not consider the new council the beginning of political reorganization.[67]

These concessions neatly foreshadowed issues that would come to dominate Cherokee-American relations in the postwar era. The provision granting citizenship to former Cherokee slaves, for example, while on the surface quite clear, set in motion what proved to be a tortuous effort to determine precisely who qualified for the tribal rolls. The treaty specified that former slaves desiring Cherokee citizenship should present themselves by January 1867. During the war, however, many Cherokee slaves had fled the territory or had been taken out by their owners, and some freed people who otherwise qualified did not make it back in time. Others had trouble proving that they had been Cherokee slaves, while some of those claiming citizenship had never been owned by Cherokees but had migrated to the Indian Territory after the war in hopes of securing land.[68] Many Cherokees, meanwhile, balked at the notion that freed people should receive the same rights and benefits as Indian citizens. They accepted the treaty's freedmen articles as a condition of resuming relations with the United States but never fully accepted black people as equal members of the tribe. As the anthropologist Circe Sturm suggests, nineteenth-century Cherokees defined the nation in racial terms. They identified Cherokee blood as the foundation of the national community, and they assumed that the freed people lacked that blood. As a result, black people in the nation, even those who clearly fell within the treaty provisions, often found themselves with a second-class status.[69]

Economic factors tended to drive the freedman controversy – in particular, questions of black access to tribal resources. On several occasions in the decade after the war, for instance, Cherokee leaders proposed granting citizenship to former slaves who had missed the January 1867 deadline. The National Council repeatedly rejected this idea, the majority's rationale being that admitting more freed people than absolutely necessary would unacceptably reduce the land and treaty money available to future generations of Cherokees. Later, at the end of the 1870s, a more disruptive version of this argument developed when Cherokees sold a portion of the Outlet to the United States. In drawing up a roll of those eligible for a share of the payment, the tribe excluded the freed people. American officials and the freed people themselves condemned this as a violation of the 1866 treaty and set out to win for the black citizens their part of the payment. The resulting legal battle raged on and off for more than a decade. From a political standpoint, the great danger of the freedman issue was its tendency to draw federal interference in internal Cherokee affairs. Tribal leaders insisted that citizenship was an issue that the Cherokee government alone had the right to address. Yet when the tribal government acted toward the former slaves in ways that could be interpreted as treaty violations, it invited the United States to intercede.[70]

The question of railroads in the Indian Territory likewise became a source of great trouble for the nation's leaders. Railroads brought American intruders into the Indian country, while railroad companies joined the constellation of interests seeking the dismantling of the Indian nations and the opening of the territory to American settlement. Congress offered railroad companies grants of land in the Indian Territory that could be claimed if and when the tribes relinquished their titles, an action that all but ensured that the railroad companies would become the Indians' enemies. Within a few years after the treaty, Cherokee leaders were regularly decrying the railroad as the nation's greatest foe. The railroads, meanwhile, were the first representatives of the modern corporation to come to Indian Territory. As a later chapter explains, the corporation's arrival altered in some fundamental ways the conditions in which tribal leaders operated.[71]

Finally, the idea of turning the Indian Territory into a regular American possession became the central issue in the Cherokees' relations with the United States. From the end of the war until it was supplanted by allotment in the 1880s, territorialization was the answer to the Indian question continually offered by members of Congress, frontier politicians, and Indian Bureau officials. Despite almost unanimous opposition among the people of the Five Tribes, bills to reorganize the Indian Territory appeared in Washington almost yearly. Denouncing those bills formed the context for much of the Cherokees' political writing for the next two decades.[72]

Ironically, the problem that seemed the most intractable during treaty negotiations – the Cherokees' "ancient feud" – faded from sight within a few years of the war. John Ross's final service to his people was to die almost immediately after signing the treaty of 1866, his removal setting in motion a realignment of Cherokee politics. By 1867 a portion of Ross's following, culturally conservative subsistence farmers led by Union Army veteran Lewis Downing, had joined with former Confederates to create a new dominant bloc in electoral politics. This coalition succeeded in electing Downing principal chief over Ross's nephew and heir, William Potter Ross. The Downing Party, as it came to be known, allied Southern Cherokee leaders like William Penn Adair and William P. Boudinot with Keetoowahs, whom the Confederates had lately attacked as Ross Party terrorists. With John Ross gone and Cherokee politics no longer divided along the old factional lines, the disputes born of removal faded, and never again in the nineteenth century was a division of the Cherokee homeland seriously contemplated.[73]

As rapprochement occurred between the belligerents in the Cherokees' Civil War, agreement emerged as well on the point of interpreting the conflict. Cherokee leaders continued to invoke the war in their messages and appeals to non-Indians, but not surprisingly almost all mention of southern alliances or Confederate enlistment or even the tribe's internal conflict faded from Cherokee writings. Instead, it was the Ross Party's story of loyalty and suffering that became the official memory of the war. Delegates in the 1870s and beyond reminded American authorities that "population considered, the Cherokee Nation furnished more men to the Union cause than any one of the States, and suffered greater loss by death in battle, on the march, and in camps."[74] Likewise, they made certain that no one forgot the misery experienced by their people. "The war of rebellion," an 1880 message recalled, "swept over our country like a terrible tornado, and extinguished nearly one-half of our people and destroyed our homes or made them desolate, and deprived our people of nearly every single bit of personal property."[75] Even when those writing had themselves fought with the Confederacy, service and sacrifice in the Union cause dominated recollections of the war.

Continuing the tendency present in the 1860s, these writings depicted the war as a phenomenon almost completely external to the Cherokees, a scourge emanating from the United States. Here lay the necessity of remembering the conflict. Cherokee leaders recounted the history of the war years in documents arguing against proposals and policies they viewed as new dangers on a par with the conflict, in particular territorialization. In that context, the war became an example of what happened when American authorities forgot their country's obligations to the Indians. When they violated treaties or failed to protect the Cherokees, disaster followed. By contrast, when the Cherokees were left unmolested they prospered and progressed. Even after the vast destruction of the war, one memorial recalled, "they were not discouraged; but like brave men, with few tools and slender resources, set to work in earnest to regain a competency."[76] Pushing from their accounts the complicated history of Confederate sympathy and guerilla warfare, Cherokee representatives made the war a lesson in the imperative of a well-protected Indian nationhood.

Loyalty, suffering, protection – these are hardly terms one associates with the political relationship between one sovereign nation and another. Yet these were the words with which Cherokee leaders attempted not only to explain the Civil War but to imagine a basis for their people's continued national autonomy. In the end, they wrote as if nationhood were a debt white America owed the Cherokees for their devotion and misery during the war – a debt accrued, in fact, over the whole history of American betrayal and Cherokee constancy. If this were something less than true sovereignty, it was considerably more than the ward's role that American authorities would press upon Indian people with increasing intensity in the remainder of the nineteenth century.

3

The Cherokees' Peace Policy

In February 1877 the *Cherokee Advocate* published a short essay to mark the end of the presidency of Ulysses S. Grant. By most standards, Grant's departure from Washington that spring was not a triumphant one. The revelation of corruption at the highest levels of government had marked his second term, and by the time he retired he had become an emblem of weak leadership and scandal. Yet Cherokee editor William P. Boudinot gave a positive, even heroic, portrayal of the outgoing president. From an Indian point of view, Grant had proven himself to be a worthy leader. "We feel like expressing for ourselves and for our whole nation," Boudinot wrote, "the high and sincere gratitude we must all feel for the humane and conscientious consideration he has, first and last, expressed and shown for the rights of a race it was just as easy . . . to neglect, if not oppress." Boudinot recognized that Grant had become the target of much "partisan heat," but he argued that the president's Indian policy demonstrated his true statesmanship. "We cannot help thinking that a man's character must be largely consistent with itself, and that the qualities of justice, humanity, fair dealing and wisdom that General Grant has so plainly shown in dealing with the Indians, are equally prominent as motives governing his policy and course in other directions, and that history will surely place him among the first and best of American Presidents."[1]

As it happened, Boudinot was wrong about the judgments of history, but his lavish praise of Grant points to an important aspect of Cherokee relations with the United States in the years following the Civil War.

During that period, Cherokee leaders found an Indian policy that they could support. The "peace policy," the Grant administration's campaign to end warfare on the plains and reform the Indian Service, won the public approval of Cherokee representatives. Principal chiefs and delegates to Washington lauded it as a sign that at last corruption and oppression in Indian relations were to be replaced with justice and Christian love. They portrayed the reform effort as a step toward reversing the decline of the Indian race and furthering the civilization process. If the United States remained true to Grant's principles, they suggested, its Indian question would soon disappear as all the tribes came to benefit from the blessings of civilized life already enjoyed by the Cherokees.

In supporting the peace policy, however, Cherokee leaders changed it. They took a thoroughly paternalistic program and turned it into an endorsement of Indian autonomy. While the peace policy's subject was an individual ward coaxed toward assimilation by benevolent whites, the Cherokees wrote of Indian nations improving themselves free of damaging interference from white America. Cherokee leaders created their own peace policy, one rooted in the model of Indian-American power relations implied earlier in their writings about the Civil War.

As Francis Paul Prucha has written, the peace policy was more a "state of mind" than a consistent set of initiatives.[2] It reflected a conviction among policy makers and "friends of the Indian" that the established practices in Indian affairs had failed and that new methods were necessary if Native people were to be saved from extinction. Peace-policy advocates blamed frontier violence and Indian degradation on the cupidity of white Americans and expressed remorse at the crimes that had accompanied westward expansion. At the same time the "mind" of the peace policy held that the failures could be reversed if kindness and justice replaced greed and violence in American Indian relations. Expansion could continue cleansed of brutality if the right people with the right values managed the Indians. The peace policy, then, involved an awareness of the dark side of American expansion coupled with a renewed faith that civilization would reconcile Indian people to conquest.[3]

The peace policy began as a reaction to violence in the West during the Civil War years. The attacks carried out in 1862 by reservation Sioux in Minnesota, warfare on the central plains, and the Colorado militia's massacre of peaceful Cheyennes and Arapahos at Sand Creek created among eastern Americans a sense that Indian affairs were in a state of crisis. The Sand Creek Massacre, in particular, was taken as evidence that American Indian policy had to be changed. Newspapers throughout the eastern states published descriptions of the attack, many of them sharply critical of the militia's actions, while Congress's Joint Committee on the Conduct of the War investigated the matter and submitted a report condemning the militia and its leaders. Accounts of the massacre tended to focus on Indian suffering and presented the Cheyennes and Arapahos as innocent victims of murderous frontier whites. Sand Creek became a powerful symbol that something was deeply wrong in American Indian affairs and a rallying cry for reformers for years to come.[4]

At the end of the Civil War, two government commissions were appointed to gather information on the state of the frontier and the Indian population and to recommend changes in policy. In 1865 the "Doolittle Committee," a joint congressional commission led by Senator James R. Doolittle of Wisconsin, observed conditions at various Indian agencies and gathered the opinions of military officers, agents, and other frontier Americans. Its report described an impoverished Indian population being driven toward extinction "by disease; by intemperance; by wars, among themselves and with the whites; by the steady and resistless emigration of white men into the territories of the west."[5] It blamed continued warfare on the desperate conditions in which western Indians lived and on the crimes committed against them by frontier Americans. Most Indian wars, the commission asserted, were caused by "the aggressions of lawless white men, always to be found on the frontier, or the boundary between savage and civilized life."[6] As the Sand Creek Massacre had demonstrated, frontier whites were willing to wage wars of extermination against Indians.[7]

The second and more important deputation was the "Peace Commission" of 1867. Organized in response to renewed warfare on the plains, in particular the hostilities involving the Sioux in the Powder River country, the Peace Commission was composed of military officers, politicians, and civilian friends of the Indian. They were instructed by Congress to investigate the causes of the current warfare and to negotiate new treaties. In making those treaties, the commissioners were to assign lands to the various tribes to be occupied as permanent homes from which white settlement would be barred. That is, the Indian country was to be broken up into clearly defined tribal territories more closely resembling the modern image of an Indian reservation.[8]

The commissioners had some success as peacemakers, but their more significant contribution was the report they submitted to Congress in January 1868.[9] That document, written by the civilian members of the commission, validated calls for reform and became a blueprint for the peace policy. In even sharper terms than had the Doolittle Committee, the commissioners blamed non-Indians for the persistence of warfare in the West. The fundamental cause of Indian wars was injustice – in particular the dishonest appropriation of tribal lands. "Have we been uniformly unjust?" the commissioners asked. "We answer unhesitatingly, yes!"[10] Greedy frontiersmen, in collusion with corrupt federal agents, consistently defrauded Indians and incited violence. Once blood was drawn, those same frontiersmen cried out for the United States Army to punish the Indians and drive them from their lands. That situation, repeated again and again through the course of American history, had resulted in the Indians' reduction to a small desperate remnant. If something were not done soon, even the remnant would disappear.[11] Most Americans, the commissioners asserted, were kindly disposed toward the western Indians, but few citizens outside the frontier states and territories paid any attention to Indian affairs. "When the progress of settlement reaches the Indian's home, the only question is, 'how best to get his lands.' When they are obtained the Indian is lost sight of."[12] Few people knew enough or cared enough about the condition of the Indians to demand justice, so the bloody cycle continued.

The solution to the crisis lay in the reform of the Indian Bureau and a renewed effort to civilize Native peoples. Frontier expansion could take place without injustice and violence, the commissioners implied, but it required the presence of agents and administrators who were thoroughly dedicated to protecting the Indians and guiding them toward civilization. Tribes should be placed on reservations away from frontier communities. There missionaries and teachers could instruct Indians in agriculture, the English language, and Christianity. Reservation Indians would adopt the good elements of American civilization while being protected from the bad. Over time, the survivors of the Indian race would be saved from extinction and, when they were ready, drawn into the broader American population.[13]

The commissioners suggested several specific measures designed to reorient American policy toward the goals of reform and Indian civilization. All agents and superintendents were to be removed from office to allow a review of their characters and performance. Dedicated capable officers were to be returned to their positions, while the dishonest and incompetent were to be replaced. The Trade and Intercourse Laws were to be reviewed and altered to protect Indian people more effectively and regulate their interaction with frontier Americans more closely. Finally, in order to promote Indian civilization, cash payments and annuities were to be replaced with tools, farming implements, and domestic animals. That is, the United States was to meet its treaty obligations in a manner that encouraged the transformation of Indian people into American farmers and workers.[14]

Those suggestions were hardly radical; they amounted to a variation on removal with special attention paid to the civilizing mission. After portraying United States Indian relations as an almost complete failure, the commissioners reaffirmed most of the old ideas in Indian affairs. Reform-minded Americans, however, responded with great enthusiasm, their reactions providing evidence in support of Prucha's belief that the peace policy was about changing attitudes more than laws. "I welcomed this Report almost with tears of joy," wrote the well-known author Lydia Maria Child. In her essay, "An Appeal for the Indians," Child declared: "We have, at last, an Official Document which manifests something like a right spirit toward the poor Indians!"[15] Child directed the "humane and thinking people" of America to read the findings and endorsed, in particular, the commissioners' emphasis on education. Through patient instruction, she affirmed, white Americans could save the Indians.[16] Meanwhile, philanthropists and church organizations flooded Congress with petitions in support of the Peace Commission report. Quakers, in particular, urged Congress to implement the report's recommendations immediately, their memorials insisting that if abuses within the Indian Bureau were ended, America's Indian problems would quickly fade.[17]

As even the brief discussion above suggests, particular ideas and symbols recurred in the writings of the postwar reform effort. Most petitions and reports depicted past American Indian relations as an almost unbroken history of failure and crime. As the *New York Times*, an early supporter of the peace policy, put it: "Baseness, cupidity, treachery and pillage have characterized our treatment of the Indians since the days of the Pilgrim Fathers." Frontier expansion had set in motion a terrible cycle of abuse and violence. White Americans stole from each new tribe they encountered, and their crimes eventually drove the Indians to retaliate. Once the blood of a white person was shed, the United States waged unlimited war upon the offending tribe. Conflicts that began with the greed of white Americans ended with the death and dispossession of Indians.[18] The one bright spot in the history of Indian affairs was the career of William Penn. Penn appeared frequently in postwar reform statements as a kind of patron saint of the peace policy. Reformers invoked the memory of his amicable relations with Pennsylvania tribes as evidence that justice and peace provided the best foundation for Indian affairs. "Had the views of William Penn been faithfully carried out," Lydia Maria Child speculated, "we should doubtless see a very different state of things from that which now exists."[19]

Essential to that model of history was a second theme: reformers' condemnation of frontier whites. An image of the white savage appeared continually in reformers' writings. Existing between primitive and civilized worlds, the white savage embodied unrestrained greed and violence. He represented the dark side of the energetic character that propelled Americans westward. Such men were the cause of nearly all Indian wars, reformers intoned time and again, and no less than the Indians themselves, these frontier Americans required careful regulation.[20] Coupled with the criticism of frontier whites, however, was faith in the good intentions of the rest of the American population. Most Americans desired fair treatment for the Indians, reformers insisted. The challenge of reform was to make the feelings of the good-hearted multitude the basis of policy, rather than continue to allow the actions of the greedy few to define Indian relations. As the reformer John Beeson stated several years before the inauguration of the peace policy: "As soon as our people calmly consider the matter, and in their quiet moments review what has passed, their generous emotions will burst forth; and as with the voice of one man we shall all exclaim: 'Those evils shall be repressed.'"[21]

Change had to take place immediately, many reform documents suggested, or else soon there might not be any Indians left to protect. One of the defining characteristics of postwar reform writings was an apocalyptic tone. Conditions among the tribes were so poor, and American society was moving and developing so quickly, that the remaining Indians would soon be extinct if the government and good-hearted whites did not act immediately. Of course, the prediction of Indian extinction and the image of the "disappearing savage" were quite old. But postwar reformers seemed to believe that the Indians' final disappearance was immediately at hand. With the settlement of the West, there was no place to which Indians could be driven. White America had one last chance to answer its Indian question. As a Quaker petition put it, unless a fundamental reform were made now, "the same bloody work of extermination of the various Indian tribes will still go on, as hitherto, until not one red man shall be left alive on the American soil, and the vials of a just retribution shall be poured out in full measure upon our guilty land."[22]

The moral terms here echoed those employed by an earlier generation of Christian "friends of the Indian," the ministers and missionaries who had helped in the fight against removal. Like Jeremiah Evarts in the late 1820s, postwar reformers defined Indian policy as an ethical test for Americans. Would they at last behave humanely toward the Indians, or would they allow the worst of their countrymen to destroy them? Turning a blind eye to the cycle of frontier violence was sinful, with American passivity amounting to participation in that violence. Like the removal-era missionaries, reformers sought to rouse Americans, to make them aware of the dangers that a repressive Indian policy posed to the national character. One reason that the Cherokees responded positively to the peace policy may have been that its advocates spoke a language with which tribal leaders were thoroughly familiar.

Indians themselves were only vaguely present in the reformers' writings. They appeared almost exclusively as objects acted upon by others. If the white savage represented unrestrained action, Indian savagery was of a more passive variety. Indians were victims of American expansion, a "once-powerful race" driven toward extinction by forces they could not control. Or else they appeared as the meek charges of kindly agents; they were racial children yearning for knowledge of civilization. Even their acts of resistance – their retaliation against abusive frontiersmen and the wars they waged against the United States – were less the actions of thinking human beings than consequences of ill-formed American policies. Success or failure in Indian relations and the survival or extinction of the Indians themselves were matters to be determined solely by white Americans.[23] With this outlook came the likelihood of coercion. Reformers suggested that the return of justice to Indian affairs would create conditions in which Indian people would naturally choose civilization. If they failed to make that choice, agents and missionaries could push them in the correct direction. Always lurking in the reformers' language of sympathy and fairness was their certainty that white Americans knew what was right for Native peoples, and their suspicion that an answer to America's Indian question might have to be imposed upon the Indians.[24]

Within two years of the publication of the Peace Commission's report, its ideas and general outlook had been embraced by the new Grant administration and transformed into official policy. Grant himself had given little indication prior to his election that he would seek changes in Indian affairs. But influenced by individual reformers and the general atmosphere of crisis, he made several important innovations soon after taking office.[25] First, he removed all Indian agents and replaced them with army officers and men nominated by Quaker organizations. Later, when Congress barred military men from holding Indian Bureau positions, Grant offered other churches the opportunity to nominate agents. Eventually, the Interior Department and church leaders parceled out more than seventy Indian Bureau jobs among members of the major Christian denominations and missionary societies. The new Christian agents, it was thought, would be less corruptible than their predecessors and better able to protect their charges from frontier whites. They would also be more committed to the civilizing mission.[26]

Second, Grant sponsored the creation of the Board of Indian Commissioners. This was to be a group of high-minded Christian men from outside government who would oversee Indian affairs. The idea of such a review board had been around for some time, and it had become a favorite proposal of reform advocates during the Civil War years.[27] The members of the Board would scrutinize the work of Indian Bureau officers, oversee the disbursement of federal funds for the tribes, and advise the president on Indian policy. Being wealthy men, they would serve without pay, and the independence they enjoyed would keep them immune to bribery and political pressure. The law establishing the Board did not specify a relationship between the commissioners and organized religion, but in practice members tended to be prominent laymen from the major Protestant denominations. The Board, then, represented an additional way in which the peace policy offered the Christian churches roles in reforming Indian affairs.[28]

The Grant administration made those changes within the framework of the developing reservation policy. Grant and the reformers accepted the long-standing practice of separating tribes from white settlements and regulating contact between Indian people and non-Indian Americans. They embraced, as well, the more recent idea of steadily reducing the territory held by Indians and concentrating the tribes on a small number of reservations. Reducing their lands would encourage Plains Indians to abandon nomadic hunting economies and pursue agriculture, while concentrating the tribes would make it easier to regulate interaction between Indians and western Americans. Both practices, of course, would also accommodate the westward expansion of the American population. The reservation became the setting in which the new godly agents would return justice to Indian affairs and revive the campaign for Indian civilization.[29]

Historians of the Cherokees typically do not discuss the peace policy. William G. McLoughlin, for example, mentions the Grant administration's reforms only once in his treatment of the postwar era.[30] This is understandable, as the Five Tribes figured only marginally in the plans of reform advocates. The movement to change American Indian policy emerged from public revulsion at continued war on the plains, which took the form of conflicts involving "wild" tribes like the Sioux and the Comanches. Those tribes constituted the test of American Indian relations after 1865, much as the Cherokees had served as the test of the removal campaign earlier in the century. The Five Tribes did sometimes appear in the major peace policy documents, but they tended to represent a sideshow rather than the main event.[31]

The policy initiative of greatest concern to the Cherokees during this time was the effort to reorganize the Indian Territory politically, and that effort diverged in an important way from the peace policy. In the decade and a half following the war, Congress considered a long succession of bills to turn the Indian Territory into a full-fledged possession of the United States. With these "Oklahoma bills," as they were sometimes called, legislators sought to end the area's anomalous political status and apply to it the federal government's standard territorial law. The change would bring the dismantling of existing tribal governments and most likely involve the opening of part of the country to non-Indian settlement. The reorganized territory would retain some Indian reservations, but civilized peoples like the Cherokees would become American citizens.[32]

Political reorganization shared the ultimate goal of the peace policy, the absorption of Indian tribes into non-Indian America. In the case of Five Tribes, however, the method of achieving that goal was not the protection of Indians from whites but their rapid incorporation into the United States. In retrospect, that distinction may seem unimportant, since the aim of both policies was eventual Indian assimilation. It proved very significant, however, to Cherokee leaders, who opposed reorganization as an act that would destroy their nation's political autonomy. They and the leaders of the other civilized tribes insisted that the Indian Territory should remain a collection of separate nations. The only territorial government they would accept was the "General Council," the legislative body authorized under the treaties of 1866 and consisting of the representatives of the various tribes of the Indian Territory. Further changes in the territory's political structure, the Five Tribes argued, were, at that point, unnecessary and ill-advised.[33]

Although civilized Indians were thought to require different methods than their "wild" cousins, reformers did assign the Cherokees several supporting roles in the peace policy's great work. For one thing, it was expected that the Indian Territory would become one of the principal locations in which Indian tribes would be concentrated. As it had in the antebellum era, the territory would be a destination for removed tribes, and the civilized Indians would provide some of these newcomers with land. The federal government created reservations for groups of Pawnees, Poncas, and other tribes, using land purchased from the Cherokees. There was even talk of moving the Lakota Sioux to a former Cherokee area.[34] Reformers sometimes argued that the presence of the civilized tribes made the Indian Territory an especially favorable arena for the reservation policy. The civilized tribes would aid in the work of teaching "wild" Indians by providing models of proper behavior. They would demonstrate the benefits of progress to recently pacified groups.[35]

Reformers, meanwhile, drew their own variety of inspiration from the Cherokees. Peace policy advocates pointed to the tribe as proof that the civilization of Indians was possible. Before the war the Cherokees "were perhaps the richest people, per capita, in the world," declared Commissioner of Indian Affairs N. G. Taylor in 1868. And they rose to that position because of two developments. First, the game in their homeland died off, which forced the Cherokees to "resort to agriculture" (the Cherokees, of course, had been farmers long before Europeans showed up). At the same time, missionaries brought Christianity to the tribe. The same two processes, Taylor maintained, could bring civilization to the "wild" Indians of the West.[36] For peace-policy advocates, the Cherokees' most important role was symbolic. As reformers directed their attention to the nomadic tribes of the plains, they invoked the civilized tribes of the Indian Territory as evidence that their goals and methods were correct.[37]

The Cherokees, then, were not the main focus of the peace policy, but they served as emblems of the promise of reform. To a great extent that simply confirmed what some Cherokees had been arguing for decades: that their nation proved the susceptibility of Indians to progress. Cherokee leaders, however, responded to the reform movement's emergence by finding within it roles for their people that were far more than figurative. They took for the Cherokees the authority to contribute to discussions of American Indian policy and to decide what was and was not wise and just in Indian affairs. Moreover, they defined their people as crucial actors in the peace policy's application, necessary agents of reform. And when they made themselves participants in the reform effort, they shifted its meaning.

Among the tribe's postwar politicians, several stand out as interpreters of the peace policy. William Penn Adair was the Cherokees' most important spokesman during this time, a delegate almost every year from 1868 to 1880 and (in the words of the *Cherokee Advocate*) the "acknowledged leader of all the Indians at the Capital of the United States."[38] A well-educated lawyer, he produced some of the most thorough Cherokee analyses of American Indian policy. Adair was a leader of the Southern Party, the dissidents who had joined the Confederacy early in the Civil War. Adair himself received a Confederate commission and served as quartermaster for Stand Watie's regiment. Like many of the Southern Party, he belonged to a family that had supported removal. His father, George Washington Adair, had signed the Treaty of New Echota, and the Adairs were related to the Ridge family. William

Penn shared his relations' hatred for John Ross and his faction and participated avidly in the effort to depose the old chief at the close of the war. His opposition to the dominant party, however, did not dim his Cherokee nationalism. The Civil War, in fact, strengthened his commitment to the Indian nation. The Southern Party felt betrayed by the Confederacy, which had promised support but then had left its Indian allies exposed to the vengeance of pro-Union Cherokees and federal troops. Adair concluded that Indians simply could not trust whites, strengthening his conviction that the Cherokees had to remain separate and autonomous. He gained the opportunity to act on that conviction in the late 1860s when he and other Southern Party leaders allied with Lewis Downing, full-blood leader and erstwhile Ross supporter, to form a new political movement. When the Downing Party gained control of the Cherokee government in the 1867 elections, Adair, the longtime dissident, found himself laboring as an official representative of the tribe.[39]

Interestingly enough, the most prominent spokesman, next to Adair, during the years of the peace policy was one of his most bitter rivals, William Potter Ross. This Ross, as earlier chapters have noted, was the old chief's nephew – a sister's son, a highly significant relationship in the Cherokees' traditional kinship ways. John Ross singled William out early as a potential asset to the tribe and sponsored a very extensive non-Indian education. He sent his nephew to a mission school and several private academies in the South and then ultimately to Princeton University. In the 1840s and 1850s William put that schooling to use as clerk of the Cherokee National Council and as editor of the *Cherokee Advocate*, the national newspaper that replaced the *Phoenix* after removal. In the Civil War, true to his uncle's policies, he served on both sides, enlisting first in the Confederate Army (he was present at the Battle of Pea Ridge) and then switching over to work for the Union's Cherokee Home Guards in the sutler's store at Fort Gibson. He was his uncle's acknowledged heir and was duly appointed principal chief after John Ross's death. But when his turn to lead came, he was unable to keep the old party together. The alliance founded by Adair and Downing voted him out, and when he was again appointed principal chief after Downing's death, Downing's followers rallied and defeated him once more. Despite political repudiation, William Potter Ross remained useful to the Cherokee Nation as a frequent delegate to Washington and as a tribal representative when American officials visited the Indian Territory. In these roles, he joined Adair in examining American policy and arguing for the maintenance of Cherokee nationhood.[40]

Two other interpreters of the peace policy deserve mention here. William P. Boudinot and John Lynch Adair edited the *Cherokee Advocate* during the reform-effort years. From that vantage point, they had a chance to comment frequently on the peace policy, the territorial bills, and Indian relations in general. Like William Penn Adair, they had belonged to the Southern Cherokees, fighting with the Confederacy and working against the Ross Party. Boudinot's younger brother was the famous Elias C. Boudinot, a Southern Party leader who came away from the Civil War advocating the immediate incorporation of the civilized tribes into the United States. That position earned the younger Boudinot a great deal of attention from white advocates of territorialization, and scorn from most of his fellow Cherokees. William, as it happened, favored William Penn Adair's politics over those of his brother. He and John Lynch Adair were nationalists and opponents of American interference in the Cherokees' internal affairs, positions they expressed in the *Advocate* and in occasional stints as tribal delegates.[41]

For these Cherokee representatives, the most straightforward response to the peace policy was to support it publicly, to become Indian witnesses to the propriety of the reformers' ideas. In memorials and letters and in personal visits, delegates thanked President Grant for his dedication to a "benign Indian policy" and assured him that the Indians considered him "one of the best friends to them they ever knew."[42] The *Advocate* reprinted presidential messages defending the peace policy, as well as editorials from American newspapers that supported the administration's approach to Indian affairs.[43] Cherokees testified to the success of the reform effort, claiming that warfare on the plains was decreasing and that the "wild" tribes were being won over to progress and civilization.[44] In a letter to Grant at the time of his retirement, Cherokee delegates summed up their approval. Grant's actions toward the Indians, they stated, had shown "an earnest wish for their advancement in the arts and pursuits of civilized life; a conscientious regard for their rights and the full purpose to enforce in their behalf the obligations of the United States." This treatment had proven successful. "The results have been peace among themselves and among others far as their influence reached, increased confidence in the pledges of protection given them and steady progress in knowledge and industry."[45]

Cherokee support, however, did not extend to the policy initiative that concerned the Five Tribes most directly, political reorganization of the Indian Territory. In fact, Cherokee leaders insisted that territorialization was in direct conflict with the peace policy. In their efforts to defeat the Oklahoma bills, Cherokee representatives argued that reorganization would represent the dismantling of the reform effort. Grant himself supported the idea of turning the Indian Territory into a full-fledged territory of the United States, and he told Cherokee delegates as much on a number of occasions.[46] But Cherokee leaders portrayed reorganization as a dire threat to the Grant administration's benign approach to Indian affairs.

One of the most vivid examples of that argument appeared in a memorial issued by Cherokee, Creek, and Choctaw delegates in the spring of 1870.[47] The document expressed opposition to a territorial bill then under consideration in the Senate, a bill that to the delegates' dismay enjoyed wide support. "When we reached Washington about the first of January last," the delegates recalled, "we found a thoroughly organized party operating against every Indian interest."

The most persistent efforts were being made to intensify public feeling against us as a race, and at one time it seemed that we would be overwhelmed. Denounced without stint, and hunted with remorseless ferocity, it appeared that no age, sex or condition would be spared, no rights of property respected, nor the slightest regard paid to the most solemn obligations of your government. Yet the leaders of this cruel warfare were for a while concealed under the specious pretext of being instigated [sic] solely by a desire to benefit the Indians.[48]

The men promoting territorialization were the enemies of the Five Tribes, "the speculator and land pirate," who sought to profit from the theft of Indian lands. That being the case, reorganization was a radical departure from the Grant administration's doctrine in Indian affairs. It was "a policy vastly different from the peace policy of the President; the first a policy of war and extermination; the last a policy of peace and preservation."[49] Far from encouraging the further progress of the Indians, territorialization would work their speedy annihilation.

We will venture the prediction that if you establish over us such a government as the bill provides for, your officers would not get into our Territory before it would be overrun by squatters, who would look to them for protection. Indeed, they would regard their very appointment as an invitation to go, and if Congress were to place an army around our borders they could not be kept back. We have been taught in too many instances, not to be admonished by the lesson that where squatters have the slightest pretext to take possession of Indian lands they do it. . . . Do you ask, senators, what the result would be? Every trouble between an Indian and a white man would be laid to the fault of the Indian. Nothing would please the squatters and their confederates better than to get up difficulties, and they would get them up. A cruel, relentless, and exterminating war would follow. . . . We think we hazard nothing in saying that in nineteen out of twenty cases of hostility between Indians and whites, it was engendered by the class of persons we have just described, or the failure of the government to keep its treaty stipulations.[50]

This language echoed earlier Cherokee writings. In particular, the lurid description of fraud and persecution was reminiscent of Cherokee statements in the last few years of the struggle against removal. Here, no less than in the late 1830s, unwise federal policy portended Indian destruction. At the same time, and what is more striking, the delegates wrote in the contemporary language of reform. They duplicated the reformers' habit of classifying initiatives in Indian affairs as either hostile policies or peaceful policies, and they placed territorialization squarely in the hostile category. The territorial campaign was an Indian war, one no less terrible for being fought by lawyers and lobbyists. The Indians were to be "hunted with remorseless ferocity" by evil men who would spare "no age, sex or condition." This could have come directly from newspaper accounts of the Sand Creek Massacre, the petition defining reorganization as an act equivalent to the slaughter of innocents. In identifying the authors of this legislative race war, the delegates pointed to precisely the bad frontier whites whom reformers so often condemned. Reorganization was a policy of squatters and speculators, the kind of Americans from whom the Grant administration had pledged to protect Indians. In making that claim, the delegates invoked the reformers' model of the history of Indian affairs. Territorialization, they suggested, would bring the resumption of the evil cycle that had so long dominated American Indian relations. An invitation to ill-intentioned whites, it would lead to outrages against Indians, which in turn would bring about a devastating war that even the civilized tribes could not hope to survive.

The general characteristics of the 1870 petition can be found in many other anti-territorial writings. Cherokee representatives consistently identified reorganization as an act of violence. As one letter put it, the territorial bills represented a "threatening and aggressive policy" and were "understood by all to be but entering wedges to disrupt [the Five Tribes'] present political status and relations in order to render it practicable to speculate in lands."[51] The interests behind the territorial effort were the Indians' enemies, corrupt whites hoping to profit at the expense of the Indian Territory tribes. Cherokees described such people variously as "Goths and Vandals," "scalawags and cut-throats," and "hungry comorants."[52] There were thousands of frontier Americans lurking on the borders of the Indian Territory, leaders observed, waiting for the smallest excuse to invade. If the tribal governments were dismantled and the land opened to white settlement, whites would rush in to defraud and abuse the Indians. In the end, territorialization would lead to the disappearance of the civilized tribes. As Cherokee leaders argued repeatedly, what was at stake in the territorial issue was ultimately the very survival of the people of the Indian Territory. "The establishment of such a government over us," another petition from 1870 assured the Congress, "would work our certain and speedy extinction by subjecting us to the absolute rule of a people foreign to us in blood, language, customs, traditions, and interests."[53] Even when they did not directly invoke the Grant administration's reforms, Cherokee leaders expressed opposition to territorial bills using the basic terms of the peace policy.

President Grant's own support for territorialization was an obvious problem, one that Cherokee spokesmen tried to reason away on various occasions. In December 1872, for example, Grant stated that he wanted a new United States government for the Indian Territory at a time when Congress was considering an Oklahoma bill. In the *Advocate*, William P. Boudinot responded by arguing that Grant's general support for territorial reorganization could not be construed as support for the specific law under debate. Grant's policy, he noted, was to afford Indian tribes just and fair treatment. At the very least, justice meant adherence to the treaties, and the Five Tribes' treaties strictly prohibited a change in their governments without their consent. The goal of bringing the civilized tribes under a United States territorial government might be consistent with the general spirit of the peace policy, but it could never be achieved except through an act of aggression that would violate that spirit.[54] Moreover, Boudinot pointed out that reorganization would render the Indian Territory useless as a place in which to concentrate removed Indian tribes, since it would serve as an invitation to every white person on the borders to rush in and seize land. "The President would have this country reserved as a home for the Red men and would accordingly have it filled up with the Red race to the exclusion of the White 'for a term of years' at least."[55] Regardless of the president's feelings about the reorganization idea, the act – like all such proposals – violated the peace policy.

As the statements quoted so far suggest, Cherokee representatives emphasized two particular elements of the postwar reforms. First, they applauded the promise of justice and heartily endorsed the notion that fair dealing on the part of the United States was the necessary first step toward perfecting Indian affairs. Not surprisingly, they took the promise to mean that the United States would adhere strictly to the treaties. That was an important conclusion, since from a Cherokee perspective the treaties were in jeopardy during this period. In addition to producing the Oklahoma bills, the federal government in the 1870s officially abandoned treaty making with Indian tribes, a development that Cherokees watched with great anxiety. White reformers generally agreed with the decision to end the treaty process, but Cherokees hoped that the peace policy would ensure adherence to agreements already on the books.[56] Second, chiefs and delegates focused on the peace policy's commitment to the separation of Indian tribes from frontier whites. The peace policy was meant to fix problems that reformers felt were caused by "wild" Indians coming into contact with unprincipled Americans. Cherokee leaders applied that purpose to their own situation and insisted that separation, at least for the time being, was necessary even for civilized tribes.

In embracing the latter doctrine, Cherokee representatives took several positions that invite further analysis. For one thing, delegates during this period added strong appeals to racial difference to their arguments for the maintenance of a distinct Indian Territory. In an 1870 report back to the Cherokee Nation, William Penn Adair explained the reasoning that he and other delegates had used to protest territorial bills and "to show-up the Indian question in its true light." They had informed their white audiences "that the innate genius of the Indian race was radically different from that of the white one; that the two races were, therefore, by nature antagonistic to each other, and could not be *forced* into an immediate commingling as one political community without a '*war of races*,' which could have but one logical result, viz., the *deterioration* and *destruction* of the weaker party, the *Indians*." The only way to contain that natural antagonism was to safeguard "the separate and distinct political existence of the Indians."[57] As a later memorial put it, "when whites and Indians are indiscriminately commingled in one political community, the Indians have always perished."[58]

To some extent, statements like these simply reiterated the basic argument for reservations. Indian tribes and whites had to be kept separate to avoid destructive conflict. The appeal to "innate genius" and natural antagonism, however, struck a different note. Documents like Adair's report suggested a more profound gulf between Indians and whites than a variance in levels of civilization. They suggested that the fundamental nature of the races made their respective members incompatible. That line of reasoning, of course, was common in discussions of Indian affairs. European Americans, however, were usually the ones to express it, and it generally implied unhappy conclusions for the Indians in question. For whites, profound racial difference suggested permanent Indian inferiority, and that belief easily became a justification for coercion or evidence that extinction was the Indian race's destiny.[59] Making the Cherokees' use of that language doubly interesting was the tribe's long history of absorbing members of other races. By the 1870s the nation had incorporated Indian people from several other tribes (Delawares, Shawnees, and Creeks) and hosted a substantial non-Indian population. There were African American citizens, former Cherokee slaves and their families. There were also growing numbers of whites who either married into the tribe or entered the nation legally as workers or tenants on Indian land. And most famously there were intruders from surrounding states, squatters hoping to gain possession of tribal property. The Cherokee Nation was a multiracial country, a fact that would seem to clash with the claim that racial mixing led to Indian annihilation.[60]

There are several ways to read the racial argument. William G. McLoughlin suggests that its appearance reflected the rising "ethnic nationalism" of the "full-blood" faction that controlled the Cherokee government at various points during this period.[61] He may be correct, since the presence of former slaves and white newcomers was becoming an increasingly bitter issue in the tribe's internal politics. Ethnic nationalism may have seeped into the messages employed in the Cherokees' external relations as well. It is important to note, however, that very few of the individuals writing these statements were full-bloods, either biologically or in terms of cultural traditionalism. Adair and the others were nationalists, but they were members of the mixed-race, bicultural population. In suggesting that there existed an innate antagonism between Indians and whites, they erased the history of "commingling" that had produced their own families and community.

The anthropologist Circe Sturm's work suggests a somewhat different explanation. Sturm argues that when Cherokees in the early nineteenth century adopted the European American concept of the nation-state, they adopted as well the assumption that nationhood was tied to race. Cherokees, by this way of thinking, shared a common stock or blood that provided the foundation of their political community. This idea proved useful in creating a centralized political system and in rallying Cherokee people to defend the nation against the United States. Despite the growing diversity of the population, Cherokees maintained this idea of the nation in the second half of the nineteenth century. Sturm's work suggests that when leaders like Adair appealed to "innate difference" in the 1870s memorials, they were not expressing a new full-blood nationalism so much as a variation of this older racial ideology, a nationalism of Cherokee blood in whatever quantity. The increasing complexity of the Cherokee Nation's populace may have made this ideology more appealing in the postwar era. Identifying the nation with Cherokee blood helped leaders like Adair maintain common ground with more traditional Cherokees, while pushing intermarried whites and the black citizens to the margins. Viewed in this manner, the racial ideology's tendency to erase complexity is precisely what preserved its relevance. As Sturm would point out, however, marginalizing those who were not Cherokees by blood came at a price. The freed people, for example, generally supported territorialization, and their unequal treatment by the tribal government did nothing to change that position. Continued adherence to the racial definition of nationhood precluded the development of alternative understandings, ideas of the nation that might have drawn the diverse citizenry together.[62]

From the standpoint of the tribe's federal relations, the racial argument offered a similar mix of benefits and problems. In describing a natural gulf between the races, delegates reduced Cherokee-American relations to the simplest possible terms. They ignored the tribe's tangled multiethnic past and present and made the issues of the 1870s elements of an age-old clash of radically different peoples. That is, they took the question of keeping Indians separate out of the realm of policy and made it part of an unchanging order. The presence of so many non-Indians in the nation, however, was bound to undermine the argument that Indians and whites could never mix. Later in the century, allotment advocates would cite the territory's growing non-Indian population to prove that preserving tribal autonomy was pointless. Why protect Indian nationhood, if the nations were full of non-Indians? Indian Territory communities themselves refuted arguments based on ideas of "innate difference." What leaders like Adair wanted was not racial separation, but self-government. The "commingling" that worried them was the kind that would take place if the tribal government fell and the Indian Territory were opened to unregulated American settlement, the problem being not so much Indian-white mixing as the loss of Cherokee control. Racial arguments, by themselves, could neither explain nor resolve that problem.

Equally intriguing, Cherokee writings in the postwar era frequently offered a positive memory of removal. Delegates recalled Andrew Jackson's Indian policy as having been the first step toward the just and humane approach of President Grant. Again, William Penn Adair provides the best example. In an 1876 address made to the House Committee on Territories, Adair depicted removal as a sympathetic response to the rapid decline of the Indians since colonization. In the early nineteenth century, Adair recalled, the Indian population was rapidly falling, and "the relic of the Indian race was scattered to the four winds throughout the domain of the United States, with laws, customs, and habits foreign and antagonistic to those of whites." Witnessing this dire situation, "humanitarians, Christians, and statesmen conceived of the notion of maturing some new plan to rescue the few remaining Indians from destruction."[63] The new plan, of course, was removal, an idea nurtured by statesmen like Jefferson and supported by "the growing sentiment in favor of the Indians among the great masses of your people."[64] The Removal Act of 1830 set the new plan in motion and, more important for Adair, became the basis of the reforms after the Civil War. "This act," Adair stated, "is . . . really the foundation of the present 'Indian policy.'"[65]

Removal advocates had indeed asserted that migration was the only way to save the Indians. In the 1820s and 1830s, Lewis Cass, Andrew Jackson, and lesser-known proponents had argued that contact with the people of the frontier had brought degradation and decline to eastern tribes like the Cherokees and that continued interaction could only lead to their disappearance. A generation later, Adair invoked that humanitarian argument as the primary inspiration for the policy and made it the center of a new, positive memory of removal.[66]

If the goal of removal had been to arrest Indian decline, it had worked wonderfully – at least that was how Cherokee leaders following the Civil War presented matters. Separated from the European American frontier, the peoples of the Indian Territory had survived and prospered. Adair noted that the Cherokee population had grown steadily from removal until the outbreak of the Civil War, reversing the decline of the pre-removal era.[67] Elsewhere, he made the same point and then added a familiar list of civilized achievements, attained in this case thanks to migration. Since their "establishment outside of any State or Territory," he wrote, the Five Tribes "have regular written governments, . . . with flourishing schools and churches established throughout their countries, so that, without *one cent of cost* to the United States, those Indian nations have advanced in civilization more rapidly than any other people ever did during the same length of time." Meanwhile, he continued, "their brethren in the States . . . have deteriorated in numbers and intelligence, and are regarded by the communities in which they reside more as a *nuisance* than otherwise."[68] The reference to Indians' costing the United States money is worth noting here. Adair suggested that removal had made his people less dependent, and he explicitly linked this greater autonomy to the civilization process. While postwar reformers typically addressed Indian people as government wards, Adair saw the trend of the previous half century's Indian policy as pointing toward tribal autonomy.

By 1876 the account of the tribe's improvement had long been a staple of Cherokee political writing; however, removal had commonly appeared as an obstacle to progress. The Cherokees had kept on the road to civilization in spite of removal, representatives explained in the years following the Trail of Tears. That the Cherokees had endured the crime of forced migration testified to the their profound commitment to peace with the United States, while their continued progress despite the trauma of removal demonstrated their great capacity for advancement.[69] That memory still appeared in postwar Cherokee writings,[70] but just as often Cherokee leaders invoked the newer positive account. They chose not to recall the fraud and coercion employed by Georgia and the United States in sending the Cherokees west, or the suffering of the Cherokees during migration. Instead, they identified removal strictly as a humane response to Indian decline and as the policy that had saved their people and others from disappearance.

It should not be surprising, perhaps, to find that memory in William Penn Adair's writings. His family, after all, had belonged to the Treaty Party. He probably took the success of the tribe in the West as vindication of his family's decision and as evidence against their old enemies. At least in part, the new image of removal can be traced to the postwar political realignment that had brought men like Adair into prominence in the Cherokee government.

Equally important, the new memory helped align the Cherokees and the other civilized tribes with the peace policy. As Adair remembered it, removal had developed under conditions almost identical to those that had inspired the postwar reform movement. The Indians of the East had been in a desperate state, teetering on the edge of extinction. Sympathetic Americans, like the reformers of the postwar years, had responded by working to separate the endangered Indians from the frontier, the source of corruption and the setting for conflict. The peace policy, in truth, had begun in the Southeast, "inaugurated by President Jackson, and . . . improved by General Grant."[71]

Removal, furthermore, had bequeathed to the Cherokees of later years the 1830 Removal Act and the Treaty of New Echota. While members of John Ross's Party and generation understandably had condemned those documents as criminal, both proved useful to tribal leaders after the Civil War. The 1830 act, as Cherokees read it, guaranteed that the removed tribes would remain forever outside the states and territories of the American republic – a boon to those fighting yearly Oklahoma bills. The treaty, meanwhile, promised the Cherokees permanent landholding in the West. It was commonplace for postwar writings to cite the two documents as evidence that the Cherokee Nation was beyond the authority of the American government, that policies like territorialization were contrary to the whole history of the tribe's American relations. When tribal leaders temporarily cleansed removal of the stain of coercion and suffering, the removal-era documents and the policy itself became bulwarks of Cherokee independence rather than symbols of American duplicity.[72]

If Adair and other postwar Cherokees celebrated the Grant administration's commitment to keeping Indians and whites separate, they ignored the element of the peace policy that was most celebrated among whites – the new Christian agents. Cherokee leaders never asked for a member of the Grant administration's new cadre of missionary-bureaucrats, and they rarely even discussed this aspect of the peace policy in their correspondence with the American government. On several occasions, in fact, they and the leaders of the other civilized tribes pointed out that they preferred not to have any agents at all. After the Civil War, there was only one bureaucrat assigned to the Five Tribes, the officer in charge of the Union Agency in Muskogee, Creek Nation. Indian leaders argued that even this one agent was unnecessary.[73] They failed to carry that point, although for a time in the 1870s it seemed that one of their own rank might be appointed as Union agent. The Indian Bureau considered William Potter Ross for the position, a move that the *Advocate* supported as a sign of respect for the people of the Indian Territory.[74] Tribal leaders preferred that relations with the United States be carried out on a government-to-government basis. Indian governments would communicate with the Indian office, the president, and Congress through direct correspondence or through the delegates appointed by the tribal councils. Ross at one point suggested that the best situation would be for the Cherokees to maintain an agent to the United States, a permanent ambassador in Washington, D.C.[75]

Several of the Five Tribes' treaties provided for the election of a delegate to the House of Representatives, something that might have rendered agents unnecessary. As mentioned earlier, the Treaty of New Echota contained such an article, and the 1866 treaty with the Choctaws and Chickasaws similarly authorized the sending of an Indian Territory delegate to Congress. The Five Tribes' opponents, however, embraced this idea and in doing so tainted it before nationalist Indian leaders could turn it to their own purposes. Advocates of territorialization cited the treaty provisions as proof that the tribes had already agreed to reorganize politically and thus that Congress was within its rights to pass an Oklahoma bill. Ordinary American territories, after all, elected such delegates. In signing a treaty with a delegate article, the argument ran, tribes like the Cherokees had themselves started the process of merging with the United States.[76] Construed in this way, congressional representation became too dangerous for most tribal leaders to consider. On several occasions during this period, Congress debated bills to create the office of Indian Territory delegate. The Five Tribes protested against these bills, arguing that the initiative would lead to their people being forced to accept United States citizenship and the dismantling of their own governments. They also pointed out that the treaties made the delegate optional rather than obligatory, and they explained that they were not yet prepared to exercise this particular option.[77] One of the few Cherokees to support the delegate idea publicly was William P. Boudinot. He suggested in the *Advocate* that a congressional representative would be quite useful, if it could be disentangled from efforts to denationalize the tribes.[78]

If the peace policy's new agents were missing, so too were the Indian wards that reformers envisioned. Tribal representatives rejected, often in quite vehement terms, the idea that their people were the foster children of the United States. Americans, they complained, assumed that Indians were recipients of charity living on federal lands at the pleasure of the government.[79] That might have been true of some tribes, but certainly not of their own nation. The Cherokees did not receive charity from the United States; they received payments agreed upon in the treaties. That money represented recompense for the large, valuable landholdings that the Cherokees had ceded to the United States over the years – something very different from alms. The government and people of the United States benefited greatly from the possession of those lands and would continue to benefit, as Boudinot noted, "while grass grows and water runs in Alabama and Georgia."[80] The fact that treaty payments kept the Cherokee government and other institutions operating could not be construed to mean that the Cherokees were dependent upon the United States. Being the proceeds of legitimate transactions, the funds rightfully belonged to the tribe. "The Cherokees," John Lynch Adair stated plainly, "never were dependent upon the Government further than a creditor is dependent upon a debtor."[81]

In a similar manner, Cherokee leaders reminded non-Indians that the United States government had no legitimate stake in Cherokee land. Americans, they feared, thought of all Indian territory as being equivalent to federal property. By this line of reasoning, tribes did not truly own their land the way that an American farmer owned his farm. They merely "occupied" it at the discretion of the United States. Removal advocates had used that argument earlier in the century, leading the Cherokees to suspect (quite correctly) that Americans considered Indian land titles to be of a lesser order than American ones.[82] They replied by insisting that the Cherokees themselves constituted the sole owner of their land. The government had never given them any land, just as they had never received government charity. They had purchased their section of the Indian Territory, paying for it with their old homes in the East. Leaders frequently reminded their audiences that the Cherokees held patents for their land. During the removal era the federal government had issued the patents to reassure the Indians that their possession of the new lands, unlike that of the old, was secure. One of the Cherokee patents, delegates usually pointed out, had been signed by President Martin Van Buren, the heir to Andrew Jackson himself. It was on file in Washington for anyone to see. It proved that their people were not "occupants" of their land but full proprietors.[83]

The rejection of ward status took on a particularly interesting cast during debates over territorial reorganization. One of the arguments made by the supporters of the Oklahoma bills was that the Five Tribes, having become civilized, were now ready to merge with the general

American population. To maintain their present isolation was to keep them needlessly in the restrictive role of dependents.[84] In spring 1870 a multi-tribal delegation led by Adair and Principal Chief Lewis Downing answered that argument in especially clear terms in responding to debate in Congress over a territorial bill. Yes, they acknowledged, their people were civilized. But they were not, nor had they ever been, wards. "Wards! In what sense does he mean?" they asked. "We defy the honorable gentleman, or any other gentleman, to show that we are costing the government of the United States a single dollar in the way of contribution or charity."[85] The civilized Indians' lack of American citizenship did not mean that they were trapped in a debilitating state of dependence. In fact, their present status – protected from frontier whites but outside the authority of American governments – was the proper one and the one that they preferred. The heart of the matter was this: advocates of territorial reorganization identified a choice of only two positions for Native Americans in the West. Indian people could be United States citizens, or they could be government dependents. Cherokee leaders and those of the other civilized tribes recognized a third choice – Indians could be citizens of their own autonomous political communities.

Replacing wardship with tribal autonomy radically altered the meaning of the peace policy as it applied to the Indian Territory. Rather than a school for Indian children run by selfless agents, the Indian Territory was to be a collection of autonomous tribes, "a Federal Republic of Indian States," in the phrase of one Cherokee delegation. The United States government would protect the Indian Territory from frontier whites and effect the migration there of additional Indian peoples in accordance with the reservation policy. The United States, however, would stop short of exercising political authority. That it would leave to the individual tribal governments and the multi-tribal General Council provided for in the treaties of 1866. The Indians would be self-governing. Generally, Adair and other leaders promised that at some time in the future this situation would give way to the incorporation of the territory into the union as one or more predominantly Native American states. For the time being, however, the Indian Territory had to remain separate – not as the white reformers' government-run reservation but as a largely independent alliance of Indian nations.[86]

That status, Cherokee leaders insisted, was not only their preferred basis for relations, but was also the best available answer to the Indian question. Leaders argued that only independent tribes could achieve the peace policy's goals – the end of Indian wars, the rescue of the Indian race from extermination, and the furthering of the civilization process. For the Five Tribes, the maintenance of autonomy and nationhood represented an opportunity to continue their progress. Protected from the machinations of corrupt Americans, the most civilized members of the tribes would have the chance to teach those among their people who lagged behind. The Indians themselves would do the work of the peace policy by instructing "the less intelligent class" among them in the ways of civilized life. A letter from Cherokee delegates to the House Committee on Indian Affairs explained: "They [the delegates] feel that the ultimate destiny of their people will be to become connected with the mighty Government of the United States . . . and they feel the great importance of preparing their people for that great event, by cultivating them, and teaching them (as they must by degrees) all the arts and sciences of civilized life, as well as the precepts of morality and religion, and to this end they earnestly ask for *time* to educate their people and to train them."[87] In messages like this, Cherokee leaders assumed the teacher's role that white reformers had given to agents and missionaries. They promised that if the Indian Territory were left alone, the Cherokees themselves would push toward the completion of their civilization process. "They have demonstrated their capability of civilization and are rapidly solving the problem of the so-called Indian 'question,'" William Potter Ross told senators in arguing against territorialization. "Do not destroy them now."[88]

The maintenance of the Indian Territory, moreover, would help the United States deal with its more pressing Indian problem – the tribes of the plains. Cherokee representatives promised that if left unmolested they would labor to bring progress to the Plains Indians. Echoing a theme from the immediate post-removal years, they suggested that the Five Tribes were the natural leaders of the Indian race and that if left secure in their governments and land ownership they would exert "a wide influence over their wild brethren of the plains."[89] As the United States removed additional tribes to the Indian Territory, the civilized Indians would show them the benefits of peace and progress. As Boudinot explained in the *Advocate*, "the Nations to which all the rest look up with respect and deference – the civilized Tribes of the Indian Territory – would proceed to give the advice, and make proposals to their less favored brethren."[90] The civilized Indians, in fact, were better suited to instruct the wild tribes than were white agents and missionaries, since conflict with Americans had left the Plains Indians suspicious of whites. "We stand in relation to them as older brothers of the same family, as natural allies. . . . The white people stand in the relation of antagonists in interest, from whom this trouble, perplexity, and danger is expected to come."[91] Cherokees offered their own people as the best possible agents of civilization in the West.

In short, the Adairs, Boudinot, and Ross promised Americans that the peace policy could indeed triumph. Indian wars could become a thing of the past and progress could come to the Plains tribes. The agents of that success, however, would not be the Christian bureaucrats envisioned by postwar reformers but the civilized Indians and their autonomous political institutions. The leaders of the Five Tribes embraced the idea that the civilized Indians would serve as examples to their "less favored brethren," and they made that role a far more active one than reformers had envisioned. Leaders cast their people not only as models to be copied by the "wild" tribes, but as crucial instruments of the peace policy. They moved their people from the margins of the reform effort in Indian affairs to its center. All the while, they insisted that if progress were to continue, the tribes of the Indian Territory would have to remain autonomous. The civilized Indians could serve as teachers and agents of the peace policy only if the efforts to dissolve the Indian governments and open the territory to white settlement ceased. "The experiment so far has been a success," a multi-tribal petition stated, but "much still remains to be done to enable the masses of our people to meet and endure white competition." If the United States forced changes upon the Indians now, "the masses, and above all, the wild tribes just coming in, will be scattered and ruined, and become homeless outcasts and vagabonds."[92]

The peace policy dominated American Indian affairs for only a brief time. Almost immediately from its inception, it became a target of critics who characterized the reformers' approach as ill-informed, quixotic, and dangerous to both Americans and the Indians themselves. Making matters worse, several corruption scandals tarnished the Indian Bureau and undermined reformers' faith in the Indian agent as an instrument of peace and civilization. And most damaging of all, the peace policy did not in fact bring peace to the West – the Cherokee delegates' claims notwithstanding. The period saw some of the most brutal Indian warfare of the nineteenth century. All this undermined the peace policy, and in the 1880s new reforms emerged to take its place.[93]

For the Cherokees, however, the peace policy was far more significant than the brevity of its heyday would suggest. It was one of the few American policies that Cherokee leaders steadfastly endorsed. They embraced its promise of justice and humanity, and they echoed its language of crisis and redemption. They identified it as the culmination of all of white America's experience with the Indians since the early republic – at last, a wise and fair course of action. From their self-appointed position as the elder brothers of the Indian race, they accepted the peace policy for the "wild" Indians of the plains and welcomed the prospect of the United States's removing new tribes to the Indian Territory. Even after white reformers had begun to turn away from the Grant administration's approach, Cherokee representatives identified it as the one answer to the Indian question.

During the 1870s, two institutions appeared in the Indian Territory that embodied the Cherokees' version of the peace policy: the General Council already mentioned and the Indian International Fair. Both arose at the instigation of European Americans, yet in the hands of tribal leaders, in particular Creeks and Cherokees, both served the cause of Indian autonomy. Like the peace policy itself, these American imports proved susceptible to reinterpretation. As the next two chapters explain, the council and the fair became institutional expressions of the possibility, indeed the necessity, of the Indian nation's survival in the late nineteenth century.

4

The Okmulgee Council

For the tribal leaders present, it must have seemed a historic moment, the turning of a corner in American Indian affairs. In December 1870 an intertribal council met at Okmulgee, Creek Nation, and debated the idea of chartering a new government for the Indian Territory. This was an explosive topic, since by this time pressure was building upon the tribes to accept reorganization as a territory of the United States. None of the Indians at Okmulgee wanted that. No one wanted the kind of government stipulated by American territorial law, with its appointed executives and judges and its promise that land would be opened to non-Indian homesteading. Yet to those assembled in the Creek capital that winter, it appeared that it might be possible to come up with something better, a territorial government (as one member put it) "of their *own choice*." There was a strong president in Washington who spoke of reforming Indian policy. There were philanthropists and missionaries, Americans of seemingly good conscience, demanding justice for the Indians. The council itself was being funded by the United States Congress, an action that may have signaled confidence in the Indians' ability to direct their own affairs. Perhaps the time was right for tribal leaders to build a new and stronger political structure, a government that, in the words of the council's official record, could "blend in one harmonious system the whole of them at the same time that it preserves a just and impartial regard for their respective rights." By the time the council adjourned, members had written and approved a constitution creating an independent confederacy of tribes. They had come up with a plan that, if ratified and enacted, would preserve the Indian Territory as a refuge for Native American peoples and place it almost entirely beyond the reach of non-Indian authorities. As they returned to their homes, tribal representatives may have believed that they had just solved the Indian question.[1]

The body that produced that potentially radical document was the General Council of the Indian Territory, and oddly enough it had been the American government's idea. The Okmulgee Council, as it was commonly known, was born in the treaty talks that reestablished relations between the United States and the Five Tribes at the end of the Civil War. As an earlier chapter noted, American officials in 1865 demanded that the Indians take clear steps toward accepting United States territorial law as a condition of their return to the good graces of the federal government. The tribes resisted that demand, with Indian leaders fearing that the imposition of territorial law would bring the destruction of their independent governments. In the end, however, the Five Tribes agreed to participate in a permanent, multi-tribal council for the territory.[2]

American officials believed that a general council would lead to the Indian country's amalgamation into the United States. It would be the first step in creating a government identical to those of other American territories. But as it happened, the institution simply became a new site of the existing struggle over tribal autonomy and Indian nations. While the federal government tried to make the council a mechanism by which the territory's special political status would be dismantled, council members attempted to perfect that status through the new body. Indian leaders used the council to combat threats to tribal governments and landholding, and they tried to use it to strengthen the Indians' control over the territory. When the intent of the council's members became clear, Congress moved to eliminate the institution. For a brief time, however, the Okmulgee Council offered tribal leaders an opportunity to express their own conception of the Indian Territory's future, one that began with the preservation of Indian nationhood.

The creation of the Okmulgee Council renewed an antebellum tradition of intertribal meetings in the Indian Territory. Beginning in the 1830s, tribal leaders, most often Cherokees and Creeks, organized conferences to discuss matters common to the newly removed communities. There were two goals at these early meetings: standardizing relations among the Five Tribes and seeking peace with the "wild" Indians of the region. In the summer of 1839 and again in 1843, the Cherokees convened councils at Tahlequah aimed at establishing common procedures among the Five Tribes in the areas of criminal justice, tribal citizenship, and relations with the United States. They hoped to minimize opportunities for conflict and to make sure that all the removed Indians were committed to preserving the new western homeland from further assault by the United States or its citizens.[3] Creek chiefs, meanwhile, used similar councils to open relations with some of the peoples of the southwestern plains. At several meetings in the 1840s and 1850s, Creeks led the way in working out peace agreements between the removed tribes and the Comanches, Pawnees, and Kiowas. They also encouraged warring tribes (the Osages and Pawnees, for example) to settle their disputes. And they recommended to the Plains Indians that they abandon buffalo hunting and join the civilized tribes in making the Indian Territory an agricultural region, an effort appreciatively noted by Indian Bureau officials. In their organization and leadership of such councils, the Creeks developed what the historian Angie Debo called an "all-embracing internationalism," a commitment to seeking intertribal unity and using cooperative action to protect and improve the Indian Territory.[4] After the Civil War, the architects of the Okmulgee Council would attempt to build on that legacy by investing the internationalism of the Creeks and Cherokees in a permanent governmental structure.

Although all the Five Tribes had agreed to a general council by August 1866, four years passed before the first meeting. The problem was treaty money, or more specifically the federal government's failure to come up with the money promised by its treaty negotiators. The United States had pledged to fund the new institution, but Congress hesitated to make the necessary appropriation. While this reflected a general impulse to retrench at the end of the war, there was probably an additional motive specific to the Indian Territory. By the time Congress started considering the general council, the flood of bills to territorialize the Five Tribes' country had begun, and supporters of those bills may have worked against the council. L. N. Robinson, the superintendent of the Indian Bureau's southern department, believed this to be the case. He suspected western congressmen of blocking the funds out of apprehension that the new assembly would interfere with the effort to force reorganization upon the tribes. Whether or not this was true, territorializers surely considered a full-fledged United States government preferable to the council anticipated in the treaties. Some argued, in fact, that the treaty provisions regarding a general council constituted tribal acceptance of reorganization. If that were the case, why settle for an institution that would not necessarily lead to the speedy integration of the Indian country into the United States?[5]

In contrast to legislators' reluctance, Indian Bureau officials often supported the council quite fervently. Superintendent Robinson championed the idea in his reports, as did his superior in Washington, Commissioner Ely S. Parker. They noted that the Indians were eager for the new assembly, and they urged its inauguration as one of the most beneficial actions that the federal government could take on behalf of the Indians. In Robinson's words, "Too much importance cannot be attached to the organization of this council."[6] That enthusiasm was related to the general spirit of reform then at work in Indian affairs. In backing the council, Robinson and Parker identified it as an instrument of the emerging peace policy. The council, they anticipated, would show the Indians that they could trust the United States, and it would give them confidence in the possession of their lands. That "feeling of security," as Parker put it, would be conducive to the civilizing process. Moreover, the assembly would command the attention of other tribes, who, seeing the improvements made in the Indian Territory, would be drawn to emulate their civilized brothers. The council's presence might even help the federal government convince additional tribes to move to the Indian Territory. With that optimistic outlook, Robinson and Parker placed the general council at the center of the campaign to build a better foundation for American Indian affairs.[7]

Congress finally responded to the Bureau in July 1870 and appropriated the necessary funds.[8] Even before that act, however, the Five Tribes had begun to move on their own toward cooperation. In June 1870 a multi-tribal conference met at Okmulgee. Called by Samuel Checote, principal chief of the Creeks, it was a response to the continued presence of territorial bills in Congress. Not surprisingly, the Creeks and Cherokees dominated the meeting, with Checote setting the agenda and Cherokee William Potter Ross serving as president. No Choctaws answered Checote's invitation (a "subject of both remark and regret," according to the *Cherokee Advocate*), but Seminole and Osage delegations were present, along with one Chickasaw representative. The delegates reaffirmed the antebellum guidelines for intertribal relations and added a provision that the principal chief of any of the participating nations might call a meeting in the future. Moreover, they drafted a strong message to the government of the United States expressing their peoples' unwillingness to accept territorialization. The meeting offered a clear signal that the Five Tribes intended to use such meetings to combat threats to Indian landholding and nationhood.[9]

Two months later, the first official council finally convened at Okmulgee, presided over by Enoch Hoag, a Quaker peace-policy advocate and newly appointed Bureau superintendent. Although the Indians reportedly had been anxious for the council to begin, the turnout of delegates was disappointing. The Cherokees and Creeks sent full complements, with William Potter Ross leading the Cherokee delegation, but none of the other civilized tribes appointed representatives. The Chickasaws wrote to Okmulgee, apologizing and explaining that the announcement of the meeting had arrived too late for them to select a delegation. The Choctaws, meanwhile, simply ignored the announcement, their council neither appointing representatives nor authorizing the principal chief to do so. Several of the smaller Indian Territory tribes sent a single delegate each, but with three of the five major nations absent, it was clear that little business could be conducted.

After only three days the council adjourned until the first week of December.[10]

In the intervening months, both tribal leaders and the Indian Bureau worked to convince more of the region's peoples to participate. United States officials, for example, advised the Choctaws and Chickasaws that they would stand in violation of their 1866 treaties if they did not attend.[11] These efforts bore fruit as the December meeting attracted over fifty delegates representing a dozen different Indian Territory groups, including all five of the civilized tribes. As usual, the Creeks and Cherokees were the strongest presence at Okmulgee, but with the delegates of so many tribes attending, the meeting was truly a general council of the Indian Territory. The one disappointment in terms of attendance was the absence of representatives from the Plains tribes. At the September meeting, the council had ordered invitations sent to the Kiowas, Comanches, Cheyennes, Arapahos, and other groups. None, however, answered the call.[12]

Once it was truly operating, the council found enough work to fill two full weeks, with even reluctant members like the Choctaws participating actively. Delegates addressed a variety of issues, from the state of Indian agriculture to the work of the Board of Indian Commissioners. The main business, however, was the drafting of a constitution, a document that would not only define and perpetuate the assembly but create a full-fledged governmental organization for the Indian Territory. This project was urged upon the delegates by Commissioner Parker, who traveled to Okmulgee to address the meeting. Parker told the assembly that the new council was an opportunity for the Indians to gain true self-government. The tribes were there to form an administration of their own, in which "they would hold the power of regulating the affairs of the territory in their own hands." And if they did the job correctly, he advised, the new organization "would end the fear which now troubled them so much, of having a territorial government forced upon them."[13] Surely these were welcome words for the delegates, who may have taken from Parker's speech a promise that the Indian Bureau shared their opposition to territorialization. As would soon become clear, however, federal officials and tribal leaders possessed very different ideas of what proper self-government for the Indian Territory should mean.

After some initial discussion, the council appointed a twelve-man committee, led by William Potter Ross, to draft a constitution.[14] The committee returned a finished document three days later. Modeled on American state and federal constitutions, it provided for a governor, a two-house legislature, and a three-judge supreme court (with each judge also serving on the bench of one of three district courts). Envisioning a kind of tribal federalism, the committee kept the powers of these new authorities limited and clearly delineated. The legislature was authorized to deal with trade and intercourse among Indian nations, criminal matters involving more than one nation, and the common defense of the territory. It could also raise revenue for the territorial government, provided taxation was applied uniformly to all tribes. The judiciary, meanwhile, was not to interfere with the laws or jurisdiction of the individual nations. The district and supreme courts would judge only those cases arising from multi-tribal matters and regarding laws passed by the territorial government. Ross and his committee thus took care to assure the individual tribes that this new organization would not infringe upon their rights and established customs as separate peoples.[15]

The equation for assigning representatives in the territorial assembly pointed to the dominance of the new government by large tribes like the Cherokees and Creeks. Each nation would receive one seat in the senate per two thousand citizens. Small tribes would be grouped together, with the Ottawas, Peorias, and Quapaws, for example, electing one senator among them. The house of representatives would consist of one member per nation, plus an additional member for every one thousand citizens (rounding up from five hundred and one). Under this scheme, the Cherokees, who by conservative estimates numbered around fourteen thousand after the war, would elect at least seven senators and fifteen representatives. A small group like the Shawnees, meanwhile, would receive two representatives and one senator (which they would share with the Wyandots and Senecas) for their seven hundred members.[16]

Crucially, there was no mention of United States influence in the selection of the governor or judges, office holders that the president would have appointed in an ordinary American territory. The voters of the various tribes alone would select the governor, while the governor (with the advice and consent of the Indian Territory senate) would choose the judges. Likewise, the constitution did not provide for the election of a delegate to the American Congress, a feature of standard territorial law and something provided for in several of the Five Tribes' treaties. In fact, there was no mention whatsoever of the United States's having a hand in the direction of the Indian Territory. The schedule of the constitution did not even provide for United States approval of the new organization; ratification was to be solely an Indian matter. The constitutional committee may have assumed that the treaties of 1866, in providing for the general council, represented all the American approval necessary.[17]

As these last features suggest, Ross and the other framers intended to create an alternative to a United States territorial government, their goal being an organization largely independent of Washington. "The opposition of all Indians to any form of Territorial Government that has been proposed by the Congress of the United States is too notorious to require any comment," the resolution appointing the constitutional committee stated. "It is firmly and ineradicably imbedded in their very nature. They cling to their homes, to their laws, to their customs, to their National and personal independence, with the tenacity of life itself."[18] Like the meeting called by Checote earlier in the year, this multi-tribal organization was meant specifically to combat dangerous policies emanating from the American capital. As a Cherokee delegation later wrote, it was meant to be "one of the chief safe guards of our people against a Territorial Government."[19] Far from embracing territorialization, the General Council would put the issue to rest by creating a government that would place the Indian Territory beyond the reach of Congress.

The Grant administration and peace-policy advocates welcomed the Okmulgee Constitution, as it soon came to be known. The Board of Indian Commissioners, several of whom attended the December session, greeted it as nothing short of a sign from God. "The hand of Providence," they enthused, "has opened the eyes of these tribes to see this opportunity, just at the time that the Government and the public sentiment of the country are especially enlisted in their behalf." The council represented "the beginning of a new epoch in the history of the red man."[20] Commissioner Parker, Secretary of the Interior Columbus Delano, and the president himself used less ecstatic terms, but they similarly expressed satisfaction and optimism at the work of the Okmulgee delegates. In particular they anticipated that the new organization would convince other tribes to move to the Indian Territory, thus solving the Indian question for at least a portion of the West. Like the Board of Indian Commissioners, Grant and his lieutenants saw the constitution as evidence that the reform effort in American Indian affairs was working.[21]

In embracing Okmulgee, however, the Grant administration violated the central principle informing the Indians' work. Before any of the Indian Territory nations could act upon the constitution, the president submitted it to Congress with the suggestion that it be amended to conform to standard territorial law. This would involve not only the presidential appointment of judges and the governor, but federal veto power over acts passed by the territorial legislature.[22] Begun as an effort to elude territorial bills, the Okmulgee Constitution was itself to become in essence a territorial bill. Moreover, the president's message opened the possibility that federal authorities could interfere again once the new structure was in place. If Congress could unilaterally alter the compact, what would stop it from making further changes in Indian government or landholding in the future? Grant's action effectively killed the constitution. The Cherokee National Council refused to consider it, afraid that if the Indians ratified the new government it would initiate a slide toward the destruction of tribal independence and the opening of the Indian homelands to settlers. As the *Cherokee Advocate* put the matter, "Its adoption is now regarded as a handle to the ax that is to fell entire forests of Indian nationalities." Many of the other tribes balked as well. Among the large nations, only the Creeks accepted the document, their faith in internationalism overcoming their distrust of Congress. But Creek support was not enough, and any hope of ratifying the constitution quickly faded once the president's recommendations became known.[23]

Rejected by its makers, the Okmulgee Constitution became a minor episode in the history of postwar Indian affairs. It was an episode, however, that illustrated several important points. For one thing, Grant and Delano clearly believed that unilaterally amending the constitution would not contradict the peace policy. They believed, in fact, that they were perfecting the document as an instrument of the new reform effort in Indian relations. An amended constitution, they felt, would grant the Indian Territory peoples a better form of self-government than they could ever enjoy under their own tribal institutions, while American law would offer greater protection for their homes and property than they enjoyed at present. These achievements, Grant and his councilors believed, would not only be good for the peoples currently settled in the territory but would draw the attention and admiration of other tribes. Seeing the security and peace to be had within an Indian-dominated United States territory, Native people across the West would consent to move there, thus eliminating opportunities for frontier conflict elsewhere. The Indian Territory would become a mechanism for pacifying the remaining western tribes and bringing them under American authority. All this could be done without violating at least the spirit of the treaties, since the territory would remain almost exclusively an Indian homeland, "the last refuge of the race," as peace-policy advocates liked to call it. Amending the Okmulgee Constitution, then, became an act embodying the peace policy's promise of justice for Native Americans.[24]

That outlook, it is worth noting, made the effort to alter the constitution into a different form of territorialization than was foreseen in many of the Oklahoma bills submitted to Congress. These tended to leave open the question of whether additional tribes would be moved to the territory or whether unused land would simply be opened for settlement under standard American law regarding the public domain. Tribal leaders quite logically interpreted the bills as efforts to instigate land runs in their territory, as well as attempts to dispose of the Indian governments. The Grant administration, on the other hand, wanted to maintain barriers to non-Indian settlement to the extent that the open land was to be given to new migrant tribes. The ultimate goal was for the territory to develop into a predominantly Indian state, a full-fledged member of the Union but one with a particular racial identity.[25]

For many Native leaders, however, this distinction was irrelevant. Territorialization of any kind without tribal approval was a violation of the treaties and an assault upon the Indians themselves. As discussed earlier in this study, tribal representatives generally interpreted the peace policy as a new pledge to honor the treaties and with them Indian nationhood. Humanity and justice began with the United States's keeping its promises. That being the case, any attempt by Washington to impose political reorganization immediately placed the Grant administration on the side of the peace policy's enemies – land speculators, savage frontier whites, and unscrupulous border politicians. What was more, Grant had handed the tribes over to Congress, the source of so many threats to the Indian Territory in the postwar era. Quite reasonably, tribal leaders doubted that the peace and security promised by Grant could be won through congressional action. More likely, the amended Okmulgee Constitution would open a door through which new troubles would come to the territory.

In handling the Okmulgee Constitution, the Grant administration blended respect for Indian self-determination with paternalism. Grant believed he was offering the people of the territory self-government within the United States – something far better than what they possessed as semi-independent nations. But he proposed to bestow this gift in a fundamentally paternalistic manner, by "fixing" an Indian charter specifically meant to prevent territorialization. In effect, he attempted to grant the tribes self-government by denying it in the immediate situation. Interestingly, the tribal leaders who rejected the constitution did something similar. They abandoned the document in the name of Indian independence and nationhood. Yet in the absence of an Indian Territory government, their people remained dependent upon the president for protection. Tribal leaders ended up clinging to the Great Father on the understanding that a territorial government would leave them in the much more dangerous hands of Congress. The Okmulgee Constitution, which everyone involved hoped would clarify the political status of the Indian Territory tribes, became a further example of the fundamental contradiction at work in the tribes' affairs: the coexistence of Indian dependence and tribal sovereignty.

Despite the failure of the constitution, the Okmulgee Council continued to meet. Tribal representatives gathered at least once annually for the next five years, and Congress continued to support the council financially, as stipulated in the treaties. Without being part of a new government structure, the council during these years possessed virtually no formal power. It could not legislate for the territory or enforce any decisions it made on behalf of the member nations except through the nations' individual governments. Yet it served a number of important functions for the Indian Territory tribes, especially in regard to their relations with the United States. For one thing, it became a new instrument for expressing tribal opposition to territorialization, the allotment of Indian land, and other policy initiatives that threatened Indian independence and nationhood. A regular part of each session's business was the selection of a "committee on United States relations," the main purpose of which was to draft statements to Congress and the president. These committees returned protest memorials that, if anything, were more forceful than those of the individual tribal governments. In 1872, for example, the council charged that "the spirit of avarice of 1830–35" (that is, the greed that had inspired the removal policy) was again at work in Indian affairs. Frontier interests conspired for the purpose of "disrupting every Indian nationality," while anti-Indian legislators wrote bills aimed at breaking the treaties and imposing upon the Indians a government not of their own choice. At stake in this case was nothing short of the persistence of the Indian race. The opening of the Territory to whites threatened the Five Tribes with "degradation and ultimate extinction," and if the civilized Indians were annihilated, the rest of the continent's Native people would soon follow. "Remember that the hopes and destiny of the race, are measurably interwoven with the fate of the five original nations of this country. . . . Our destiny is one, that we must all stand or fall together."[26]

In this and other statements, the council expressed many of the common themes of Five Tribes relations with the United States in the postwar era. Members argued that Indian survival required Indian nationhood and thus that territorialization was nothing short of an act of war. They attacked the white savages of the frontier. They offered themselves, the "elder brothers of the race," as spokesmen for all Indians.[27] The council, then, became an additional voice broadcasting to the United States the demand for tribal autonomy. In fact, the council may have been more effective than any tool at tribal leaders' disposal. One of the difficulties the representatives of the Five Tribes faced was that American authorities frequently challenged their legitimacy. Their adversaries continually renewed the old argument that the chiefs of the civilized tribes seldom acted for the Indians' good. The chiefs, it was said, were self-interested schemers, cunning "half-breeds" who manipulated the "ignorant full-bloods" to serve their own ends. That image of the civilized Indian leader was always available to Americans – legislators, Indian Bureau officials, newspaper editors – who disagreed with the positions taken by the tribal governments. It was a ready-made excuse for the dismissal of tribal political statements. Thus, congressmen and western newspapers charged that the leaders of the Five Tribes kept their people in the dark about the great benefits that inclusion in the United States and the vigorous promotion of railroads offered. They argued that the statements made against territorialization or allotment reflected merely the feelings of a greedy Indian elite rather than those of the common people. Tribal delegates to Washington, in particular, were open to abuse. They lived well in the capital on the treaty funds of their tribes. Their opposition to changes in policy was said to be animated principally by a desire to maintain the system that let them drain their people's wealth in this manner.

The Okmulgee Council may have been partially immune to these charges. Although its members represented the tribal governments no less than did the delegates to Washington, the council itself was sanctioned and supported by the Indian Bureau and Congress. The council, or something like it, had been the United States government's idea in the first place. High-ranking federal officials presided over its meetings (an Indian Bureau superintendent generally acting as president) and even higher officials visited or sent greetings to Okmulgee. This particular relationship with the federal government may have granted the council an authority that the Washington delegates or even the tribal chiefs lacked. The Okmulgee assembly, by the federal government's own terms, was the official voice of the people of the Indian Territory. At any rate, the institution's potential to grant greater legitimacy to Indian positions was likely one of its attractive features from a tribal point of view.

Beyond composing explicitly political messages, the council generated certain kinds of information about the Indian Territory. Committees on agriculture and education produced reports each session detailing the state of the member nations' farming and schools. These documents were then included in the published proceedings of the council. Typically, the committees would write a few paragraphs on each tribe, tallying the number of acres under the plow or used as pasture, listing the number of schools and pupils attending, and indicating whether those numbers represented improvement or decline. "Choctaws are one of the Five Nations of the Indian Territory," the agriculture report for 1873 read. "They are civil, friendly, intelligent, industrious and wealthy. They cultivate sixty-five thousand acres of land. They raise the cereals; plant gardens and set out fruit trees which bear the apple, peach, pear and cherry. . . . They are enlarging farms and building fences. Cotton and cattle bring them cash. They are improving native stock by mixing pure breeds imported from the States."[28] Most of the descriptions, like the passage above, indicated that agriculture and education were improving steadily among the Indians. In 1872 the Creeks' new boarding schools were "bidding fair to become not only a great blessing, but a bright honor to the Creek Nation," while in the Cherokee country, "many of the farmers are using the most improved farming utensils, and the general tendency of education and agriculture is very encouraging."[29] Even the smaller tribes with little money were seen to be improving. The Wyandots had only one school, run by missionaries, and no tribal funds explicitly marked for education; the council reported, "The cause of education among them, however, is encouraging." Some of the Wyandots had attended schools outside their country, and most wanted their children to have opportunities to learn. Overstating the matter somewhat, the committee concluded that despite the tribe's lack of school money, "The Wyandottes are, to a great extent, an educated people."[30]

The reports also discussed Indian proposals for improving the territory's farms and schools. In 1872 the committee on agriculture suggested that the council work with the various tribal governments to form agricultural societies, institutions that would help bring modern farming practices to the territory. This idea eventually led the Okmulgee Council to support the founding of the Indian International Fair, an annual event described in the next chapter. The following year the council discussed building an "International Literary and Industrial College," a high school like the Cherokee seminaries that would be supported by all the Indian Territory nations. Including these proposals in the official proceedings of the council, the committees on agricultural and education broadcast the Indians' zeal for improvement.[31]

Statistics on schools, crop yields, and livestock herds were common in the records of tribal relations, but for several reasons these particular reports are worth noting. First, the information generated at Okmulgee came from an Indian-controlled institution. This would have been significant to many tribal leaders. The Cherokees and Five Tribes during this period constantly endeavored to present "true information" about the Indian Territory to federal officials and other non-Indian Americans. Delegations to Washington were expensive and controversial, but they were necessary in order to present a true picture of the Territory to Congress and the president and to remind the powerful Americans of their treaties with Indian nations. Newspapers like the *Cherokee Advocate* and the Creek Nation's *Indian Journal* not only kept readers within the Indian country informed, but traveled east to educate curious Americans and to counter racist propaganda. In publishing the education and agriculture reports, the Okmulgee Council took on a role parallel to that of the delegates' missions to the capital. It became a tool by which Native people attempted to shape Americans' knowledge of the Indian Territory and its inhabitants.

Moreover, in writing about farms and schools, the Okmulgee Council took hold of two important signs of Native civilization, signs invoked in one way or another by almost all participants in the debates over American Indian affairs. Typically, the expansion of agriculture and increased school attendance were taken to be evidence of successful federal policy. Improvement in these areas meant that the Indian Bureau's officers were performing well and that the directives they implemented were wise. The Okmulgee Council's agriculture and education reports, in fact, were quite similar to the descriptions sent by federal Indian agents in their annual messages to the Bureau, documents that continually assured Washington of the agents' steady success.[32] When the council wrote of improving education and agriculture, it likewise affirmed the propriety of existing relations – or at least tribal leaders' interpretation of them. It offered the information on schools and farms as evidence that the Indian Territory's current political status was the correct one. Success in these areas proved that the territory should remain a loosely confederated group of Indian nations, protected by treaty and withheld from non-Indian settlement.

At times the Okmulgee reports made that message explicit, and with it the political nature of all writing on the topics of Indian agriculture and education. The committees generally capped their descriptions of tribal improvement by noting that the chief obstacle to further progress came from Washington rather than from the tribes themselves. As the 1872 report put it, "We sadly deplore the fact that a feeling of insecurity in our possessions, caused by the agitation of the question in Congress, of opening this country to white settlement, greatly retards our agricultural advancement."[33] The prospect of being overrun by white Americans and of seeing their nationalities destroyed left the citizens of the Indian Territory demoralized and less willing to continue in the work of civilization. Echoing some of the rhetoric of the peace policy, the council members insisted that Indian improvement required protection and respect for Indian rights.

On several occasions members attempted to expand the Okmulgee Council's role as a medium for spreading knowledge of the territory. In 1873 the council proposed sending lecturers to American towns and cities. Itinerant preachers of the Indian question, their duty would be "to travel through the United States, and deliver lectures, and employ other means as may seem proper to further enlighten the public mind upon the Indian problem of the Indian Territory." They would also solicit donations for the support of Indian agriculture and the tribal schools. The resolution concerning this matter passed during the 1873 session, but it appears that the council never gathered the necessary funds to implement the program.[34] In a similar action two years later, council members raised the idea of mounting an official Indian Territory display at the 1876 Centennial Exhibition at Philadelphia, America's first major world's fair. As the next chapter explains, this too foundered for lack of adequate funding, although several of the Five Tribes did send small exhibits.[35] While these efforts failed, the fact that they developed at all indicates the extent to which those at Okmulgee valued the council (with or without a constitution) as a means of broadcasting a proper picture of the Territory to the citizens of the United States.

If tribal leaders fit the Okmulgee Council to existing needs in their relations with white America, they also tried to make the council useful to the United States in at least one important way. From almost the first session, the council attempted to act as a mediator between the federal government and some of the nomadic tribes of the plains. As mentioned earlier, maintaining peaceful relations with Plains Indians was one of the main purposes of the territory's antebellum conferences, especially those directed by the Creeks. In those cases, however, the focus was on mediating between plains peoples and the five emigrant nations. In the 1870s, the Okmulgee Council altered and embellished that old role to establish itself as something like an independent Indian agency. Each year it invited groups like the Southern Cheyennes and Arapahos to attend the council's meetings, where they would confer with leaders of the Five Tribes and the federal officials present. Council

members offered themselves as advisers to the Indians of the southern plains, their first recommendation being "to refrain from acts of
hostility among themselves, and with the people of the United States."
They proposed to help the Plains tribes establish "permanently friendly
relations with the [United States] Government." And they presented
their nations as models for the Plains Indians, examples of how Native people could survive and prosper even in the midst of the rapid
expansion of non-Indian settlement.[36]

Not surprisingly, tribal leaders often emphasized this aspect of the
council's work in their messages to non-Indians. Okmulgee was a
"school of government for our wilder brethren" and a "civilizing influence" upon the people of the plains. It was a "Peace-Maker" in that
members continually counseled Plains tribes to give up warfare and
to defend themselves with schools and agriculture instead of the gun.
Indian leaders acknowledged the Grant administration's hope that the
council would help pacify the Plains Indians, and whenever possible
they offered proof that this was in fact taking place. "This council
has already been the means of saving a hundred times its cost to the
Government by its influence in preserving peace on the plains," one
statement read, "and we are confident of its ability for great usefulness
in the same field in the future." In effect, leaders promised that the
council was performing much of the Indian Bureau's work for it on
the plains and would continue to do so if left to operate.[37]

Playing this mediator's role, the Okmulgee Council became involved
in one of the most famous western conflicts of the post – Civil War era,
the struggle over southern range land that culminated in the Red River
War of 1874–75.[38] This episode deserves to be described in some detail,
for while the civilized tribes could not prevent the war, the effort testified to their commitment to the peacemaking aspect of the council's
work. At issue were raids conducted by Kiowas and Comanches against
white settlements and hunting parties in Texas. Such hostilities had occurred off and on since the 1840s, when Texans began to encroach upon
lands claimed by the Indians as hunting territory. For two decades the
Kiowas and Comanches, along with elements of several other tribes,
had the better of this sporadic warfare, with the Indians successfully

plundering Texans and beating back whatever organized campaigns were sent against them. At the close of the Civil War, however, the United States Army established a stronger presence on the southern plains, and the federal government drew the Kiowas and their allies into negotiations to settle the old conflict. In the 1867 Treaty of Medicine Lodge Creek, tribal leaders agreed to accept a reservation in the Indian Territory and to give up their claims to much of their old hunting land. Federal officials hoped that this would be the end of the matter, but events proved otherwise. Not long after the signing of the treaty, poor conditions on the reservation and the continued killing of the buffalo by white hunters drew elements of both tribes back to war. Although many older recognized chiefs opposed it, raiding persisted, and the crisis deepened through the 1860s and into the next decade.[39]

It was an intensification of these hostilities that drew the Okmulgee Council into the conflict. In May 1871, American authorities arrested three Kiowa war leaders – Satanta, Big Tree, and Satank, the last of whom was killed while attempting to escape soon after. When Satanta and Big Tree were carried to Texas, convicted of murder, and sentenced to life imprisonment, Kiowas, joined at times by Comanches and others, reacted by stepping up their raids. In the spring and summer of 1872, they moved against white settlements all along the Texas frontier, killing settlers, stealing their property, and taking a number of children captive. On several occasions they threatened their own United States agency at Fort Sill.[40] The region's army commanders wanted to mount a punitive campaign in response to these attacks, but the Indian Bureau instead opted to arrange new peace talks for later that summer. Bureau officials understood that if the raiding continued it would only be a matter of time before the United States mounted a full-scale war, and they wanted another chance (perhaps a last chance) to make the Indians themselves accept this. Toward that end, the Bureau planned to take a group of tribal leaders to Washington in an effort to impress upon the Indians the vast extent of American power and thus the hopelessness of continued opposition to the Great Father's will. In preparation for the journey, Superintendent Enoch Hoag organized preliminary talks for late July at Fort Cobb, an abandoned army post located near Anadarko on the Wichita reservation. It was here, at the preliminary meeting, that the civilized tribes entered the picture.[41]

The Okmulgee Council had already made overtures to the Kiowas and Comanches, a delegation having traveled to the plains the previous year.[42] At the session in June 1872, Hoag alerted the assembly to the deepening crisis and asked that it again take action. The council agreed and quickly drew up a committee consisting of delegates from the Five Tribes, along with the leaders of bands served by the Wichita Indian agency. The Cherokees appointed were Daniel H. Ross (William Potter Ross's brother), James Vann, and Eli Smith. A month later these delegates, calling themselves the "Indian Peace Commission," assembled at Fort Cobb.[43] There, over the course of about ten days, they met with representatives of most of the major groups of the southern plains, including many of the Kiowas and Comanches responsible for the most recent raiding. They informed the Plains Indian leaders of the precariousness of their situation, insisting that the Fort Cobb talks represented "the last call," a final chance to avoid a full-scale war. They urged them to return the captive children and stolen property and invited them to join the party traveling to the American capital. In return, they promised that the military would not bother their people while they were away, and they suggested to the Kiowas that if they cooperated, the Americans would be willing to discuss the release of Satanta and Big Tree.[44]

The talks at Fort Cobb yielded mixed results. Some of the Plains Indians present scoffed at the delegates, dismissing them as "white Indians" unworthy of their attention. "They are an old dirty inefficient looking set," one Comanche said. "We don't take much stock in them."[45] On the other hand, the commission succeeded in gaining at least its immediate objectives, so clearly someone was listening. The commission helped the Indian Bureau assemble a good-sized group of plains leaders for the journey to Washington – no small feat, as rising tensions had left many Indians reluctant to deal with white officials. It also managed to win some white prisoners' release. And it helped the Kiowas gain eventual freedom for Satanta and Big Tree. The talks provided the Kiowas with an opportunity to appeal for their leaders' release, which in turn encouraged the Indian Bureau to adopt that goal in the hope that the return of the chiefs would placate some of the raiders.[46]

Concentrating on the positive signs, the Indian commissioners and the Okmulgee Council declared complete victory. "The labors of this Peace Commission," one report stated, "have been fruitful of the most happy results to all of the parties in interest. In the emphatic words of the leading Kiowa raiders, '*The war was cut right off.*'" The Kiowas, the report continued, now understood the vast power of the United States. "They know . . . that their only safety for the future is in peace – peace with all." When the imprisoned chiefs came home, it said, "We believe that like the noted chief of the Sioux – Red Cloud – Satanta will hereafter be the steadfast friend and advocate of peace."[47]

Satanta, in fact, ceased to be an important war leader after his parole in 1873; however, the council's optimism regarding the future of Indian relations on the southern plains proved misplaced. During the winter of 1873–74, raiding by Kiowas, along with Comanches and some Cheyennes, began anew. The return of Satanta and Big Tree had not ended the destruction of the buffalo nor made reservation life any more attractive, and some Indians persisted in seeking plunder and revenge. By the summer of 1874 violence had escalated to the point that President Grant at last authorized the punitive war that the military desired. Loosed upon the southern plains, the United States Army sought out and attacked any Indians whom they found away from their agencies, with soldiers destroying food supplies, seizing horses, and occasionally engaging warriors in combat. By the end of a long winter of this kind of harassment, almost all the militant leaders surrendered, and for the Kiowas and their allies the reservation era began in earnest.[48] The Okmulgee Council continued to involve itself in the crisis during this time. It sent additional delegates to meet with the leaders of Plains tribes, and it tried to act as an advocate for bands that had remained peaceful. At the end of the conflict, for example, the council supported the effort to gain the release of Indian prisoners held without trial at Fort Marion in St. Augustine, Florida. But once the military campaign had begun, the council could do little to shape the course of events.[49]

As the army broke the last of the hostile Kiowas and Comanches, legislators in Washington moved to eliminate the Okmulgee Council. In making the Indian Bureau's appropriation for 1876, Congress omitted the funds necessary to hold the council's next session. At a time when the tribes themselves were often in desperate financial straits, this action dealt a death blow to the new institution. Indian leaders and delegates protested, of course. They reminded lawmakers that the council and its budget had been created by treaties duly ratified in the Senate and that Congress was thus bound to provide proper funding. Such arguments changed nothing, however. The yearly "Indian bills" never again included an appropriation for the council, and no further meetings were held.[50] The immediate reason for the funds' omission is unclear. Cherokees blamed the lobbyists working in Washington in support of the Oklahoma bills, and indeed pressure was mounting during this time to force territorialization upon the tribes. The year that Congress stripped the council of its funds, no less than thirteen territorial bills were introduced. Meanwhile, the council had lost some of its old admirers. By 1875 the commissioner of Indian affairs was Edward P. Smith, who believed that Congress should throw aside the treaties and reorganize the Territory unilaterally. Likewise, the Board of Indian Commissioners had lost faith in the Okmulgee experiment by this time. In 1874 many of the Board's members had resigned, frustrated with what they considered the government's failure to act upon their suggestions. Their replacements included men less willing to listen to tribal representatives, and a committee sent west by the new board returned a report advocating territorialization. With the support of the Indian affairs establishment fading, there was no one in the government to protest revoking the council's appropriation.[51]

At the same time, the opposition of the council itself to territorialization was growing stronger, and this may have further encouraged legislators to defund the institution. Indian leaders insisted that the council represented an independent Indian confederacy, the definitive expression of the tribes' unwillingness to accept a United States government. As they had said all along, the Okmulgee Council was not a step toward territorialization but an alternative to it.[52] As if to underline that fact, the council in its final meeting drafted a new constitution, one that, like the charter of 1870, excluded the federal government from the selection of officers or the governing of the Indian country. For many in Congress, an Okmulgee Council that would not facilitate territorialization must have seemed worse than useless, an obstacle to progress.[53]

In the years following the council's demise, tribal leaders discussed the possibility of reviving the institution, either by convincing Congress to resume support or by maintaining an assembly funded by the Indian treasuries. Restoration failed, however, and some in the tribal governments seem to have preferred that outcome. The prospect of a new Indian Territory association always entailed the danger that Congress would use it as an excuse for imposing a United States government. Having been threatened in this manner after the passage of the 1870 constitution, leaders hesitated to offer Congress new opportunities for mischief. The Five Tribes, however, continued to sponsor international conferences, meetings that could fulfill some of the purposes formerly met by the Okmulgee Council but that did not pose the risks of a new permanent institution. The late 1870s saw mass meetings to protest the "boomer" invasions, schemes to bring illegal settlers into the territory in hopes of forcing the federal government to open the Indian country. Later, there were numerous conferences held to express opposition to allotment. The intertribal meeting, the practice of marshaling the tribes to produce a unified Indian voice, remained one of the chief political tactics available to the people of the territory. But those meetings never again became an effort to create a multi-tribal confederacy or government.[54]

By almost any standard, the Okmulgee Council was a failure. It did not leave the tribes more secure in their governments and landholding, nor did it clarify their contradictory political status. It drew the attention of the nomadic tribes but fell short in its efforts to act as a "peace medium" on the southern plains. At the time of its disappearance, officials in Washington and even some Indian leaders believed that it might do more harm than good. Yet if the council changed little, its efforts merit consideration as evidence of tribal leaders' analysis of their political situation. For six years, Okmulgee provided a setting in which Indian people acted out their own ideas of proper relations between tribes and the United States. The council produced momentary views of how Indian leaders might have altered conditions in the territory had they possessed sufficient power. That being the case, one can draw from the Okmulgee Council's short life an Indian model of American Indian affairs.

That model begins with the altered role that council members envisioned for the federal government, a role best described as the territory's gatekeeper. The United States would protect the borders of the Indian Territory, with federal authority barring intruders and preserving the country as an Indian homeland. The United States would also continue to be a source of capital for the tribes, to the extent that all treaties would remain in force and treaty payments would still be made. The power of the federal government, however, would stop at the border of the Indian country. In the system laid out in the Okmulgee Constitution, policies for the Territory would be set exclusively by the intertribal legislature or the individual Indian governments. Likewise, Indian authorities and institutions would handle law enforcement, although the United States would most likely remain responsible for bringing its own citizens to justice when they committed crimes in the Indian country. The president and Congress would exercise no influence in the selection of the territory's political officers and would play no formal role in making laws for the tribes. In fact, the treaty process would be the one remaining route by which the United States could affect the territory's internal affairs. American authorities could seek new international agreements with the Indians, but otherwise their role would be strictly to protect the territory from American citizens.

Earlier chapters have described a similar conception of federal power at work in Cherokee reactions to the Civil War and the peace policy. Cherokee leaders welcomed the stronger federal presence of the late 1860s and 1870s, but they placed strict limits on the actions that American authorities could legitimately perform with their augmented power. Properly exercised, federal power would restrain the greed and treachery of an expansive America. It would protect the Indian nations so that Native peoples could work out their own destinies. When protection turned into an effort to control Indian people, however, an opening was created that allowed all that greed and treachery to enter the Territory and destroy the tribes. A strong federal government was necessary, but as a sentinel rather than a manager. The Okmulgee Council and constitution attempted to ratify this idea of federal power, and in doing so they further broadcast the rather ironic image of the United States expressed by Cherokee leaders during this period. The council looked to the emergence of a federal government more active in Indian affairs, to the extent that it saw the Territory's future as dependent upon federal policing of the borders. Yet this federal government was also more restrained, insofar as it could do almost nothing legitimately to influence conditions within the Territory. Its power had to be exerted exclusively to curb its own population's destructive impulses.

As tribal leaders saw it, American officials could afford to leave the Indian Territory alone, because the Okmulgee Council was prepared to assume responsibility for its internal affairs. In fact, the council's activities and proposals suggest that members envisioned its assuming most Indian Bureau functions. Agents' yearly reports, for example, would be unnecessary when the Indian Territory had its own government to speak for the tribes. The representatives at Okmulgee would investigate conditions in the Territory for the Great Father, with Indians themselves explaining their needs and desires. More important, the council would oversee the civilizing mission, relieving the Indian Bureau of one of its main responsibilities. Okmulgee would urge Indian people to progress in agriculture, industry, and education through its reports on the territory and its sponsorship of new institutions like the proposed industrial training school. Presumably, missionaries and other agents of civilization would continue to work with some Indian Territory groups, but there would no longer be a need for federal officials to involve themselves directly in Indian advancement. Finally, the council would continue its work as an intermediary for the federal government in its relations with the peoples of the plains. Indian leaders would convey to Plains Indians the necessity of maintaining peace with the United States and of giving up nomadic hunting for agriculture. They would offer the Plains tribes homes in a territory that, thanks to the Okmulgee Constitution, was safe from American invasion and beyond the grasp of a capricious Congress. With the Indians of the West concentrated in a single region administered by Native institutions and officers, there would be little need for an Indian Bureau at all.

To be sure, this model of future relations did not untangle the knot of Indian nationhood. Even in the council's most sanguine visions, the maintenance of tribal sovereignty relied upon the United States government's power; that is, the Indians remained dependent. When tribal leaders looked to the council to replace the Indian Bureau, however, they imagined a future in which dependence no longer truly mattered. The ultimate promise of the Okmulgee Council was that it would take the Indian question out of American hands. Pacifying the plains and carrying out the civilization mission, the council would allow the federal government to remove itself almost entirely from the management of Indian people. In return, American authorities would simply have to protect the Territory, something that they had repeatedly sworn in the treaties to do anyway. Indian dependence, in this scheme of things, was almost beside the point. The council imagined a partnership in which a Native solution to the Indian question would suit the needs of both the tribes and the United States.

It is unclear whether members of the Okmulgee Council foresaw the territory's remaining permanently detached from non-Indian America, or whether the confederacy of tribes was a step toward eventual inclusion in the United States. They seem to have hoped that an autonomous status could be maintained at least long enough to allow newly removed tribes to occupy the unpopulated portions of the Territory. Eliminating "surplus" land, it was thought, would remove one major reason for Americans to tamper with the treaties. It would help grant the tribes the security that peace-policy advocates identified as important but could never deliver. And with Indian landholding safe, the Territory could potentially move toward some kind of amalgamation with the United States. According to an argument made by both tribal leaders and American reformers, Indian people would progress once they were secure in their property, and eventually they would be ready for American citizenship. The Indian Territory could then enter the Union without risk. Much as the Grant administration had hoped, the Territory would become a Native American state – a full member of the nation while still an Indian refuge and homeland. Perhaps council members viewed this kind of statehood as the Territory's ultimate destiny. It was an end, however, that could only be reached through the preservation of Indian nationhood in the immediate future.

5

The Indian International Fairs

I would be glad to see the people in the States take a greater interest in the Fairs of these people than they have heretofore. They deserve it. If you don't believe it, go and see for yourselves. Go amongst them and don't be afraid to take your wives down with you. See and enjoy the beautiful country and the delightful climate. See for yourselves the intelligence they have, and the wonderful advancement they have made and test their hospitality. My word for it you will find ladies and gentlemen among the Indians, and you will form acquaintances among them, as I have done, whose acquaintance you may be proud to claim in any country.

J. W. Archer, a resident of Indiana, was writing of the Indian International Fair, a multi-tribal gathering held annually at Muskogee, Creek Nation, during much of the late nineteenth century. Archer had attended the fair while traveling through the Indian Territory in the autumn of 1881, and upon returning home he wrote about it for an Indiana newspaper. He described an event that in most respects resembled the county agricultural fairs held each year across his own state. There were exhibits of corn and wheat grown in the Indian nations, livestock, and "some very good cotton." There was a "ladies' department" displaying needlework and canned fruits and preserves. Merchants had placed farm machinery on display for inspection. The fact that this was an *Indian* fair, however, set the gathering apart in Archer's mind. When performed by the Territory's Native American residents, the typical fairground activities took on new meaning as

149

markers of Indian civilization. Archer had not expected to meet "ladies and gentlemen" in the territory, and he suggested that the truly remarkable aspect of the fair was the extent to which those in attendance did not match white Americans' popular images of the western tribes. "The man who goes to the Indian Territory to find the dime-novel Indian," Archer observed, "will be badly fooled."[1]

I, too, find the Indian International Fair remarkable, but for a somewhat different reason. In the late nineteenth century, Americans maintained a variety of cultural forms concerned with producing images of Indians, from the dime novels that Archer mentioned to the early Wild West show. Among these media were America's own international expositions, the world's fairs, which almost always included exhibits of Indian objects and Indian people. These expositions displayed Indians in ways that reinforced white ethnocentrism and justified American conquest. Indians appeared as colorful primitives and relics of the past, or else they were the dutiful wards of enlightened white authorities, children receiving much-needed instruction. Native Americans themselves appear to have exercised very little influence over how their images were employed.[2] Placed in that context, the Muskogee fair seems different and noteworthy. Although most of its original organizers were white merchants interested primarily in bettering their town's commerce, Native Americans participated in ways that allowed them to shape the fair's depiction of Indian people and the Indian Territory. In particular, Cherokees and other members of the Five Tribes made the fair serve their paramount political goal, the maintenance of the Territory as a collection of independent Indian nations. As Archer's letter suggests, they did this by crafting images of Indian progress. They used the fair to amplify one of their most common political arguments: that Indian advancement proved the wisdom of preserving tribal autonomy.

The Indian International Fair existed for about twenty years, from 1874 through the early 1890s.[3] Held in the autumn, it ran for four days in an area of open fields on the outskirts of Muskogee. The first meeting took place in a tent located at what is now the corner of Cherokee and

Cincinnati Streets, but organizers later moved the event to a permanent site further east. By the late 1870s, the fairgrounds were entirely fenced and contained barns for livestock, a one-mile racetrack, and a two-story circular exhibit hall known as the "Floral Pavilion" (or, more prosaically, the "Dinner Bucket"). Contemporary newspapers described these facilities as simple but trim and well maintained, and correspondents usually compared them favorably to county fairgrounds in the surrounding states. During the meet, flags representing the Five Tribes flew from the main exhibit hall, while a tall central flagstaff displayed the stars and stripes. Inside the hall, banners announced the various Indian peoples participating in the fair, as well as the Territory's black population, and cedar and evergreen branches decorated the building's wooden posts and rafters. Just outside the pavilion, organizers erected a platform for music performances and speeches, hanging a banner reading "Fairs to Encourage Agriculture" above it.[4]

By all accounts, the event drew large crowds. "Everybody came except those with a price on their heads or who were dodging the marshals," one visitor recalled.[5] While I have yet to find exact figures, commentators who made estimates reported that several thousand people attended the fair each year. In 1878 a group of visiting United States congressmen guessed that the number was as high as twenty thousand for that year's meet.[6] Muskogee had several small hotels and boardinghouses for those who could afford them, but most visitors camped on site, setting up tents and lodges on and around the fairground. Many accounts mention this camp (and in particular the presence of Plains Indians) as one of the more striking features of the event. "They were a picturesque group with their gaily colored blankets . . . and their imposing head-dress," the Cherokee Ella Robinson remembered many years later. "The Indians always welcomed visitors to their tepees and it was my delight as a small child in company with my little cousins, the Ross children, to wander among their camps."[7] Others emphasized the variety of peoples represented at the fair, noting that the visitors included Indians of many different nations, black and white residents of the territory, and fairgoers from neighboring states. It was "a crowd of wonderfully mixed colors," one observer concluded. The "mixing of colors," however, had its limits. Black visitors were not allowed to sleep within the fair enclosure itself but were relegated to the surrounding fields at the end of each day.[8]

Muskogee was a new town at the time of the fair's inauguration, having been established in the early months of 1872. Its primary reason for existence was as a depot on the newly arrived Missouri, Kansas, and Texas railroad line (MK&T, or "Katy"), the first of the two railroads that the Five Tribes had agreed after the Civil War to allow through the Territory. Although Muskogee was part of the Creek Nation, there were relatively few Creeks living there. Its population consisted mostly of whites, both United States citizens and individuals who had married into an Indian nation, and African Americans, men and women formerly held as slaves in the Territory. A number of Cherokee families lived there as well. This seems like a strange mix for a Creek town, but in fact many new settlements that sprouted along the railroad lines were similar in character. Railroad construction brought in laborers from outside the Territory, some of whom stayed, while the new towns became destinations for a variety of people – Indian, black, and white – seeking economic opportunity. In the case of Muskogee, the Creek government did little to regulate who acquired land in the town, so for a time Muskogee was an open door for outsiders, who migrated there hoping to cash in on the boom anticipated with the Katy's arrival. During its early years, then, Muskogee was a foreign place as far as some Creeks were concerned, a part of their nation in geographic terms alone.[9]

The creators of the fair reflected this character. They were merchants and entrepreneurs, mostly white men, who hoped the event would increase trade and attract capital from the border states into the Indian country. The group was led by John A. Foreman, president of the fair association, and Joshua Ross, secretary. Foreman owned a mill and was one of Muskogee's most prominent businessmen. A white man, he was not a citizen of any Indian Territory nation. During the Civil War Foreman had spent time in the Territory as an officer in the Indian Home Guards, Union regiments made up of Native American recruits. After the fighting he had settled in the Indian country, entering legally under a license to trade in the Creek Nation. Eventually he became one of Muskogee's town fathers, doing his best to take advantage of the presence of the Katy. Ross was a Cherokee living in the Creek country. Born in Arkansas but raised in the Indian Territory, Ross attended Cherokee public schools, the Cherokee Male Seminary, and the university at Fayetteville, Arkansas. Married to a Creek woman, he moved to Muskogee in the early 1870s, drawn like Foreman by the railroad. He opened a general store near the Katy station and developed a substantial business selling goods to travelers and those settling in the expanding town. In starting the International Fair, Foreman and Ross played the classic role of frontier boosters, drumming up business and advertising the commercial potential of their growing community.[10]

Those origins led the historian Angie Debo to label the International Fair a "white man's project," an expression of Muskogee's "alien spirit." While its organizers expected Indian people to visit the fair, the event's main purpose was to serve the economic interests of a group of men whom many Creeks considered interlopers. Foreman was the chief example. An outsider eager to take advantage of an Indian Territory boomtown, he was regarded by some Creeks as a carpetbagger. Foreman flaunted the Creek government's authority for the sake of his personal economic interests, first by illegally raising sheep and then by promoting unauthorized railroad development. The latter action in particular won Foreman a great many enemies in his adopted homeland. Creek leaders, in fact, complained frequently to the Indian Bureau about Foreman's business practices.[11]

If many of the organizers came from outside the Indian nations, so too did most of the fairground activities. In a summary of the first fair, Joshua Ross listed exhibits and entertainment that might have been found at any county fair in the United States: speeches by officers of the fair association and visiting dignitaries, brass-band music, horse racing, and exhibits of grain, fruit, livestock, and women's needlework.[12] Subsequent fairs offered similar attractions. The equestrian events, the fair's most popular feature, may have seemed particularly Indian in appearance. Some commentators described them as demonstrations of the "wild" Indians' riding skill. Races and riding contests, however, were standard (if sometimes controversial) entertainment at county and state fairs in the United States, and there is little evidence that the Indian International Fair departed from the American model in this area. Perhaps the sole exhibit at the fair that could be called culturally Native American was the "Indian work" exhibit, in which participants competed in categories like "best buffalo robe," and which one year included a contest (sponsored by the local Indian Bureau agent) for the best collection of tribal "relics."[13]

Debo's doubts, then, were warranted; however, she disposed of the event too quickly. John A. Foreman may have been a white man with dubious business interests, but plenty of Indian people participated in the International Fair, Joshua Ross being the most obvious example. Debo dismissed him as "mostly white," and indeed he was a "mixed-blood." But he was also a member of the Cherokees' most prominent family, the son of John Ross's brother Andrew, and George Lowrey's sister Susan. Andrew Ross's support for removal in the 1830s may have left his son estranged from his politically powerful relatives; however, Joshua Ross was considered trustworthy enough by the Cherokee government to be made, at various points in his career, the clerk of the tribal senate, a teacher at the Cherokee Male Seminary, and a delegate to the Okmulgee Council. His daughter remembered him as having spoken the Cherokee language fluently, suggesting a tie to the traditional culture.[14]

A look at the International Fair's lists of judges, officers, speakers, and premium winners, meanwhile, shows that both Indians and whites were involved in most aspects of the event. A number of prominent Cherokees, for example, bought stock in the fair association soon after its founding, among them future principal chiefs Dennis Wolfe Bushyhead and Colonel Johnson Harris. Harris and the Creek chief Legus C. Perryman served as superintendents and judges, along with prominent Cherokees like Daniel H. Ross. Cherokee leaders William Potter Ross and William Penn Adair gave speeches at several of the fairs, as did the Choctaws' Coleman Cole and Allen Wright and the Seminoles' John Jumper. Well-known Creeks such as Daniel N. McIntosh, Samuel Checote, and Napoleon B. Moore participated, with Moore serving many years as the fair association's treasurer. To be sure, most of these men belonged to the Indian Territory's bicultural population, a group Debo sometimes held in suspicion. They were educated and involved in commercial agriculture and trade. But they undoubtedly represented their Indian nations.[15]

Moreover, Native American fair officers like Joshua Ross and Napoleon Moore outlasted Foreman, whose career in the Territory was cut short by the Creek government in the early 1880s. Foreman had continued his illegal business ventures during his tenure as president of the fair association, despite the Creeks' protests. He then further enraged tribal leaders by involving himself in the Creeks' internal politics, which were in a particularly fractious state in these years. During the American Civil War, the Creeks (like the Cherokees) had divided into Northern and Southern parties, and after 1865 disputes over changes in the tribe's political system sustained the conflict. On several occasions, the Creeks came close to renewing their civil war, most notably in the early 1880s in the "Green Peach War," a brief insurrection by Creek dissidents allied with former slaves.[16] Foreman, according to formal Creek appeals to the Indian Bureau, helped sustain these troubles by encouraging rebellious Creeks in their efforts to replace the tribal government. Foreman denied the charges, but Creek leaders determined to drive him from the nation. In November 1881 the tribal legislature passed a law requiring that the officers of the fair association be Indians. Around the same time, the Creek government began demanding Foreman's removal from the Territory, a position supported by John Q. Tufts, the United States Indian agent in Muskogee. For a while Foreman resisted, preparing to sue to remain in the Territory, but he seems to have relented sometime in 1884. By the opening of that year's fair in late September, Robert L. Owen, a Cherokee citizen (and later Oklahoma senator), was president of the association, and Foreman was preparing to move to Texas.[17]

Finally, as I have already suggested, a great many Indian people attended the fair. Contemporary accounts identified not only Creek and Cherokee visitors but representatives of other nearby tribes, such as the Peorias and Osages, and members of a number of plains groups, including the Cheyennes, Arapahos, Comanches, and Kiowas. The Indian Bureau encouraged Plains Indians, in particular, to attend, and some years allocated funds to buy provisions for these visitors. On several occasions, plains leaders took part in the event formally, as in 1875 when the Kiowa chief Kicking Bird made a speech at the fair at the invitation of the Okmulgee Council.

Rather than dismissing the event as alien to the Indians of the Territory, it is better to ask what the Indian people (and for my purposes, Cherokee leaders in particular) who did participate saw in the International Fair and what they attempted to gain from it.[18]

A good place to start in answering that question is with a fairground address made by William Penn Adair in 1878. Reprinted in the Creek Nation newspaper, the *Indian Journal*, the speech was a long, somewhat rambling disquisition on the theme of Native American progress. Adair discussed the biblical revelation of mankind's essential unity, with its lesson that Indians possessed the same capabilities as whites. He offered an extensive review of the Cherokees' progressive history, from the arrival of de Soto (who found that the southeastern Indians were farmers and thus already partially civilized) to the tribe's remarkable advances in the nineteenth century. And as he did each year in his work as a delegate to Washington, he gave evidence of his people's highly civilized present state: their schools ("the Indian Nations . . . excelled most of the states and territories of the Union" in providing education), Christian churches ("no people on earth are more religious than the Indians of this country"), and proofs of industry ("54 stores, 22 mills, and 65 smithshops owned and conducted by their own citizens"). The Cherokees and the Territory's other tribes, Adair assured fairgoers, were carrying out their paramount duty in the postwar era, their "duty to push our people forward in civilization."[19]

The Indian International Fair contributed significantly to this great mission of progress. The fair was "A school of Instruction" for the people of the Indian Territory. "Here all classes of our people, the civilized, the semi-civilized and the nomadic have an opportunity of coming together once a year, as friends, and to interchange ideas of improvement in all the varied pursuits of civilization." Learning from one another and from their white and black neighbors, the Indians who attended the fair became better farmers, stock raisers, homemakers, and craftsmen. As another Cherokee put it, the fair was a "civilizer."[20]

It was a school, as well, for non-Indians. "To people not acquainted with our true capacity and condition," Adair noted, "the idea of our having such a fair is at least novel if not incredible. As a general rule the white people, especially those not well informed and at a remote distance from us, are apt to class all Indians alike; and with the Indian they generally associate the tomahawk and scalping knife [and] a ruthless disposition – regardless of his situation."[21] The International Fair gave the Indians a chance to disabuse whites of such dangerous and unfair notions. Their attention drawn by the novelty of the event, whites could discover the truth about the Indians – that they were peaceful, well disposed toward the United States, and progressing rapidly.

Education at the fair, Adair suggested, contributed to the Indians' efforts to maintain self-government and possession of their lands. Americans enlightened at the fair might become political allies of the tribe, while Indians who attended became better able to defend their land and political rights. Adair explained the latter point with regard to the Plains tribes. "Some of our brethren from the Plains have heretofore attended this Fair with good results," he noted, "and we trust that no pains will be spared hereafter to induce them to continue their attendance so they, like our leading Nations, may be blessed with all the comforts and powers of enlightened people and thereby be able to unite with the civilized Nations in holding and defending our common country."[22] In Adair's view progress brought to the tribes a stronger commitment to preserving the Indian Territory, and the political skills with which to pursue that goal. In this scheme of things the International Fair was the equivalent of the Okmulgee Council, a forum that brought the tribes together in the name of both self-improvement and self-defense. Regardless of its origins, then, for Adair the event served important purposes for the Indian Territory tribes, making it in his view "essentially an Indian institution."[23]

As an educational institution, the fair reflected both the influence of its American models and the peculiarities of American Indian relations. Agricultural societies had spread and flourished in the Northeast and Midwest beginning around 1840 precisely as "schools of instruction" for American farmers. With expanded transportation systems, increased demand resulting from urban growth, and improved agricultural technology, mid-century farmers found themselves operating in increasingly complex economic systems. The agricultural fair served as a clearinghouse for information about markets and machinery and provided a forum in which farmers, factors, and merchants could discuss their complementary pursuits.[24]

The Muskogee fair served roughly the same functions for commercial farmers in the Indian Territory; however, when Indian leaders like Adair spoke of education, they had issues that ran deeper than economics in mind. Education held a special place in the language of nineteenth-century American Indian affairs, with the school often appearing in discussions of the Indian question as the key to the future. Government agents and philanthropists identified the ability of Native Americans to learn their way out of their existing cultures as the chief test of whether Indians as a race were destined for survival or extinction. Many Cherokee leaders, for their part, embraced education as a crucial act of defense. Schooling equal to that enjoyed by non-Indians promised to help the Cherokees hold their own in a world dominated by European Americans. In Cherokee political rhetoric, the school stood alongside the treaties as bulwarks of Indian rights and interests. If the International Fair were truly a "school of instruction," it was an institution that guarded the Indians' autonomy, as well as encouraged their economic proficiency.[25]

The manner in which the fair taught its participants may have been important from an Indian perspective. For white philanthropists and government officials, the education of Indians often implied their strict control by European American teachers, reservation agents, and missionaries. This was especially true in the post – Civil War era, which saw the full emergence of the wardship model in American Indian relations. That model placed virtually all Indian people in the role of unruly children whose best interests lay in submitting to white instructors. The idea of Indian education, then, frequently implied a particular power dynamic during this period and one especially unfavorable for the Indian people in question.[26] In this context, what is interesting about the International Fair is that while it involved the transfer of knowledge from whites to Native Americans, it did not demand that the former control the latter. It did not require that the Indians be the wards of those providing instruction. "We owe our improvement in almost every respect to what is practiced and produced elsewhere, and our knowledge of it," wrote William P. Boudinot in discussing the fair in the *Cherokee Advocate*. That being the case, the fair was a welcome development, since it offered Indians "the opportunity of seeing for themselves what is a great source of wealth to farmers outside our limits."[27] The fair as educator was a parallel institution to the Cherokees' national school system; it prepared Cherokees to compete with non-Indians without subjecting them to non-Indian control. It promised instruction without domination.

Equally important was the other kind of education that Adair mentioned in his address. As I have discussed in previous chapters, tribal leaders in this period were continually trying to teach white Americans about the Indian Territory. Delegates to Washington, for example, often described their work as an ongoing effort to enlighten American authorities about their peoples' rights and desires, "to educate them into our interests," as Adair had written in 1870.[28] They clung to the hope that if Americans could be made to understand the Territory, they might end their assaults on tribal autonomy and land. The fair at Muskogee offered tribal leaders a further opportunity for this kind of teaching, particularly when visitors from "the states" included politicians and Indian Bureau officers. When Adair made his 1878 address, several congressmen were among his listeners. They were members of a special subcommittee established to consider the so-called transfer question, the issue of shifting responsibility for Indian relations back to the War Department.[29] They came to Muskogee to gather testimony and to observe the condition of the Indian Territory and its people. A year later, Carl Schurz, secretary of the interior in the

Hayes administration, attended, and the Cherokee government that year invited President Hayes himself. On other occasions visitors included the commissioner of Indian affairs, who used the event to hold talks with the representatives of the Plains tribes in attendance, and the federal commissioner of agriculture. And in almost all years the Muskogee fair was good for visits by at least a border-state politician or two (the governor of Kansas, for example) and several lower-level representatives of the Indian Bureau.[30]

The presence of these authorities turned the fair into a forum for debating the Indian question and the future of the territory. In 1878, Indians at the fair used the visit of the congressional committee to express their unwillingness to accept territorialization. "Every citizen of the Indian country present," the *Cherokee Advocate* reported, "numbering thousands of representative men from all the Nations and Tribes of this whole country, passed a series of resolutions in the presence of the Committee, declaring that the Indians wanted no change whatever, in their present condition." According to the *Advocate*, the congressmen agreed that change was unnecessary and "said in plain words that we should be left '*severely*' alone."[31] A year later, the fair became an occasion for discussing illegal white settlement in the Indian Territory and the threat of an invasion by "boomers." Interior Secretary Schurz, the fair's guest of honor, promised that the government would continue to observe its treaties but advised that since land-hungry Americans could not be held off forever, the Indians should accept political reorganization and allotment of their communal lands. Presumably, the leaders of the Indian national governments, with whom Schurz conferred during his visit, informed the secretary of their people's continued opposition to those policies.[32] In 1882 the fair even doubled as an intertribal council. Leaders of the Five Tribes met every day in the main pavilion, and delegates from each nation addressed the crowds.[33]

Thus, the gathering at Muskogee became a medium through which the people of the Indian nations, as one account put it, broadcast their "wants and grievances."[34] This is particularly interesting in that at least some of the fair's original architects surely favored reorganizing the Territory and denationalizing the tribes. John A. Foreman, as an

American citizen and a businessman, may well have hoped that the fair would speed the opening of the Indian Territory. Certainly, a rush of new settlers would have improved commerce at his mill and brightened the prospects of the other Muskogee merchants who participated in the fair association's founding. By drawing American citizens to Muskogee and advertising the Indian country's natural and potential wealth, the fair stood to win new converts to the cause of territorialization. If this logic figured in the thinking of the fair's organizers, it is especially important that Indian representatives made the event a means of expressing their unwillingness to let the Territory become part of the United States. The participation of Indian leaders may have represented an effort to grant a potentially dangerous institution a more benign function and meaning.

In addition to allowing direct political argument, the fair taught visitors through images. Newspaper accounts and oral histories tended to emphasize three impressions left by the event: the colorful presence of the "wild" Plains Indians, the civilized and "nearly white" appearance of fairgoers from the Five Tribes, and the peacefulness with which all – wild and civilized Indians, blacks, and whites – attended the fair together. The overall picture was one of orderly Indian advancement. Encountering Indian people of all "stages of civilization" and finding all at peace with one another and with their non-Indian neighbors, visitors received a lesson in progress.[35]

Take for example the fair's opening ceremonies. In the 1870s the fair began with the impressively named "Grand March of the Nations."[36] This was a parade of representatives of the various Indian Territory peoples, organized, according to newspaper accounts, "in order of their advancement in civilization, each bearing a banner with an appropriate motto."[37] In the 1875 procession, the Sedalia Silver Cornet Band led the way, followed by the women who would compete in the riding contests, a group that included members of the civilized tribes, women of the Territory's black population, and the "ladies of the plains." Next came the tribal representatives. The Cherokees marched first, carrying a banner that read, "Agriculture and the source of wealth," followed by the Creeks, whose banner read, "Charity for all, malice toward none" and "Firmness in the right." Groups representing the Peorias and Osages walked behind, the Peorias' banner reading, "We would learn a better way," and the Osages', "Come and see the figure of the plow and follow me." Rounding out the Indian section were the plains delegates and their banners: Comanches with "We wish to learn" and "Preserve our liberties"; Kiowas proclaiming "We need schools, cows and plows"; Arapahos with "The farm better than the chase"; and Cheyennes carrying the banner, "Peace with all people." The Cincinnati, Arkansas, brass band followed the Indians, then the "colored delegation" (maintaining the fairground's racial segregation), another band, and finally "citizens on horseback and in carriages."[38]

I do not know who came up with the Grand March of the Nations. It served the fair organizers' needs to the extent that it was a curiosity, a spectacle to draw attention and visitors to Muskogee. The historian Theda Perdue implies that the association was interested in drawing Plains Indians to the fair because the merchants wanted "wild" Indians present as attractions.[39] Or perhaps it was the idea of an Indian agent. Of constant concern for Indian Bureau officers was the need to demonstrate that they were succeeding in convincing Indian people of the superiority of European American ways. Certainly there could be little better evidence of this than a group of Comanches carrying a sign reading, "We want to learn."

At the same time, the Grand March offered an image that illustrated rather neatly several things that leaders of the Cherokee Nation wanted understood about the Indian Territory. Cherokee leaders wanted it known that their people were civilized. Here they were in Muskogee proclaiming themselves to be farmers. They identified their people as the elder brothers of the Indians, steadily drawing their less advanced siblings toward civilization. In the parade, one encountered a physical representation of that idea, Cherokees and Creeks literally leading all other tribes, with the other Indians declaring their eagerness for instruction. Chiefs and delegates always insisted that the Indian Territory (when left alone by whites) was a place of peace and order. The parade made that argument manifest, with each group of Indian Territory residents occupying its place in order of advancement, and all marching to the same music. Joining in the Grand March, Indian representatives became walking evidence for Cherokee leaders' most time-honored themes: the possibility of Indian civilization and the ongoing success of the civilizing mission in an Indian Territory made up of separate nations.

Other forms of Indian participation bolstered this image of peaceful progress. The Cherokees and Creeks, for example, exhibited their school systems at the fair. In 1876 the Cherokee Board of Education provided for three of its commissioners to attend, along with several "representative native teachers," instructors from the two Cherokee high schools, and ten students of the Cherokee Orphan Asylum. The board also sent invitations to other school administrators in the Territory asking them to meet at the fair to discuss "the different school systems and their practical workings." Similar actions were taken in other years during the 1870s.[40] Meanwhile, the fair itself featured an "Educational Department," in which Indian Territory students competed for prizes in essay writing, declamation, and singing.[41] Several years' fairs also hosted meetings of the Territory's Sabbath-school organizations and temperance societies.[42] And simply by exhibiting produce, stock, or housewares at the fair, Indian people testified to their progress. With items ranging from "Indian work" to the latest American-made farm machinery, fair exhibits offered something akin to the Grand March of the Nations – a graphic depiction of the Indian civilization process's various stages. When Cherokees or members of other tribes entered their work or animals, they placed themselves in that picture. They showed themselves to be engaged in the movement toward civilization. And they did so not as wards of the federal government, but as citizens of autonomous Indian communities.

Order and progress, of course, could serve several different causes when it came to Indian affairs. For officials of the Indian Bureau, the lesson of the International Fair may have been that the tribes were nearing the point at which they would be ready to assimilate into the greater American populace. Similarly, proponents of territorialization could find evidence at the fair that it was no longer necessary for the government to wall off the Indian country in the name of protecting the tribes. The Indians could take care of themselves in a full-fledged and thoroughly settled territory of the United States. In the context of Cherokee claims to autonomy, however, the image broadcast by the fair could have quite the opposite meaning. Cherokee political rhetoric tied the success of the civilization process to the preservation of Indian nationhood. A threat to tribal autonomy was a threat to Cherokee civilization as well. Conversely, all the things that signaled progress in the culture of Indian affairs – Christian churches, schools, commerce, and agriculture – became signs of Cherokee competence to exercise self-determination. In these terms, the International Fair's pageant of order and progress was an argument for Indian nationhood. By participating, Indian people identified themselves as capable of self-government.

The fair also fit well within the Cherokees' version of the peace policy. Here were all the various tribes, from the Cheyennes to the Creeks, mingling together peacefully, as if to illustrate the feasibility of concentrating Native peoples in the Indian Territory. These tribes all declared themselves to be committed to the civilization process and demonstrated their progress in spectacles like the Grand March. The fair itself was a "civilizer," educating people in commerce and agriculture. And all this was done without touching the treaty relation or the barriers between Indian tribes and non-Indian America. The International Fair displayed the essence of the Cherokees' peace policy: it promised to help the United States achieve its goals in Indian affairs without jeopardizing Indian autonomy. In fact it promised to strengthen the independence of the Indian country, if, like William Penn Adair, one believed that as the Plains tribes progressed they would join their neighbors in defending the territory. The fair offered a glimpse of what the Indian Territory might become if allowed to develop as a league of Indian nations.

The Indian International Fair, then, was both a "white man's project" and an "Indian institution." The event founded by John A. Foreman proved to be a medium through which some Native Americans could communicate their own conceptions of Indian affairs. Did American visitors accept those political messages? The visiting congressmen and cabinet secretaries seem not to have modified their positions on territorialization, so perhaps the answer is no. J. W. Archer, however, appears to have understood. The Hoosier traveler concluded his account of the fair by stating, "I will ask our next Congressman-elect . . . to look into the Indian question, and when he is in Congress to help them with his voice and vote against those who desire to rob them of their beautiful country."[43] The leaders of the Five Tribes, who labored to turn the fair to their own political purposes, could hardly have scripted a better verdict.

The fair at Muskogee belongs to the history of the Indian Territory and late-nineteenth-century Indian affairs. But it is also deserves attention as part of a separate and somewhat broader historical subject – the developing American practice of formally displaying Indian life. Around the time that the Muskogee fair began, the United States hosted the first of its world's fairs, international expositions that included extensive Native American exhibits. Fair organizers considered Indian displays necessities, both because they were popular with visitors and because they contributed powerfully to the vision of the world that the expositions broadcast. While it is obvious that the world's fairs operated on a much grander scale and in different circumstances than did the Indian Territory event, they invite comparison. Both involved efforts to shape the image of Native Americans and to use that image to serve particular ideological ends.

At the first world's fair held in the United States, Philadelphia's 1876 Centennial Exhibition, the Smithsonian used one-third of its allotted space for an Indian display. It offered visitors cases filled with pottery and tools, models of aboriginal Indian housing, photographs of Indians, and life-size wax figures in tribal costumes. Later expositions featured similar collections of representative objects but, in addition, boasted living exhibits of Indian people. At the Columbian Exposition in Chicago in 1893, organizers established model Indian villages on and around the Midway, a long strip of land extending west from the White City (as the main fairground was known) and devoted largely to food and entertainment concessions. Here, visitors to the fair could observe and interact with Dakota Sioux, Apaches, Navajos, and members of other tribes recruited for the occasion by Indian Bureau agents. Five years later in Omaha, there was an even grander attraction called the Indian Congress. Billed as the largest Indian exhibit ever and as a final chance to see truly aboriginal Americans before they disappeared, the congress was a combination museum and Wild West show. Like the fair's displays of artifacts, it was meant to be educational. Its most popular feature, however, proved to be sham battles, complete with scalping and the torture of captives.[44]

Like the message that William Penn Adair applied to Muskogee, the paramount theme of the world's fairs was progress. The Centennial Exhibition was meant to celebrate the United States's quick rise to the status of a great power, and the wealth of the new industrial age, while the Columbian Exposition documented the Americas' transformation since 1492. The Omaha fair announced the maturation of the trans-Mississippi West.[45] Indian exhibits contributed to the progress theme in several ways, most often by providing an image of primitivism that fairgoers might contrast with the civilized United States. Ethnologists designed the displays to illustrate the stages through which human societies were thought to pass as they evolved. The work proceeded from the idea that one could rank cultures according to a linear scale of civilization, with modern America representing the advanced end of the continuum. The Indian exhibits demonstrated the progressive nature of American society by showing the primal state that Western man had long since left behind.[46] In addition, the fairs sometimes displayed Indian people as American wards. Several fairs, for example, included model schools, at which visitors could observe Indian children being taught by whites. Such exhibits contributed to the overall theme of progress by depicting a primitive people's rise from savagery and by reaffirming modern America as the end of improvement. Along the way, of course, they also affirmed the correctness of the wardship relation in Indian affairs.[47]

Ethnologists in this period usually believed that any culture could evolve; Indians just happened to be at the beginning of the process. The fairs, however, tended to present progress as the special trait of whites, raising the question of whether Native Americans were capable of truly escaping their primitivism. Chicago's Columbian Exposition provides an example. The center of the fair, the White City, was meant to be a vision of the utopia that mankind might create in America. It truly was a *white* city, however, for many of the non-European exhibits were placed on the Midway, outside the main fairground. The Midway itself offered what one visitor called "a sliding scale of humanity." As fairgoers left the White City, they moved through a line of attractions that became gradually less "white" and less civilized, with the outermost exhibits being the camps of people thought to be the most savage, Africans and American Indians. In this and other expositions, Indians were depicted as an inferior and dying race as much as a primitive but evolving one. In the fairs' vision of the world, progress was frequently synonymous with white racial supremacy.[48]

The Native Americans who participated in the fair at Muskogee surely would have rejected such stark racism (at least when applied to themselves). Yet as the description above suggests, the image of Native Americans presented at the world's fairs was at times quite similar to that offered at the Indian Territory gathering. Both varieties of exposition visualized progress as a linear path stretching from primal savagery to enlightened civilization. One could place Indian societies here and there along that line, an idea that Muskogee's Grand March of the Nations illustrated as vividly as did anything at the American expositions. Moreover, both agreed on the basic attributes of civilization. Christianity, industry, agriculture, and formal education – these were the things that distinguished the advancing Indian from the doomed savage. Sometimes these accomplishments were even represented in the same manner, as in the practice of putting Indian schools and students on display. And of course modern America in both cases provided the standard of enlightenment against which Indian tribes were judged. The United States was the point at the civilized end of the cultural spectrum, the goal toward which less advanced peoples progressed.

Both types of fair tended to support the legitimacy of established authorities and power relations in their respective spheres. At the world's fairs, utopian visions of order and prosperity suggested that the political, social, and economic structure of the United States was correct and unassailable. In particular, the expositions endorsed the new industrial corporation as an essential element of American progress.[49] Muskogee, meanwhile, gave the leaders of the Five Tribes an opportunity to demonstrate their worthiness as "elder brothers" of the Indians and to display the benefits of keeping the Indian Territory in its existing state. The International Fair tended to confirm Cherokee leaders' assumption that they were the guides and spokesmen for their entire race, while it cast the Plains tribes and former slaves in the role of dutiful followers. In addition, with its celebration of "advanced" Indians, the fair endorsed the leadership of men like William Penn Adair, educated members of the Cherokees' commercial class, in a period when that leadership was challenged several times by movements of Cherokee-speaking subsistence farmers. The International Fair, like the American expositions, suggested that the people it represented were unified, traveling the proper path, and led by the proper authorities.

Yet the status quo defended at Muskogee included Indian nationhood and autonomy, and this made for a crucial difference. Among the types of power legitimized in the world's fairs was that of European Americans to decide the fate of other peoples. As depicted in the American expositions, the primitivism of Indian tribes made the conquest of North America by a progressive people a natural and necessary act. Indian "savagery" also justified the holding of Native Americans as wards of the federal government. Progress demanded that white American authorities control and direct the lives of less advanced races. In later fairs this view of the world would include other non-Europeans in America's overseas empire – the people of the Philippines, for example.[50] At Muskogee, however, the United States's position as the vanguard of civilization did not confer upon white Americans the right to control Indian people. The members of the civilized tribes who participated in the International Fair coupled their acceptance of a European American model of progress with an insistence that the Indians of the territory be left alone politically. White Americans could help the Indians by providing examples of civilized

168

life and by supporting progressive institutions shaped by the Indians themselves, such as the fair . But control and prescription would only undermine Indian civilization. Further acts of conquest would destroy the authority granted to white America by its civilized status.

Comparing these two displays of Native American life, then, reveals an argument over acceptable forms of American power and the relationship between civilization and authority in Indian affairs. At the Centennial and the Columbian Exposition, the authority granted to white America by its vanguard status was of an active nature – it was the authority to conquer and command. In the Indian Territory event, leaders of the Five Tribes suggested that such authority was ideally passive, an indirect influence. For it to operate, Indian tribes had to be allowed to use the American model themselves. Or to put the matter in somewhat broader terms, the vision of Indian relations that the Five Tribes invested in the International Fair maintained at least a narrow realm in which Indian people could act on their own behalf – a possibility that the exhibits at the world's fairs seemed expressly designed to dismiss.

The two sides of the argument, it is worth noting, almost met in 1876 in Philadelphia. As mentioned in the last chapter, the leaders of the Indian Territory nations wanted to participate in the Centennial Exhibition. A year before it opened, the Okmulgee Council sent to the fair's organizers a request for "encouragement and assistance" in mounting "a proper representation at [the] centennial of the Indian interests and advancements."[51] The council members seem to have had in mind not merely a visit to the fair or the inclusion of Five Tribes material in the Smithsonian's ethnology displays, but some kind of official exhibit. They identified in the Centennial another opportunity to broadcast their preferred picture of the Territory and its Indian nations. Had the idea come to fruition, the exhibit would have proven a fascinating anomaly. In a forum in which white authorities carefully crafted representations of "the Indian," there would have stood an Indian image created by a group of Native Americans themselves.

As it turned out, the Okmulgee Council's proposal barely advanced beyond the planning stage. The Centennial organizers offered plenty of encouragement in response to the council's request. They approved the idea of an Indian Territory representation and sent the leaders at Okmulgee an official invitation. But they did not provide assistance, at least not in monetary form. The council, whose own budget and existence were at risk at this point, was left urging the individual tribes to appropriate the necessary funds. None appear to have taken this advice.[52] In the end, some Creek and Cherokee material did make it to Philadelphia – photographs of the Cherokee public buildings, for example, and work by Creek schoolchildren.[53] But it fell far short of the "proper representation" envisioned by the Okmulgee Council. The full exhibit, it seems, fell victim to the strained finances of the tribal governments during this period.[54]

"Alas that it is not larger," a correspondent to the *Indian Journal* said of the Creek and Cherokee display in Philadelphia. "We have lost much of a golden opportunity."[55] Indeed, when the Okmulgee Council failed to mount its exhibit at the Centennial, it surrendered one of the few chances that Native Americans ever possessed to speak formally for themselves at America's international expositions. Instead, the Indian displays, and the image of "the Indian" that they broadcast, remained European American creations. The fair at Muskogee was a different matter. It provided nowhere near as grand a platform as the Centennial, but it offered a forum for discussion of the Indian question that, unlike most, was amenable to Indian influence. Being exhibitors as well as exhibits, Indian participants exerted a measure of control over how the fair displayed their people. To be sure, a spectacle like the Grand March of the Nations was no more accurate a depiction of Indian life than was Omaha's Indian Congress. It was an idealized vision of order and improvement based upon an ethnocentric conception of progress. Yet it was an ideal that served Indian, as well as European American, needs. The International Fair allowed some Native Americans to broadcast the message that wardship was not the only alternative to extinction for Indian people. It gave them another way to claim a future for Indian autonomy and nationhood.

In the International Fair, Cherokees helped adapt a European American institution to serve the cause of Indian nationhood. A similar process, meanwhile, was occurring in Cherokee leaders' political language, which adapted to new conditions in the postwar era. During this time, the social and economic changes wrought by America's industrialization produced new dangers for the Indian Territory. As the remainder of this study explains, however, Cherokee leaders found in the culture of industrial America new arguments for the maintenance of the Indian nation.

6

Demagogues, Political Bummers, Scalawags, and Railroad Corporations

"What is the world coming to?" asked the editor of the *Cherokee Advocate* in early 1878. George W. Johnson had just learned that a group of Protestant ministers, once reliable allies of the Indians, had testified in favor of territorialization before the Board of Indian Commissioners. How could Christian preachers, he wondered, promote policies that required the government to commit the sin of breaking treaty promises? Perhaps the ministers had been confused or ill-informed. Likely, however, there was a more sinister explanation for the their testimony.

Preachers who have no more of the milk of human kindness in their bosoms than to want the government of the United States to destroy us, certainly do not profess the word of God – but to preach in the interests of demagogues, political bummers, and scalawags, and railroad corporations. It may be that those preachers we refer to have their expenses paid, and are paid a pretty liberal salary to lobby at Washington for our destruction and in the interest of railroads and federal office seekers. Of course they have as much right to do this as other lobbyists have – but all we ask is for them not to urge our destruction under the guise of Christianity, but for them to let the world know that they are working for money and not souls. [1]

Convinced by the end of the column that the ministers indeed had been corrupted and "bought up" by railroad companies, the editor reached an apocalyptic conclusion. "It is the time that the world should be purged of her sins again – and we think it ought to be burnt out, as the Bible says it will be burned next time. Nothing less than burning could wipe such disgraces from the earth."[2]

With its usual fervor, the *Advocate* here expressed a theme common to Cherokee political writing. In the decades following the Civil War, a new foe – the railroad corporation – joined the grasping frontier whites and border-state congressmen on the Cherokees' list of enemies. Chiefs and delegates during this time continually inveighed against what they labeled the evil scheming of railroads and their representatives. They identified the railroad as their chief adversary, the most powerful interest seeking the destruction of Indian nationhood. Moreover, as the editorial just quoted suggests, they located the railroad interest behind the actions of other opponents. They insisted that wealthy corporations operating secretly and corruptly were responsible for the continual assaults on tribal autonomy and landholding. The railroad appeared in Cherokee writings as the center of a conspiracy to defraud the Indians and dismantle their governments.

Several historians have written about corporate activity in the Indian Territory in the post – Civil War era, America's period of rapid industrialization. Generally speaking they have identified the arrival of the American corporation as an event that deepened Indian dependency and contributed significantly to the dismantling of the Indian nations. While circumstances at times led companies to ally with tribal governments, the overall effect of the corporate presence was the further erosion of Indian sovereignty.[3] I will draw on that scholarship, but I want to tell a different story. This chapter explores the ways in which the railroad issue fit into and influenced Cherokee claims to nationhood. Cherokee leaders did not stop asserting their people's national status when the first tracks appeared in the Indian Territory. They adapted their claims to the new environment brought by American industrialization. When they wrote of the corrupt schemes of railroad men, they drew from late-nineteenth-century America a new set of symbols and ideas to explain the need for Indian autonomy. Industrialization, even as it unleashed new threats, offered Cherokee leaders fresh ways of imagining a future for the nation.

The prospect of railroad development in the Indian Territory first arose not long after the Trail of Tears. In the 1840s political and economic leaders in Texas and Missouri (and later in Kansas) began to demand railroad rights-of-way through the Indian country in order to link the southwest to the population centers of the United States. Stock raisers in Texas, for example, complained that an Indian Territory devoid of rails represented a barrier between their grazing lands and American markets. Since the nearest railroad terminals were in Missouri, cattlemen had to drive their herds through the Indian Territory before they could gain access to the broader American economy. Meanwhile, early proponents of a southern transcontinental railroad recognized in the Indian Territory a logical route to the Pacific Coast. As would be the case in later years, railroad advocates charged that the Indian Territory and its peoples stood in the way of the necessary progress of the United States. Regardless of treaties or the intercourse laws, they insisted, Indian nations could not be allowed to obstruct American economic expansion.[4]

John Ross and the Cherokee government during these years took a typically wary position on the question of railroads. Cherokee leaders rejected several offers by individual companies to establish lines and depots in the nation, and they maintained that the land sales necessary to facilitate such arrangements could be carried out only through the treaty process. At the same time, some believed that the Cherokees would eventually have to accept railroad development in their nation. In his 1857 annual message, Ross stated: "We cannot be insensible to the spirit of the age in which we live, nor to the circumstances which surround our lot, with a population increasing rapidly and rife with the impulses of restless progress and acquisition." The Cherokees would have to adapt to the changes taking place among their European American neighbors, but perhaps with vigilance and care they could keep that process within the bounds of the treaty relationship and Cherokee sovereignty.[5]

The railroad issue remained unresolved at the start of the Civil War, and conflict outside and within the Cherokee Nation quickly overshadowed questions of adapting to American industrialization. At

the close of hostilities, however, the issue abruptly returned to Cherokee affairs in a far more urgent form. In the treaty negotiations that
reestablished relations between Washington and the Five Tribes, the
United States demanded that the Indians accept railroad rights-of-way
through their country. Finding their bargaining position weakened by
the war and viewing as inevitable some kind of development, tribal
delegates agreed. The treaties finalized in 1866 allowed for two lines
through the Indian Territory, one north-to-south line originating in
Kansas and one east-to-west line out of either Missouri or Arkansas.
Four railroad companies responded by mounting vigorous campaigns
to secure the rights-of-way along with federal aid to construct the
roads. The Atlantic and Pacific Railroad proposed to build the east-to-
west line along a route that would run through the Cherokee and Creek
Nations. The ultimate goal of the company was to connect St. Louis
to San Francisco, the most important commercial center in the Far
West. Three companies, meanwhile, competed for the right to build
the north-to-south line: the Kansas and Neosho Valley (later renamed
the Missouri River, Fort Scott, and Gulf); the Leavenworth, Lawrence,
and Galveston; and the Union Pacific, Southern Branch (later renamed
the Missouri, Kansas, and Texas, or "Katy"). Congress specified that the
first company to lay track to the southern border of Kansas would win
the right-of-way, a decision that prompted a race to set the first rail
in the Indian Territory. The Katy won the competition; in June 1870 it
crossed into the Cherokee Nation near the Neosho River.[6]

When Cherokee leaders agreed to the rights-of-way, they hoped
that the railroads could develop without threatening the tribe's land
ownership or autonomy. In essence they held to John Ross's position
of cautious accommodation. To this end, the National Council took
several actions designed to gain for the Cherokees the power to control
railroad development within their borders. In October 1866 the council
authorized a $500,000 stock subscription to the Union Pacific, South-
ern Branch, to be purchased with the proceeds of land sales specified in
the 1866 treaty. The council also allowed a bonus to be granted to aid in
construction and provided for the sale of building materials payable in
cash or additional stock. In return for this cooperation and generosity,

the Cherokees requested two seats on the railroad's board of directors and the right to regulate the rates charged for carrying freight and passengers through the nation.[7] Several years later, the council went even further and called for the creation of a Cherokee-run railroad. Partly modeled on Choctaw and Chickasaw efforts to charter their own railroad companies, the Cherokee railroad would accept non-Indian investment and employ non-Indian builders, but it would be under the control of Cherokee directors. The stock subscription and the Native railroad idea suggest that for a time leaders believed that they could strike a balance between the demands for railroad development and the necessity of maintaining their nation's autonomy. The council attempted to lead the railroad-building process and channel the era's "restless progress" in directions acceptable to the Cherokees.[8]

The hope of accommodation, however, faded quickly, and by the early 1870s all but a few Cherokee leaders had adopted hostile attitudes toward the railroads under construction in their country. Cherokee political writings of this period began to identify the railroad corporation as the Indians' greatest enemy, a force that threatened to destroy the Nation and the Cherokee people themselves. A number of factors accounted for this shift in outlook. First, the Cherokee government's efforts to gain control of railroad development failed completely. The Indian Bureau's disapproval of the stock subscription act, along with delays in assigning the right-of-way, resulted in the National Council's revoking the offer at the end of 1867. The plan to create a Cherokee-run railroad similarly fell through when the federal government refused to approve the new company's charter. The idea resurfaced from time to time over the following decade, but each time, the Indian railroad died in the planning stages. Denied the opportunity to experiment and shape railroad development according to their needs, Cherokees faced the prospect of powerful interests operating in the Nation without being accountable to the tribe.[9]

Meanwhile, it became clear that the railroad companies favored the dismantling of the tribal governments and the opening of the country to non-Indian settlement. The revival of the railroad issue coincided with the intensification of efforts to territorialize the Five Tribes, to subject them to a United States territorial government and allow unrestricted non-Indian settlement on at least some of their lands. Railroad corporations, both those already operating in the Indian Territory and others hoping for a way in, became important supporters of the "Oklahoma bills" that appeared in Congress yearly. They sent lobbyists to Washington to push for reorganization and made sure that western congressmen in particular understood the benefits that would come from the passage of an Oklahoma bill. Their directors testified before the Committees on Territories and Indian Affairs to the necessity of opening the country to American progress. Like many of the officials and politicians involved in Indian relations, the men running the railroads assumed that reorganization was inevitable. They threw their lot in with the territorializers rather than with tribal governments struggling to preserve what most Americans considered a doomed Indian sovereignty.[10]

There were at least two powerful economic reasons for the railroads to support territorialization. First, railroad builders suspected that without a rapid increase in the population of the territory – achievable only through the opening of the Indian country to unrestricted settlement – their companies would not attract enough business to make running a line through the Indian Territory worthwhile. As the two authorized corporations lay track through the Indian nations, their lobbyists and executives complained that the Indians were too few in number and their economies too backward to support railroads. A dearth of customers threatened the companies if the federal government did not reorganize the Territory soon.[11] Second, there were the "conditional land grants." During the Civil War, Congress had begun the practice of offering corporations grants of public land as an incentive to build railroads through the West. Alternating sections were handed out along the major western lines. This policy, however, could not be applied directly to the Indian Territory railroads, since by treaty the land in question belonged to the various tribes. Instead, Congress promised that the companies operating in the Territory would receive land grants as soon as the Indian titles were extinguished. The Atlantic and Pacific, for example, was to receive twenty alternating sections per mile on either side of the track. Although the intent was to encourage construction, the bills also created a clear incentive for the railroad companies to support territorialization. Most likely, the reorganization of the Indian Territory would involve "unused" portions of the tribes' communal lands' becoming part of the American public domain – that is, the extinguishing of Indian titles. Such a change would potentially allow the railroads to claim a portion of the new territory. For the Cherokees, the conditional grants were the most obvious sign that the railroad men stood with the territorializers, the enemies of Indian sovereignty.[12]

The Cherokees' political realignment in the late 1860s may also have intensified the anti-railroad rhetoric coming from Tahlequah. Lewis Downing, elected principal chief in 1867, represented the interests of Cherokee-speaking subsistence farmers, Cherokees who had adopted less of the economy and culture of non-Indian America than had English-speaking bicultural families like the Rosses, Boudinots, and Adairs. Downing was also a leader among the Keetoowahs, the full-blood society dedicated to maintaining the treaties and keeping the Cherokees' communal lands intact. H. Craig Miner and William G. McLoughlin suggest that Downing's constituency opposed the railroads in stronger terms than did the nation's businessmen and commercial farmers. If so, Downing's election may have hastened the development of hostility on the part of the Cherokee government. By the end of the 1860s, however, distrust of the railroad companies became a majority position in the Cherokee Nation, with members of nearly all parties and factions criticizing the roads.[13]

Cherokee attacks on the railroad corporations adhered to a fairly consistent pattern from the late 1860s through the 1880s. Typically they focused on the conditional grants, with delegates arguing that it was the promise of free land that had transformed the railroad from an agent of progress into a dire threat to the Indian nations. An 1876 memorial to Congress provides an example. Led by Cherokee Daniel H. Ross, representatives of four of the Five Tribes explained the necessity of repealing the conditional grants. Using an argument that by the mid-1870s had become a standard refrain, they began by insisting that Congress lacked the authority to make decisions about Indian Territory land. "That our Nations have bought and paid for, and own the lands they occupy, is a matter of history that really covers no debatable ground." Landholding among the Five Tribes was not a matter of "Indian title," a simple right of possession at the convenience of the federal government. When they purchased the territory with their old eastern homes, the tribes placed their land beyond the grasp of Congress, which could no more offer corporations parts of the Indian Territory than the farms owned by American citizens. From the very beginning, then, the conditional grants were a mistake.[14]

They proved a costly mistake, however, for once in place the offer of Indian land became "a premium for the destruction" of the Indian nations.[15] The delegates estimated that the grants, if allowed to take effect, would amount to twenty-three million acres. Facing such a windfall, the railroad corporations naturally directed all their energies toward eliminating the Five Tribes' titles to the country. And when it became obvious that the Indians would never willingly give up their land, the railroads turned to territorialization. The railroad companies, delegates charged, were the engines of the territorialization campaign. Their agents kept the idea continually before Congress, even though the treaties stated clearly that the Territory could not be reorganized without the agreement of the Indian nations. They invented all sorts of arguments to sway congressional and public opinion toward their position, but ultimately territorialization was nothing but a great swindle, an effort to tear apart the Indian nations for the benefit of a few businessmen. "These parties plead humanity, religion, and civilization as the necessity for such a change, in order to mislead our best friends in Congress to favor such a measure," they noted. "The real motive 'behind the scenes,' that prompts the agitation of the measure, doubtless, is the hope of getting, without paying for the same, 23,000,000 acres of our lands, to the exclusion, not only of its owners, the Indians, but also of 'actual settlers'" (that is, homesteaders, rather than speculators).[16] The delegates went on to estimate that since the lands in question were "the finest in the whole country" they would be worth at least ten dollars per acre. Given that there were about two hundred individuals interested in the two railroads, by the delegates' math each stood to gain $1,150,000 from the dismantling and dispossession of the Indian nations. "Have you ever heard of such a gigantic speculation, in any country?" they asked. "Even the 'credit mobilier,' that startled the whole country, pales in comparison with it."[17] The reorganization campaign was a "railroad job," an effort to fool Congress into taking action that would trigger the conditional grants and hand over much of the Indian Territory to a few private interests. Congress could easily prevent this fraud, however, by repealing the grants. "If the legislation we have asked for should be promptly enacted by you, we do not believe you would be so often importuned and annoyed by railroad parties and land grabbers with the continued cry, that religion, Christianity, humanity, civilization, and 'manifest destiny,' require the establishment of a U.S. Territorial Government."[18]

The general themes expressed in the 1874 memorial appeared in the majority of the anti-railroad documents. Indian representatives characterized the conditional grants as a mistake rather than a knowing attack by the government. "We are satisfied," an 1880 pamphlet stated, "that these acts would never have been passed through Congress had they not been rushed through in quick succession at a time when Congress was absorbed in healing up the wounds of the war of the rebellion."[19] Had legislators paused to consider the acts thoroughly, they would have realized that the conditional grants violated their public trust. After all, the whole weight of federal law and the treaties was behind the continued protection of the Indian nations' communal lands. Delegates absolved Congress of blame for having promised the conditional grants and in the process suggested that the "mistake" of 1866 could easily be reversed.[20]

Likewise, anti-railroad statements almost always identified the companies that stood to benefit from the grants as the chief sources of the territorialization campaign. Just as Congress had not truly wanted to break the government's treaty promises in 1866, the American people in the 1870s and 1880s did not want to see the Cherokees and other civilized tribes destroyed for the benefit of railroad men. "We are unwilling to believe that the great masses of your good people would encourage or sanction any movement that would sacrifice their pledges to us by destroying our existing rights and prosperity," stated an 1876 petition to Congress from the Cherokee Nation's Flint District. "But we do believe that certain railroad companies, who claim conditional grants of our land, are the prime means in endeavoring to get Congress to legislate for us contrary to our existing rights and prosperity."[21] If it were not for the "plundering schemes of giant corporations," incited by the conditional grants, the territorial question would most likely fade away. Thus, Indian representatives found in the land grants an explanation that focused culpability for the Oklahoma bills on a narrow interest – the "Railroad-Territorial Bandits" – rather than the broader American population or the United States government.[22]

Chiefs and delegates found and singled out for special criticism an even smaller group within the railroad party: lobbyists. This criticism formed a third near-universal theme. "Wealthy bankers and Rail Road stock holders, the attorney for the Foreign bond holders, the Agents of Companies who sought special grants for Roads in process of Construction, and for roads built or partially so whose owners seek enlargement of their present franchise" – such were the adversaries that Cherokee representatives found working diligently in Washington to sway the opinions of congressmen and Indian Bureau officials.[23] Delegates denounced the lobbyists as the people personally responsible for keeping the territorial issue and the conditional grants alive. Lobbyists hung about the capital year after year to pester legislators with talk of territorialization. They allied with other interests, such as land speculators and squatters, seeking to rob the Indians. Pursuing their unwholesome ends, they spun fallacious legal arguments to convince congressmen that the treaties allowed territorialization, and spread terrible lies about the Indians to justify the dismantling of their governments. "There was nothing too low for these territorializers to resort to accomplish the passage of an Oklahoma, or similar bill," the *Cherokee Advocate* reported after the close of one legislative session. "We were pictured to Congress by renegades and tricksters as being lawless, uncivilized, as assassins, murderers and thieves, not being capable of attending to our own affairs, and too mean to be allowed to attend our own affairs. All these things were pitted against us for the hope of accomplishing our destruction."[24] And when mere lying failed, some suggested, the railroad lobby sought to secure an Oklahoma bill through bribery. In the late 1870s, the Advocate claimed that the railroads were spreading their bonds among congressmen to secure votes. "It is said that such bonds have great powers of ubiquity, and frequently crawl about loose, and hide themselves in folks old britches pockets. It may be that some of them can be found in unexpected quarters in Washington where they 'will do the most good.' "[25] In Cherokee writings, the lobby was the corrupter of weak politicians and the deceiver of honest ones. It was the embodiment of the dangers of unchecked railroad power.[26]

Finally, Cherokee leaders frequently reminded non-Indians that the railroad was a problem in the United States, too. "The terror of the great masses of people," railroads speculated in land and drove up prices. They maintained scandalously high rates for their services, endangering the livelihood of ordinary American farmers. And they brought corruption to American politics with their bribes and secret deals. The Indians observed all this, delegates explained, and consequently were convinced that uncontrolled railroads would destroy their nations.

During the past ten years we have not been heedless spectators of the struggles in State and national legislatures to force great railroad corporations to loosen their hold upon lands of which, as stated, they gained illegal possession, to the great detriment and loss of thousands of cultivators of the soil. These events are known to the world, and force us to believe that if white men with their great numbers, their knowledge of the language and the laws of the land, are not always able to guard the public domain against the unauthorized grasp of railroad corporations, the Indians of the Territory would have still fewer chances of success; for they would have to fight the same battle with less knowledge, with weaker weapons, and with fewer men.[27]

Another message put the matter in more blunt terms. "Soulless railroad corporations" had already "sucked the very life-blood out of your own people [and] now turn their eyes upon our beautiful country." Americans' own terrible experience with the railroads should have made them the Indians' allies in seeking to control so rapacious a force.[28]

The overall effect of the anti-railroad argument was to identify a very great danger emanating from a narrow interest. The railroad companies sought to overthrow the Indian nations and pauperize the Indian people. They threatened to disgrace the American republic by corrupting its statesmen. Incorrigibly venal, their agents would go to any lengths and spin any lie in pursuit of financial gain. Yet these hazards came from only a small number of corporations and their employees – and from an interest already suspect among the people of the United States. In fact, the issue might have been largely avoided had Congress not mistakenly made the conditional grants. Cherokee attacks on the railroads displayed a strange mix of almost hysterical warnings, and assurances that the railroad problem could easily be solved.

Several historians have offered interpretations of the anti-railroad rhetoric. Jeffrey Burton suggests that Cherokee leaders focused on the railroads and the conditional grants as a way of marshaling public opinion within the Cherokee Nation. He argues that continually raising the threat of a corporate land grab helped Cherokee authorities maintain popular opposition to territorialization and support for the Cherokee government.[29] Burton has a point. Delegates' reports back to the Cherokee Nation from the American capital were often full of dramatic descriptions of the battles between railroad lobbyists and the Indian representatives. The reports implied that the only thing standing between the tribe and annihilation was the persuasiveness of Cherokee leaders and the government they represented. The railroad threat may have convinced some wavering Cherokees to support their government's opposition to territorialization and other changes in Cherokee status. If nothing else, the railroad threat justified the great expense of sending delegates, a practice that drained the national treasury and was a perennial subject of complaint among the Cherokees.[30] This explanation, however, is at best a partial one, for the anti-railroad argument was not just for Cherokee consumption.

184

Leaders continually attacked the railroads in the messages sent to the American government and in their various other statements meant for non-Indian audiences. Clearly, they were trying to persuade people outside the Indian Territory as well as their own citizens.

William G. McLoughlin presents a broader explanation. He includes the anti-railroad rhetoric in his evidence for the development of "Cherokee populism" in the 1870s. During this time, McLoughlin argues, full-blood subsistence farmers came to dominate the Downing party and worked to make it an instrument of their class interest. They did so out of anger at what they considered the dangerous policies pursued by commercial farmers and businessmen. For example, they hoped to rein in the practice of commercial farmers and herders claiming very large tracts of the nation's communal property, something that the subsistence class considered a perversion of the tribe's land system. They also wanted to keep Cherokee citizens from employing large numbers of "permit laborers," workers brought in from the United States. Permit labor threatened to fill the Nation with non-Indians while helping commercial farmers control ever-larger tracts of land. Growing dissatisfaction over issues such as these ultimately prompted what McLoughlin calls a "full blood rebellion" in the election of 1875. Identifying itself as a movement of the Cherokee masses, the Downing party elected Charles Thompson, known as a full-blood spokesman, to the principal chief's office. McLoughlin sees in his election the triumph of Cherokee populism, the taking of power by the Cherokee "working class."[31]

McLoughlin's populism thesis is useful when it comes to the internal economic questions dividing subsistence farmers and the commercial class. The argument over permit labor, for example, truly fits McLoughlin's model. The thesis falls short, however, when it comes to the railroad issue. McLoughlin points to Thompson's condemnation of the railroad companies as evidence of his populism.[32] Thompson's attacks, however, were nearly identical to those issued by such men as William Potter Ross, the Downing party's hated opponent, and William Penn Adair, a Downing party spokesman but a mixed-race Cherokee and a member of an elite commercial family. Moreover, the major shift in Cherokee government rhetoric from tentative support for railroad development to bitter opposition came in the late 1860s rather than in the wake of the Downing Party's victory of 1875. Cherokee chiefs and delegates were using the "populist" anti-railroad language years before Thompson's election. Although a few well-known Cherokees such as Elias C. Boudinot joined forces with the railroads, most Cherokee leaders, across the parties and factions, expressed distrust of the railroad companies throughout the 1870s and 1880s. If anything, the railroad issue fit the pattern of tribal politics typical of the John Ross era, in which more traditional small farmers would ally with wealthier bicultural Cherokees against a common, national enemy. That agreement, in fact, may have been one of the reasons for the pervasiveness of the anti-railroad argument. At a time when politics in the nation were growing more contentious, the railroad was a subject on which all but a few marginal figures could agree.[33]

Both Burton and McLoughlin explain the anti-railroad position in terms of internal Cherokee politics. That perspective is necessary, but it is important also to see the argument as part of Cherokees' ongoing effort to explain their nationhood to non-Indian Americans. Chiefs and delegates, after all, made their attacks on the railroad companies in writings meant to convince Americans that the Cherokees were and should remain a nation. If the railroad threat became an almost ubiquitous theme in these writings, Cherokee leaders surely hoped it would strike a chord with non-Indians and encourage them to recognize tribal sovereignty.

Viewing the railroad argument in this manner, one first notices how closely it fit the existing patterns of Cherokee protest. The practice of locating the source of threats to the nation in a small corrupt party was not new to discussions of the railroad issue. As earlier chapters have suggested, Cherokee writings displayed a general tendency to divide white America into an anti-Indian minority and a much larger majority sympathetic to the tribes. During the removal crisis, Cherokees argued that greedy Georgians were trying to destroy the treaties against the desires of both the Cherokees themselves and most of the American population. Later, chiefs and delegates endorsed the peace policy's assumption that the problems of the frontier were the fault of a few disreputable whites. The railroad, then, conformed to a long-established role in Cherokee writings: the evil interest that sought to violate the good faith of the United States against the true wishes of the American people.

The conditional grants made the railroads particularly well suited for that role. As long as the promises of 1866 remained part of American law, chiefs and delegates could depict policies like territorialization as the cause of the greedy few. The Oklahoma bills could not possibly reflect the will of the American majority, because territorialization would benefit only the railroad companies and their investors. Many of those investors, in fact, were not even United States citizens but rather European bondholders.[34] Americans who supported territorialization either had been fooled by the lies of railroad agents or were party to the corporations' schemes. Writing of the grants in this manner answered one of the primary arguments for reorganizing the territory and opening it for settlement – the position that American farmers needed and possessed a moral claim upon "surplus" Indian lands. Territorialization would not give the poor farmer easy access to land, Indian leaders maintained, because all the best property would be snapped up by the railroads as part of the conditional grants. New settlers in the territory would have to buy their land from the railroad companies rather than obtain it free through the homestead laws. As the *Cherokee Advocate* explained, "They would have to pay railroad prices for their lands, and what they are, the people of the West have had a dear experience." As Indian leaders viewed the matter, territorializers could not legitimately invoke the needs of settlers, or any other claim on behalf of the American masses, as long as the conditional grants were on the books.[35]

If the railroad threat fit an old Cherokee argument, it also allowed leaders to tie their defense of the nation to crucial developments in the postwar United States. When Cherokees wrote of "railroad jobs," scheming lobbyists, and the bribing of legislators, they placed the tribe's struggles in the context of one of the era's great public issues – corruption in the midst of industrial development. This was, after all, the

Gilded Age, a time when many Americans suspected their governments were for sale, with corporations in a rapidly industrializing economy serving as ready buyers. In the decades following the war, a long series of scandals came to light that suggested corruption was a matter of regular business in American politics, and many of the worst cases involved precisely the interests that Cherokee leaders so often decried: railroad corporations and their lawyers and lobbyists. The practice of federal and state authorities using land grants, bonds, and stock purchases to promote railroad development created a situation in which government support could appear to be (and sometimes was) for sale to the richest companies with the cleverest agents. Railroad aid was the single greatest source of scandal during the Gilded Age, "the main course at the Great Barbecue."[36]

Political historians have long debated the true extent of public malfeasance in this period. At present the consensus seems to be that the image of government as a wide-open field for corruption was exaggerated. Bribery and influence peddling did take place, but the relationship between government and corporations was usually more confused than corrupt. Industrialization left public officials with a great many new tasks and concerns, promoting railroad building among them. In the absence of modern bureaucracies and well-defined standards for guiding government-business relations, decisions were made in a haphazard manner that easily took on the appearance of corruption.[37] That appearance, however, may have been more important than the reality behind it. The historian Mark W. Summers has examined corruption as a topic of public discussion in the postwar era. He finds that Americans in this period exhibited a remarkably intense awareness of the possibility of dishonesty in their officials. While many of the era's scandals could be explained in terms other than corruption, Americans presumed their leaders were thoroughly rotten until proven otherwise. This public mindfulness of corruption, Summers suggests, did as much as venal practices themselves to fix the era's enduring image.[38]

In accounting for that phenomenon, Summers pays special attention to the American press. Journalists, he finds, kept corruption permanently before the public eye. The traditional party-run newspapers found scandal in every action of their political opponents, while the newer independent press took as its special mission the ferreting out of dishonesty in high places. Independent journalism in particular played an important role. Papers such as Horace Greeley's New York *Tribune* made the exposure of public "rings" and shady "jobs" the measure of their integrity; finding scandal was a crucial part of their service to the public. That approach, however, ended up promoting an image of politics and government in which dishonesty was assumed. Summers argues that American newspapers during this period broadcast the idea that corruption was imbedded in the basic operations of government, that in fact the government's business *was* corruption. American politics might still look like a democratic system of regular elections and open debate, but in fact the real political process was clandestine and operated on bribes and secret deals.[39]

Popular literature affirmed that message. There was a fad for political novels in the last decades of the nineteenth century, and the subject was almost always scandal. The most famous example was Mark Twain and Charles Dudley Warner's *The Gilded Age* (1873), but a host of other writers used fiction to expose and criticize the sorry state of American government. Popular novelists like John Hume presented damning portraits of the big-city political machine and the spoils system. Hamlin Garland depicted railroad development as a corrupt alliance between venal officeholders and dishonest capitalists. Henry Adams condemned American politicians as shallow opportunists unworthy of the people's trust.[40] This literature, like the Cherokee memorials, reserved especially harsh treatment for corporate lobbyists. They were the corrupters, the people who handed out the bribes. Their presence made certain that the government's attention would be focused on special legislation on behalf of wealthy companies rather than the needs of the people. In the most striking of these portrayals, the lobbyist is literally a demon from hell. Darius Dorman, in John W. De Forest's *Honest John Vane* (1875), is "a goblin fresh from the lower regions," whose "exceedingly smutty soul" manifests itself in a permanent coating of dirt on his skin.[41] Dorman bribes legislators for the sheer joy of it. He wants their souls as much as their votes. With men like this hanging about Washington, it is impossible for politicians to remain committed to the public good. "The real business of your legislators is running party politics," Dorman explains to a young congressman, "clearing scores with your fuglemen, protecting vested interests which can pay for it, voting relief bills for a percentage of the relief, and subsidizing great schemes for a share of the subsidy." To hope for something better is naive. "It's the common thing in Washington, and it's got to be the correct thing, and *you* can't change it."[42]

Ultimately, this literature, and the corruption issue itself, was an expression of anxiety. It indicated a fear on the part of some Americans that, in an age of industrial development and powerful corporations, democracy had been forgotten. In this regard, the issue corresponds to Alan Trachtenberg's notion of cultural ambivalence during industrialization. Trachtenberg famously argues that the rise of the modern industrial corporation engendered deep conflicts and contradictions in American culture. Rapid economic change called into doubt Americans' established ways of understanding their world, a shifting of categories that yielded both excitement and dismay. On the one hand, Americans embraced economic progress and dreamed new utopias of wealth and technology. They saw in the corporation a force that would bring prosperity and power unimaginable in the past to the United States. On the other hand, they worried that in the headlong rush of economic development cherished American principles were falling by the wayside. Old ideals like individual liberty and equality of opportunity seemed to possess little relevance in a world recreated according to the rules of efficiency and maximum production. The great question of the postwar era was whether America could be "incorporated" and remain America in any meaningful sense. The corruption issue was part of that question. In their willingness to believe in the venality of their leaders, Americans expressed their fear that modernization meant the end of government by the people.[43]

All this discussion of newspapers and novels and the worries of late-nineteenth-century Americans may seem far removed from the Cherokees' struggle for sovereignty. Yet when chiefs and delegates attacked the railroads as the Indian nation's great enemy, they addressed precisely the anxiety revealed in *Honest John Vane.* To dismantle the Indian nations, they suggested, would be to surrender to the grasping spirit of the new age. It would demonstrate that Americans were committed more to the interests of "Railroad-Territorial Bandits" than to justice and the promises made by their forebears. Americans, if they wanted to prove themselves still worthy of their heritage, would help the Cherokees defend their nationhood. Cherokee leaders, of course, had been offering warnings of this sort for a very long time. In Cherokee writings the tribe's American neighbors were always on the verge of violating their own most sacred principles. The corruption issue, however, and the ambivalence inspired by industrialization gave that old theme a new and more powerful resonance in the postwar era.

In addition, the corruption issue gave Cherokee leaders themselves a new political language. Cherokee writings, especially the editorials of the *Advocate*, echoed the language of scandal. Attacks on the railroads spoke continually of secret deals and conspiracies and contained imagery that would have fit the most lurid of De Forest's passages. Delegates called territorialization an "abortion" and a "deformed babe . . . dropped as a bastard" in Congress, its father being the railroad. Cherokees likened railroad agents to dogs, buzzards, and the Hessians employed by the British during the American Revolution. Like De Forest's character Dorman, railroad lobbyists appeared as creatures from hell in Cherokee writings.[44] Moreover, corruption at the hands of railroad men became a blanket explanation for any and all threats to Cherokee nationhood – just as the secret deal, in the view of the independent press, could explain almost anything in American public life. When North Carolina Cherokees petitioned for a share of the western nation's treaty money, delegates argued that the eastern Indians had been bought up by the "ring." The ever-vigilant lobbyists and lawyers had found in the North Carolina claim an opportunity to compel Congress to violate the treaties, a step toward the dismantling of the nation. Likewise, Cherokee leaders identified as a "railroad job" an effort in the 1870s to expand the jurisdiction of American courts in the Indian Territory, an indirect and more insidious attack but one with the same origin as the Oklahoma bills. And of course anyone who supported territorialization could be charged with being a paid railroad lackey. Congressmen, American newspapers, and the few Cherokees who openly advocated a change in the status of the Indian Territory were all dismissed as tools of a corrupt ring powered by railroad money.[45]

At the same time, Cherokee leaders did not take their condemnation as far as did some American commentators. The independent press and the political novelists often implied that American government was so thoroughly venal that it was too late to restore democracy. As Darius Dorman says, "*You* can't change it." They also suggested that the root of the problem lay in the American people themselves, in the weakness of their commitment to the ideals of the republic. Shallow and grasping in their own right, Americans received the politicians they deserved.[46] The Indian Territory representatives held back from that conclusion. As vituperative as were their attacks on the "territorial ring" and the railroad lobby, they always maintained that the American majority and even most American leaders desired justice for the Indians. As the *Advocate* said of reorganization, "There could never be found enough dishonest Congressmen in the United States to perpetrate so great a wrong."[47] They stuck to their traditional practice of dividing their neighbors into a small group of villains and the well-meaning (if easily and continually misinformed) masses, and they searched for signs that the second group was turning against the first. When pro-territorial congressmen lost elections, for example, Cherokee representatives saw in their defeat the American public's reawakening to justice.[48] Reading the Cherokees' petitions and pamphlets, one encounters Indian leaders expressing considerably more faith in Americans and their institutions than did many Americans themselves.

That constancy seems odd, but it can be explained. As Mark W. Summers notes, an obvious judgment to draw from the long parade of scandals was that government in the United States could do no good. The system had become so mired in venality that the best course was to limit its power and thus its ability to cause harm. Summers argues that the corruption issue destroyed the belief, born of the Civil War and emancipation, that government could be a tool of progress and reform. It undermined the active state created during the war years and aided in the revival of laissez-faire principles.[49] The Cherokees could not share in this dismissal of American political institutions. They needed the federal government to support Indian nationhood. They needed Washington to be an agent of justice in Indian affairs. A weak federal government was as much a threat to their people's continued independence as were too-powerful railroads. It made sense that while Cherokee writings continually invoked corruption as a dire threat, they also affirmed the ability of American institutions to pull themselves from the muck.

In an important way, the railroad was an ideal adversary for the Cherokees, and this more than anything else may explain the ubiquity of the anti-railroad argument. The conditional grants and the actions of the companies interested in them closely matched much of what Cherokee leaders had been saying for generations. Yet the railroad also provided a way for delegates and chiefs to make the defense of Indian nationhood relevant in the rapidly changing post – Civil War world. In the context of the corruption issue, the struggle over the Cherokee Nation became an episode of a broader effort to maintain democracy in the new industrial era. The territorial campaign was not only the work of a greedy scheming interest but also a tool of the most dangerous power of the age. Those working for the passage of an Oklahoma bill were not only unrepresentative of the American majority but were also Americans' well-known enemies, "the railroad kinds [who] have wielded the iron rod over their own distressed people about as long as they can stand it."[50] The message was that if Americans supported the right of the Cherokees to remain an independent nation, they would do more than offer aid to a long-suffering people, sympathy to the "vanishing race." They would also help check the dangerous forces unleashed by their own economic revolution.

If the railroad served as a bridge from the old Cherokee arguments to the new industrial era, some Cherokee writers found a very different use for the idea of the corporation. As the historian H. Craig Miner notes, Cherokee leaders were capable of making deals with American companies when it suited their purposes. The most famous example was the Cherokee government's leasing of a vast stretch of territory to the Cherokee Strip Live Stock Association. It was hoped that such leasing arrangements would help the tribe increase the national treasury and keep control of its underused land, thus turning the corporation from a threat into an ally.[51]

Something similar occurred on the level of ideas and language. There were ways, some argued, in which Indian tribes were identical to corporations; perhaps corporations could be looked to as models for the survival of autonomous Indian communities. William P. Boudinot, as editor of the *Cherokee Advocate* in the 1870s, offered the clearest statements of this theme. Boudinot frequently argued that as a property owner the Cherokee Nation occupied a status equivalent to that of a chartered corporation, and he felt that American recognition of that status would help the Cherokees defend themselves.[52] The key to this position was the editor's belief that the tribe was dangerously reliant on the American president for protection of its land. Although the Cherokees possessed a clear title to their property, they continually found themselves begging the president to thwart efforts to steal from the tribe. Their land, it seemed, was only as safe as the executive's willingness to protect it. As Boudinot wrote in one issue, this situation was analogous to a "despotism." "To the people of the United States, [the president] is a Chief Magistrate. To the Red men, he is an Emperor, and it does not help matters to call him 'Great Father.' He holds the destiny of the Red men in his hands."[53]

In Boudinot's view the problem was that the Cherokees lacked access to American courts, and it was here that the idea of tribes as corporations entered. Plenty of American companies, railroads in particular, owned lands that amounted to communal property – just like the lands of the Cherokee Nation. Yet those companies did not seem to be as vulnerable to plundering schemes as were the Indians. "We have a title as a corporation called the Cherokee Nation," Boudinot observed. "Now if the Cherokee Nation was a railroad company having just such a title with possession of property, it would have no difficulty in keeping that possession secure. . . . What is the reason then [that] it is not as easy for this Nation, and others of the territory having similar titles, to use this title for their defense and security as it is for the thousand and one other corporations or companies owning land?"[54] The answer was that the Cherokees could not bring suit against their adversaries through the American legal system. While railroad companies could take legal action in defense of their rights, the Cherokees had to rely upon the president. For Cherokee land to be truly secure, Boudinot argued, the tribe needed the same recourse to United States law as was enjoyed by American corporations.[55]

The attraction of this approach, as the editor saw it, was that it would require very little of either federal authorities or the Cherokees themselves. On the federal side, Congress could simply pass a law recognizing that in their land ownership the tribe possessed the same legal standing and rights as a corporation. For the Cherokees no change would be necessary other than a willingness to use the American legal system. On other occasions, one should note, Boudinot suggested that the tribe should voluntarily replace its communal land system with ownership in severalty, making sure to allot all the territory so as to leave no "surplus" to tempt non-Indians.[56] In this case, he foresaw the Cherokees continuing to hold their lands in common; however, now both their lands and their nationhood would be far better protected. Boudinot suggested that earlier chiefs, had they anticipated the problems of the 1870s, would have inserted such a provision into the treaties that removed and reestablished the nation. With that, they would have spared present-day Cherokees the burden of constantly reminding Congress and the president of Indian rights. Cherokees would have gained the ability to assert their rights for themselves.[57]

Boudinot found in the corporation a model of how the Cherokee Nation might retain at least some of its autonomy in the new industrial era. Concerned about tribal sovereignty, Cherokees typically opposed the extension of United States legal authority beyond what was explicitly allowed in the treaties. The editor felt, however, that in this case American law would help safeguard the nation. He suggested that the tribe could maintain two distinct relationships with the United States: the first as a corporation with lands deeded by the federal government and the second as an Indian nation possessing treaties with Washington. The first relationship, in fact, would strengthen the second. In making their lands secure, the Cherokees would take away their enemies' chief incentive for destroying the treaties. So while Boudinot's plan would place the Cherokees more completely under American law, it would also grant them weapons necessary for the nation's further defense.[58]

It was highly ironic that the railroad – the target of so many of the *Advocate*'s tirades – provided the inspiration for this argument. But as Boudinot frequently pointed out, railroads bore an essential similarity to the Indian Territory nations when it came to land. "Many Railroad Companies have millions more acres granted to them than the Cherokees have included in their deed. And Railroad land is in many cases equally uncultivated and unoccupied. . . . [But] they are enabled to retain exclusive possession not only against trespassers, but against Congress."[59] If the railroads could keep Congress from breaking its promises and dividing up their "communal" lands, then so too could the Cherokees.

The idea of the tribe as corporation, however, cut both ways, as the Cherokees sometimes became targets of precisely the kind of rhetoric that they directed at the railroads, especially in cases of individual Cherokee citizens' assembling large holdings from the tribe's communal lands. As noted earlier, this practice was the subject of debate within the Cherokee Nation, especially when some citizens brought non-Indians from neighboring states to work their land. Although most Cherokees who opposed the practice also opposed altering the land system, advocates of territorial reorganization and allotment raised the issue on behalf of their own cause. They argued that a small group of "monopolists" dominated the Indian nations. Taking for themselves the wealth of the country, the monopolists kept the Indian masses poor and backward while withholding valuable land from needy American farmers. Worse, this same interest was responsible for leasing vast tracts of land to American corporations such as the Cherokee Strip Live Stock Association, further limiting the opportunities available to "honest laborers." Only the dismantling of the nations could rescue the Indians and put the Territory to its proper use as homestead land for both Indian and non-Indian families.[60]

Resolutions adopted by an 1888 convention held in Kansas City provide an example of this argument. Delegates from the states bordering the Indian Territory claimed that arable land in the Indian nations was "almost exclusively in the hands of half-breeds and so-called 'squaw men,'" whose holdings were "almost unlimited," and who amassed "large wealth of which the full-bred Indian receive[d] no share." Congress, the delegates speculated, might have long ago corrected this situation by opening the Indian Territory for settlement and extending American laws over it. The lies of the Indian leaders and their white allies, however, prevented lawmakers from seeing the true state of affairs. "The machinations, the intrigues, and the influence of interested leaders, beneficiaries of monopoly contracts, and 'squaw men' have obscured the truth as to the wishes of the main body of Indians. These persons have control of many sources of profit and power, which they are determined not to surrender; it is they who have opposed all attempts for the correction of the evils of isolation and degradation; it is they who are opposed to every form of civilization which may protect and elevate the great mass of these people." And it was not only the Indian masses who were hurt by the power of the tribal leaders. "The pioneer settler" suffered as well. "He knows that the fertile public lands are about exhausted," the resolutions explained, but "the pioneer settler . . . is still looking for a home for himself and his family." To leave the Indian Territory in the hands of the greedy elite was an injustice toward both the majority of the Indian population and the honest farmers of the United States. "Interested and powerful individuals, corporations, and combinations should no longer be permitted to stand in the way of the best interests of the great mass of the people."[61]

In this and other petitions and pamphlets, territorial reorganization became a populist cause, with Indian leaders on the side of corporations and speculators. These writings depicted chiefs and delegates in terms virtually identical to those that the Indians applied to the railroads. The Indian leaders were a corrupt and wealthy interest, one that conspired against the common people and deceived American authorities. Indian delegates, by this reasoning, were no better than corporate lobbyists. They were professional liars sent to harass and confuse Congress. Territorial advocates added and adapted those themes to older arguments: that the Five Tribes chiefs were "scheming mixed-bloods" rather than "real Indians" and that Indian leaders maintained authority by keeping their people ignorant. In particular, they used the image of the deceitful corporation to bolster the argument that the honest American farmer had a right to underused Indian land. That a devil's alliance of tribal oligarchs and American corporations controlled the Indian country made the exclusion of homesteaders even more offensive. As one petition put it, "The landless, homeless people of this country have greater, more sacred rights to the soil, than speculators . . . be they Indians or white men."[62]

This line of attack, interestingly, was not used exclusively by Westerners or other Americans who stood to gain from opening the Indian country. The papers of the House and Senate Committees on Territories from the 1880s contain memorials from throughout the United States exhibiting essentially the same position as the Kansas City resolutions. The document just quoted, for example, came from the town of Eddyville, New York. Moreover, dozens of Midwestern chapters of the Knights of Labor petitioned Congress for territorialization and allotment. They urged that the Indian country be opened "to the end that speculators shall cease their control" of the land. The presence of the Knights of Labor in this debate suggests the ease with which Americans could identify in the Indian Territory fight larger issues tied to the era's rapid economic change. In the Knights' petitions, the territorial campaign became an effort to secure justice for ordinary working people, a goal that the Knights envisioned themselves pursuing in virtually all areas of American life. Like the Cherokee leaders themselves, territorializers could make the question of the Indian country's future an aspect of the broader struggle to control the ill effects of industrialization. However, now it was the Indian nations that stood with a narrow interest empowered by economic development, Indian leaders who denied justice to the "honest laborer" in the new machine age.[63]

The corporation, then, influenced Cherokee claims to nationhood in multiple and sometimes conflicting ways. With the conditional grants, the railroad company became the great enemy of Cherokee sovereignty, the ultimate example of a small interested party seeking to overthrow the treaties. Yet for some the railroad was also a model for the Cherokee Nation, its relationship with the federal government suggesting new ways of safeguarding tribal autonomy. The issue of corporate-inspired corruption in American politics provided chiefs and delegates with a powerful language that could be employed in their defense of the nation. That same language, however, could be made to serve the cause of territorialization and allotment when Indian leaders behaved like modern businessmen. And while Cherokee leaders raised the specter of corrupt political jobs and "the ring" to protect Indian sovereignty, in doing so they added their voices to a chorus that may have destroyed Americans' faith in government power – power that the Cherokees needed federal officials to exert on their behalf if the Indian nation were to survive.

It was fitting, however, that the corporation's influence should have proven so varied. When the railroad arrived in the Indian Territory, it brought new elements of American culture to bear upon the Cherokees' relations with the United States, and among these were Americans' ambivalent responses to industrialization. Cherokee leaders debated the railroad issue with non-Indians capable of viewing industrial corporations as both agents of progress and mortal threats to liberty and democracy. In the end, Cherokees appealed to both sides of that ambivalence in seeking to nullify the danger to Indian nationhood that the railroad posed. The corporation became enemy and ally, menace and model, as Cherokees searched for room in the new industrial order for autonomous Indian tribes.

That they could undertake such a search at all is perhaps the most interesting aspect of the encounter with the railroad. The struggles of Native American peoples in the West in the late nineteenth century can seem marginal and barely relevant to the vast economic and social transformation occurring in the United States. Groups like the Cherokees can appear to be simply waiting for their neighbor's revolutions to sweep them away. Yet when they wrote of the railroads, Cherokees placed the Indian Territory and Indian nationhood at the center of the era's epochal changes. They made support for Cherokee autonomy a test of whether or not industrialization had corrupted Americans. That theme would remain prominent in Cherokee writings as the tribe faced its final political ordeal of the nineteenth century, the allotment campaign.

7

"This New Phase of the Indian Question"

The historian Nell Irvin Painter writes of the late nineteenth century as an age of "sweeping panaceas." It was a time when the great changes wrought by industrialization inspired in many Americans both deep anxieties and the hope that a utopia could be created if only the right reform were found and implemented. Henry George's single tax, free coinage of silver, the Populists' sub-treasury: these were simple but all-embracing answers to the problems of the modern era. They promised at a single blow to end class conflict, ensure that the wealth of the new order was distributed equitably, and spare future generations from the kind of terrifying economic collapse experienced in 1873 and again twenty years later. The outlook informing these programs, Painter suggests, was apocalyptic. Americans in the late nineteenth century faced a choice between allowing their nation to become an industrial hell and building what George predicted would be the "City of God on earth." The breadth of the reformers' visions matched the depth of the crises they detected in American society.[1]

Cherokees who followed their neighbors' freewheeling discussions of political economy would have found this outlook familiar. Indian people had long been the target of simple but sweeping reforms, and the choices offered to them by government officials and "friends of the Indian" – civilization or disappearance – were every bit as apocalyptic as those perceived by the industrial visionaries. Native Americans were forever standing on the edge of extinction, and yet their redemption was always at hand in the form of one or another new policy that promised at last to set them on the road to civilization. The progress of white America threatened their very existence, yet with a few changes they could be carried along by the current of the nineteenth century rather than drown in it. Cherokees and other Indian people were at home in an age of panaceas.

In the last two decades of the century, Cherokees found themselves fighting the greatest of the simple answers to the Indian question – the allotment campaign. Although the idea of breaking up common tribal lands had long been a point of discussion, during this time it became the most celebrated and most actively pursued policy initiative in Indian affairs. Ignoring Indian objections, as well as the dubious record of earlier allotment experiments, politicians and philanthropists heralded land in severalty as the thing that would finally, definitively solve the nation's Indian problems. In allotment, they promised, they had discovered the catalyst for the rapid civilization of the Indians and their absorption into the general populace of the United States.

As most accounts of Cherokee history explain, the assault upon common land was the act that finally brought about the dissolution of the Cherokee Nation. With severalty came the end of independent tribal government, the extension of American law over the Cherokees, the opening of the Indian country to American citizens, and eventually (early in the next century) the Cherokees' inclusion in the new state of Oklahoma. Allotment, in other words, initiated a thorough dismantling of the separate status that was the foundation of Cherokee autonomy. Yet if resistance to allotment turned out to be a losing battle, it was one that inspired a great deal of creative political thought on the part of tribal leaders. The allotment campaign forced chiefs and delegates to find new, positive justification for common landholding and Indian nationhood. And in the end they found it in a surprising place: the industrializing economy that had become the subject of the era's more famous debates and conflicts. They suggested that the great changes taking place among their neighbors made the preservation of the Indians' common lands, and with them Indian nationhood, more important than ever. The arguments they crafted in this regard did not stop allotment, but in them one may observe Cherokee representatives entering the discussions carried out by utopian thinkers, labor leaders, and agrarian radicals and charting a future for the autonomous Indian nation in modern, industrial America.

As previous chapters have argued, the peace policy and the reservation – or the Cherokees' interpretations of them – lay at the heart of tribal leaders' postwar political thought. Although the Grant administration's reform effort seems little more than a footnote in the history of Indian affairs, for Cherokee leaders at the time it was an epochal development. They took the reformers' promise of justice to mean that the United States would at last fully honor its treaty promises, while talk of returning humanity to Indian affairs suggested that the federal government would protect the Cherokees from the violence and chicanery of white Americans. They welcomed as well the reinvigoration of the civilizing mission, for who could speak with greater authority on the subject of Indian civilization than the Cherokees? And most important, tribal leaders embraced the notion that Indian survival and progress required continued separation, Cherokees turning that idea into an American endorsement of Indian nationhood. The peace policy, in short, offered Cherokees hope that their people would be allowed to "work out their own destiny," as leaders sometimes put it. It was evidence that the Great Father was coming around to the Cherokees' own way of thinking.

In retrospect, that hope can seem rather naive. Knowing that allotment and denationalization were rapidly approaching, it can be difficult to take Cherokee leaders' professions of faith in the United States seriously. Until the allotment policy's triumph, however, Cherokee chiefs and delegates could claim success in opposing efforts to alter or do away with the reservation. They found allies among American authorities, people whom the Cherokees could persuade. In William Penn Adair's phrase, it was possible "to educate them into our interests."[2] And as long as that was the case, tribal leaders had reason for optimism.

Take for example the "transfer question." Between 1865 and 1880, Congress considered granting the United States Army responsibility for

Indian affairs on several occasions. The idea was to transfer the Indian Bureau from the Interior Department back to the War Department, which had overseen Indian relations prior to 1849. The War Department, it was expected, would then replace civilian agents with army officers. The reasoning here was that the only way to ensure peace and progress in the West was through the direct control and management of Indian tribes, a task missionaries and philanthropists were simply incapable of performing. Such thinking refuted the basic assumption of the peace policy, that kindness and the civilizing mission were the keys to keeping order on the frontier. It also implied that the cause of frontier warfare was not white injustice but Indian savagery.[3] Corruption in the Indian Bureau provided a further argument for transfer. Evidence of agents' embezzling funds and cheating the Indians under their supervision led some reformers, including a number of Indian people, to argue that military officers could return honesty, as well as discipline, to the Indian service. For example, Sarah Winnemucca, the Paiute writer and activist, advocated transfer as an answer to the "Indian ring." The army, she hoped, would clean out the bureau and work to improve reservation conditions.[4] Most Indian Bureau officials, who were of course civilians, opposed transfer, but continued warfare in the West kept the idea alive. With each new conflict, critics demanded that Indian affairs should be a military matter as long as violence persisted. In particular, the clashes involving the Sioux during this period offered powerful ammunition for transfer advocates. The Sioux had received special attention from the architects of the peace policy, and the failure of civilian agents to control them led critics within and outside the military to argue that "wild" Indians could be handled only by the army.[5]

Cherokees followed the wars from the Indian Territory and in some cases participated in efforts to resolve hostilities. Keeping to their version of the peace policy, they generally blamed continued warfare on frontier whites and the failure of federal authorities to deal justly with Indians. In the case of the Sioux, William P. Boudinot argued that resistance was understandable and justified. In its treaties with the Sioux, the United States had promised the Indians possession of lands that were now overrun with "a rough and reckless population" of greedy whites. Warfare was the predictable result, a consequence of "atrocities naturally following the contemptuous hatred of Indians and disregard of Indian rights on [the] part of the invaders." The Sioux war was little more than a new example of the old cycle of frontier violence.[6] The Battle of the Little Bighorn, for its part, was a tragedy, but one that could not be blamed upon the Indians. Custer was the attacker, Boudinot reminded readers. He and his men died at the hands of people who were merely defending themselves. In a column printed a few weeks after the fight, the editor suggested that the key to Custer's defeat was that he had grown used to slaughtering peaceful bands of Indians. "Unfortunately for him they [Sitting Bull's warriors] were *not* of that class. He made the mistake so often made of confounding all Indians alike. . . . This time it was General Custer. Before it was Black Kettle. Next time it may be Sitting Bull or General Crook."[7] The lesson of the Sioux war was not that the United States should change its Indian policy, handing Indian affairs over to military men like Custer. It was that the United States should stand by its obligations and treat Indians with the justice that the peace policy was meant to ensure.[8]

Cherokee delegates, and those of the other civilized tribes, broadcast this opposition to transfer in their annual journeys to Washington.[9] And when the Indian Bureau succeeded in defeating transfer proposals, they took credit for the victory. Their testimony as Indian spokesmen, they reported, armed their allies in Congress and the Interior Department with irrefutable arguments against military oversight. In 1876, for example, William Penn Adair told the Cherokee National Council that the positions that he and his fellow delegates struck were instrumental in turning the majority of congressmen against that year's transfer bill. "They were used with signal effect, by our friends, against the measure, and unquestionably had great weight in deciding the result in favor of the Indian race."[10] As that passage suggests, the delegates came away from the transfer debates with a positive assessment of the state of American Indian relations. The defeat of the various bills demonstrated that the Indians still had friends in Congress, men who wanted the United States to act justly toward the tribes and nations. More important, the debates seemed to demonstrate that the delegates of the civilized tribes could persuade American authorities. The delegates almost certainly overestimated their influence. Needing to justify the expense of sending representatives to the East each year, they tended to inflate the importance of their actions. The Cherokees in Washington, however, appear to have been genuinely impressed with the goodwill shown to them by some members of the House and Senate. From the perspective of the capital during the debates over transfer, it looked as if American authorities could be made to understand the Cherokees' political needs and goals.[11]

How very different was the allotment campaign. Even as the transfer issue was being laid to rest, allotment emerged as an alternative solution to America's persistent problems with Indian tribes. Like transfer, it was meant to supplant the peace policy, with both campaigns growing out of a perception of the failure of the earlier reforms. But unlike transfer, by the 1880s allotment enjoyed almost unanimous support among those involved in American Indian affairs, leaving little room for Cherokees and others to influence debate. This was perhaps the crucial development from an Indian point of view. For most Cherokees, allotment differed little from transfer, territorial reorganization, or any of the other dangerous postwar initiatives. It was an unwanted innovation that would undermine the treaties, cost the tribe scarce resources, and set the Indians up for abuse at the hands of Americans. It promised to deny the Cherokees the ability to determine their own future. Yet unlike the earlier proposals, allotment in the 1880s appeared to be winning over even the most tractable of Indian friends. The delegates' sanguine picture of Indian affairs faded as the ranks of Cherokee opponents seemed to expand from a few corrupt interests – a railroad company or a handful of crude western politicians – to include almost all of America.

One can trace the Cherokees' awareness of the allotment issue by looking at the official instructions issued by the National Council to delegates to the United States. These lists of orders serve as annual snapshots of tribal leaders' most important political concerns and give one a sense of how council members perceived the various policy innovations proposed in the late nineteenth century. During the 1870s, the instructions always began by directing the delegates "to protest against, and oppose, by all lawful and available means, the passage . . . of any bill or measure for the establishment of any sort of a territorial or provincial government over the Cherokee Nation." This reflected tribal leaders' sense that territorialization was the primary political threat. In the early 1880s, that standard injunction still headed the instructions, but it was joined (sometimes in the same very long sentence) by an order to fight any effort to alter the Cherokee system of landholding. A few years later the instructions began to invoke allotment directly in a mandate to combat bills that would impose land in severalty upon the Cherokees or other peoples of the Indian Territory.[12] Severalty, meanwhile, also came to occupy a more prominent place in the delegates' reports back to the nation. Where in the past men like Adair and Daniel H. Ross had trumpeted their defeat of the latest Oklahoma bills, a note of uncertainty entered with regard to allotment. "The policy so strenuously advocated a few years since of organizing the Indian Country into Territories of the United States seems to have undergone a radical change," wrote delegates Hiram T. Landrum and Richard M. Wolfe in 1884. "It is now proposed to partition the Indian lands, allowing the Indians individually, a fixed number of acres, and selling any surplus to whites, with the right of residence, and the extension of state and territorial laws over all." This policy, they continued, was winning a great many supporters, "among them thousands of the best men and women in the United States." The Cherokees, they concluded, needed "to carefully watch this new phase of the Indian question, lest in its development, we in common with others, are made victims of a great wrong."[13] Reading the official correspondence that traveled between Washington and Tahlequah, one finds the allotment campaign's presence growing steadily in tribal leaders' political field of vision.

Strictly speaking, Landrum and Wolfe were incorrect in calling allotment a "new phase" in American Indian affairs. Along with Christianity, a command of the English language, and knowledge of the American economy, land in severalty had long been thought a prerequisite for Indian amalgamation into the European American world. By the early national period, some had come to consider it the most important of the changes involved in the civilization process. The ownership of individual property and the impulse to defend and increase one's property were said to form the foundation of American society. Without individual land, Native Americans would never develop the energy and self-interest necessary to survive in the United States. Following this line of reasoning, treaties during the antebellum period had often featured some limited form of allotment, and by the Civil War most new treaties included an American offer to start surveying tribal lands when the Indian people in question agreed that they were ready for ownership in severalty.[14]

Yet for most of the century, allotment remained one goal among many. The architects of the peace policy, for example, shared the belief in the necessity of individual land. Their immediate concern, however, was halting frontier warfare and improving the existing system of reservations. Likewise, proponents of Indian Territory reorganization looked to the ending of communal property, the Oklahoma bills generally providing for some form of allotment. But, again, allotment was not the central purpose of the initiative. It was something that would take place as a logical outgrowth of the new policy. What happened in the late 1870s and 1880s was that reformers, politicians, and government officials came to embrace allotment as the main mechanism by which America's Indian question would be put to rest once and for all.

A number of developments contributed to that change. For one thing, as the threat of frontier warfare faded, the Indian question itself underwent a partial transformation. As long as new Indian wars appeared likely, even those who objected to the reservation policy could see the logic of maintaining tribes on separate islands under the observation of American agents. By the early 1880s, however, most of the "hostiles" of the West had been subdued, and preventing warfare no longer seemed the overriding concern that it had been a few years earlier. That change encouraged policy makers and friends of the Indian to turn their full attention to the goal of assimilation, and many quite logically saw the tribes' separation as an obstacle to attaining that end.

This raises an interesting point regarding the Cherokees and the Five Tribes. It suggests that warfare involving other Native peoples was one of the factors that granted them the space necessary to continue their experiments in nationhood in the postwar era. While warfare or the threat of it persisted, the reservation remained useful. And as long as the reservation remained, Cherokees had a chance to shape it into an Indian nation.[15]

While the reserves were beginning to seem unnecessary, there occurred a number of well-publicized events in the West that raised doubts about the humanity of the reservation policy. In 1878 a group of Cheyennes moved away from their agency when a shortage of government supplies left them near starvation. Their flight turned into a battle when United States troops were sent to bring them back. Eventually the troops fulfilled their mission but only after the deaths of dozens of Cheyennes, soldiers, and white settlers. At about the same time, Standing Bear's band of Poncas tried to escape poor conditions in the Indian Territory, where the Poncas had been relocated against their will. Their flight did not end in bloodshed but in a celebrated court case in which a United States district judge prevented federal troops from returning the Poncas to the Indian Territory. This period also saw the efforts of the Nez Perce to return to their traditional lands in Oregon from the poor Indian Territory reservation assigned to them following their military defeat. All those events were widely reported in the East, and they cast a harsh light upon Indian reservations and the reservation policy. Where peace policy advocates had envisioned the reservations as schools and safe havens, cases like those of the Cheyennes and Poncas suggested that the reservations were in fact prisons.[16]

To make matters worse, charges of corruption dogged the Indian Bureau. Stories circulated in the press concerning Indian agents stealing from the bureau, accepting bribes, and taking kickbacks on government contracts. Not even the commissioner of Indian affairs could escape attack. In early 1880 Commissioner E. A. Hayt had to resign after being charged with covering up abuses in the Indian service in Arizona in order to protect his friends. The peace policy had failed to eliminate corruption in the Indian service with its new cadre of Christian agents, and many who observed the scandals concluded that corruption was endemic to the reservation system. The new agents had not reformed the reservation; the reservation had corrupted the agents.[17]

Finally, the issue was made especially urgent by the broader social and economic changes in the United States. The pace of progress appeared to be quicker in the 1870s and 1880s than it had been before the war. In an age of expanding cities and growing industrial production, the cultural distance that Indians had to travel to conform to the standards of modern America seemed to be growing greater day by day. There was no longer sufficient time, allotment proponents argued, to bring Native peoples slowly into civilization. The point had been reached at which only swift, immediate advances could save them.[18]

Among the most important allotment advocates were eastern reformers and philanthropists, the people whom the Cherokee delegates in 1884 called "the best men and women in the United States." These were the sort of Christian humanitarians who had earlier supported the peace policy and promoted the reservation as a refuge for persecuted Indians. In response to the wars and scandals of the 1870s, many reformers turned to rapid assimilation as the only hope for Native people. They formed new organizations like Boston's Indian Citizenship Committee and Philadelphia's Indian Rights Association and began to press federal officials and lawmakers to break up the reservations. Along with land in severalty, the reformers wanted to grant United States citizenship to the Indians and provide a universal school system to separate children from their tribal cultures. But allotment was the key – the first step and the catalyst for the broader transformation of Indian people into Christian Americans.[19]

This faith in allotment seems odd in retrospect. How could a parcel of land work such revolutions? The reformers, however, believed that without individual property Indians could never suitably maintain the most basic human relationships. They suggested, for example, that communalism denied Indian men their full adult masculinity and kept them from creating proper families. "The highest right of man is the right to be a man," wrote Merrill E. Gates, an educator and member of the Board of Indian Commissioners in the 1880s. Common property kept Indians from attaining true masculinity, Gates reasoned, because it "cuts the nerve of all that manful effort which political economy teaches us proceeds from the desire for wealth." Likewise, since the tribe supported its members with the common property, men did not have to provide for their families. There was no reason, in fact, for Indians to have families, as European Americans defined them. This, in turn, perverted all other relations among the Indians, according to Gates, since "the family is God's unit of society." Thus, without individual property, there could be no true manhood and no adequate family life, and in the absence of these, society itself lacked a foundation. America had to give Indian men land of their own so that they could make homes for their families. This then would create the setting in which the civilizing and "Americanizing" of the Indians could be quickly completed.[20]

In the case of the Five Tribes, allotment advocates found an additional set of arguments for severalty, insisting that communal land was the root cause of a variety of Indian Territory problems. The tribal systems, they maintained, left too much land unoccupied, and this encouraged unscrupulous Americans to enter Indian country illegally. These intruders existed outside the authority of both American and tribal governments, committed crimes almost impossible to punish, and denied the use of land to both Indian people and the honest American farmers who might have homesteaded the territory were it fully integrated into the United States. The most spectacular examples of this phenomenon were the "boomer" conspiracies, plans for organized invasions of the Indian Territory that first appeared in the late 1870s. These schemes involved small armies of squatters attempting to stake claim to large sections of tribal land in hopes of forcing the federal government to open the territory officially. While federal authorities squelched the invasions (much to the delight of Indian leaders), allotment advocates took the boomers as evidence that the communal land system invited trouble.[21]

If intruders were a problem, many of those who made use of communal lands legally were even worse. Critics of the Five Tribes identified an unholy trinity of interests whom they believed exploited the land system: corporations that leased tribal territory, white men who married into the tribes, and mixed-race tribal leaders. While the federal government excluded American farmers from the territory, "squaw men" and "half-breeds" grew rich by amassing vast holdings of land and by leasing tribal property to corporations like the Cherokee Strip Live Stock Association. This was a particularly fascinating line of argument, insofar as it combined the old distrust of the civilized tribes' "clever mixed-bloods" with an attack on the monopoly capitalism of the industrial era. Fear of miscegenation merged with outrage at unfair economic privilege. As one pamphlet argued, no honest white man would seek wealth by marrying into an Indian tribe. "The American pioneer . . . would not, if he could, leave his family and enter this Territory as a 'squaw man' – he would not surrender his Anglo-Saxon pride of race to enter anywhere, for land or gold." That being the case, the worst sort of men had come to control the rich resource that was the Indian Territory. And they exercised that control to the detriment not only of the honest pioneer but of the great majority of Indians as well. While the bulk of the tribes' wealth went to support a few privileged individuals and companies, the Indian masses still lived in poverty, too ignorant to know that they were being robbed. Allotment supporters thus identified a shared cause between the honest small farmer of the United States and the "poor full bloods." Both required the dethroning of the territory's corporate and tribal rulers.[22]

Worst of all, communal landholding, according to allotment advocates, kept the Indian masses in a state of savagery. This was perhaps their most damning argument. The Five Tribes had long maintained that their history of self-directed progress justified their being left alone to continue the work of civilization. By the late 1870s allotment supporters refused to entertain that position. The more circumspect argued that while it was true that the Five Tribes had advanced rapidly in the antebellum era, in the years since the Civil War they had slipped backward. Others simply denied that any tribe could change on its own. "The Indians remain in the bonds of their ancient barbarism," a group of border state businessmen argued. It was as simple as that.[23]

Beginning in 1879 a series of congressional bills translated the reasoning of allotment enthusiasts into legislative form. In essence, these bills identified the division of communal lands as the United States's most important Indian policy goal and empowered the president to pursue it. Typically, they stated that when the president deemed a reservation suitable for agriculture, he could order the surveying of the land and its allotment to individual Indians. Different bills offered different equations dictating how much land each person would receive, but generally allotments were to be some variation on the 160-acre quarter section, the traditional unit of American land law. Indian people would select their parcels of land, and once the Interior Department gave its approval, they would receive patents. These titles would specify that the land in question could not be alienated for a number of years, usually twenty-five. The idea here was to give Native Americans a grace period of continued federal protection, during which they would make the transition from members of a tribe to individualized Americans.

The bills specified or suggested several additional changes that were to occur when Indians accepted land in severalty. Any surplus territory would be sold to the federal government, the price to be set through negotiations with the Interior Department. If the surplus were suitable for farming, it would fall under the homestead laws and be opened to settlers. In addition, allotment would mark the end of independent tribal government and law. Indians would become citizens of the United States, and tribal councils (allotment supporters assumed) would be maintained only as long as it took to settle business related to the elimination of communal property. The laws of the United States would be extended over the new American citizens. The acceptance of individual land, then, would inaugurate a process whereby all the formal barriers that separated Native Americans from the general population of the United States would fall. Although close to eight years passed between the introduction of the first general allotment bill and the signing of the Dawes Act, the beginning of congressional debate on the matter offered the definitive sign that the peace policy and Americans' faith in the reservation were dead.[24]

Cherokee leaders observed all this with considerable anxiety. Thanks to Indian opposition, the severalty bills introduced between 1879 and 1887 usually excluded the Five Tribes from their provisions. This was true of the Dawes Act, a fact that Cherokee delegates reported to the nation with some relief. It was clear, however, that allotment was a policy that the Indian Affairs establishment wanted to see applied to all. Indeed, many advocates believed that the progressive Five Tribes should have been the first to accept private land. Even before the Dawes Act was signed, then, tribal leaders in the Indian Territory recognized that they would soon become targets of the new campaign.[25]

Within the Cherokee Nation, allotment was the topic of considerable debate. Some influential Cherokees had been urging their people to accept land in severalty for years prior to the appearance of the first general allotment bills. William P. Boudinot, for example, during his off-and-on tenure as editor of the *Advocate*, frequently suggested that the Cherokees break up their communal lands through their own action. This, he hoped, would end the continual agitation to open the territory and would grant his people more easily defended titles to their lands. Boudinot's version of allotment, however, did not foresee any surplus territory being handed over to white homesteaders, and it would be carried out without destroying tribal government. More important, it was something that only the Cherokees themselves could do; it could not be imposed upon them. In Boudinot's terms allotment was primarily a defensive measure.[26]

Some Cherokees, especially as time passed and pressure from allotment advocates mounted, went further than Boudinot and accepted that the United States had the right and duty to allot tribal lands for the Indians. Boudinot's brother Elias, for example, continued to call for the dismantling of the tribal governments and in the late 1870s and 1880s became a highly visible Indian advocate of allotment.[27] Spencer Stephens, another long-standing critic of the Cherokee government, likewise argued publicly for division of the tribal lands. In 1882 he wrote a pamphlet calling upon the United States to act to incorporate the Indians as speedily as possible into the American body politic and economy. Indian nationhood, he suggested, was no longer a viable proposition. The Cherokees' only hope was to gain security and peace as individuals within the United States. The federal government could help the Cherokees and other tribes achieve this by throwing all its weight behind educating Indians and by allotting the land as soon as they seemed ready. Even Stephens, however, insisted that allotment should not be done in violation of treaties – that is, the Cherokees had to ask for it first. Stephens, a former superintendent of Cherokee schools, hoped that a vigorous education campaign would soon result in all Cherokees' accepting the idea of private property. Caught between his conviction that Indian nationhood was a farce and his respect for the treaties, Stephens fell back upon the civilizing mission as the answer to the Indian question.[28]

By the 1880s, then, a minority within the Cherokee Nation supported some form of allotment. The Cherokee government, however, remained opposed to any change in the tribe's landholding or political status. The two major political parties, National and Downing, each proclaimed their commitment to landholding in common, and changes in government leadership did not alter the official stand on severalty. It was said, in fact, that some candidates who personally supported allotment declined to make landholding an issue in elections. They deferred to the majority view.[29] Delegates to Washington, meanwhile, regardless of their own feelings about landholding, stuck to the national line. While the Cherokees themselves entertained a variety of positions on allotment, the Cherokee Nation was consistently and officially opposed.

In explaining that opposition, leaders and delegates invariably began with the treaties and the patents that the Cherokees held on their common lands. As they had in opposing the Oklahoma bills, they insisted that the United States simply had no right to tell the Cherokees how to use their property. They had purchased their lands and held as strong a title to them as they ever could hold. Allotment advocates, tribal leaders noted, liked to characterize all Indian land as ultimately belonging to the federal government, with the tribes merely using it at the president's pleasure. The patents granted after removal, however, proved that this was not true of the Cherokees and the other civilized tribes. In moving to the West, the tribes had purchased their new homes with the old and thus were not the president's tenants. To be sure, the 1866 treaties allowed for allotment, but only when the Indians themselves asked for it. As the Cherokees saw it, this was little more than a further acknowledgment of their exclusive ownership of the land. Until the Indians decided to accept severalty, there was nothing that the United States could legitimately do.[30]

Legality aside, allotment was a terrible idea because the communal land system, leaders insisted, protected tribes from the dishonest individuals and interests that always sought to prey upon Indian people. It was an "ancient safeguard . . . against fraudulent devices." To divide the lands was to invite every swindler in the West to rush in and cheat the poor, weak, and uneducated. Precisely that concern, delegates sometimes recalled, had helped motivate Cherokees in the 1830s to accept removal. "Our fathers knew the evils of holding land in severalty," the *Advocate* explained in 1879, and they allowed themselves to be pushed beyond the Mississippi to avoid it. Little had changed since Andrew Jackson's day. If the United States forced allotment upon the Cherokee Nation now, one statement predicted, "two-thirds of her citizens would be homeless wanderers in a few years."[31]

At particular risk were the "less civilized" of the Cherokees, often characterized as full-bloods. "All experience," an 1880 memorial argued, "shows that our present tenure to our lands is, by far, the safest for weak and unenlightened Indians like the majority of our people are."[32] There were still a great many members of the Five Tribes who were incapable of coping with unrestricted interaction with white Americans. That being the case, it was best to keep to the traditional and proven land system. Cherokee, Creek, and Chickasaw representatives offered a version of this argument in an appeal to President Grover Cleveland during the congressional debates over the Dawes Act. "Ownership of land in common has been a part of the tribal policy of Indians from time immemorial," they reminded the president. "It is with them a religion as well as a law of property. . . . In the transition of any race from the savage state to civilization, the highest welfare of the people can be assured only by a common ownership of the soil. Ownership in severalty must necessarily result in the acquisition of the great body of the lands by a few strong and unscrupulous hands, with poverty and misery for the masses of the people."[33] In messages like these, tribal leaders maintained that they needed more time to teach their people before changes like allotment could be accepted. Where in the past they had argued that their progressive achievements gave them the right to be left alone, here they suggested that the still-uncivilized state of many of their people necessitated their being left alone.

It is interesting to note that the allotment debate in the Indian Territory often took the form of an argument over what was best for full-bloods or the "Indian masses." Allotment advocates contended that this group had to be granted homesteads in order to liberate them from the tribal governments and mixed-race aristocrats. They identified full-bloods as the true Indians, the ones for whom policy should be made, while assuming that they were ignorant, culturally backward, and susceptible to exploitation. They conflated biological ancestry with identity and culture, a tendency that some scholars argue reflected the rise of eugenics in scientific thinking about race. In this equation, greater Indian blood quantum (to use a term coined later) made an individual more authentically Native and more deserving of tribal resources, but it also meant that the individual was less competent. While the mixed-bloods could hold their own, the "real Indians" needed paternalistic agents and humanitarians to protect them.[34]

Cherokee leaders employed a similar full-blood image, but used it to argue against allotment. The full-bloods were "weak and unenlightened." They were vulnerable. They were the Indians whose welfare had to be kept in mind when discussing policy. Yet Cherokees insisted that their own system protected the full-bloods better than could any scheme devised by the Indian Bureau or eastern philanthropists. Common land and tribal government shielded them from fraud and abuse; thus, until the full-bloods were ready for non-Indian competition, the Cherokee system should remain in place. Full-blood spokesmen themselves often affirmed this basic argument. In the 1890s, the Keetoowah Society, the organization of culturally conservative Cherokees, became more active in resisting allotment. They based their opposition on the treaties, but they also argued that their people were not yet ready to leave the protection provided by tribal government and common land.[35] Cherokees seem not to have believed that "blood" literally determined identity. When describing full-blood "weaknesses" they generally cited a lack of proficiency in English and familiarity with the market economy, matters related to experience and things that could be taught. By using the language of blood, however, they tended to affirm the connection between biological descent and culture.

After the triumph of the allotment policy, the practice of categorizing Indian people by blood would have devastating effects upon Native Americans. Officials implementing the Dawes Act used blood quantum to exclude some Indian people from receiving land, denying allotments to those who could not demonstrate that they were at least one-half Indian by blood. For the Five Tribes, the United States would use blood quantum in the early twentieth century to determine how much protection allotments required. Under a 1908 law, those who were less than one-half Indian by blood were assumed to be civilized enough to pay taxes and sell their land. The language of blood became a tool with which to manipulate and often dispossess Native people. While allotment was still under debate, however, speaking that language could be a source of authority – for Indian people as well as for American reformers.[36]

Allotment's dangers, tribal leaders suggested, should have been evident to American policy makers. After all, allotment on a smaller scale had been tried repeatedly in the past, and it had resulted in precisely the abuse and loss of property that worried contemporary chiefs and delegates. "Their own experience," an 1878 memorial said of the Five Tribes, "tells them exactly what the system of allotment and citizenship means." The Cherokees' treaties in 1817 and 1819 had included allotment provisions, as had those of the Choctaws in 1830 and the Creeks in 1832. But the anticipated benefits had never been seen. "Hundreds of Indians entitled to patents for land under these Treaties have never received a single acre. Many more whose rights were recognized by the Government were shamefully wronged by the whites and to this day have been unable to obtain relief or redress."[37] Other tribes, Cherokees assured their readers, could tell similar tales of fraud and property loss. In an 1880 letter, William Penn Adair listed fourteen tribes and bands that had accepted individual land between 1839 and 1868. "Only one succeeded in taking care of themselves – the Brothertown band, in Wisconsin." The United States had offered these Indians allotment as a way of permanently securing their land and as a step toward self-sufficiency. The consequences, however, had been impoverishment and deeper dependence. "It is a demonstrated fact," Adair concluded, "that Indians, as a general thing, do not succeed or prosper as citizens of the United States with tenure in severalty."[38]

The historian Francis Paul Prucha notes that participants in the allotment campaign tended to overlook the policy's rather muddled history. Convinced that they had found the answer to most of the country's Indian problems, they promoted severalty with an "almost blind enthusiasm . . . despite considerable evidence from the previous half-century of experience that allotment had been a mixed blessing."[39] By frequently invoking these earlier cases, Indian leaders attempted to puncture the campaign's air of certainty. They portrayed allotment as an experiment (a term Cherokees often applied to the policy) at best and an experiment that had failed more trials than it had passed.

On several occasions, Cherokees took pains to remind their audiences of a number of small tribes that had experienced allotment in Kansas and subsequently moved to the Indian Territory. That state's recent history, they suggested, should be enough to convince anyone that dividing reservations resulted only in suffering for Native people. Not long before the passage of the Dawes Act, Elias C. Boudinot (William P. Boudinot's son, not William's pro-allotment brother of the same name) told the story in the *Advocate*. "[Kansas] when admitted to the Union promised everything that was fair to the Indians within her borders. Where are these Indians to-day – the Delawares, Shawnees, Pottowotomies, Kaws, Osages and others? They are *not* in Kansas. They *are* in the Indian Territory." And they were driven there, Boudinot recalled, by precisely the conditions that Congress now wanted to impose generally. "They tested to their satisfaction, and sorrow too, [the] plan of civilizing Indians under the operations of State laws – with lands in severalty and a good white farmer at the call of every Indian homesteader who needed his help. The 'layman and missionary' white farmers soon wearied of the presence of their Indian neighbors and went to work to drive them out and possess their lands and homes." Here the allotment debate became an argument over the nature of frontier whites. Were they honest laborers deserving access to Indian lands, or the crude swindlers from which the peace policy had tried to protect the Indians? In the experience of the Kansas tribes, they were the latter. Rather than serve as models of civilized life, the newcomers used every means at their disposal to cheat the Indians and gain control of their property. Before long, "existence became so intolerable that in sheer despair they gave up all and fled to an Indian community for protection, which they found in the Indian Territory where lands are held in common and where they are now doing well."[40] The lesson was clear to anyone not blinded by the extravagant theories of eastern philanthropists: landholding in common was one of the last shields that Indian people possessed against white America's demonstrated rapacity.

One potentially significant problem with the protection argument was the presence in the Five Tribes' country of so many of these dreaded frontier whites – intruders, legally admitted laborers, and intermarried citizens. Common land did not prevent these non-Indians from entering in large numbers, and by 1890 a federal census estimated that whites far outnumbered Indians.[41] In these circumstances, what kind of protection did tribal government and common land afford? Cherokee leaders tended to skirt the issue of whites in the nation, preferring to focus more narrowly on the intruder question. The treaties obligated the United States to remove American citizens who entered the Indian country illegally, and the Cherokee government frequently petitioned federal authorities to perform this duty. Tribal spokesmen blamed white intruders for much of the crime and disorder in the nation, adhering to the time-honored practice of locating the sources of most Indian trouble outside the boundaries of the Indian nation. They suggested that if the United States would keep its promises and remove the intruders, the Cherokees could live with the non-Indians' residing legally in the territory.[42]

On the occasions when they referred directly to the intermarried citizens and permit workers, they generally described them as useful additions to the nation. As the *Advocate* explained the matter in 1879, "We have no objection to teachers, preachers and mechanics, or those who come here and remain by permission. Our objections are against those who are 'intruders' who come here and 'squat' without leave or license." Honest white men, the *Advocate* continued, had always been the Cherokees' welcome friends. "We are indebted to good worthy white men for all that we are in civilization and education. Teachers, preachers, farmers and mechanics, who came here in the olden time with habits of industry and morality, many of whom intermarried and reared families – to these white men we are under many obligations."[43] The practice of bringing in outsiders to work Cherokee land, tribal leaders admitted, was a problem when it became too extensive. They believed, however, that the Cherokees' own laws and government were up to the task of dealing with the issue, if federal officials would help the tribe rid itself of unwanted Americans. It was primarily an internal matter. At any rate, conditions in the nation would be immeasurably worse if tribal government and common landholding were eliminated. The difficulty of keeping bad whites out of the Indian country, they argued, could hardly be resolved by destroying the existing protective barriers.[44]

As tribal leaders invoked the dire consequences of allotment, they also offered a positive argument for communalism. The Cherokee land system, they maintained, was the one best suited to their people's condition and environment. More important, it compared favorably to the economy of the United States, where industrialization threatened Americans with the kind of abuse and impoverishment that tribal leaders anticipated would follow the division of their lands. Allotment in these terms represented the destruction of a good and proven system in favor of one the merits of which were far from certain.

Dennis Wolfe Bushyhead, the Cherokees' principal chief from 1879 to 1887, wrote or led the delegations that produced the most forceful statements of this position. He was especially well suited for this role, having gained extensive experience with both American and tribal economies by the time he was elected chief. After education at mission schools, a private academy in New Jersey, and Princeton University, he had spent a good part of his early adulthood in California trying to cash in on the Gold Rush and the broader economic boom it inaugurated. After returning to the Cherokee Nation in the late 1860s, he had assumed direction of his family's store at Fort Gibson and gained a solid enough reputation as a businessman that he was chosen to be the tribe's treasurer in 1871. He spent seven years in that office, until his selection as the National Party's candidate for chief. While few doubted his financial acumen, Bushyhead's economic policies garnered significant criticism. He was an advocate, for instance, of leasing tribal land to cattle interests, and he helped secure the lease of the tribe's western Outlet to the Cherokee Strip Live Stock Association. Opponents within the Cherokee Nation argued that this policy amounted to an invitation to white intruders and in practical terms the ceding of tribal land. Some American politicians and journalists, meanwhile, charged that the lease was simply illegal, since by treaty the United States was entitled to purchase the Outlet from the tribe. Bushyhead, then, faced charges of corruption even as he and his fellow tribal spokesmen questioned the fairness of America's economic system.[45]

Cherokees, of course, were not the only people in the late nineteenth century casting doubt upon the organization of the American economy. They broadcast their positive interpretation of communal land at a time when political economy was the subject of avid debate among their neighbors in the United States. Concentration in American industry, the emergence of a large population of permanent wage laborers, and in particular the great and increasing disparity between the rich and poor led many Americans to wonder whether democracy and individual liberty could survive in a modern economy.[46] As Bushyhead reminded congressmen in one memorial, the United States was proposing to force allotment upon the Indians "at the very time when grave questions [were] being discussed among the white population of the United States as to the wisdom of making the land a chattel, and the football of speculators and corporations."[47] The Cherokees' positive defense of communal land represented a Native American contribution to the political economy debates, albeit one translated through the goal of maintaining the Indian nation.

As explained by Bushyhead and others, communalism's positive attributes ranged from the practical to the more abstract. Cherokee representatives often pointed out that the quality of their land was such that it could not support the kind of small farms envisioned in the typical allotment scheme. Most of the territory was grazing land, and a quarter section of it would not suffice to support a family. "No man can afford to live by stock-raising and herding who is restricted to 160 or even 320 acres, especially on lands away from water," explained the memorial of an 1881 delegation led by Bushyhead. "The herds must be sufficiently large to justify the care of them."[48] Dividing these lands into quarter sections would ensure that the Indians never profited by them. The allotments would sit useless until their owners sold out, most likely to some speculator or corporation. Far from encouraging self-sufficiency, severalty would make economic independence almost impossible by rendering useless the tribes' single greatest resource. In contrast, communal landholding fit the business of stock raising perfectly. The Indians could rent the land out (as they did the Outlet) with all tribal members receiving a share of the proceeds, or they could raise herds upon it themselves. In short, common lands preserved the economic value of the territory for its Native American owners.[49]

Tribal spokesmen further suggested that herding was the endeavor that best suited the majority of their people and in making this argument wed an old idea of Indian progress to their analysis of the contemporary economy. Most Cherokees, they implied, occupied an intermediate stage between savagery and civilization. While they were not ready for individual farms, they were more than capable of working as herders. The same was true of other western Indians. According to an 1884 memorial, "The least civilized of the Indians can soon be taught to raise cattle and sheep, and in this way can eminently serve the interests of American civilization."[50] Force them onto individual allotments

223

where stock raising was impossible, and one ensured that they would progress no further. Some Cherokee memorials cited the example of the Navajos as evidence. In Navajo country, one observed, "not more than one acre in twenty is suitable for cultivation." The Navajos lived "by pastoral pursuits," maintaining large herds of sheep, cattle, and horses. "By this business," delegates reported, "they live comfortably, exporting wool and livestock. By sectionizing and reducing them to 160 acres, you would pauperize and ruin a people who are adding to your productive industries."[51]

As the last chapter explained, Cherokee leaders sometimes identified the Indian nation as being the equivalent of a corporation. The nation was a collective enterprise with certain economic resources in which all members possessed an interest. The argument regarding stock raising and common property would seem to fit that manner of thinking. Herding was the most logical enterprise for the Indian nation/corporation. It suited the environment of the territory; many Cherokees already possessed the necessary skills and knowledge to work at it; and its products could be marketed profitably in the American economy. Yet stock raising did not require any substantial change in either the tenure of Cherokee property or the tribe's political status. If one could believe Cherokee leaders, land in common and Indian nationhood in fact nurtured the enterprise. Herding offered a way of adapting communalism, and with it Cherokee nationhood, to the economy of the modernizing United States. In it lay a promise that the tribe's customs and autonomy could be made relevant and useful in the late nineteenth century.

No matter what the Cherokees did with their land, however, their system provided clear advantages over property ownership in the United States – or so tribal leaders insisted. By law, a Cherokee citizen could occupy and work any unused tract of the national domain. Ownership of the land would remain with the nation, but the individual would own, and could sell, any improvements made on the land. As the allotment campaign continued, chiefs and delegates increasingly described that arrangement as an almost perfect foundation for economic life. In the words of one principal chief, it was "the best form of government, not only for the Indian in his helpless condition in wrestling with the Anglo-Saxon race for his existence on the face of this earth, but the best government for all mankind."[52] The nation's laws, they argued, allowed individuals to experience all the advantages that came with private property. Yet because the land itself could not be sold, the Cherokee system eliminated the possibility of speculation and monopoly. It ensured, ultimately, that all citizens had an opportunity to possess and improve a farm and that no one in the nation need be poor. "The only difference between your land system and ours," Bushyhead wrote, "is that the unoccupied surface of the earth is not a chattel to be sold and speculated in by those who do not use it." In the Cherokee system, "so long as one acre of our domain is unoccupied, any Cherokee who wishes to cultivate it can do so, and make a home, which is his."[53]

As the reference to the home implies, the positive view of common land answered, among other things, the gender argument broadcast by pro-allotment reformers – the position that common property warped the home and masculinity by denying men an incentive to work for their families. The Cherokee system did in fact motivate men to strive and accumulate wealth, tribal leaders insisted. It not only allowed but encouraged them to make homes for their families. "In the sense that one man has as much right as another to get a decent and happy living for himself and his family by the sweat of his brow, in that sense and in no other, is the land of the Cherokee Nation *common property*," the *Advocate* explained in the late 1880s. "A man's home, a man's improvements, a man's property of all descriptions are as inviolably his, and as rigidly secured to him and his heirs by the laws of this Nation, as the same kind of property is to anybody else in the world under any other Government. . . . Every rational and worthy incentive to labor is as actively at work among the Cherokees as among other people on earth." The one thing restrained by the Cherokee system was "the baleful passion of greed, the indulgence in which is so much encouraged by being allowed full exercise by other so-called civilized governments."[54] The Cherokee system did not eliminate the need for Cherokee men to build homes and provide for their families.

It ensured that everyone had a chance to do these things, while helping men defend their families and property against the avarice of others.

Chiefs and delegates contrasted that situation with life in the United States, where (as an early anti-allotment memorial put it) "hundreds and thousands of our white neighbors have been crushed and ruined, and others to-day are struggling for an existence."[55] While the Cherokee Nation safeguarded economic opportunity for all its citizens, the United States after the Civil War had shown itself to be a country where many never had a chance to rise above poverty. Bushyhead made this comparison in a March 1881 letter to the *New York Independent.* He was responding to an essay printed earlier in the newspaper in which an anonymous writer claiming to be a Cherokee had urged the United States to dismantle the Five Tribes' governments and allot the common lands. The principal chief replied by providing a familiar list of the Cherokees' civilized achievements: over one hundred primary schools, the two Cherokee seminaries, the orphan asylum, and so on. He then explained that when allotment advocates called for the division of the common lands they were asking the Cherokees to jeopardize that success for the sake of a dangerous experiment. "There are those who wish us well," he acknowledged, "who are carried away by the doctrine of 'land in severalty.' I would say to them that to provide that our land shall be made a chattel . . . is not the best way of civilizing Indians." The Cherokees already possessed a landholding system that suited their needs. Any citizen could cultivate and improve any unused land, but they were not permitted to sell the land itself. The soil, "like the air and waters, is the heritage of the people." That system was clearly preferable to landholding in the United States. If allotment were imposed, Bushyhead continued, "our domain would soon drift into the hands of a few, and our poor people in a few years would become like your poor people, most of whom, if they died tomorrow, do not own a foot of the earth's surface in which they could be buried. If this is the phase of your civilization to which you are at present so nervously inviting us, can you wonder if we pause to study the present tendencies and probable future of this fearfully anti-republican system[?]" In other words, the American economy of the late nineteenth century, in its full dimensions at least, was not a "phase of civilization" that any Cherokee could desire. "We are neither socialists nor communists," the chief concluded, "but we have a land system which we believe to be better than any you can devise for us. . . . Cannot you leave us alone to try our plan, while you are trying yours?"[56]

Writings like these seldom referred directly to industrialization in the United States. Chiefs and delegates still attacked the railroads and other corporations, but they generally did not mention urban growth, the spread of factory production, or the other changes that were remaking America in the late nineteenth century. Those changes, however, provided the essential context for the development of the positive argument for common land. The economic upheavals of the postwar era allowed Cherokees to portray not only allotment but the American political economy itself as an uncertain thing, an experiment. And as the statements already quoted demonstrate, chiefs and delegates found plenty of evidence that for many Americans the experiment was a failure. The implication was that by the end of the century the United States itself had ceased to provide many of its citizens with the freedom and opportunity that were thought to be that nation's great promise. The Cherokees, however, having preserved their homeland as a common treasury for all, could still make good on the ideals that they had learned from their neighbors. While the United States became ever less American, the Cherokee Nation, protected and without allotment, remained a refuge of genuine equality.

The *Cherokee Advocate*, during William P. Boudinot's final stint as editor, gave perhaps the best expression of that theme. In 1889 a short essay titled "The Cherokee Constitution" explained that while both the American and Cherokee systems promised citizens life, liberty, and the pursuit of happiness, only in the Cherokee Nation was that promise fulfilled for all. According to the *Advocate*, "A hundred years of experience has proven that the American Constitution and Government will not accomplish that purpose. The wealth of the few has become more and more enormous – the poverty of the many, more widespread and hopeless, since the famous declaration was made by Jefferson that all men are created free and equal." In the Cherokee Nation, however, this had not been the case. The laws regarding landholding guaranteed that every citizen had the opportunity to benefit from "the gifts of the Creator, common to all." This was what Jefferson had meant by equality, the *Advocate* asserted, but only in the Indian nation had the founding father's principle been put into action. As a result, the Cherokees at the end of the nineteenth century did not suffer from the economic extremes found among their unfortunate neighbors. "Unlimited ease, or enormous and disproportionate wealth among them is impossible; and it is equally true that the dreadful concomitants of the riches; idleness and luxury of the favored few . . . the poverty, the ill-paid or excessive labor or enforced idleness, the suffering and wretchedness of the unregarded many are impossible also among the Cherokees. Thus is the Cherokee government shunning a rock upon which all other governments have been, or are being, wrecked." Far from a problem to be solved through allotment, Cherokee landholding was the one system that could still promise free opportunity to all.[57] As a commission led by Bushyhead later put it, "on account of that one notable feature [land in common], which exemplifies the golden rule in government, thoughtful Cherokees consider the Cherokee government the best, the most just and equal in the world."[58]

The language that Cherokee leaders used in these writings was strikingly similar to that of the most forceful American critics of the new industrial order. Henry George, for example, in his widely read *Progress and Poverty*, identified the individual ownership of land as the root cause of destitution in the United States. Strictly private landholding always led to monopoly, and this in turn brought about the appalling gulf between the wealthy few and the masses in contemporary America. That situation, George strenuously argued, represented a rejection of the ideals upon which the nation had been founded. "The great republic of the modern world has adopted at the beginning of its career an institution that ruined the republics of antiquity," George wrote. Americans, "a people who proclaim the inalienable rights of all men to life, liberty, and the pursuit of happiness have accepted without question a principle, which, in denying the equal and inalienable right to the soil, finally denies the equal right to life and liberty."[59] The

Knights of Labor similarly inveighed against absolute ownership of land, and like George some of the organization's leaders identified the "land question" as the problem from which all others grew. "The land is the heritage of God," declared Terrence Powderly in an 1882 speech. "He gave it to *all* his people. If He intended it for all His people, then no man or set of men has a right to monopolize it." Later he stated, "If I ever come to believe in individual, absolute ownership in land, I must, in order to be consistent, believe that the man who owns the land owns the people who live on it as well. . . . Such a doctrine is monstrous."[60]

This is not to say that Cherokee leaders declared common cause with radical labor unions or any particular American reformer. Nor does it mean that reformers looked to the Indian Territory for examples of proper systems of landholding. American students of the land question, in fact, were just as likely to view the Indian Territory as an example of the evils of monopoly, with land reformers joining with allotment advocates in calling for an end to the reign of tribal aristocrats and their corporate partners.[61] The parallels in language, however, suggest that Americans' debates over political economy helped tribal leaders find new ways of defending common lands and Indian nationhood. George, the Knights, and other radicals and reformers wanted to reorder the American economy so that its new power would serve the many rather than the few. The Cherokees' implication was that in their own country they already had an institution that could achieve that goal. Using a phrase that the Knights would employ in their "Preamble," an early Five Tribes memorial against severalty stated, "We believe that system which is promotive of the greatest good to the greatest number is the true system for the guidance of God's creatures." The Cherokees possessed such a system; it was the economy of the United States that was proving to be of questionable value.[62]

This portrayal of communal landholding answered some of the charges that allotment advocates commonly leveled against the Cherokees. Common lands were not an obstacle to Indian civilization; they were a shield that protected Indian people while they progressed. The tribe's common property did not encourage the monopolizing of land. On the contrary, it ensured that monopolies of the sort continually being created in the United States had no place in the Indian nation. The full-bloods were not victims of tribal aristocrats but beneficiaries of what may have been the last truly republican system on the continent. But the positive argument did something more. In describing their nation as a place where free enterprise existed but could not be abused, they made landholding in common a modern thing, a practice that made sense in the industrial age. Common land, they suggested, was the institution that would allow the Cherokees to benefit from the new economy of the late nineteenth century without experiencing the traumas that the birth of that economy seemed to be inflicting upon so many Americans. Common land, it seems, was necessary in the age of capital, perhaps more so than ever before. That idea is significant, because for most of those involved in discussions of allotment, communalism was the very antithesis of modernity. Whether they endorsed allotment or not, participants tended to identify landholding in common as a pre-Columbian custom, a savage practice to which the Indians, by nature or by choice, had clung. It was at best a preliminary stage to the Indians' accepting a fully civilized economic life. Five Tribes' leaders themselves often adhered to that definition. They promised that in time all their people would be ready for severalty and would naturally embrace it. Or else they admitted that for better or for worse allotment was part of their destiny. Yet present alongside that reasoning was this different, more radical thought: that perhaps the changes witnessed by the postwar United States had made the tribal relic something logical and desirable in the modern era. Landholding in common, from this perspective, was not a fading survival of ancient life but a living institution, one revitalized by the uncertainty of the times.

Cherokee leaders continued to broadcast these arguments into the 1890s, as pressure mounted on the Five Tribes to accept severalty and denationalization. In fact, two developments offered them fresh evidence of the essential correctness of their system. First, beginning in 1889, there was the creation and settlement of the new Oklahoma Territory. Congress created this entity from land cessions promised by the Five Tribes in the 1866 treaties. Those agreements had stipulated that the lands were to be used to accommodate new tribes moved to the Indian Territory. In the wake of the peace policy's demise, however, and in response to the clamoring of westerners for a new frontier, the federal government decided to overlook that provision. Congress authorized homesteading in the "Oklahoma District," and on April 22, 1889, the first great Oklahoma land run occurred. A year later, a territorial government was created. From a Cherokee point of view, the dishonesty with which the Oklahoma Territory was created, along with the chaos of the run, demonstrated the ruin invited by weakening the barriers between the Indian nation and white America. There was "no lover of his country," Cherokee delegates explained in the early 1890s, "but would deprecate the repetition of the scenes attending the opening of Oklahoma, the Cherokee Strip, the location of the capital at Guthrie, as well as subsequent occurrences of pauperism, fraud, and crime."[63] To make matters worse, Oklahomans and some members of Congress wanted to merge the new territory with the country of the Five Tribes, bringing both into the Union as a single state. A protest from the Cherokee National Council replied to this idea by expressing the tribe's "supreme contempt for the white persons who are not content with the disgrace brought by them upon their own race and nation in the recent transaction in the opening of that territory . . . but whose dishonesty and greed seek also to pervert and destroy the autonomy of the Five Civilized Indian Nations." The Cherokees, the council added, "compare favorably in education and morality with those of neighboring states, and might be regarded as models when viewed in comparison with the heterogeneous elements attempting their union with Oklahoma." What benefit could the Indians derive from sharing a state with such people?[64]

Second, the American economy in the early 1890s became an even less attractive model than in the previous decade. In 1893 a financial panic plunged the United States into a prolonged depression. Some 20 percent of American workers found themselves unemployed, and an already troubled agricultural economy sank into stagnation. The civilized economic system in which American authorities were so anxious to include the Cherokees was seen to be on the verge of coming apart. Cherokee representatives seldom referred directly to the crisis in their writings against allotment, but they did continue to invoke poverty in the United States as evidence of the benefits of landholding in common. "People who are so anxious to see this country allotted and made a state," the *Advocate* suggested in 1894, "should read of the destitution and misery among the people of the states." How could the Indians expect to profit from inclusion in the United States when so many of that country's citizens were being crushed? It is impossible to say how closely tribal leaders followed the economic developments in the United States, but whatever knowledge they possessed of the American depression surely heightened their fears concerning the consequences of allotment. If nothing else, it is a great irony (in a history full of irony) that federal authorities moved to draw the Cherokees at last into the United States at precisely the moment in the nineteenth century when America had the least to offer.[65]

Questionable in their timing or not, allotment advocates in the mid-1890s finally began to force their program on the Indian Territory. In 1893 Congress created the Commission to the Five Civilized Tribes, charged with negotiating agreements for the extinguishing of national land titles. President Grover Cleveland appointed the now-retired Senator Henry L. Dawes to head the commission, and in early 1894 the federal representatives made their way to the Indian Territory. The Cherokee National Council responded by appointing commissioners of its own, instructing them to confer with the Americans but to resist allotment and any change in tribal government. The council also sent Cherokee delegates to several intertribal conferences, meetings at which the Five Tribes declared their united opposition to allotment and their unwillingness to negotiate. As a memorial from one of these conferences explained, tribal leaders had no intention of participating in the "ruin and annihilation" of their people. "If the die is cast you must do these things yourselves and not ask and expect us to aid you in reducing ourselves to homeless wandering paupers." With the tribes unwilling to consider the American proposals, the talks sputtered, and the commissioners ended their first visit to Indian Territory with little to show for their efforts.[66]

The Dawes Commission's approach at this time was to assure the Indians that they had a say in determining their future, while threatening them politely. In May 1894, for example, Commissioner Meredith Kidd wrote to C. J. Harris, the Cherokees' principal chief, to discuss setting up a meeting between the commission and the Cherokees' representatives. To ensure that the Indians understood the situation, he informed Harris that allotment and a change of government were coming one way or another. The Cherokees had the choice of either making a generous agreement with the Dawes Commission or having allotment forced upon them through "drastic measures by the government of the United States."[67] Along the same lines, the Americans insisted that the United States was no longer capable of protecting the Five Tribes' rights. This amounted to a warning that if the Indians did not strike a deal with the commission, they would face the unhindered assaults of squatters, corporations, and Congress.[68]

Cherokee leaders, for their part, responded to the commission by reviewing the arguments against allotment and stalling as best they could. When the Americans submitted a formal proposal to the Cherokee government in July 1894, C. J. Harris asked that sufficient time be granted for the National Council and the Cherokee people to consider the matter, implying that this could take quite a while. He also suggested that if the Americans wanted new negotiations with the Cherokees, it would be best to resolve existing issues first – the removal of intruders, for example, and the settlement of old claims. To avoid carrying out standing commitments while asking for an allotment pact implied bad faith on the part of the Americans. "The impression prevails," Harris noted, "that it is the policy of your government to harass the Nations into a compliance with its wishes by delaying, if nothing more, the performance of its most solemn obligations to them."[69] The National Council reiterated that point several months later in a formal statement to the Dawes Commission. The United States should remove the intruders, as the treaties required, before asking for new negotiations. The council also reminded the commissioners that common landholding was written into the Cherokee constitution; thus, it would require an amendment before any change could be discussed. The tribe and the United States would have to take a number of time-consuming preliminary steps before negotiations could be freely and fairly entered.[70]

The Dawes Commission, however, was in no mood to wait. Soon after their return to Washington, the Americans submitted a highly negative report on the Indian Territory and added further damning testimony before congressional committees and the meetings of reform organizations. Conditions in the Indian country, they said, had deteriorated horribly. The territory was completely overrun by whites; some illegal intruders and others Americans invited by the Indians. These whites, along with the tribal elites, were exploiting the wealth of the common land while the full-bloods were excluded from benefiting from their patrimony. A handful of mixed-bloods and intermarried whites dominated the tribal governments, which they used for corrupt purposes. American citizens in the territory lacked a voice in government and access to schools and other services, as did many non-Cherokee tribal citizens, among them the freed people. Crime was on the rise everywhere, and the territory was fast approaching a state of anarchy. If the Indians continued to resist negotiations, the commission suggested, changes in land and government would have to be imposed upon the tribes unilaterally.[71]

Soon after the release of this report, new Cherokee delegates arrived in Washington and set out to control the damage. They followed the Dawes Commission around the capital as it met with the various congressional committees and with officials of the Interior Department, the Indians attempting to refute the commissioners' arguments before they had a chance to sink in. The delegates insisted that Dawes and his associates had been misinformed about the Indian country. They had put too much credence in the testimony of frontier whites, who were willing to say anything to speed the opening of the territory. "The misfortune of the commissioners," delegate Walter A. Duncan told the House judiciary committee, "was to go there and catch the rumors floating in the air, put forth from the little newspapers and people working for the dissolution of our country. They swarmed around them and put in their complaints, saying, Here is an Indian who has done so and so; there is a rich man who has a fine house . . . therefore, down with the Indian Territory."[72] While giving a full hearing to these dishonest elements, the commissioners tried to intimidate the Indian citizens and their legitimate representatives. They came "with a sword in one hand and the proposition of the Government in the other," as Duncan put it, with the commissioners insisting that if the tribes did not negotiate, Congress would force the matter. Starting this way, the commissioners themselves ensured that the Indians would resist.[73]

Yes, the delegates admitted, there was crime in the territory, but no more than in surrounding states. At any rate, all the worst criminals were white intruders, people whom the treaties obliged the United States to remove. It was true that Americans in the territory could not send their children to Cherokee schools; however, they had known this would be the case when they entered, and there were church and private schools open to all. It was also true that some tribal citizens had built up prosperous farms, but this did not mean that the land was monopolized. The Cherokee constitution allowed the National Council to regulate landholding to ensure that all had access. If monopoly ever threatened, the people had the power to correct the matter through their government. As for the full-bloods needing rescue, the delegates noted that traditional Cherokees themselves opposed allotment. One delegate, Roach Young, came as a full-blood representative, and, speaking through translators, he offered support for the positions taken by the other delegates. Young and the delegation as a whole stuck to the position that the full-bloods were not yet ready for allotment and American citizenship. They asked that the treaties be maintained until the Cherokees themselves decided that they were ready and asked for a change.[74]

In reporting back to the nation, the delegates urged the tribal government to stand firm. They recognized, however, that the Cherokees were facing very long odds. "It did seem as if the world were about to rise in arms against us," they wrote, describing their time in Washington. The Capitol and executive buildings were full of lawyers and lobbyists pressing for the end of tribal government, and copies of pro-allotment newspapers were everywhere. No one seemed to be willing to consider the Indians' side of the matter, not even the Cherokees' old friends. "Many of the great dailies, that a few years ago pleaded so persistently for the liberation of the slaves, are now insisting upon 'opening' our country," they noted, adding later that "even the heavy quarterlies, such as the North American Review, are being operated in the interests of our enemies." And the churches, which had once been Indian allies, were silent when it came to the rights of the Five Tribes. "No church assembly now passes resolutions against a violation of our treaties." The delegates did their best to broadcast the arguments against allotment, but they were outnumbered and faced with an enemy possessed of "a zeal that knows no pause." Quoting Tom Paine, they concluded that "as far as the Indian people are concerned, these are the days that try men's souls."[75]

The Dawes Commission went west again in the spring of 1895, but it achieved little more than it had the previous year. There were signs of weakening among the Choctaws, but otherwise the Five Tribes continued to resist and stall.[76] At this point, however, Congress came to the commissioners' aid. First, it proposed to extend the jurisdiction of federal courts over all people and all matters in the Indian Territory. The Five Tribes' treaties, in fact, authorized the creation of federal courts, but the Indians' own legal systems were to retain jurisdiction over cases involving only tribal citizens. As Cherokee leaders pointed out, the House and Senate were attempting to eliminate an entire branch of their government.[77] Even more threatening, Congress responded to the Dawes Commission's difficulties by authorizing it to begin surveying the lands and drawing up rolls for each tribe. In other words, it empowered the commission to begin the allotment process with or without the Indians' agreement or cooperation.[78]

In response to these actions, the tribes at last began to negotiate in earnest, and by 1898 all but the Cherokees had made allotment agreements. These still had to be ratified (a tortuous process in several cases), but after years of mostly futile effort, the Dawes Commission had finally made real progress. The Cherokee National Council appointed a new group of commissioners in 1896 and authorized it to deal with the Americans, but the talks, which took place in the spring and summer of 1897, ended in stalemate. For the Cherokees there were several sticking points. First, the Interior Department ordered the Dawes Commission to reserve 157,000 acres of tribal land to meet a claim by Delawares adopted as Cherokee citizens after the Civil War. The Cherokees demanded that that if allotment had to happen, then all the tribal land should be distributed equally to Cherokee citizens. The Delaware citizens of the nation would each receive a share, but this would amount to far less than the acreage that they claimed they were due. Second, the old issue of conditional land grants to railroads resurfaced. Midway through the 1897 talks, lawyers for the Missouri, Kansas, and Texas Railroad, the Cherokees' old enemy, informed the commissioners that they intended to sue for their conditional grants as soon as allotment began. By the Cherokees' reckoning, this could amount to as much as eight hundred thousand acres. Finally, there was the issue of the federal courts' jurisdiction. Congress had made good on its threat to extend the authority of U.S. courts, passing an act to that effect set to begin operating on the first day of 1898. The Cherokees insisted that their government, including the tribal courts, should remain in place until allotment was completed, something the Dawes Commission itself had promised. Eliminating whole branches of tribal government midway through the process would leave the Indians unprotected and invite abuse.[79]

Despite these issues, some of the Cherokee negotiators in 1897 still hoped to come to terms with the Dawes Commission. Former chief Bushyhead, for example, argued that they should make the best deal possible and then let the National Council and the Cherokee people decide how to proceed. He also held that the troublesome issues could be worked out satisfactorily in further talks and in federal courts. Others, however, insisted that the Americans had shown bad faith throughout and that there was no way that the Cherokees could negotiate. Walter A. Duncan, in particular, found the Dawes Commission's actions insulting, charging that the Americans had treated the Cherokees like dogs and slaves. "It is agreed on all hands that we have beat them on all questions," he noted. "We have beaten them in diplomacy all along, and it is only when they do something arbitrarily that they beat the Cherokee Nation." Referring to a sponsor of the federal court bill, he added, "I don't care if Berry transcends Jupiter with the grip of Heaven's lightening in his fist. I will not give in."[80] All the Cherokee representatives, meanwhile, recognized that, regardless of the terms, any allotment agreement would likely be opposed by many of their people. In the midst of the 1897 talks, the Keetoowah Society passed a set of resolutions opposing severalty and the end of tribal government. Around the same time, the Keetoowahs petitioned President William McKinley, declaring that the full-blood population was unanimously opposed to allotment. They noted that their children were in school and would be ready when they grew up to become American citizens, but they asked that the change be delayed until their own genera-tion was gone. Between the Americans' underhanded tactics and the Keetoowahs' opposition, it is not surprising that Cherokee negotia-tors failed to decide upon a course of action. They ended their 1897 meetings by simply stating that they could not treat under the present circumstances.[81]

It took the strongest possible federal action – short of sending in the army – to break the deadlock. The Curtis Act, passed in June 1898, abolished tribal laws, confirmed the extension of federal jurisdiction, and declared the residents of the Indian Territory to be under American authority. Principal Chief Samuel Mayes and the tribe's lawyers briefly pursued the idea of bringing a test of the new law to the Supreme Court (the Curtis Act, after all, violated the treaties), but they must have known that their time was almost up.[82] As the Dawes Commis-sion later reported, "the Cherokees now began to realize the sensations of 'a man without a country'" and started to bend.[83] In November 1898, the National Council appointed a new set of negotiators, and meetings with the Dawes Commission resumed the following month. Even under this considerable pressure, Cherokee representatives tried to win concessions from the Americans. They proposed, for example, that the allotments granted to freed people be limited to forty acres and that black citizens receive no per capita payments, articles that continued the well-established practice of trying to limit black citizens' access to tribal resources. They worked to have the Delaware and railroad land claims kept out of the agreement. They revived the idea of the Cherokees' sending a delegate to Congress, asking that they be allowed to elect a tribal representative until such time as they were included in a new state. They protested when it was suggested that only English speakers would be allowed to sit on juries, requesting that court proceedings remain bilingual. And what was most creative, they submitted a plan whereby Cherokees who so desired would be able to select adjoining allotments, which they would then hold collectively under a corporate title. Had it survived, this proposal, which was meant as a concession to the full-bloods, would have empowered culturally conservative communities to preserve common landholding and a vestige of the tribe as an institution.[84]

None of those provisions made it into the document signed by the Cherokees and the Dawes Commission in January 1899, but in several respects the agreement was still a generous settlement (at least by allotment policy terms). Each Cherokee citizen was to receive the equivalent of 120 acres of the average allotable land, and the agreement stipulated that no excess tribal land other than townsites would be sold. Cherokees charged with crimes would be tried in courts located within the boundaries of the old nation, and Congress was urged to establish more courts within Cherokee communities. Presumably, these articles were meant to guard against Cherokees' being subjected to courts dominated by non-Indians. Particularly interesting was a provision that, had it gone into effect, would have altered the political landscape of the West. The Americans promised that unless the Cherokees consented they would never be included in a territory or state except one created from the lands of the Five Tribes. That is, Oklahoma and the Indian Territory would almost certainly enter the Union as separate states.[85]

The Cherokees ratified this agreement in a hurried special election at the end of January, but apparently it conceded too much to the Indians for the taste of American legislators. Congress refused to act upon it, and the Dawes Commission went back to try again. Negotiations resumed in 1900, and a second agreement was made. But this time many Cherokees disapproved of the terms. Some feared that under the deal's enrollment provisions illegal intruders might receive land, while others felt the proposed allotments were too small. The agreement limited each citizen to a "homestead" of forty acres, inalienable and untaxed for twenty-one years, and added forty more acres that could be sold (what later came to be called "surplus"). The provisions regarding courts and state government were removed, which probably helped turn Cherokees against the document. The Keetoowah Society, meanwhile, declared its opposition to any allotment at all. In November 1900 a convention of Keetoowahs at Tahlequah passed resolutions urging Cherokees to resist having their names placed on the allotment rolls. The Dawes Commission, they declared, had no right to make such rolls without Cherokee consent. Moreover, they rejected the idea that freed people and intermarried whites had a right to Cherokee land. In adopting them, the tribe had granted them political and civil rights, but the land belonged exclusively to Cherokees by blood. Some of the freed people, it should be noted, did possess Cherokee ancestry, but Cherokees tended to categorize them as strictly non-Indian. When a second special election was held in April 1901, the tribe voted the new agreement down.[86]

One last set of negotiations took place in 1902 under increasingly coercive conditions. By this time, the Interior Department had ordered the closing of the tribal rolls, and federal authorities had begun to sell the property of the Cherokee government. It seemed allotment was going to take place with or without the tribe, and at this point even some of those who had earlier resisted enrollment began to submit. In July the Cherokee and American governments again completed terms. Each tribal citizen would receive the forty-acre homestead, but the surplus was increased to seventy acres. Homesteads would be inalienable and untaxed for twenty-one years; surplus would be inalienable for five years. The favorable articles regarding courts and state government remained absent. The 157,000 acres demanded by the Delawares were set aside until a federal court ruled on the claim. Intermarried whites and the freed people were to receive full allotments, although they ended up being enrolled separately. The rolls were scheduled to be closed in September 1902, and the tribal government was to cease to exist on March 4, 1906. The tribe and the United States ratified this agreement in August 1902, although by this point Cherokees may have considered ratification little more than an empty formality. The United States had forced the tribe's submission, no less than it had the removal of the Cherokee majority in the 1830s.[87]

Yet even after this apparent end, there were last-ditch efforts to maintain a semblance of the old Indian Territory. Among the Cherokees, a faction of Keetoowahs, known as Nighthawks, continued to resist enrollment. Affirming the sacredness of the treaties, they refused to believe that the United States would break its word as long as the Cherokees themselves remained true to the old agreements. They tied their resistance, meanwhile, to the preservation and revival of elements of Cherokee religion and other traditional practices. The Nighthawk Keetoowahs sought in the older Cherokee culture the power to continue the struggle against allotment after the tribe's elected leaders had given up.[88] Other Indians adopted a different strategy. Many of the Five Tribes' leaders allied with a segment of the white population of the Indian Territory in an effort to secure separate statehood for the area that is now eastern Oklahoma. If they had to give up the Indian nation, they hoped at least to keep the homelands of the Five Tribes distinct from Oklahoma. By the turn of the century the Oklahoma Territory had a large population, and tribal leaders feared (quite correctly) that if their people were thrown together with that population in a single state, the Indians' interests would suffer. They participated in a campaign to create two states: one from the Oklahoma Territory and the second from the lands of the Five Tribes. In 1905 a convention met at Muskogee and wrote up a constitution for the new state of Sequoyah.[89]

Both of these efforts failed. Many of the Nighthawks eventually relented and accepted enrollment and individual lands or else found that allotments had been created for them. As many as two thousand Cherokees refused to claim their lands, but they could not stop the implementation of the policy. The Sequoyah constitution, although supported by most of the citizens of the Five Tribes, never came to a vote in Congress. In fact, it probably accelerated the movement toward single statehood. It became one of the models used by the convention that drafted the constitution for the one state of Oklahoma in late 1906 and early 1907.[90]

As tribal leaders' resolve weakened, the kind of writings explored in this study, writings in which Cherokees explained the necessity and possibility of Indian nationhood, faded from the record. More concerned with winning the most favorable terms possible for tribal dissolution, they no longer took the time to imagine a future for the Indian nation within America. That project would await later generations of Indian people in the new century.

Epilogue

In opposing allotment, the leaders of the Five Tribes predicted that land in severalty and the end of tribal government would impoverish their people, rather than make them into self-sufficient American farmers. Dishonest frontier whites would rush into the former Nations and do everything possible to steal the land once the protection of common title was removed. Only well-educated Indians and those experienced with the American economy and law would be able to protect themselves and take advantage of the benefits promised by the policy's advocates. The majority, the "common Indians" for whom eastern philanthropists expressed such sympathy, would be ruined.

That forecast proved all too accurate. Some members of the Five Tribes did, in fact, prosper with land in severalty and American citizenship. A few rose to the ranks of Oklahoma's political and economic elite. But many more found themselves preyed upon by their new neighbors (and sometimes by their own people), caught up in what Angie Debo called an "orgy of plunder and exploitation probably unparalleled in American history."[1] As Debo meticulously documented in research conducted in the 1930s, the Americans drawn to the Indian Territory included enough thieves and unethical lawyers and businessmen to make tribal leaders' most dire predictions come true. At the end of the Civil War, the Five Tribes owned more than nineteen million acres of land. By the end of the allotment era, the great majority of this land was owned by non-Indians.[2]

Early on, while most allotments remained inalienable, leasing offered the easiest way to gain control of Indian property. Grafters, as they came to be known, sought out uneducated and inexperienced Indians and offered to help them select their surplus, the allotted land separate from the forty-acre homesteads. They then proposed to lease the land in question, usually at extremely low rates. Successful grafters were able to group multiple leases, which they then rented at a profit to a third party. Some entrepreneurs, meanwhile, invented methods of circumventing the restrictions on land sales. Leases would sometimes include provisions granting the renter ownership of the land when the allottee died; in other cases land dealers would convince allottees to sign power-of-attorney instruments giving the dealer the right to sell the land whenever restrictions ended. Some businessmen simply drew up deeds and bought allotments, believing that in time their ownership would be upheld in American courts. [3]

While this lucrative business proceeded, Congress greatly expanded the grafters' opportunities by easing restrictions on some allotted land. In 1904 a new federal law declared alienable the surplus belonging to adult white and black allottees (though homesteads still could not be sold). The same act allowed the secretary of the interior to remove restrictions on the surplus of adult Indians considered competent to handle their property. Four years later, a second act removed all remaining restrictions on white and black allottees and did the same for Native Americans who were less than one-half Indian by blood. Those who were between one-half and three-quarters Indian by blood were authorized to sell their surplus, while land belonging to Indians with a blood quantum of three-fourths or greater remained completely inalienable. [4]

Between them, these two laws made over thirteen million acres eligible for sale, and their passage set off a frenzy of activity, as speculators raced to find allottees willing to part with their property at low prices. "Picturesque scenes were enacted in the county seats," Debo wrote. "The object of the land buyers was to bring as many allottees as possible to town, entertain them royally, and secure deeds and record them before a rival dealer could record a similar instrument." [5] Land that could not be bought could still be exploited through the judicial system. Children with allotments fell within the jurisdiction of Oklahoma's county courts, probate judges having authority to appoint guardians to manage the minors' property. These children numbered around sixty thousand, and their property, including oil valuation, was worth at least $150 million. Handling children's land became a profitable enterprise, with guardians leasing the property for agriculture or mineral development and pocketing most or all proceeds. Guardianship appointments became a form of political spoils as county judges paid supporters off with Indian wards.[6]

The Indian Bureau and the reform organizations were not idle during this period. When scandalous activities came to light, they made sincere efforts to adjust the allotment system and correct abuses. As Debo noted, however, attempts to fix the problems often seemed to create new avenues for cheating, while complicating an already confusing situation. Advocacy on behalf of exploited Indians, meanwhile, was often resisted by Oklahoma's political leaders. Already suspicious of the Indian Bureau's influence in the state, they reacted jealously to anything that looked like interference in their affairs. Defending Indians invariably brought conflict, while it did not always help the allottees.[7]

In light of all this, it is worth remembering that the Five Tribes had offered the United States an alternative. Tribal leaders in the late nineteenth century had urged the federal government to remove the intruders and to help them maintain their borders. With this constructive use of American power secured, they believed, the tribes could be left to manage their own internal affairs. Regulating frontier Americans in this way would have been a monumental task for federal authorities, but would it have been more difficult or complicated than allotment? Land in severalty and American citizenship were meant to simplify Indian affairs by eliminating the differences between Indians and other sorts of Americans. As it happened, the policy made the Indian Bureau's work far more complex, too complex to be performed effectively by even the most diligent and well-meaning officers. From this perspective, helping the Five Tribes maintain their separation seems not only a more just policy than allotment but a more practical one as well.

At the end of the 1930s, Debo surveyed the wreck of the old Indian Territory and remarked, "It is highly improbable that any of these five extinct Indian republics will ever collect its scattered members and regain its lost autonomy."[8] Yet little more than a generation after she wrote those words, the highly improbable happened. The Cherokees and their sister Nations in eastern Oklahoma reassembled and by the close of the twentieth century stood on as firm political ground as they had enjoyed since the Civil War. Having described the dismantling of the nineteenth-century Cherokee Nation, I should end by marking its reemergence.

Allotment failed to extinguish the tribe as a political entity. Tribal government was supposed to disappear in 1906, but as the date approached, there remained much unsettled business with the United States. The allotment process was not yet finished, and Indian leaders requested that some kind of extension be granted. The Five Tribes Act, passed by Congress in 1906, provided that the federal government assume most of the tribal governments' duties but retained the chiefs and tribal attorneys, posts that were to be filled by presidential appointees. Even after allotment had been completed, federal officials found it convenient to preserve this vestige of the old Indian Nations for administrative purposes. The irony here, as Rennard and William Strickland point out, is that a policy begun as an effort to eliminate Indian tribes ended up confirming their continued existence, in however constrained a form. Indian Territory leaders had long contended that the tribal governments were the most effective institutions through which the United States could pursue its legitimate Indian policy goals. Federal authorities seem to have accepted a version of that argument at the moment when they had hoped to dispense with the tribe forever.[9]

Indian people, meanwhile, preserved remnants of their national institutions on their own. Most of the Five Tribes held informal councils, and culturally conservative Indians maintained organizations that sometimes acted like the old tribal governments. Among the Cherokees, a number of different versions of the Keetoowah Society survived. These independent groups selected their own officers and held their own councils. At times, they tried to represent the Cherokees in dealing with the Interior Department or Indian Bureau, offering their elected leaders as alternatives to the appointed tribal executives. Perhaps more important, the various Keetoowah organizations kept alive a Cherokee sense of being a people, a sense that a distinct tribal community existed despite political reorganization and the loss of the land.[10]

Developments in the 1930s and 1940s then set the stage for the revival of tribal government and the reassertion of Cherokee sovereignty. Under John Collier, Franklin Roosevelt's commissioner of Indian affairs, the Indian Bureau reversed course, ending the allotment policy and fostering what Debo called "the new trend." In 1934 Collier and Interior Secretary Harold Ickes convinced Congress to pass the Indian Reorganization Act (IRA), which allowed for the creation of new tribal governments and set aside funds for the recovery of Indian lands and for economic development programs. Oklahoma's political leaders, led by Senator Elmer Thomas, opposed the law and managed to secure an amendment excluding the state from its provisions. Thomas contended that the IRA would prove a step backward for Oklahoma Indians, most of whom neither possessed reservations nor required special status. He was supported in this position by many non-Indian Oklahomans, most of the state's newspapers, and a number of influential Native Americans, such as Cherokee Congressman William Wirt Hastings.[11]

Other Oklahoma Indians, however, wanted the IRA, or at least endorsed the general goals of land recovery and greater autonomy for Native communities. A convention of Keetoowahs, for example, passed resolutions urging the application of the law to Oklahoma, as did similar meetings in other tribes. Several of the Five Tribes' appointed leaders likewise declared their support for the law. Responding to Indian opinion, Thomas secured new legislation to bring some of the principles of the IRA to the state. Passed in 1936, the Oklahoma Indian Welfare Act (OIWA) allowed the Interior Department to purchase land for Indians, and it created a fund to provide economic development loans. It also allowed groups of Native Americans to draw up constitutions and incorporate, forming organizations that, once chartered, could manage funds and hold property collectively. This last provision, it is worth noting, was quite similar to an article that the Cherokees had sought in negotiations with the Dawes Commission. As the last chapter mentioned, tribal representatives in 1899 proposed that groups of Cherokees be allowed to take adjoining allotments, which would then be held in common under a corporate charter.[12]

The 1936 law did little to alleviate the poverty of Oklahoma Indians, but it encouraged some to begin working for political change. At the end of the decade, three Creek towns incorporated under the OIWA and gained recognition as distinct political communities, actions that revived the tribe's tradition of town autonomy. Around the same time, some of the Keetoowahs began to explore a similar move. Several Keetoowah organizations joined in drafting a new constitution and electing a common set of officers. They then asked that the federal government acknowledge them as a new tribal organization under the terms of the OIWA. In 1946, after repeated requests, Congress granted them recognition as the United Keetoowah Band of Cherokees. In the following years, the band would sometimes act in conjunction with the federally appointed tribal executives, while at other times it worked to establish itself as an alternative Cherokee government. Democratically elected, the band's leaders believed that they enjoyed greater legitimacy than did the appointees and that they were better able to speak for the Cherokee people.[13]

During this time, the appointed leaders were also moving toward recreating tribal government. In July 1948 Principal Chief Bartley Milam called a national convention at Tahlequah, the main function of which was to create a Cherokee executive committee – in essence, a new tribal council. Milam and others in the tribe felt that an expanded administration could help Cherokees deal with local and state governments while allowing greater participation in federal welfare and economic-development programs. Equally important, the Cherokees needed tribal officers and a legal team to prosecute lawsuits against the United States. Two years earlier, Congress had created the Indian Claims Commission (ICC), an agency before which tribes could litigate past grievances against the federal government. The Cherokees had several potential claims, the most important of which concerned the terms by which the United States had compelled the tribe to part with the Outlet lands at the end of the nineteenth century. Among the first duties of the new executive committee was to begin the process of filing with the ICC.[14]

Milam died less than a year after the convention, and President Harry Truman, at the executive committee's urging, appointed W. W. Keeler as the new principal chief. Keeler would occupy the office for almost three decades, becoming, in Rennard and William Strickland's words, "the most powerful, enigmatic, and controversial Cherokee tribal leader since John Ross."[15] Keeler was the president and CEO of the Phillips Petroleum Corporation, and he brought to the Cherokee leadership great personal influence and national connections. He proved quite successful at drawing federal funds to the tribe, particularly those available through Lyndon Johnson's Great Society programs, and under his leadership the Cherokee administration became a powerful economic and political force in northeastern Oklahoma. Some in the tribe, however, felt that Keeler failed to understand the needs and desires of culturally conservative Cherokees and that his administration empowered the tribe's more acculturated members at the expense of traditional communities. In addition, at several points during the Keeler era tribal officers faced charges of mismanaging Cherokee funds and concealing their activities. Today, opinion in Oklahoma is still sharply divided regarding the longtime chief and his legacy.[16]

One thing, however, is certain about the Keeler administration: under its authority, a functioning Cherokee state reemerged. In the early 1960s, the ICC ruled in favor of the tribe's Outlet claim and awarded the Cherokees over $14 million. Most of this money was distributed per capita to Cherokee citizens by blood, but several million dollars were left in the hands of the chief.[17] Keeler and his associates used this new capital to invest in numerous tribal projects, among them the Cherokee National Historical Society, an enterprise that drew tourism to the area while encouraging nationalism among Cherokee people. The Great Society and War on Poverty, meanwhile, provided funds with which the Keeler government established and administered a variety of additional programs. Thus, with the help of the United States, the Cherokee executives laid the foundation for a new tribal structure. Over the course of the decade, they found themselves heading a growing Cherokee bureaucracy overseeing an expanding collection of projects and services.[18]

As new tribal institutions evolved, the Cherokees recreated a representative national government. In the late 1960s, responding in part to criticism of the undemocratic nature of the Cherokee leadership, Keeler and the executive committee established a system of community representatives. These were elected local delegates who eventually replaced the executive committee as the chief's advisers. Next, Cherokee officials joined with other eastern Oklahoma Indians in requesting federal legislation authorizing the Five Tribes to resume electing their principal chiefs. Congress passed the necessary act, and in August 1971 Cherokees voted in their first nationwide election since 1903. Keeler, running against five other candidates, won by a very broad margin. Finally, the chief completed the transformation by calling for a new Cherokee constitution, one that would return to the tribe a fully realized democratic government. A national committee drafted the document, which established a fifteen-member tribal council, a judicial tribunal, and an executive consisting of principal and deputy chiefs and a cabinet. In 1976 this easily won ratification by Cherokee voters in a special election. With that act, the Cherokees regained a status similar to their status in the nineteenth century, that of a functioning Indian republic.[19]

Today, the Cherokees' nineteenth-century political experiment continues. To be sure, the system established in the 1970s has not always run smoothly. As with other democratic governments, there have been disputed elections and bruising internal fights. In the late 1990s the Cherokees experienced a major political crisis when allegations that the principal chief had misappropriated funds led to a long, angry standoff between the chief and the tribal judiciary.[20] Yet the Cherokees have won back the right to determine among themselves the answers to their problems. To paraphrase nineteenth-century delegates, they have regained the right to find their own destiny. And if the nightmare of allotment suggests anything, it is that the future for Indian peoples has to begin with this kind of autonomy. In 2003, Cherokees were preparing to vote on a new constitution, one that expanded the council and judiciary and attempted to provide greater balance among the branches of government. Cherokee leaders were working to eliminate an article in the earlier constitution that required federal approval of amendments, a move that, when completed, would represent a significant reassertion of tribal sovereignty. The tribe had recently opened a new office in Washington to coordinate lobbying and watch over Congress and the Indian Bureau – something William Penn Adair or Dennis Bushyhead would have immediately understood. Tribal leaders were even exploring the old idea of securing a Cherokee delegate to the U.S. House of Representatives, a treaty provision long dormant but never dead. Cherokees were carrying on the work of the nineteenth century, the work of adapting the Indian nation to a changing modern America.[21]

NOTES

Abbreviations

GM   Gilcrease Museum, Tulsa, Oklahoma
NA   National Archives, Washington DC
OHS   Oklahoma Historical Society, Oklahoma City
WHC   Western History Collection, University of Oklahoma, Norman

INTRODUCTION

1. "Indian Territory" was never a formal political entity in the way that, say, Kansas was a territory of the United States. The term here refers to the lands in what is today Oklahoma that were bought by the Cherokees, Choctaws, Chickasaws, Creeks, and Seminoles in exchange for their eastern homelands. The capitalization reflects common nineteenth-century usage.

2. Letter of W. P. Adair, Cherokee Delegate, Addressed to His People, September 20, 1870, folder 3792, roll 38, Cherokee Nation Papers, WHC, 1.

3. Letter of W. P. Adair, September 20, 1870, 4.

4. Letter of W. P. Adair, September 20, 1870, 7–8.

5. For example, Walter H. Conser, Jr., "John Ross and the Cherokee Resistance Campaign, 1833–1838," *Journal of Southern History* 44 (May 1978): 191–212; William G. McLoughlin, *Cherokees and Missionaries, 1789–1839* (New Haven CT: Yale University Press, 1984); William G. McLoughlin, *Cherokee Renascence in the New Republic* (Princeton NJ: Princeton University Press, 1986); William G. McLoughlin, *After the Trail of Tears: The Cherokees' Struggle for Sovereignty, 1839–1880* (Chapel Hill: University of North Carolina Press, 1993); H. Craig Miner, *The Corporation and the Indian: Tribal Sovereignty and Industrial Civilization in Indian Territory, 1865–1907* (1976, reprint; Norman: University of Oklahoma Press, 1988); Rennard Strickland and William Strickland, "Beyond the Trail of Tears: One Hundred Fifty Years of Cherokee Survival," in *Cherokee Removal: Before and After*, ed. William Anderson (Athens: University of Georgia Press, 1991), 112–38; Morris L. Wardell, *A Political History of the Cherokee Nation, 1838–1907* (1938, reprint; Norman: University of Oklahoma Press, 1977).

6. For example, Arnold Krupat, "Figures and the Law: Rhetorical Readings of Congressional and Cherokee Texts," in *Ethnocriticism: Ethnography, Literature, History* (Berkeley and Los Angeles: University of California Press, 1992), 129–63; Theda Perdue, ed., *Cherokee Editor: The Writings of Elias Boudinot* (Knoxville: University of Tennessee Press, 1993).

7. Francis Paul Prucha's work offers this perspective in a particularly strong fashion. See Francis Paul Prucha, *The Great Father: The United States Government and the American Indians* (Lincoln: University of Nebraska Press, 1984); Francis Paul Prucha, *American Indian Treaties: The History of a Political Anomaly* (Berkeley and Los Angeles: University of California Press, 1994).

8. Prucha, *Great Father*, 2: 609–757; Frederick E. Hoxie, *A Final Promise: The Campaign to Assimilate the Indians, 1880–1920* (Lincoln: University of Nebraska Press, 1984).

9. Alan Trachtenberg, *The Incorporation of America: Culture and Society in the Gilded Age* (New York: Hill and Wang, 1982).

10. Krupat, "Figures and the Law."

11. Bhabha's most important essays have been collected in Homi K. Bhabha, *The Location of Culture* (London: Routledge, 1994). I will cite this collection rather than the original journal articles. I have also made use of several writers who have commented on Bhabha's work: Robert Young, *White Mythologies: Writing History and the West* (London: Routledge, 1990), especially chapter 8; Jenny Sharpe, "Figures of Colonial Resistance," *Modern Fiction Studies* 35 (Spring 1989): 137–55.

12. Bhabha explains his idea of the "ambivalence of colonial discourse" most clearly in "Of Mimicry and Man: The Ambivalence of Colonial Discourse" and "Signs Taken for Wonders: Questions of Ambivalence and Authority under a Tree Outside of Delhi, May, 1817," in Bhabha, *Location of Culture*, 85–92, 102–22. Bhabha's concern for ambivalence developed in part from his critique of Edward Said's *Orientalism*. Bhabha criticized Said for overlooking division and contradiction within orientalist discourse – for describing orientalism as a hegemonic discourse that could only be attacked from the outside. As Bhabha saw it, Said's own analysis implied the existence of internal dissention. Bhabha attempted to turn this problem into a positive line of investigation by focusing on ambivalence within European stereotyping and suggesting that the existence of such ambivalence implied the possibility of resistance by colonized peoples. Homi K. Bhabha, "Difference,

Discrimination, and the Discourse of Colonialism," in *The Politics of Theory*, ed. Francis Barker et al. (Colchester, England: University of Essex, 1983), 194–211. See also Young, *White Mythologies*, 141–45.

13. Bhabha, "Signs Taken for Wonders," 111.

14. Bhabha writes that the authority of a colonial power is never fixed. It is always problematic. "To be authoritative, its [the colonial power's] rules of recognition must represent consensual knowledge or opinion; to be powerful, these rules of recognition must be breached in order to represent the exorbitant objects of discrimination that lie beyond its purview." Bhabha, "Signs Taken for Wonders," 111.

15. McLoughlin, *Cherokee Renascence*, 306.

16. The Cherokee Nation Papers housed in the Western History Collection at Oklahoma University (Norman) and the Cherokee National Records housed at the Oklahoma Historical Society (Oklahoma City) contain most of these bills from the post–Civil War era. See, for example, Act Instructing the Delegation, December 4, 1873, Cherokee National Records, federal relations, roll 77, OHS; Act Instructing the Delegation, December 12, 1878, folder 491, roll 5, Cherokee Nation Papers, WHC.

17. Gary E. Moulton, *John Ross: Cherokee Chief* (Athens: University of Georgia Press, 1978), 1–33.

18. Paul Kelton, "William Penn Adair: Cherokee Slaveholder and Indian Freedom Advocate," *Chronicles of Oklahoma* 77 (Spring 1999): 22–39.

19. The term "Five Civilized Tribes" is problematic, insofar as it suggests that the Creeks, Cherokees, Choctaws, Seminoles, and Chickasaws experienced a uniform and thorough cultural transformation in the nineteenth century. The term ignores the great complexity of southeastern Indian cultural history. I prefer simply "Five Tribes," although whenever possible I use individual tribal names.

1. THE LONG AND INTIMATE CONNECTION

1. The best accounts of Cherokee removal appear in the following: William G. McLoughlin, *Cherokees and Missionaries, 1789–1839* (New Haven CT: Yale University Press, 1984); William G. McLoughlin, *Cherokee Renascence in the New Republic* (Princeton NJ: Princeton University Press, 1986); Thurman Wilkins, *Cherokee Tragedy: The Ridge Family and the Decimation of a People* (1970, revised; Norman: University of Oklahoma Press, 1986); Gary Moulton,

John Ross: Cherokee Chief (Athens: University of Georgia Press, 1978); Theda Perdue, "The Conflict Within," in *Cherokee Removal: Before and After*, ed. William Anderson, (Athens: University of Georgia Press, 1991) 48–63; Walter H. Conser, Jr., "John Ross and the Cherokee Resistance Campaign, 1833–1838," *Journal of Southern History* 44 (May 1978): 191–212. For the removal policy, see Francis Paul Prucha, *American Indian Policy in the Formative Years* (Cambridge MA: Harvard University Press, 1962); Ronald Satz, *American Indian Policy in the Jacksonian Era* (Lincoln: University of Nebraska Press, 1975); Grant Forman, *Indian Removal* (Norman: University of Oklahoma Press, 1938); Mary Young, "Indian Removal and the Attack on Tribal Autonomy: The Cherokee Case," in *Indians of the Lower South: Past and Present*, ed. John Mahon (Pensacola FL: Gulf Coast History and Humanities Conference, 1975), 125–42.

2. For activities of the various delegations during the removal crisis of the late 1820s and 1830s, see McLoughlin, *Cherokee Renascence*, 411–47. See also Principal Chief John Ross's messages to the Cherokee people in *The Papers of Chief John Ross*, ed. Gary Moulton, 2 vols. (Norman: University of Oklahoma Press, 1985). (Hereafter cited as *Ross Papers*.) For example: Annual Message, October 14, 1829, *Ross Papers*, 1:169–73; To the Cherokees, April 14, 1831, *Ross Papers*, 1:215–19. For instructions to delegates from the Cherokee government, see, for example, To Richard Taylor, John Ridge, and William S. Coodey, November 19, 1830, December 1, 1831, *Ross Papers*, 1:206–207, 232–33.

3. McLoughlin finds the beginning of the Cherokees' development as lobbyists and practitioners of public relations in the removal crisis of 1817–19. McLoughlin, *Cherokee Renascence*, 278–79.

4. To the Senate and House of Representatives, February 22, 1837, *Ross Papers*, 1:471.

5. Robert Berkhofer, *The White Man's Indian: Images of the American Indian from Columbus to the Present* (New York: Knopf, 1978), 38–49; Francis Paul Prucha, *The Great Father: The United States Government and the American Indians* (Lincoln: University of Nebraska Press, 1984), 35–60.

6. Prucha, *Great Father*, 89–158; Bernard Sheehan, *Seeds of Extinction: Jeffersonian Philanthropy and the American Indian* (Chapel Hill: University of North Carolina Press, 1973), 4–11, 15–44, 119–47; Robert E. Bieder, *Science Encounters the Indian, 1820–1880: The Early Years of American Ethnology* (Norman: University of Oklahoma Press, 1986), 7–11; Ronald Takaki, *Iron Cages: Race and Culture in Nineteenth – Century America* (New York: Knopf, 1979),

55–65. Herman J. Viola, *Thomas L. McKenney: Architect of America's Early Indian Policy, 1816–1830* (Chicago: Sage Books, 1974), 6–46.

7. McLoughlin, *Cherokee Renascence*, 21–29, 34–40; McLoughlin, *Cherokees and Missionaries*, 34–36, 101–106, 143–44, 150–53.

8. McLoughlin, *Cherokee Renascence*, 58–76; McLoughlin, *Cherokees and Missionaries*, 124–49; Theda Perdue, *Cherokee Women: Gender and Culture Change, 1700–1835* (Lincoln: University of Nebraska Press, 1998), 115–34.

9. Theda Perdue, *"Mixed Blood" Indians: Racial Construction in the Early South* (Athens: University of Georgia Press, 2003), 33–69; Moulton, *John Ross*, 2–14.

10. McLoughlin, *Cherokee Renascence*, 139–42, 224–27, 284–95, 394–401; Rennard Strickland, *Fire and the Spirits: Cherokee Law from Clan to Court* (Norman: University of Oklahoma Press, 1975), 40–66; Duane Champagne, *Social Order and Political Change: Constitutional Governments among the Cherokee, the Choctaw, the Chickasaw, and the Creek* (Stanford CA: Stanford University Press, 1992), 92–107, 127–43. Champagne argues that while the bicultural Cherokees led in the transformation of Cherokee law and institutions, they did so only with the approval of the great majority of the tribe. There was broad consensus in favor of political change, which the bicultural Cherokees, with their special experience, were able to translate into practice.

11. Prucha, *Great Father*, 195–97.

12. Prucha, *Great Father*, 186, 197–98; McLoughlin, *Cherokee Renascence*, 217–20; Carl J. Vipperman, "Forcibly If We Must: The Georgia Case for the Cherokee Removal, 1802–1832," *Journal of Cherokee Studies* 3 (Spring 1978): 104–11. For the legal doctrines regarding Native American land rights and ownership, see Tim Allen Garrison, *The Legal Ideology of Removal: The Southern Judiciary and the Sovereignty of Native American Nations* (Athens: University of Georgia Press, 2002), 59–102.

13. Prucha, *Great Father*, 79–88; McLoughlin, *Cherokee Renascence*, 203–205; Francis Paul Prucha, *American Indian Treaties: The History of a Political Anomaly* (Berkeley and Los Angeles: University of California Press, 1994), 152–55.

14. Sheehan, *Seeds of Extinction*, 148–81; Viola, *Thomas L. McKenney*, 185–99; Brian W. Dippie, *The Vanishing American: White Attitudes and U.S. Indian Policy* (Middletown CT: Wesleyan University Press, 1982), 165–90.

15. Prucha, *Great Father*, 183–89; McLoughlin, *Cherokee Renascence*, 128–37, 147–67, 221–59.

16. McLoughlin, *Cherokee Renascence*, 128–62, 221–57.

17. McLoughlin, *Cherokee Renascence*, 292, 302–308; Champagne, *Social Order and Political Change*, 129–36.

18. McLoughlin, *Cherokee Renascence*, 223–26, 394–401, 413–28; McLoughlin, *Cherokees and Missionaries*, 266–86; John A. Andrew, III, *From Revivals to Removal: Jeremiah Evarts, the Cherokee Nation, and the Search for the Soul of America* (Athens: University of Georgia Press, 1992), 169–228.

19. Theda Perdue, ed., *Cherokee Editor: The Writings of Elias Boudinot* (Athens: University of Georgia Press, 1983), 3–25.

20. Prucha, *Great Father*, 191–94; Moulton, *John Ross*, 34–40.; McLoughlin, *Cherokees and Missionaries*, 240–54; Andrew, *From Revivals to Removal*, 184–91. Evarts's "William Penn" essays are reprinted in *Cherokee Removal: The "William Penn" Essays and Other Writings by Jeremiah Evarts*, ed. Francis Paul Prucha (Knoxville: University of Tennessee Press, 1981).

21. Jill Norgren, *The Cherokee Cases: The Confrontation of Law and Politics* (New York: McGraw – Hill, 1996), 49–62, 98–111; Garrison, *Legal Ideology of Removal*, 125–50.

22. Norgren, *Cherokee Cases*, 112–22; Garrison, *Legal Ideology of Removal*, 169–97.

23. The law regarding the practical exercise of federal power over the states in cases like these was unclear. When Georgia refused to free the prisoners, Jackson cited this problem as his reason for not enforcing the court's decision. In essence, a technicality allowed him to ignore the decision while maintaining the appearance of legal propriety. Norgren, *Cherokee Cases*, 123–33.

24. Prucha, *American Indian Policy in the Formative Years*, 233–49; Ronald N. Satz, "Rhetoric versus Reality: The Indian Policy of Andrew Jackson," in Anderson, *Cherokee Removal*, 29–54; Francis Paul Prucha, "Andrew Jackson's Indian Policy: A Reassessment," *Journal of American History* 56 (December 1969): 527–39.

25. To Hugh Montgomery, July 20, 1830, *Ross Papers*, 1:193.

26. To William Carroll, August 29, 1829, *Ross Papers*, 1:167.

27. To Hugh Montgomery, November 25, 1830, *Ross Papers*, 1:208; To Lewis Cass, February 14, 1833, *Ross Papers*, 1:261–64; To Andrew Jackson, March 12, 1834, *Ross Papers*, 1:277–79; *Cherokee Phoenix*, April 16, 1831, in Perdue, ed., *Cherokee Editor*, 125–27.

28. *Cherokee Phoenix*, November 12, 1831, in Perdue, *Cherokee Editor*, 141.

29. *Cherokee Phoenix*, January 28, June 17, 1829, in Perdue, *Cherokee Editor*,

104, 108–9; To Andrew Jackson, March 12, 1834, *Ross Papers*, 1:277–79; Memorial to the Senate and House of Representatives, May 17, 1834, *Ross Papers*, 1:290–92.

30. I base this on the genealogies compiled by the early Cherokee historian Emmet Starr. Emmet Starr, *History of the Cherokee Indians and Their Legends and Folklore* (Oklahoma City: Warden, 1921), 350, 366–68, 410–11; Moulton, *John Ross*, 1–7; Carolyn Thomas Foreman, "The Coodey Family of the Indian Territory," *Chronicles of Oklahoma* 25 (Spring 1947): 323–25.

31. Starr, *History of the Cherokee Indians*, 50–53, 103, 263–64, 295; Foreman, "Coodey Family," 326–35.

32. To the Senate and House of Representatives, February 27, 1829, *Ross Papers*, 1:157.

33. Moulton, *John Ross*, 37–38.

34. To the Senate and House of Representatives, February 27, 1829, *Ross Papers*, 1:154–55.

35. *Ross Papers*, 1:155.

36. *Ross Papers*, 1:156.

37. *Ross Papers*, 1:155–56.

38. *Ross Papers*, 1:157.

39. *Ross Papers*, 1:156.

40. Norgren, *Cherokee Cases*, 49–60.

41. Robert A. Williams, Jr., *Linking Arms Together: American Indian Visions of Law and Peace, 1600–1800* (New York: Routledge, 1999), 32–51.

42. For example, To William Carroll, August 29, 1829, *Ross Papers*, 1:167–68; To Andrew Jackson, March 12, 1834, *Ross Papers*, 1:277–78; To the Senate and House of Representatives, June 21, 1836, *Ross Papers*, 1:440–41; To the Senate and House of Representatives, February 22, 1837, *Ross Papers*, 1:473; To Martin Van Buren, March 16, 1837, *Ross Papers*, 1:481.

43. Williams, *Linking Arms Together*, 83–97.

44. Robert H. Abzug, *Cosmos Crumbling: American Reform and the Religious Imagination* (New York: Oxford University Press, 1994), 3–8, 30–35, 79–80, 127–28.

45. Prucha, ed., *Cherokee Removal*, 50.

46. Prucha, ed., *Cherokee Removal*, 51.

47. Andrew, *From Revivals to Removal*, 3–5, 169–98.

48. To David Crockett, January 13, 1831, *Ross Papers*, 1:210–11.

49. *Cherokee Phoenix*, May 15, 1830, in Perdue, *Cherokee Editor*, 118.

50. Sacvan Bercovitch, *The American Jeremiad* (Madison: University of Wisconsin Press, 1978), 141–75; Sacvan Bercovitch, *The Rites of Assent: Transformations in the Symbolic Construction of America* (New York: Routledge, 1993), 38–64. See also Fred Somkin, *Unquiet Eagle: Memory and Desire in the Idea of American Freedom* (Ithaca NY: Cornell University Press, 1967), 1–54, 131–209; Michael Kammen, *A Season of Youth: The American Revolution and the Historical Imagination* (New York: Knopf, 1978), 15–58; Harry L. Watson, *Liberty and Power: The Politics of Jacksonian America* (New York: Hill and Wang, 1990), 28–62.

51. Sheehan, *Seeds of Extinction*, 4–11, 15–44, 119–47; Berkhofer, *White Man's Indian*, 38–49, 142–45, 149–51.

52. Elias Boudinot, "An Address to the Whites Delivered in the First Presbyterian Church," May 26, 1826, in Perdue, *Cherokee Editor*, 71–79; *Cherokee Phoenix*, January 28, 1829, November 12, 1831, in Perdue, *Cherokee Editor*, 103–5, 140–42; Memorial to the Senate and House of Representatives, May 17, 1834, *Ross Papers*, 1:290–91.

53. See, for example, [Lewis Cass], "Documents and Proceedings Relating to the Formation and Progress of a Board in the City of New York, for the Emigration, Preservation, and Improvement of the Aborigines of America," *North American Review* 30 (January 1830): 64–77, 116–21; Andrew Jackson, Annual Message, December 8, 1829, in *Messages of General Andrew Jackson* (Concord NH, 1837), 59–61.

54. Bieder, *Science Encounters the Indian*, 11–15, 55–103; William Stanton, *The Leopard's Spots: Scientific Attitudes toward Race in America, 1815–59* (Chicago: University of Chicago Press, 1960) 24–44, 65–72; Reginald Horsman, *Race and Manifest Destiny: The Origins of American Racial Anglo – Saxonism* (Cambridge MA: Harvard University Press, 1981), 117–57.

55. Berkhofer, *White Man's Indian*, 86–96; Dippie, *Vanishing American*, 21–25; Lucy Maddox, *Removals: Nineteenth-Century American Literature and the Politics of Indian Affairs* (New York: Oxford University Press, 1991). See also David Murray, *Forked Tongues: Speech, Writing, and Representation in North American Indian Texts* (Bloomington: Indiana University Press, 1991) and Frank W. Griffin, "Walking 'the Same Path': Indian Voices and the Issues of Removal" (PhD diss., University of North Carolina, Greensboro, 1994).

56. To the House and Senate of the United States, February 27, 1829, *Ross Papers*, 1:155, 157.

57. To Andrew Jackson, March 12, 1834, *Ross Papers*, 1:277–78.

58. *Cherokee Phoenix*, January 28, 1829, in Perdue, *Cherokee Editor*, 105.

59. Thurman Wilkins, *Cherokee Tragedy*, 228–53; Theda Perdue, "The Conflict Within," in Anderson, *Cherokee Removal*, 55–74; Moulton, *John Ross*, 50–57.

60. Moulton, *John Ross*, 55, 59–60; To Lewis Cass, February 14, February 25, 1835, *Ross Papers*, 1:321–23, 324–27.

61. Wilkins, *Cherokee Tragedy*, 254–78; Moulton, *John Ross*, 65–77; Prucha, *American Indian Treaties*, 177–82.

62. To Martin Van Buren, March 16, 1837, *Ross Papers*, 1:481.

63. To Lewis Cass, June 16, 1834, *Ross Papers*, 1:295.

64. To the Senate and House of Representatives, September 28, 1836, *Ross Papers*, 1:459.

65. To the Senate and House of Representatives, June 21, 1836, *Ross Papers*, 1:427–28.

66. To the Senate and House of Representatives, February 22, 1837, *Ross Papers*, 1:471–72.

67. This conclusion echoes Arnold Krupat's analysis of several Cherokee memorials from the 1830s. Krupat argues that the memorials replaced "America's 'official' tragic narrative of Indian decline" with an "ironic counternarrative" of Cherokee victimization. Arnold Krupat, "Figures and the Law: Rhetorical Readings of Congressional and Cherokee Texts," in *Ethnocriticism: Ethnography, History, and Literature*, ed. Arnold Krupat, 160–63 (Berkeley and Los Angeles, University of California Press, 1992).

68. Grant Foreman, *Indian Removal* (Norman: University of Oklahoma Press, 1938), 279–312; Moulton, *John Ross*, 95–106; Russell Thornton, *The Cherokees: A Population History* (Lincoln: University of Nebraska Press, 1990), 63–76; Kenneth Penn Davis, "The Cherokee Removal, 1835–1838," *Tennessee Historical Quarterly* 32 (Winter 1975): 311–30.

69. Morris L. Wardell, *A Political History of the Cherokee Nation, 1838–1907* (1938, revised; Norman: University of Oklahoma Press, 1977), 12–16, 40–46; William G. McLoughlin, *After the Trail of Tears: The Cherokees' Struggle for Sovereignty, 1830–1880* (Chapel Hill: University of North Carolina Press, 1993), 1–10.

70. Wardell, *Political History of the Cherokee Nation*, 16–19, 54–55, 62–67; McLoughlin, *After the Trail of Tears*, 11–45; Kenneth Franks, *Stand Watie and the Agony of the Cherokee Nation* (Memphis: Memphis State University Press, 1979), 80–82.

71. Rogers, Bell, and Watie to Poinsett, January 22, 1840, 26th Cong., 1st sess., H. Doc. 188 (Serial 366), 42–43; Memorial of the Treaty Party of Cherokee Indians, April 13, 1844, 28th Cong., 1st sess., H. Doc. 234 (Serial 443), 1–16; Treaty Party Delegates to Medill, March, 1846, 29th Cong., 1st sess., H. Doc. 185 (Serial 485), 73–76; Report of the National Council of Old Settlers, February 7, 1840, 26th Cong., 1st sess., S. Doc. 347 (Serial 359), 55–58; Memorial of Rogers, Carey, and Rogers, March 30, 1844, 28th Cong., 1st sess., H. Doc. 235 (Serial 443), 1–36; Agents of the Western Cherokees to Marcy, November 1, 1845, 29th Cong., 1st sess., H. Doc.185 (Serial 485), 30–40.

72. To William Wilkins, May 14, 1844, *Ross Papers*, 2:201.

73. To the Senate and House of Representatives, February 28, 1840, *Ross Papers*, 2:6–17; To John Bell and the House Committee on Indian Affairs, April 20, 1840, *Ross Papers*, 2:23–39; To William Wilkins, May 14, 1844, *Ross Papers*, 2:200–202.

74. To Starr and Downing, June 28, 1842, *Ross Papers*, 2:137; *Cherokee Advocate*, July 17, 1845. See also, *Cherokee Advocate*, November 28, 1844, November 27, 1845.

75. To John Bell, May 15, 1841, *Ross Papers*, 2:85.

76. To John Bell and the House Committee on Indian Affairs, April 20, 1840, *Ross Papers*, 2:23–39; *Cherokee Advocate*, December 18, 1844, May 22, December 4, 1845.

77. To John Bell, May 15, 1841, *Ross Papers*, 2:85.

78. To John Bell, May 15, 1841, *Ross Papers*, 2:86.

79. To the Senate and House of Representatives, February 28, 1840, *Ross Papers*, 2:7–8.

80. For example, *Cherokee Phoenix*, April 16, December 21, 1831, in Perdue, *Cherokee Editor*, 126–27, 144–45; Letter from John Ross, July 2, 1836, *Ross Papers*, 1:455–56.

81. *Cherokee Advocate*, May 28, 1846.

82. To the Senate and House of Representatives, April 30, 1846, *Ross Papers*, 2:301.

83. To the Senate and House of Representatives, February 28, 1840, *Ross Papers*, 2:8.

84. *Cherokee Advocate*, April 3, 1845.

85. Memorial of Rogers, Carey, and Rogers, March 30, 1844, 28th Cong., 1st sess., H. Doc. 235 (Serial 443), 10; Memorial of the Delegates and Repre-

sentatives of the Cherokee Nation, West, April 1, 1840, 26th Cong., 1st sess., H. Doc. 162 (Serial 366), 1–6.

86. Rogers, Bell, and Watie to Poinsett, January 22, 1840, 26th Cong., 1st sess., H. Doc. 188 (Serial 366), 42–43.

87. McLoughlin, *After the Trail of Tears*, 47–48; Grant Foreman, *The Five Civilized Tribes* (Norman: University of Oklahoma Press, 1934), 332–35.

88. McLoughlin, *After the Trail of Tears*, 48–55; Edward Everett Dale and Gaston Litton, eds., *Cherokee Cavaliers: Forty Years of Cherokee History as Told in the Correspondence of the Ridge – Watie – Boudinot Family* (1939, reprint; Norman: University of Oklahoma Press, 1995), 33.

89. McLoughlin, *After the Trail of Tears*, 56–68; Wardell, *Political History of the Cherokee Nation*, 73–74; Charles G. Royce, *The Cherokee Nation of Indians* (Chicago: Aldine, 1975), 182–86.

2. THE CIVIL WAR AND CHEROKEE NATIONHOOD

1. Memorial of Lewis Downing, March 23, 1869, 41st Cong., 1st sess., S. Doc. 16 (Serial 1399), 2; Albert Pike to the Commissioner of Indian Affairs, February 17, 1866, in "The Cherokee Question," *Chronicles of Oklahoma* 2 (Summer 1924): 179. (Hereafter cited as "The Cherokee Question.")

2. William G. McLoughlin, *After the Trail of Tears: The Cherokees' Struggle for Sovereignty, 1839–1880* (Chapel Hill: University of North Carolina Press, 1993), 59–120; Rennard Strickland and William M. Strickland, "Beyond the Trail of Tears: One Hundred Fifty Years of Cherokee Survival," in *Cherokee Removal: Before and After*, ed. William L. Anderson (Athens: University of Georgia Press, 1991), 114–15.

3. McLoughlin, *After the Trail of Tears*, 154–55; William G. McLoughlin, *Champions of the Cherokees: Evan and John B. Jones* (Princeton NJ: Princeton University Press, 1990), 337–76.

4. McLoughlin, *After the Trail of Tears*, 156–60; McLoughlin, *Champions of the Cherokees*, 344–48; Janey B. Hendrix, "Redbird Smith and the Nighthawk Keetoowahs," *Journal of Cherokee Studies* 8 (Spring 1983): 22–25. For Ross and the Cherokee government's efforts to keep the tribe out of the sectional crisis, see Annual Messages, 1856, 1860, 1861, in *The Papers of Chief John Ross*, 2 vols., ed. Gary E. Moulton, 2:395–99, 449–52, 492–95 (Norman: University of Oklahoma Press, 1985). (Hereafter cited as *Ross Papers*.)

5. To J. S. Dunham, February 1, 1861, to Henry Rector, February 22, 1861, in *Ross Papers*, 2:458–59, 464–65.

6. A. M. Wilson and J. W. Washbourne to Stand Watie, May 18, 1861, in *Cherokee Cavaliers: Forty Years of Cherokee History as Told in the Correspondence of the Ridge – Watie – Boudinot Family*, ed. Edward Everett Dale and Gaston Litton (1939, reprint; Norman: University of Oklahoma Press, 1995), 106–7. McLoughlin, *After the Trail of Tears*, 168–75.

7. Address to the Cherokees, August 21, 1861, in *Ross Papers*, 2:479–81.

8. McLoughlin, *After the Trail of Tears*, 182–90; Morris L. Wardell, *A Political History of the Cherokee Nation, 1838–1907* (1938, reprint; Norman: University of Oklahoma Press, 1977), 132–41; W. Craig Gaines, *The Confederate Cherokees: John Drew's Regiment of Mounted Rifles* (Baton Rouge: Louisiana State University Press, 1989), 11–19. See also Kenny Franks, "The Implementation of the Confederate Treaties with the Five Civilized Tribes," *Chronicles of Oklahoma* 51 (Spring 1973): 21–33; Kenneth McNeil, "Confederate Treaties with the Tribes of the Indian Territory," *Chronicles of Oklahoma* 42 (Winter 1964–65): 408–20; Paul T. Wilson, "Delegates of the Five Civilized Tribes to the Confederate Congress," *Chronicles of Oklahoma* 53 (Fall 1975): 353–66.

9. John Ross's Speech to Drew's Regiment, December 19, 1861, in "The Cherokee Question," 187. See also, Annual Message, October 9, 1861, in *Ross Papers*, 2:492–95.

10. Wardell, *Political History of the Cherokee Nation*, 138–41.

11. McLoughlin, *After the Trail of Tears*, 192–95; Gaines, *Confederate Cherokees*, 43–54; Angie Debo, *The Road to Disappearance: A History of the Creek Indians* (Norman: University of Oklahoma Press, 1941), 147–53.

12. Gaines, *Confederate Cherokees*, 74–90; Alvin Josephy, *The Civil War in the American West* (New York: Knopf, 1991), 324–48. See also, William L. Shea and Earl J. Hess, *Pea Ridge: Civil War Campaign in the West* (Chapel Hill: University of North Carolina Press, 1992); Larry C. Rampp and Donald L. Rampp, *The Civil War in the Indian Territory* (Austin: University of Texas Press, 1975).

13. McLoughlin, *After the Trail of Tears*, 205–7; Gary E. Moulton, "John Ross and W. P. Dole: A Case Study of Lincoln's Indian Policy," *Journal of the West* 12 (July 1973): 414–23; Edmund J. Danziger, Jr., "The Office of Indian Affairs and the Problem of Civil War Indian Refugees in Kansas," *Kansas Historical Quarterly* 35 (Autumn 1965): 257–75.

14. Stand Watie to Sarah C. Watie, November 12, 1863, in *Cherokee Cavaliers*, 144–45.

15. Huckleberry Downing et. al., to John Ross, January 8, 1863, in *Ross Papers*, 2:528.

16. McLoughlin, *After the Trail of Tears*, 208–17, 220; Russell Thornton, *The Cherokees: A Population History* (Lincoln: University of Nebraska Press, 1990), 90–95.

17. Official Report of the Proceedings of the Council with the Indians of the West and Southwest, September 8–21, 1865, 39th Cong., 1st sess., H. Doc. 1 (Serial 1248), 498, 502–3 (Hereafter cited as Proceedings of the Council); McLoughlin, *After the Trail of Tears*, 219. See also, Propositions Submitted to the Cherokee Delegation Regarding a New Treaty, February 24, 1866, folder 464, roll 5, Cherokee Nation Papers, WHC.

18. Proceedings of the Council, 509–11, 523–34.

19. Proceedings of the Council, 519–20, 522, 524, 527–29; Dialogue between Ross and Dennis N. Cooley, September 15, 1865, in *Ross Papers*, 2:646–48.

20. "The Cherokee Question," 141–45.

21. Albert Pike to the Commissioner of Indian Affairs, February 17, 1866, in "The Cherokee Question," 174.

22. "The Cherokee Question," 157.

23. "The Cherokee Question," 156.

24. "The Cherokee Question," 149.

25. "The Cherokee Question," 148, 155, 159.

26. See Ari Kelman, "Deadly Currents: John Ross's Decision of 1861," *Chronicles of Oklahoma* 73 (Spring 1995): 80–103.

27. See, for example, Lewis Cass, "Documents and Proceedings Relating to the Formation and Progress of a Board in the City of New York for the Emigration, Preservation, and Improvement of the Aborigines of America," *North American Review* 30 (January 1830): 71–72; Schermerhorn to Herring, August 3, 1835, in "Report from the Secretary of War . . . in Relation to the Cherokee Treaty of 1835," 1836, 25th Cong., 2d sess., S. Doc. 120, (Serial 315), 461. Theda Perdue places the development the "designing half – breed" image in the context of the antebellum era's rising tide of white supremacy. Theda Perdue, *"Mixed Blood" Indians: Racial Construction in the Early South* (Athens: University of Georgia Press, 2003), 70–90.

28. Gary Moulton, *John Ross, Cherokee Chief* (Athens: University of Georgia Press, 1978), 118–26. In 1845, agents for one group of anti – Ross Cherokees

declared of the chief: "With scarcely enough Cherokee blood in his veins to mark him as of Indian descent, he has made a majority of his deluded countrymen believe he is true to the aboriginal race." Stambaugh and Kendell to Marcy, December 10, 1845, 29th Cong., 1st sess., H. Doc. 185 (Serial 485), 57.

29. "The Cherokee Question," 161–62.

30. Bernard W. Sheehan, *Seeds of Extinction: Jeffersonian Philanthropy and the American Indian* (Chapel Hill: University of North Carolina Press, 1973), 167–72; Francis Paul Prucha, *Great Father*, 196–97; "The Cherokee Question," 162.

31. "The Cherokee Question," 164.

32. J. J. Tebbetts to the Commissioner of Indian Affairs, March 30, 1866, in "The Cherokee Question," 211.

33. Morton Keller, *Affairs of State: Public Life in Late Nineteenth Century America* (Cambridge MA: Harvard University Press, 1977), 17–30; Eric Foner, *Reconstruction: America's Unfinished Revolution* (New York: Harper and Row, 1988), 18–23.

34. Keller, *Affairs of State*, 38–46; George M. Fredrickson, *The Inner Civil War: Northern Intellectuals and the Crisis of the Union* (New York: Harper and Row, 1965), 130–50, 184–89.

35. In coming to this conclusion, I am influenced by an argument made by Richard Slotkin. Slotkin identifies in the postwar era a "new paternalism," in which the childlike identity usually reserved in nineteenth-century European American culture for non – whites (African slaves and Native Americans) came to be applied to a broader range of people – –in particular industrial workers. Richard Slotkin, *The Fatal Environment: The Myth of the Frontier in the Age of Industrialization, 1800–1890* (New York: Atheneum, 1985), 306–9.

36. Keller, *Affairs of State*, 122–61; Fredrickson, *Inner Civil War*, 98–112.

37. Slotkin, *Fatal Environment*, 281–324.

38. Proceedings of the Council, 524.

39. Proceedings of the Council, 523.

40. Proceedings of the Council, 523–24.

41. Reply of the Southern Delegates, 1866, quoted in McLoughlin, *After the Trail of Tears*, 223.

42. Proceedings of the Council, 523.

43. After the war, a number of the Southern Party's leaders, most notably W. P. Adair, became regular spokesmen for the reunited tribe in its efforts to maintain political autonomy, an indication that their effort to divide the

nation in the 1860s was not meant to be a blow against Indian nationhood per se. The most important exception was E. C. Boudinot, who became an important advocate for territorial reorganization and, later, allotment.

44. Ross to Abraham Lincoln, September 16, 1862, in *Ross Papers*, 2:516–17.

45. Statement presented by H. D. Reese, Proceedings of the Council, 506.

46. Ross to Abraham Lincoln, September 16, 1862, in *Ross Papers*, 2:517; To the Senate and House of Representatives, June 14, 1864, in *Ross Papers*, 2:590–92; To William P. Dole, January 30, 1865, in *Ross Papers*, 2:619–20. See also Gary E. Moulton, "John Ross and W. P. Dole: A Case Study of Lincoln's Indian Policy," *Journal of the West* 12 (July 1973): 414–23.

47. Statement presented by H. D. Reese, Proceedings of the Council, 507.

48. Statement presented by H. D. Reese, Proceedings of the Council, 507.

49. Memorial of the Delegates of the Cherokee Nation, 1866, Hargrett Pamphlet Collection, GM.

50. To the Senate and House of Representatives, March 2, 1865, in *Ross Papers*, 2:630.

51. McLoughlin, *After the Trail of Tears*, 208–9.

52. Memorial of the Principal Chief and Others of the Cherokee Nation, February 18, 1865, 38th Cong., 2d sess., H. Doc. 52 (Serial 1232), 1.

53. Memorial of the Principal Chief and Others of the Cherokee Nation, February 18, 1865, 38th Cong., 2d sess., H. Doc. 52 (Serial 1232), 2.

54. Memorial of the Delegates of the Cherokee Nation, 1866, Hargrett Pamphlet Collection, GM; Statement of John Ross and Evan Jones, [February 1864], in *Ross Papers*, 2:560–63.

55. For examples of Cherokee leaders describing removal in the period after 1838, see To John Bell, May 15, 1841, in *Ross Papers*, 2:84–87; To William Wilkins, July 17, 1844, in *Ross Papers*, 2:221–27; *Cherokee Advocate*, May 1, 1845.

56. To James K. Polk, November 8, 1845, in *Ross Papers*, 2:275.

57. To The Senate and House of Representatives, May 23, 1860, *Ross Papers*, 2:443.

58. Reply of the Delegates of the Cherokee Nation to the Pamphlet of the Commissioner of Indian Affairs, July 20, 1866, Hargrett Pamphlet Collection, GM, 1.

59. To the Senate and House of Representatives, March 2, 1865, in *Ross Papers*, 2:628.

60. To the Senate and House of Representatives, June 14, 1865, in *Ross Papers*, 2:590–91; To the Senate and House of Representatives, February 18,

1865, in *Ross Papers*, 2:625–26; Reply of the Delegates of the Cherokee Nation to the Pamphlet of the Commissioner of Indian Affairs, July 20, 1866, Hargrett Pamphlet Collection, GM, 3.

61. Reply of the Delegates of the Cherokee Nation to the Pamphlet of the Commissioner of Indian Affairs, July 20, 1866, Hargrett Pamphlet Collection, GM, 1–2; Memorial of the Delegates of the Cherokee Nation, 1866, Hargrett Pamphlet Collection, GM.

62. Reply of the Delegates of the Cherokee Nation to the Demands of the Commissioner of Indian Affairs, May 1866, Hargrett Pamphlet Collection, GM; To Andrew Johnson, June 28, 1866, in *Ross Papers*, 2:679–80.

63. Reply of the Delegates of the Cherokee Nation to the Pamphlet of the Commissioner of Indian Affairs, July 20, 1866, Hargrett Pamphlet Collection, GM, 1–2, 5–6.

64. Letter to the House Committee on Indian Affairs, March 21, 1866, 39th Cong., 2d sess., House Committee on Indian Affairs, RG 233, HR 39A – F11.12, NA, 2; To the Senate of the United States, June 25, 1866, folder 478, roll 5, Cherokee Nation Papers, WHC. See also, Lewis Downing to Ross and Evan Jones, [October 18, 1864], in *Ross Papers*, 2:612–14; To John B. Jones, December 16, 1865, in *Ross Papers*, 2:659–60; To Andrew Johnson, June 28, 1866, in *Ross Papers*, 2:679.

65. McLoughlin, *After the Trail of Tears*, 224–27.

66. The federal negotiators may have made the separate treaty with the Southern Party primarily as a ploy to force Loyal Cherokee leaders to make greater concessions. McLoughlin, *After the Trail of Tears*, 225–26.

67. McLoughlin, *After the Trail of Tears*, 226–27; Emmet Starr, *History of the Cherokee Indians and Their Legends and Folklore* (Oklahoma City: Warden, 1921), 167–77.

68. Katja May, *African Americans and Native Americans in the Creek and Cherokee Nations, 1830s to 1920s* (New York: Garland, 1996), 64–72; Daniel F. Littlefield, *The Cherokee Freedmen: From Emancipation to American Citizenship* (Westport CT: Greenwood, 1978) 25–30; Thomas F. Andrews, "Freedmen in Indian Territory: A Post–Civil War Dilemma," *Journal of the West* 4 (July 1965): 367–76.

69. Circe Sturm, *Blood Politics: Race, Culture, and Identity in the Cherokee Nation of Oklahoma* (Berkeley and Los Angeles: University of California Press, 2002), 52–78.

70. Littlefield, *Cherokee Freedmen*, 75–82, 119–41, 249–51; Petition, [1884],

Cherokee National Records, Freedmen, roll 81, OHS; H. Price to the Secretary of the Interior, February 12, 1884, 48th Cong., 2d sess., RG 46, Senate Committee on Indian Affairs, Sen 48A – H12, NA.

71. McLoughlin, *After the Trail of Tears*, 231–34; H. Craig Miner, *The Corporation and the Indian: Tribal Sovereignty and Industrial Civilization in the Indian Territory, 1865–1907* (1976, reprint; Norman: University of Oklahoma Press, 1988), 7–37.

72. McLoughlin, *After the Trail of Tears*, 278–79. For territorialization bills, see Roy Gittinger, *Formation of the State of Oklahoma, 1803–1906* (Norman: University of Oklahoma Press, 1939), 221–23.

73. McLoughlin, *After the Trail of Tears*, 245–50.

74. Remonstrance of the Cherokee, Creek, Choctaw, and Seminole Delegations, February 28, 1876, 44th Cong., 2d sess., Senate Committee on Territories, RG 46, Sen 44A – H24, NA, 18.

75. Memorial of Indian Delegates, February 16, 1880, 46th Cong., 2d sess., S. Doc. 41 (Serial 1890), 7; Memorial of the Cherokee Delegation, April 21, 1880, 46th Cong., 2d sess., House Committee on Indian Affairs, RG 233, HR 46A – H10.2, NA.

76. Remonstrance of the Cherokee, Creek, Choctaw, and Seminole Delegations, February 28, 1876, 19; Memorial of Lewis Downing, March 23, 1869, 41st Cong., 1st sess., S. Doc. 16 (Serial 1399); Memorial of the Delegates from the Indian Territory, April 22, 1878, folder 3854, roll 38, Cherokee Nation Papers, WHC, 2.

3. THE CHEROKEES' PEACE POLICY

1. *Cherokee Advocate*, February 17, 1877.

2. Francis Paul Prucha, *American Indian Policy in Crisis: Christian Reformers and the Indian, 1865–1900* (Norman: University of Oklahoma Press, 1976), 30.

3. This chapter's general description of the postwar reform movement and the peace policy is drawn from the work of several historians who have produced thorough studies of the topic: Prucha, *American Indian Policy in Crisis*; Robert Mardock, *The Reformers and the Indian* (Columbia: University of Missouri Press, 1971); Robert H. Keller, Jr., *American Protestantism and United States Indian Policy, 1869–82* (Lincoln: University of Nebraska Press, 1983); Christine Bolt, *American Indian Policy and American Reform* (Lon-

don: Allen and Unwin, 1987); Michael C. Coleman, *Presbyterian Missionary Attitudes toward American Indians, 1837–1893* (Jackson: University Press of Mississippi, 1985); Clyde Milner, *With Good Intentions: Quaker Work among the Pawnees, Otoes, and Omahas in the 1870s* (Lincoln: University of Nebraska Press, 1982).

4. Prucha, *American Indian Policy in Crisis*, 7–13. For criticism in the press, see *New York Times*, September 2, 1866, May 26, 1867, in *A Race at Bay: New York Times Editorials on "the Indian Problem," 1860–1900*, ed. Robert G. Hays (Carbondale: Southern Illinois University Press, 1997), 61, 133–34.

5. Condition of the Indian Tribes: Report of the Joint Special Commission, January 26, 1867, 39th Cong., 2d sess., S. Rep. 156 (Serial 1279), 3. Several years later, the Cherokees and Choctaws retained James Doolittle as legal counsel. In 1869 Doolittle submitted to the Senate on behalf of the two tribes a brief arguing for the negotiation of a new treaty in order to pay the tribes sufficiently for lands ceded for the settlement of tribes newly removed to the Indian Territory. Argument of the Hon. James R. Doolittle, April 1869, Hargrett Pamphlet Collection, GM.

6. Condition of the Indian Tribes: Report of the Joint Special Commission, January 26, 1867, 39th Cong., 2d sess., S. Rep. 156 (Serial 1279), 4.

7. Condition of the Indian Tribes: Report of the Joint Special Commission, January 26, 1867, 39th Cong., 2d sess., S. Rep. 156 (Serial 1279), 4–5; see also Donald Chaput, "Generals, Indian Agents, and Politicians: The Doolittle Survey of 1865," *Western Historical Quarterly* 3 (July 1972): 269–82.

8. Prucha, *American Indian Policy in Crisis*, 18–19.

9. Prucha, *American Indian Policy in Crisis*, 19–20.

10. Report of the Indian Peace Commissioners, January 7, 1868, 40th Cong., 2d sess., H. Doc. 97 (Serial 1337), 10.

11. Report of the Indian Peace Commissioners, January 7, 1868, 16–18.

12. Report of the Indian Peace Commissioners, January 7, 1868, 16.

13. Report of the Indian Peace Commissioners, January 7, 1868, 18–23.

14. Report of the Indian Peace Commissioners, January 7, 1868, 18–23.

15. Lydia Maria Child, "An Appeal for the Indians," *National Anti – Slavery Standard*, April 11, 18, 1868, in *Hobomok and Other Writings on Indians*, ed. Carolyn L. Karcher (New Brunswick NJ: Rutgers University Press, 1986), 216.

16. Karcher, ed., *Hobomok and Other Writings on Indians*, 229–32.

17. For example, Memorial of the Conference of Six Yearly Meetings, [1868], House Committee on Indian Affairs, 40th Cong., 2d sess., RG 233, HR 40A –

H8.2, NA; Memorial of Yearly Meetings of the Society of Friends, January 25, 1869, 40th Cong., 3d sess., H. Doc. 29 (Serial 1385).

18. *New York Times*, July 5, 1867, reprinted in Hays, *A Race at Bay*, 263. See also the first report of the Board of Indian Commissioners, November 23, 1869, printed in Report of the Commissioner of Indian Affairs, H. Doc. 1, 41st Cong., 2d sess. (Serial 1414), especially 488–90.

19. Child, "An Appeal for the Indians," 228. A group calling itself the Pennsylvania Peace Society invoked Penn as its inspiration for involving itself in Indian affairs. They told Congress that Penn's example gave them confidence that peace could be maintained with the Indians. Quaker organizations, not surprisingly, invoked Penn as evidence of their authority to comment on Indian matters and as the proper example for United States policy in the present. Petition of the Pennsylvania Peace Society, March 27, 1867, 40th Cong., 1st sess., House Committee on Indian Affairs, RG 233, HR 40A – H8.2, NA; Memorial of Six Yearly Meetings, [1868]; Prucha, *American Indian Policy in Crisis*, 47–48; Milner, *With Good Intentions*, 5–7.

20. For example, *New York Times*, May 20, 1866, June 23, 1867, December 17, 1869, in Hays, *A Race at Bay*, 27–28, 60, 213–15; Vincent Colyer, *Peace with the Apaches* (1872, reprint; Freeport NY: Books for Libraries Press, 1971) – –this is Colyer's 1871 report for the Board of Indian Commissioners on white atrocities committed against Apaches.

21. John Beeson, *A Plea for the Indians* (1857,reprint; Medford OR: Webb Research Group, 1994), 149.

22. Yearly Meeting of Friends, Longwood, Pennsylvania, [1868], 40th Cong., 2d sess., House Committee on Indian Affairs, HR40A – H8.2, NA. See also Coleman, *Presbyterian Missionary Attitudes*, 42–44.

23. Keller, *American Protestantism*, 149–66. Clyde Milner and Michael Coleman describe the paternalism of agents and missionaries involved in administering the peace policy. Milner, *With Good Intentions*; Coleman, *Presbyterian Missionary Attitudes*, especially 80–112.

24. The Peace Commission Report, for example, speculated that "strong military government" might be necessary for Indians on the reservations until they had been taught enough of civilized life to allow them to have more liberty. Report of the Peace Commission, 18–23. See also, Keller, *American Protestantism*, 27–28; Prucha, *American Indian Policy in Crisis*, 30–33.

25. Robert H. Keller, Jr., speculates about Grant's motives in launching the peace policy. Keller, *American Protestantism*, 17–30.

26. Keller, *American Protestantism*, 17–18, 27–28, 31–45.

27. Keller, *American Protestantism*, 20–22; Prucha, *American Indian Policy in Crisis*, 34.

28. Prucha, *American Indian Policy in Crisis*, 33–46.

29. Prucha, *American Indian Policy in Crisis*, 103–31.

30. William G. McLoughlin, *After the Trail of Tears: The Cherokees' Struggle for Sovereignty, 1839–1880* (Chapel Hill: University of North Carolina Press, 1993), 256.

31. This conclusion is based upon Prucha's and Keller's accounts of the peace policy and upon the peace-policy documents cited above.

32. McLoughlin, *After the Trail of Tears*, 222–29; Jeffrey Burton, *The Indian Territory and the United States, 1866–1906: Courts, Government, and the Movement for Oklahoma Statehood* (Norman: University of Oklahoma Press, 1995), 15–77; Prucha, *American Indian Policy in Crisis*, 376–80. For the bills proposing to reorganize the Indian Territory, see Roy Gittinger, *The Formation of the State of Oklahoma, 1803–1906* (Norman: University of Oklahoma Press, 1939), 221–23.

33. For the General Council, see McLoughlin, *After the Trail of Tears*, 226–27.

34. McLoughlin, *After the Trail of Tears*, 224–27; Prucha, *American Indian Policy in Crisis*, 108–109, 113–14; *Cherokee Advocate*, August 19, October 21, 1876, January 27, 1877.

35. Report of Vincent Colyer, 1869, in Report of the Commissioner of Indian Affairs, 41st Cong., 2d sess., H. Doc. 1, (Serial 1414), 512–37; Message of the President of the United States Communicating the Second Annual Report of the Board of Indian Commissioners, February 10, 1871, 41st Cong., 3d sess., S. Doc. 39 (Serial 1440).

36. Report of the Commissioner of Indian Affairs, 1868, 40th Cong., 3d sess., H. Doc. 1 (Serial 1366), 477–78.

37. For example, Report of the Board of Indian Commissioners, November 23, 1869, in Report of the Commissioner of Indian Affairs, 41st Cong., 2d sess., H. Doc. 1 (Serial 1414) 491; R. B. Macy to the Board of Indian Commissioners, June 1869, Report of the Commissioner of Indian Affairs, 552–61.

38. *Cherokee Advocate*, October 27, 1880.

39. Paul Kelton, "William Penn Adair: Cherokee Slaveholder and Indian Freedom Advocate," *Chronicles of Oklahoma* 77 (Spring 1999): 22–53; Cherrie Adair Moore, "William Penn Adair," *Chronicles of Oklahoma* 29 (Spring 1951):

32–41; Emmet Starr, *History of the Cherokee Indians and Their Legends and Folk Lore* (Oklahoma City: Warden, 1921), 296–97.

40. John Bartlett Meserve, "Chief William Potter Ross," *Chronicles of Oklahoma* 15 (March 1937): 21–29; McLoughlin, *After the Trail of Tears*, 245–48, 315–38; Act Appointing a Delegation, November 8, 1878, Delegates to Charles Thompson, November 14, 1878, Cherokee National Records, federal relations, roll 78, OHS. These last documents relate to Ross's service as a representative meeting with a special Senate committee sent to the Indian Territory to collect information regarding territorialization.

41. Emmet Starr, *History of the Cherokee Indians*, 272, 296–97, 381–82; Morris L. Wardell, *A Political History of the Cherokee Nation, 1838–1907* (1938, reprint; University of Oklahoma Press: Norman, 1977), 207–13; Thomas Burnell Colbert, "Visionary or Rogue? The Life and Legacy of Elias Cornelius Boudinot," *Chronicles of Oklahoma* 65 (Fall 1987): 268–81. W. P. Boudinot was editor from 1870 to mid – 1873, Adair from 1873 to early 1876, and then Boudinot again in 1876 and 1877.

42. Resolutions, 1874, reprinted in *Cherokee Advocate*, December 19, 1874 (The original document can be found dated December 14, 1874, Cherokee National Records, federal relations, roll 77, OHS); Letter from Delegate W. P. Boudinot, in *Cherokee Advocate*, May 30, 1874; Delegation Report, 1876, Cherokee National Records, federal relations, roll 77, OHS.

43. For example, *Cherokee Advocate*, December 21, 1872, December 26, 1874, January 16, 30, 1875, May 16, 1877.

44. Petition, May 1876, 44th Cong., 2d sess., House Committee on Indian Affairs, RG 233, HR 44A – H6.1, NA, 1–2; *Cherokee Advocate*, April 20, 1878; Delegates of the Five Civilized Tribes to Secretary of the Interior Carl Schurz, May 27, 1878, Cherokee National Records, federal relations, roll 78, OHS, 2.

45. Cherokee Delegates to U. S. Grant, February 26, 1877, Cherokee National Records, federal relations, roll 77, OHS.

46. Prucha, *American Indian Policy in Crisis*, 375–80.

47. Memorial of the Delegates of the Cherokee, Creek, and Choctaw Nations of Indians, May 23, 1870, 41st Cong., 2d sess., S. Doc. 143 (Serial 1408).

48. Memorial of the Delegates of the Cherokee, Creek, and Choctaw Nations of Indians, May 23, 1870, 1.

49. Memorial of the Delegates of the Cherokee, Creek, and Choctaw Nations of Indians, May 23, 1870, 3.

50. Memorial of the Delegates of the Cherokee, Creek, and Choctaw Nations of Indians, May 23, 1870, 4.

51. Letter of the Cherokee Delegation, June 14, 1870, 41st Cong., 2d sess., S. Doc. 154, (Serial 1408), 1.

52. *Cherokee Advocate*, January 16, 1875, May 28, 1879.

53. Petition of Citizens of the Coo – wees – coo – wee District, February, 1870, 41st Cong., 2d sess., House Committee on Indian Affairs, RG 233, HR 41A – H5.1, NA, 1–2.

54. *Cherokee Advocate*, December 21, 1872.

55. *Cherokee Advocate*, December 21, 1872.

56. Prucha, *American Indian Policy in Crisis*, 68–71; *Cherokee Advocate*, March 18, 1871.

57. Letter of W. P. Adair, Cherokee Delegate, Addressed to His People, September 20, 1870, folder 3792, roll 38, Cherokee Nation Papers, WHC, 4. (Hereafter cited as Letter of W. P. Adair.)

58. Memorial of the Indian Delegates from the Indian Territory, [1876], folder 3825, roll 38, Cherokee Nation Papers, WHC, 6.

59. Robert Berkhofer, *The White Man's Indian: Images of the Indian from Columbus to the Present* (New York: Knopf, 1978), 86–96; Robert E. Bieder, *Science Encounters the Indian, 1820–1880: The Early Years of American Ethnology* (Norman: University of Oklahoma Press, 1986), 11–15, 55–103; William Stanton, *The Leopard's Spots: Scientific Attitudes toward Race in America, 1815–59* (Chicago: University of Chicago Press, 1960), 24–44, 65–72; Ronald Takaki, *Iron Cages: Race and Culture in Nineteenth-Century America* (New York: Knopf, 1979), 100–103.

60. See Report of Committee on Territories, 1878, 45th Cong., 3d sess., S. Rep. 744 (Serial 1839); Nancy Hope Sober, *The Intruders: The Illegal Residents of the Cherokee Nation, 1866–1907* (Ponca City OK: Cherokee Books, 1991).

61. McLoughlin, *After the Trail of Tears*, 315–66, for Cherokee ethnic nationalism.

62. Circe Sturm, *Blood Politics: Race, Culture, and Identity in the Cherokee Nation of Oklahoma* (Berkeley and Los Angeles: University of California Press, 2002), 54–57, 68–78; McLoughlin, *After the Trail of Tears*, 252.

63. Remarks of W. P. Adair . . . Made before the Committee on Territories of the House of Representatives, January 31, 1876, 44th Cong., 2d sess., House Committee on Territories, RG 233, HR 44A – F36.6, NA, 4. (Hereafter cited as Remarks of W. P. Adair.)

64. Remarks of W. P. Adair, 5.

65. Remarks of W. P. Adair, 6. See also, Protest of the Delegates of the Creek, Cherokee, and Choctaw Nations, [1872], 42d Cong., 2d sess., Senate Committee on Indian Affairs, RG 46, Sen 42A – H10, NA; Memorial of the Indian Delegates, February 16, 1880, 46th Cong., 2d sess., S. Doc. 41 (Serial 1890).

66. Bernard W. Sheehan, *Seeds of Extinction: Jeffersonian Philanthropy and the American Indian* (Chapel Hill: University of North Carolina Press, 1973), 148–81; Herman J. Viola, *Thomas L. McKenney: Architect of Early American Indian Policy, 1816–1830* (Chicago: Sage Books, 1974), 185–99; Brian W. Dippie, *The Vanishing American: White Attitudes and U.S. Indian Policy* (Middletown CT: Wesleyan University Press, 1982), 165–90.

67. Remarks of W. P. Adair, 23–24.

68. Letter of W. P. Adair, September 20, 1870, 5.

69. For example, To John Bell, May 16, 1841, in *Ross Papers*, 2:85; To William Wilkins, July 17, 1844, *Ross Papers*, 2:221–27; To the Senate and House of Representatives, April 30, 1846, *Ross Papers*, 2:301; Cherokee Protest and Resolution, November 29, 1851, *Ross Papers*, 2:263; *Cherokee Advocate*, May 1, 1845.

70. See, for example, Speech of W. P. Ross, summary in Report of the Board of Indian Commissioners, Report of the Commissioner of Indian Affairs, 1871, 42d Cong., 2d sess., H. Doc. 1 (Serial 1505), 595–96.

71. Remarks of W. P. Adair, 35.

72. See, for example, Memorial of the Indian Delegates, February 16, 1880, 46th Cong., 2d sess., S. Doc. 41 (Serial 1890); Brief on Behalf of the Cherokee Nation, May 3, 1879, folder 3857, roll 38, Cherokee Nation Papers, WHC, 7; *Cherokee Advocate*, November 7, 1877. Francis Paul Prucha notes that removal gave the treaty system a "new lease on life," insofar as the policy was carried out through agreements that recognized (in however qualified a manner) the nationhood of Indian tribes and tribal ownership of land. Francis Paul Prucha, *American Indian Treaties: The History of a Political Anomaly* (Berkeley and Los Angeles: University of California Press, 1994), 182.

73. Protest by the Lawful Delegates of the Civilized Nations of Indians, March 27, 1876, 44th Cong., 2d sess., Senate Committee on Indian Affairs, RG 46, Sen 44A – H9, NA.

74. *Cherokee Advocate*, March 11, 1876; McLoughlin, *After the Trail Tears*, 344.

75. Speech of W. P. Ross, reprinted in *Cherokee Advocate*, October 17, 1874.

76. For example, Report, Senate Committee on Territories, April 27, 1870, 41st Cong., 2d sess., S. Report 131 (Serial 1409), 3.

77. Remarks of W. P. Adair, 20; Objections of the Indian Delegations, February 25, 1878, 45th Cong., 2d sess., H. Doc. 32 (Serial 1815); Delegation Report, November 7, 1878, Cherokee National Records, federal relations, roll 77, OHS; Memorial of the Indian Delegates, February 16, 1880, 46th Cong., 2d sess., S. Doc. 41 (Serial 1890); *Cherokee Advocate*, January 5, June 1, 1878.

78. *Cherokee Advocate*, March 25, 1876.

79. Brief on Behalf of the Cherokee Nation, May 3, 1879, folder 3857, roll 38, Cherokee Nation Papers, WHC, 10.

80. *Cherokee Advocate*, May 16, 1877.

81. *Cherokee Advocate*, March 21, 1874.

82. Satz, *American Indian Policy in the Jacksonian Era*, 10–11; McLoughlin, *After the Trail of Tears*, 278–80; Gittinger, *Formation of the State of Oklahoma*, 221–23.

83. Memorial of Chickasaw, Choctaw, Creek, Cherokee, and Seminole Indians, February 16, 1874, 43d Cong., 1st sess., H. Doc. 142 (Serial 1619); Remarks of W. P. Adair, 7–10; Remonstrance of the Cherokee, Creek, Choctaw, and Seminole Delegations, February 28, 1876, 44th Cong., 2d sess., Senate Committee on Territories, RG 46, Sen 44A – H24, NA; Memorial of Indian Delegates, February 16, 1880, 46th Cong., 2d sess., S. Doc. 41, (Serial 1890); *Cherokee Advocate*, November 7, 1877.

84. Prucha, *American Indian Policy in Crisis*, 376–80; Burton, *Indian Territory and the United States*, 26–71.

85. Memorial of the Delegates of the Cherokee, Creek, and Choctaw Nations, May 23, 1870, 41st Cong., 2d sess., S. Doc. 143 (Serial 1408), 10–11.

86. Proceedings of the General Council of the Indian Territory, December 6, 1870, International Council File, Section X, OHS, 9–11; Address of the Grand International Council, June 4, 1870, 41st Cong., 2d sess., S. Doc. 154 (Serial 1408); Protest of the Cherokee Nation, January 30, 1871, Hargrett Pamphlet Collection, GM, 7; Protest of the Delegates of the Creek, Cherokee, and Choctaw Nations, [1872], Senate Committee on Indian Affairs, 42d Cong., 2d sess., RG 46, Sen 42A – H10, NA; Protest of the General Indian Council, December 6, 1873, 43d Cong., 1st sess., H. Doc. 88 (Serial 1618); *Cherokee Advocate*, June 18, 1870, March 14, 1874, March 25, 1876, November 7, 1877, January 5, April 20, 1878.

87. Cherokee delegation to the Chairman of the House Committee on Indian Affairs, [1867], 39th Cong., 2d sess., House Committee on Indian Affairs, RG 233, HR 39A – F11.12, NA, 4.

88. Speech of W. P. Ross before the Senate Committee on Territories, reprinted in *Cherokee Advocate*, March 5, 1879.

89. Speech of W. P. Ross, summary in Report of the Board of Indian Commissioners, Report of the Commissioner of Indian Affairs, 1871, 42d Cong., 2d sess., H. Doc. 1 (Serial 1505), 596.

90. *Cherokee Advocate*, March 18, 1871.

91. *Cherokee Advocate*, March 18, 1871.

92. Protest of the Delegates of the Creek, Cherokee, and Choctaw Nations, [1872], 42d Cong., 2d sess., Senate Committee on Indian Affairs, Sen 42A – H10, NA, 4. This communication was reprinted as H. Doc. 51 (Serial 1525).

93. Keller, *American Protestantism*, 90–204; Mardock, *Reformers*, 192–210; Prucha, *American Indian Policy in Crisis*, 132–264.

4. THE OKMULGEE COUNCIL

1. Proceedings of the General Council of the Indian Territory, December, 1870, International Council File, Section X, Indian Archives, OHS, 9–12, 27–29. The International Council File contains typescripts of the original published proceedings (sometimes called "journals") of the Okmulgee Council meetings. (Hereafter they are cited simply as Proceedings, followed by the date of the session and page numbers.)

2. William G. McLoughlin, *After the Trail of Tears: The Cherokees' Struggle for Sovereignty, 1839–1880* (Chapel Hill: University of North Carolina Press, 1993), 219–28.

3. Angie Debo, *The Road to Disappearance: A History of the Creek People* (Norman: University of Oklahoma Press, 1941), 134–35; Address to the Indian Council, in *The Papers of Chief John Ross*, 2 vols., ed. Gary E. Moulton (Norman: University of Oklahoma Press, 1984) 2:165–66.

4. Debo, *Road to Disappearance*, 136–39; Arrell Morgan Gibson, "An Indian Territory United Nations: The Creek Council of 1845," *Chronicles of Oklahoma* 39 (Winter 1961–62): 398–413.

5. Report of the Southern Superintendent, August 1, 1869, 41st Cong., 2d sess., H. Doc. 1, (Serial 1414), 844.

6. Report of the Southern Superintendent, August 1, 1869, 844.

7. Report of the Commissioner of Indian Affairs, December 23, 1869, 41st Cong., 2d sess., H. Doc. 1 (Serial 1414), 450–51; Report of the Southern Superintendent, November 16, 1868, 40th Cong., 3d sess., H. Doc. 1 (Serial 1366), 736.

8. Report of the Commissioner of Indian Affairs, October 31, 1870, 41st Cong., 3d sess., H. Doc. 1 (Serial 1449), 471.

9. Address of the Grand International Council, June 4, 1870, 41st Cong., 2d sess., S. Doc. 154 (Serial 1408), 2–4; *Cherokee Advocate*, June 18, 1870; Debo, *Road to Disappearance*, 205.

10. Proceedings, September 1870, 1–3, 12–14.

11. Proceedings, September 1870, 12–13; Debo, *Road to Disappearance*, 205–6.

12. Proceedings, December 1870, 1–3, 28–29.

13. E. C. Parker to C. Delano, January 4, 1871, 41st Cong., 3d sess., S. Doc. 26 (Serial 1440), 3. Parker paraphrases his address to the Okmulgee Council in this letter to the secretary of the interior.

14. In addition to Ross, the Council consisted of G. W. Johnson and Riley Keys (Cherokee), Ok – tar – har – sars Harjo and G. W. Stidham (Creek), Campbell Leflore and Joseph P. Folsom (Choctaw), Colbert Carter and C. P. H. Percy (Chickasaw), John F. Brown (Seminole), Francis King (Ottawa), and Augustus Captain (Osage).

15. Constitution, December 20, 1870, 41st Cong., 3d sess., S. Doc. 26 (Serial 1440), 7–12.

16. Constitution, December 20, 1870, 7–12; Russell Thornton, *The Cherokees: A Population History* (Lincoln: University of Nebraska Press, 1990), 99–101. Representation in the lower house seems to have been based on the 1866 treaty provisions regarding representation at the first meeting of the council. Treaty of 1866, reprinted in *History of the Cherokee Indians and Their Legends and Folk Lore*, Emmet Starr (Oklahoma City: Warden, 1921), 170–71.

17. Constitution, December 20, 1870, 41st Cong., 3d sess., S. Doc. 26 (Serial 1440), 7–12. There may have been discussion of the congressional delegate issue at Okmulgee. In his address to the Council, Commissioner Parker had raised this issue, noting that there was a bill in the Senate to allow the new Council to select a delegate. As mentioned in an earlier chapter, however, Cherokee leaders were wary of the delegate issue, fearing that accepting the officer would be a step toward territorialization. The bill that Parker

mentioned was introduced by Senator James Harlan, a strongly pro – territorialization legislator. E. C. Parker to C. Delano, January 4, 1871, 41st Cong., 3d sess., S. Doc. 26 (Serial 1440), 3–4.

18. Proceedings, December 1870, 10.

19. Delegation Report, 1876, Cherokee Nation Papers, roll 77, federal relations, OHS, 27. The delegates were Daniel H. Ross, William Penn Adair, John Lynch Adair, and Rufus Ross. Their comments about the general council came in response to the congressional debate over whether to continue the Council's funding.

20. Campbell, Lang, and Farwell to Brunot, December 23, 1870, 41st Cong., 3d sess., S. Doc. 26 (Serial 1440), 6.

21. Message of the President, January 30, 1871, Delano to Grant, January 25, 1871, Parker to Delano, January 4, 1871, 41st Cong., 3d sess., S. Doc. 26 (Serial 1440), 1, 2, 3–6.

22. Message of the President, January 30, 1871, 41st Cong., 3d sess., S. Doc. 26 (Serial 1440), 1.

23. Debo, *Road to Disappearance*, 206–7; *Cherokee Advocate*, December 20, 1873.

24. Report of the Commissioner of Indian Affairs, December 23, 1869, 41st Cong., 2d sess., H. Doc. 1 (Serial 1414), 450–51; Message of the President, January 30, 1871, Delano to Grant, January 35, 1871, 41st Cong., 3d sess., S. Doc. 26 (Serial 1440), 1–2.

25. The year before the Council held its first session, Superintendent Robinson wrote, "There would be poetic justice in the embodying in the Union of one distinctly Indian State." Report of the Southern Superintendent, August 1, 1869, 41st Cong., 2d sess., H. Doc. 1 (Serial 1414), 844.

26. Proceedings, June 1872, 31–33. The committee that drafted this message consisted of J. P. Folsom (Choctaw), Daniel H. Ross and D. R. Coodey (Cherokee), Chilley McIntosh and Timothy Barnett (Creek), John F. Brown (Seminole), and Black Beaver (Delaware). Proceedings, June 1872, 9.

27. Letter of the Cherokee Delegation Transmitting an Address of the Grand International Council, June 14, 1870, 41st Cong., 2d sess., S. Doc. 154 (Serial 1408), 1–4; Memorial of the International Council, reprinted in *Cherokee Advocate*, June 18, 1871; Memorial of the General Council of the Indian Territory, December 5, 1873, 43d Cong., 1st sess., H. Doc. 85 (Serial 1618), 1–2; To the Congress of the United States, [1875], 44th Cong., 1st sess., House Committee on Indian Affairs, RG 233, HR 44A – F36.6, NA.

28. Proceedings, May 1873, 32.

29. Proceedings, June 1872, 23, 25–26.

30. Proceedings, May 1873, 38–39.

31. Proceedings, June 1872, 28; Proceedings, May 1873, 21–22.

32. See, for example, John B. Jones's agency reports, 1872, 42d Cong., 3d sess., H. Doc. 1 (Serial 1560), 616–21; 1873, 43d Cong., 1st sess., H. Doc. 1 (Serial 1601), 570–76.

33. Proceedings, June 1872, 28–29.

34. Proceedings, May 1873, 22.

35. Proceedings, September 1875, 23, 29–30.

36. Proceedings, December 1870, 23–24.

37. *Cherokee Advocate*, March 18, 1871, April 20, 1878; Speech of W. P. Ross, January 11, 1872, Report of the Board of Indian Commissioners, 42d Cong., 2d sess., H. Doc. 1 (Serial 1505); Protest of the Delegates of the Creek, Cherokee, and Choctaw Nations, January 24, 1872, 42d Cong., 2d sess., Senate Committee on Indian Affairs, RG 46, Sen 42A – H10, NA.

38. For a more thorough discussion of this episode, see Andrew Denson, "Unite with Us to Rescue the Kiowas: The Five Civilized Tribes and Warfare on the Southern Plains," *Chronicles of Oklahoma* 81 (Winter 2003–04): 458–79.

39. Robert M. Utley, *Frontier Regulars: The United States Army and the Indian, 1866–1891* (New York: MacMillan, 1973), 207–10; Donald Worcester, "Satanta," in *American Indian Leaders: Studies in Diversity*, ed. R. David Edmunds (Lincoln: University of Nebraska Press, 1980), 108–16.

40. Utley, *Frontier Regulars*, 210–11; Mildred P. Mayall, *The Kiowas* (1962, revised; Norman: University of Oklahoma Press, 1971), 257–77; Wilbur S. Nye, *Carbine and Lance: The Story of Old Fort Sill* (Norman: University of Oklahoma Press, 1942), 140–54; E. L. Gilbrath, Report, June 11, 1872, G. W. Schofield to Adjutant General's Office, June 22, 1872, Records of the Adjutant General, RG 94, M666, roll 60, NA.

41. Philip Sheridan to Adjutant General's Office, June 19, 1872, Columbus Delano to Secretary of War, July 11, 1872, Records of the Adjutant General, RG 94, M666, roll 60, NA; Columbus Delano to Francis Walker, July 16, 1872, Records of the Bureau of Indian Affairs, RG 75, M234, roll 61, NA; William T. Hagan, *United States – Comanche Relations: The Reservation Years* (New Haven CT: Yale University Press, 1976), 83–86.

42. For an account of this earlier effort, see Lawrie Tatum, *Our Red Brothers and the Peace Policy of President Ulysses S. Grant* (1899, reprint; Lincoln: University of Nebraska Press, 1970), 107–15.

43. Proceedings, June 1872, 10–11, 17–18, 20. As originally appointed, the commissioners were: Coleman Cole and J. P. Folsom, Choctaws; Eli Smith, Daniel H. Ross, and James Vann, Cherokees; Chilly McIntosh, D. M. Hodge, and Micco Hutchee, Creeks; John Jumper and Fushutchee Harjo, Seminoles; Warloup, Caddo; Black Beaver, Delaware; and Tosawa, Comanche. The Choctaw delegates, for reasons unknown to me, did not attend the actual Council. For the Creeks, Hodge was replaced by Micco Yahola. For a synopsis of Black Beaver's extraordinary life and career as a soldier, guide, tribal leader, and cultural broker, see Carolyn Thomas Foreman, "Black Beaver," *Chronicles of Oklahoma* 24 (Autumn 1946): 269–92.

44. My synopsis of the Council is based upon three reports by writers present at Fort Cobb – –a long report by Cyrus Beede, Enoch Hoag's assistant, and two shorter documents by Daniel H. Ross, who served as the secretary of the Peace Commission. Cyrus Beede to Enoch Hoag, March 30 – August 8, 1872, Bureau of Indian Affairs, RG 75, M234, roll 61, NA (the passage "the last call," p. 24); Daniel H. Ross, Report on the Indian Peace Commission, *Cherokee Advocate*, August 31, 1872; Daniel H. Ross, Report on the Proceedings of a Peace Commission, August 27, 1872, 42d Cong., 1st sess., H. Doc. 1 (Serial 1560), 579–82.

45. Cyrus Beede to Enoch Hoag, March 30 – August 8, 1872, Bureau of Indian Affairs, RG 75, M234, roll 61, NA, 34–35.

46. Cyrus Beede to Enoch Hoag, March 30 – August 8, 1872, Bureau of Indian Affairs, RG 75, M234, roll 61, NA, 59–62, 67–68; Daniel H. Ross, Report on the Indian Peace Commission, *Cherokee Advocate*, August 31, 1872; Black Beaver to Daniel H. Ross, August 19, 1872, reprinted in *Cherokee Advocate*, August 31, 1872; Report of Captain Henry Alvord, October 10, 1872, 42d Cong., 3d sess., H. Doc. 1 (Serial 1560), 513–33; Enoch Hoag to Francis Walker, January 13, 1873, Bureau of Indian Affairs, RG 75, M234, roll 62, NA; Tatum, *Our Red Brothers*, 126–27.

47. Proceedings, May 1873, 27. See also Daniel H. Ross's positive assessments of the Council in the documents cited in note 42.

48. Utley, *Frontier Regulars*, 212–13, 219–33; Nye, *Carbine and Lance*, 187–235; Mayhall, *The Kiowas*, 279–98.

49. Debo, *Road to Disappearance*, 208–10; Proceedings, September 1875, 34–39.

50. Debo, *Road to Disappearance*, 210; *Cherokee Advocate*, April 15, 1876.

51. *Cherokee Advocate*, April 20, 1878; Debo, *Road to Disappearance*, 210; Francis Paul Prucha, "The Board of Indian Commissioners and the Delegates of the Five Tribes," *Chronicles of Oklahoma* 56 (Fall 1978): 254–57. Vine Deloria, Jr., and Clifford M. Lytle argue that Indian resistance to allotment was the factor that turned Congress against the Council. In Five Tribes' writings during the mid – 1870s, however, opposition to allotment still tended to appear as only one of several objections to territorialization, rather than the primary point of contention. Vine Deloria, Jr., and Clifford M. Lytle, *The Nations Within: The Past and Future of American Indian Sovereignty* (Austin: University of Texas Press, 1984), 24–25.

52. Protest of the Creek, Cherokee, and Choctaw Nations, January 24, 1872, 42d Cong., 2d sess., H. Doc. 51 (Serial 1525), 1–3; Protest of the General Indian Council, December 6, 1873, 43d Cong., 1st sess., H. Doc. 88 (Serial 1618), 1–3; *Cherokee Advocate*, December 20, 1873, March 7, 1874, July 4, 1874.

53. Proceedings, September 1875, 7–22.

54. Creek *Indian Journal*, June 14, 28, 1877, June 5, July 17, 1879; *Cherokee Advocate*, July 18, 1877, April 20, 1878, June 11, 1879; Cherokee and Creek delegates to the Commissioner of Indian Affairs, February 2, 1877, Cherokee, Creek, and Seminole delegates to the Commissioner of Indian Affairs, February 11, 1879, Union Agency, RG 75, M234, rolls 867, 872, NA; To the President and Congress of the United States, February 21, 1894, Cherokee National Records, foreign relations, roll 81, OHS; Morris L. Wardell, *A Political History of the Cherokee Nation, 1838–1907* (1938, reprint; Norman: University of Oklahoma Press, 1977), 313–17.

5. THE INDIAN INTERNATIONAL FAIRS

1. Reprinted in the Creek *Indian Journal*, October 13, 1881, transcript in Notes on Five Nations Fairs, Grant Foreman Papers, GM, 2–4.

Relatively few of the fair association's official documents have survived. Those that remain are mostly brief letters spread about in the papers of the Five Tribes and in the correspondence files of the Bureau of Indian Affairs. There are, however, quite a few newspaper accounts available, in particular in the collection noted above. Another resource is the Indian – Pioneer History

Collection, an extensive set of oral histories taken in the 1930s by Works Progress Administration interviewers. Two sets of the collection exist, one at the Oklahoma Historical Society, the other at the University of Oklahoma, Norman. Finally, I have used the advertisements posted by fair organizers in Indian newspapers like the *Cherokee Advocate*. These often listed speakers and events, the judges of competitions, and prominent visitors.

The collection Notes on Five Nations Fairs, Grant Foreman Papers, GM, will be cited hereafter as Foreman Notes. The Indian – Pioneer History Collection will be cited as IPHC.

2. Robert W. Rydell, *All the World's a Fair: Visions of Empire at American International Expositions, 1876–1916* (Chicago: University of Chicago Press, 1984), 21–27, 55–68, 111–18.

3. I am not certain when the fair ended, but 1893 is the last year for which I have found documentation of any kind. Also, it is worth noting that the fair did not take place in 1883 and during several years in the late 1880s. Caddo *Oklahoma Star*, November 13, 1874, transcript in Foreman Notes; John Q. Tufts to Commissioner of Indian Affairs, June 30, 1884, letter no. 12440, RG 75, Bureau of Indian Affairs, letters received, NA; *Cherokee Advocate*, September 16, 1893.

4. Life of Joshua Ross, oral history of Susie Ross Martin, June 11, 1937, IPHC, 6:413; Ella Robinson, Indian International Fair, July 13, 1937, IPHC, 52:396–404; *Cherokee Advocate*, September 21, 1879; Creek *Indian Journal*, September 29, 1877, transcript in Foreman Notes.

5. Oral history of William A. Cummins, May 20, 1937, IPHC, 21:337.

6. Report of the Joint Committee Appointed to Consider the Expediency of Transferring the Indian Bureau to the War Department, January 31, 1879, 45th Cong., 3d sess., H. Report 93 (Serial 1866), 12.

7. Ella Robinson, Indian International Fair, July 13, 1937, IPHC, 52:397–98.

8. Letter of J. W. Archer, Creek *Indian Journal*, October 13, 1881, transcript in Foreman Notes; oral history of Will R. Robison, February 24, 1937, IPHC, 8:537.

9. Angie Debo, *The Road to Disappearance: A History of the Creek Indians* (Norman: University of Oklahoma Press, 1941), 198–99, 231–32; McLoughlin, *After the Trail of Tears: The Cherokees' Struggle for Sovereignty, 1839–1880* (Chapel Hill: University of North Carolina Press, 1993), 222–88; H. Craig Miner, *The Corporation and the Indian: Tribal Sovereignty and Indian Civ-*

ilization, *1865–1907* (1976, reprint; Norman: University of Oklahoma Press, 1988), 1–96.

10. John A. Foreman to Secretary of Interior, November 9, 1883, letter no. 20439, RG 75, Bureau of Indian Affairs, letters received, NA; Life of Joshua Ross, oral history of Susie Ross Martin, IPHC, 6:409–16; Debo, *Road to Disappearance*, 232; Grant Foreman, *A History of Oklahoma* (Norman: University of Oklahoma Press, 142), 120–21.

11. Debo, *Road to Disappearance*, 231–32, 241–42, 259, 278.

12. Caddo *Oklahoma Star*, November 13, 1874, transcript in Foreman Notes.

13. Muskogee *Progress*, October 22, 1875, Atoka *Vindicator*, October 25, 1876, Creek *Indian Journal*, September 29, 1877, transcripts in Foreman Notes; *Cherokee Advocate*, July 29, 1880, June 29, 1881; John Ingalls to Commissioner of Indian Affairs, August 26, 1875, handbill, [1876], RG 75, Union agency, M234, roll 865, NA; oral history of Mrs. Joseph Martin, October 20, 1937, IPHC, 60: 295–300; Ella Robinson, Indian International Fair, July 13, 1937, IPHC, 52:396–404. For horse racing at fairs in the United States, see Leslie Prosterman, *Ordinary Life, Festival Days: Aesthetics in the Midwestern County Fair* (Washington DC: Smithsonian Institution, 1995), 53.

14. Life of Joshua Ross, oral history of Susie Ross Martin, June 11, 1937, IPHC, 6: 409–16; Proceedings of the General Council of the Indian Territory, 1872, 1873, Section X, International Council File, OHS (Delegates are listed on page two of each document); Emmet Starr, *History of the Cherokee Indians and Their Legends and Folklore* (Oklahoma City: Warden, 1921), 273, 410–12.

15. *Cherokee Advocate*, March 1, 1876, October 12, 19, 1878, September 21, 1879, September 1, 1880, August 25, 1882; Creek *Indian Journal*, October 7, 1880, October 24, 1882, September 11, October 9, 1884; Resolution of the General Council of the Indian Territory [with list of stock subscribers], 1875, reprinted in Creek *Indian Journal*, October 7, 1880; Clipping from an unknown Kansas newspaper, July 29, 1875, RG 75, Union agency, M234, roll 865, NA.

16. Debo, *Road to Disappearance*, 177–83, 190–96, 268–81.

17. Commissioner of Indian Affairs to Creek Delegates, February 4, 1882, Creek National Records, federal relations, roll 35, OHS; Creek delegates to Commissioner of Indian Affairs, March 6, 1883, letter no. 4399, John Q. Tufts to Commissioner of Indian Affairs, March 25, 1883, letter no. 5300, John Q. Tufts to Commissioner of Indian Affairs, May 22, 1883, letter no. 9525, John A. Foreman to Secretary of the Interior, November 9, 1883, letter no. 20439,

Charles King (Foreman's lawyer) to Commissioner of Indian Affairs, November 9, 1883, letter no. 20556, Creek delegates to Commissioner of Indian Affairs, February 19, 1884, letter no. 3524, Robert L. Owen to Commissioner of Indian Affairs, June 1, 1884, letter no. 10665, John A. Foreman to Secretary of the Interior, March 20, 1889, letter no. 7932, RG 75, Bureau of Indian Affairs, letters received, NA.

18. Atoka *Vindicator*, September 18, 1875, Muskogee *Progress*, October 22, 1875, transcripts in Foreman Notes; *Cherokee Advocate*, October 12, 1878; John Ingalls to Commissioner or Indian Affairs, August 26, September 14, 1875, S. W. Marston to Commissioner of Indian Affairs, June 24, 1876, Commissioner of Indian Affairs to S. W. Marston, August 23, 1876, RG 75, Union agency, M234, roll 865, NA; L. G. Miles to Commissioner of Indian Affairs, July 26, 1884, letter no. 14494, E. H. Murrell to Commissioner of Indian Affairs, August 25, 1891, letter no. 31434, Joshua Ross to Commissioner of Indian Affairs, August 23, 1892, letter no. 31442, RG 75, Bureau of Indian Affairs, letters received, NA.

19. "The Indian Territory in 1878," *Chronicles of Oklahoma* 4 (September 1926): 256–57, 259–67, 269–71. This is a reprinting of Adair's address, originally published in the Creek *Indian Journal*, October 9, 16, 1878.

20. "Indian Territory in 1878," 272; *Cherokee Advocate*, October 12, 1878.

21. "Indian Territory in 1878," 256.

22. "Indian Territory in 1878," 273–74.

23. "Indian Territory in 1878," 255.

24. Allan G. Bogue, *From Prairie to Corn Belt: Farming on the Illinois and Iowa Prairies in the Nineteenth Century* (Chicago: University of Chicago Press, 1963), 193–95, 204–6. See also, Prosterman, *Ordinary Life, Festival Days*, 49–54; Fred Kniffen, "The American Agricultural Fair: The Pattern," *Annals of the Association of American Geographers* 39 (1949): 264–82; Fred Kniffen, "The American Agricultural Fair: Time and Place," *Annals of the Association of American Geographers* 41 (1951): 42–57; Warren J. Gates, "Modernizing as a Function of an Agricultural Fair: The Great Grangers' Picnic Exhibition of Williams Grove, Pennsylvania, 1873–1916," *Agricultural History* 58 (Fall 1984): 262–79.

25. Francis Paul Prucha, *The Great Father: The United States Government and the American Indians* (Lincoln: University of Nebraska Press, 1984), 285–92; McLoughlin, *After the Trail of Tears*, 86–96.

26. Prucha, *Great Father*, 687–711.

27. *Cherokee Advocate*, September 19, 1877.

28. Letter of W. P. Adair, Cherokee Delegate, Addressed to His People (pamphlet), September 20, 1870, folder 3792, roll 38, Cherokee Nation Papers, WHC, 8.

29. On a number of occasions in the 1860s and 1870s, Congress proposed transferring control of Indian affairs from the Interior Department to the War Department, which had overseen Indian relations prior to 1849. Continued warfare in the West convinced some that the civilian agency should be replaced with firm military control of the Indian population. The governments of the Five Tribes opposed transfer. Francis Paul Prucha, *American Indian Policy in Crisis: Christian Reformers and the Indian, 1865–1900* (Norman: University of Oklahoma Press, 1976), 72–102.

30. *Cherokee Advocate*, October 12, 26, 1878, October 8, 1879, January 29, 1880; Muskogee *Progress*, October 22, 1875, transcripts in Foreman Notes; Ella Robinson, Indian International Fair, July 13, 1937, IPHC, 52:402; Charles Thompson to Rutherford B. Hayes, Carl Schurz, and E. A. Hayt, August 28, 1879, E. A. Hayt to Charles Thompson, September 6, 1879, Carl Schurz to Charles Thompson, September 18, 1879, Cherokee National Records, fairs, roll 77, OHS.

31. *Cherokee Advocate*, October 12, 1878.

32. Debo, *Road to Disappearance*, 241–42; *Cherokee Advocate*, October 8, 1879.

33. *Cherokee Advocate*, August 25, 1882; Joshua Ross to D. W. Bushyhead (letter approving use of the fairgrounds for an intertribal council), August 21, 1882, Cherokee National Records, fairs, roll 77, OHS.

34. Oral history of Will R. Robison, February 24, 1937, IPHC, 8:537.

35. Letter of J. E. Brietz [editor of Ft. Smith, Arkansas, *Herald*], *Cherokee Advocate*, October 26, 1878; Atoka *Vindicator*, September 18, 1875, transcript in Foreman Notes; Letter of J. W. Archer, Creek *Indian Journal*, October 13, 1881, transcript in Foreman Notes; Ella Robinson, Indian International Fairs, July 13, 1937, IPHC, 52:397–98.

36. The parade of nations may have continued into the 1880s, but here the accounts that describe it are all from the earlier years of the fair.

37. Atoka *Vindicator*, September 18, 1875, transcript in Foreman Notes.

38. Muskogee *Progress*, October 22, 1875, transcript in Foreman Notes.

39. Theda Perdue, ed. *Nations Remembered: An Oral History of the Cherokees, Chickasaws, Choctaws, Creeks, and Seminoles in Oklahoma, 1865–1907* (Norman: University of Oklahoma Press, 1993), 68.

40. Resolution of the Board of Education, in *Cherokee Advocate*, September 16, 1876; Resolution, September 8, 1878, Minutes of the Board of Education, Cherokee National Records, schools, roll 128, OHS; Muskogee *Progress*, October 22, 1875, transcript in Foreman Notes.

41. *Cherokee Advocate*, September 21, 1879, September 1, 1880.

42. *Cherokee Advocate*, September 21, 1879.

43. *Indian Journal*, October 13, 1881, transcript in Foreman Notes, 5.

44. Robert W. Rydell, *All the World's a Fair*, 21–27, 55–68, 111–18.

45. Rydell, *All the World's a Fair*, 1–104; John G. Cawelti, "America on Display: The World's Fairs of 1876, 1893, 1933," in *The Age of Industrialism in America: Essays in Social Structure and Cultural Values*, ed. Frederic Cople Jaher (New York: Free Press, 1968), 317–63; Alan Trachtenberg, *The Incorporation of America: Culture and Society in the Gilded Age* (New York: Hill and Wang, 1982), 208–34; Neil Harris, "Great American Fairs and American Cities: The Role of Chicago's Columbian Exposition," in *Cultural Excursions: Marketing Appetites and Cultural Tastes in Modern America* (Chicago: University of Chicago Press, 1990), 111–31; Robert W. Rydell, "The Literature of International Expositions," in *The Books of the Fairs: Materials About World's Fairs, 1834–1916, in the Smithsonian Institution Libraries* (Chicago: American Library Association, 1992), 1–62.

46. Rydell, *All the World's a Fair*, 24–25, 57–60, 99–100. For evolutionary theory in American anthropology, see Curtis M. Hinsley, Jr., *Savages and Scientists: The Smithsonian Institution and the Development of American Anthropology, 1846–1910* (Washington DC: Smithsonian Institution, 1981); Robert E. Bieder, *Science Encounters the Indian, 1820–1880: The Early Years of American Ethnology* (Norman: University of Oklahoma Press, 1986), 194–246.

47. Rydell, *All the World's a Fair*, 166–67; L. G. Moses, *Wild West Shows and the Images of American Indians, 1883–1933* (Albuquerque: University of New Mexico Press, 1996), 129–67. As the title indicates, Moses deals primarily with Wild West shows. He offers, however, a very useful description of the battle between Wild West shows and the Indian Bureau for control of the Native American image, the model schools at world's fairs representing a part of that struggle. Moses aptly calls the students participating in the model schools "the government's show Indians."

48. Rydell, *All the World's a Fair*, 64–68 (quote, 65).

49. Cawelti, "America on Display," 317–21; Trachtenberg, *Incorporation of America*, 208–20.

50. Rydell, *All the World's a Fair*, 167–78.

51. Journal of the Sixth Annual General Council of the Indian Territory, September 1875, International Council File, Section X, OHS, 29.

52. Journal of the Sixth Annual General Council of the Indian Territory, 29–30. It is unclear why the fair organizers declined to offer financial support, but two suggestions can be made. First, the creators of the Indian exhibits had less money than they considered necessary, Congress having failed to meet a Smithsonian request for additional funds for use on the Centennial's Indian displays. Rydell, *All the World's a Fair*, 26. Second, the organizers had a stated preference for material from "primitive" tribes, which may have left them even less willing to use their resources on an exhibit that would feature the Five Tribes. As one organizer said of "partially civilized tribes": "their mixture with whites or negroes & their adoption of their [non – Indians'] manners & customs renders them less interesting as objects of ethnological display." Spencer Baird to Commissioner of Indian Affairs, March 9, 1876, Bureau of Indian Affairs, Record Group 75, M234, roll 54, NA.

53. Creek *Indian Journal*, August 24, September 7, 1876.

54. Delegates of the Five Civilized Tribes to the Commissioner of Indian Affairs, January 22, 1876, Bureau of Indian Affairs, Record Group 75, M234, roll 54, NA. In this letter, the delegates of the Five Tribes asked the Indian Bureau for help in mounting an exhibit and, in the process, explained that "want of funds" had so far kept them from doing so on their own.

55. Creek *Indian Journal*, September 7, 1876. This correspondent stated, however, that the Five Tribes had derived some benefit from even the small displays at Philadelphia. In particular, visitors seemed impressed by the photographs of the Cherokee public buildings: "Have I not enjoyed pointing them out and explaining them to the people who ask how many of our young men are with Sitting Bull."

6. DEMAGOGUES, POLITICAL BUMMERS, SCALAWAGS

1. *Cherokee Advocate*, January 19, 1878.

2. *Cherokee Advocate*, January 19, 1878.

3. H. Craig Miner, *The Corporation and the Indian: Tribal Sovereignty and Industrial Civilization, 1865–1907* (1976, reprint; Norman: University of Oklahoma Press, 1988); William G. McLoughlin, *After the Trail of Tears:*

The Cherokees' Struggle for Sovereignty, 1839–1880 (Chapel Hill: University of North Carolina Press, 1993), 222–88.

4. McLoughlin, *After the Trail of Tears*, 112.

5. McLoughlin, *After the Trail of Tears*, 116–17; Gary Moulton, ed., *Papers of Chief John Ross* (Norman: University of Oklahoma Press, 1988), 2:406.

6. McLoughlin, *After the Trail of Tears*, 222–27; Miner, *Corporation and the Indian*, 14–16, 29–31; Walter A. Johnson, "Brief History of the Missouri – Kansas – Texas Railroad Lines," *Chronicles of Oklahoma* 24 (Fall 1946): 340–58.

7. Miner, *Corporation and the Indian*, 21–22.

8. Miner, *Corporation and the Indian*, 24–26; Argument of Counsel for the Cherokee Nation, April 1869, Hargrett Pamphlet Collection, GM; Communication of the Delegation of the Cherokees, 1870, Second Annual Report of the Board of Indian Commissioners, 41st Cong., 3d sess., S. Doc. 39 (Serial 1440), 86–87; Memorial of the Principal Chief and Delegates of the Cherokee Nation, March 14, 1870, 41st Cong., 2d sess., S. Doc. 83 (Serial 1408), 3.

9. Miner, *Corporation and the Indian*, 26–27. For later discussion of the Cherokee – run railroad idea, see *Cherokee Advocate*, December 2, 9, 1881.

10. Miner, *Corporation and the Indian*, 77–96.

11. Railroad representatives made this argument with particular force in testimony presented to a special congressional committee sent to investigate conditions in the Indian Territory in the late 1870s. Appendix, Report on the Indian Territory, February 11, 1879, 45th Cong., 3d sess., Senate Report 744 (Serial 1839). See also C. J. Hillyer, Atlantic and Pacific Railroad and the Indian Territory, 1871, Hargrett Pamphlet Collection, GM.

12. Miner, *Corporation and the Indian*, 14–15; McLoughlin, *After the Trail of Tears*, 233–34.

13. Miner, *Corporation and the Indian*, 23, 34–35; McLoughlin, *After the Trail of Tears*, 245–48.

14. To the Congress of the United States, [1876], 44th Cong., 2d sess., House Committee on Indian Affairs, RG 233, HR 44A – F36.6, NA, 2, 9–10.

15. To the Congress of the United States, [1876], 1.

16. To the Congress of the United States, [1876], 8. The term "actual settlers" came from the official title of the 1862 Homestead Act, which referred to encouraging "actual settlers," rather than speculators, to purchase land.

17. To the Congress of the United States, [1876], 8–9.

18. To the Congress of the United States, [1876], 10–11.

19. Memorial of the Indian Delegates Petitioning for the Forfeiture of Certain Conditional Land – Grants, January 8, 1880, Hargrett Pamphlet Collection, GM, 2.

20. To the Congress of the United States, May 26, 1876, 44th Cong., 2d sess., Senate Committee on Indian Affairs, RG 46, Sen 43A – H10.1, NA, 2; *Cherokee Advocate*, May 9, 1874, May 6, 1876.

21. Petition from Flint District, Cherokee Nation, July 12, 1876, 44th Cong., 2d sess., House Committee on Indian Affairs, RG 233, HR 44A – H6.1, NA, 1.

22. Appeal of the Cherokee Delegation, March 14, 1870, 41st Cong., 2d sess., S. Doc. 83 (Serial 1408) (There is a handwritten draft of this memorial in the papers of the House Committee on Indian Affairs, RG 233, HR 41A – H5.1, NA); Protest of the Creek and Cherokee Delegations, March 3, 1873, 42d Cong., 3d sess., H. Doc. 110 (Serial 1573); Protest of the General Council of the Indian Territory, December 6, 1873, 43d Cong., 1st sess., H. Doc. 88 (Serial 1618); Speech of W. P. Ross Before the House Committee on Territories, in *Cherokee Advocate*, February 21, 1874; Answer of the Legally Authorized Delegates of the Cherokee, Creek, Choctaw, and Seminole Nations [before the House Committee on Territories], February 11, 1876, Hargrett Pamphlet Collection, GM; Reply of the Chickasaw, Choctaw, Seminole, Creek, and Cherokee Indians [before the House Committee on Territories], [1886], folder 3786, roll 38, Cherokee Nation Papers, WHC; *Cherokee Advocate*, October 18, 1873, February 28, 1874, November 30, 1878, May 14, 1879.

23. Delegation Report, 1876, Cherokee National Records, federal relations, roll 77, OHS.

24. *Cherokee Advocate*, June 29, 1878.

25. *Cherokee Advocate*, February 9, 1878.

26. *Cherokee Advocate*, October 22, 1870, April 13, 27, June 29, 1878, February 26, July 8, 1879, February 25, 1880; Petitions, July, 1876, 44th Cong., 2d sess., House Committee on Indian Affairs, RG 233, HR 44A – H6.1, NA; Memorial of Indian Delegates Petitioning for the Forfeiture of Certain Conditional Land – Grants, January 8, 1880, Hargrett Pamphlet Collection, GM.

27. Objections of the Cherokees, Chickasaws, and Creeks, Addressed to the President, May 24, 1886, folder 3826, roll 38, Cherokee Nation Papers, WHC, 4.

28. Memorial of the Indian Delegates, [1878], folder 3825, roll 38, Cherokee Nation Papers, WHC, 6; Protest of the Cherokee Nation against a Territorial Government, January 30, 1871, Hargrett Pamphlet Collection, GM, 8–9; *Cherokee Advocate*, February 9, 1878.

29. Jeffrey Burton, *Indian Territory and the United States, 1866–1906: Courts, Government, and the Movement for Oklahoma Statehood* (Norman: University of Oklahoma Press, 1995), 145–46.

30. McLoughlin, *After the Trail of Tears*, 262–63; Letter of W. P. Adair, Cherokee Delegate, Addressed to His People, September 20, 1870, folder 3792, roll 38, Cherokee Nation Papers, WHC, 1–4; Delegation Report, 1876, federal relations, Cherokee National Records, roll 77, OHS; Delegation Report, November 7, 1878, roll 78, OHS; William P. Adair and Daniel H. Ross to the Cherokee People, July 8, 1879, folder 3860, roll 38, Cherokee Nation Papers, WHC, 9–12; *Cherokee Advocate*, October 22, 1870, August 3, 1878.

31. McLoughlin, *After the Trail of Tears*, 315–38.

32. McLoughlin, *After the Trail of Tears*, 340–41.

33. Protest of Creek and Cherokee Delegates [including both Ross and Adair], March 3, 1873, 42d Cong., 3d sess., H. Doc. 110 (Serial 1573); Speech of W. P. Ross, *Cherokee Advocate*, February 21, 1874; Speech of W. P. Ross, *Cherokee Advocate*, October 17, 1874; Description of testimony by W. P. Adair and W. P. Ross before the Senate Committee on Territories, *Cherokee Advocate*, February 1, 1879.

34. Report on the Indian Territory, February 11, 1879, 45th Cong., 3d sess., S. Rep. 744 (Serial 1839); Answer of the Legally Authorized Delegates, February 11, 1876, Hargrett Pamphlet Collection, GM, 2.

35. Memorial of the General Council of the Indian Territory, December 5, 1873, 43d Cong., 1st sess., H. Doc. 85 (Serial 1618); Answer of the Legally Authorized Delegates, February 11, 1876, Hargrett Pamphlet Collection, GM; *Cherokee Advocate*, December 9, 1871, March 24, 1880.

36. This section draws a great deal from Mark W. Summers's history of the "corruption issue" in post–Civil War American politics. The book is at once a useful guide to the scandals of the 1870s and 1880s and an analysis of Americans' awareness of corruption (or the possibility of it) in their governments. Mark W. Summers, *The Era of Good Stealings* (New York: Oxford University Press, 1993). See also, Carter Goodrich, *Government Promotion of American Canals and Railroads, 1800–1899* (New York: Columbia University Press, 1960), 169–262; Thomas C. Cochran and William Miller, *The Age of Enterprise: A Social History of Industrial America* (1942, revised; New York: Harper and Row, 1961), 130–35; Carl N. Degler, *The Age of the Economic Revolution, 1876–1900* (Glenview IL: Scott and Forseman, 1967), 21–31; Lloyd

J. Mercer, *Railroads and Land Grant Policy: A Study in Government Intervention* (New York: Academic Press, 1982), 1–60; John T. Noonan, Jr., *Bribes* (New York: MacMillan, 1984), 460–500; Maury Klein, *Union Pacific: Birth of a Railroad, 1862–1893* (New York: Doubleday, 1987), 287–305. Quote from Summers, *Era of Good Stealings*, 46.

37. John Tipple, "The Robber Baron in the Gilded Age: Entrepreneur or Iconoclast?" in *The Gilded Age: A Reappraisal*, ed. H. Wayne Morgan (Syracuse NY: Syracuse University Press, 1963), 14–37; Ari Hoogenboom, "Spoilsmen and Reformers: Civil Service Reform and Public Morality," in Morgan, *The Gilded Age: A Reappraisal*, 69–90; Margaret Susan Thompson, *The "Spider Web": Congress and Lobbying in the Age of Grant* (Ithaca NY: Cornell University Press, 1985), 33–69; Summers, *Era of Good Stealings*, 89–149; Maury Klein, *Unfinished Business: The Railroad in American Life* (Hanover NH: University Press of New England, 1994), 166–86.

38. Summers, *Era of Good Stealings*, 3–74.

39. Summers, *Era of Good Stealings*, 75–85. See also F. B. Marbut, *News From the Capitol: The Story of Washington Reporting* (Carbondale: Southern Illinois University Press, 1971), 133–51; Donald A. Ritchie, *Press Gallery: Congress and the Washington Correspondents* (Cambridge MA: Harvard University Press, 1991).

40. Gordon Milne, *The American Political Novel* (Norman: University of Oklahoma Press, 1966).

41. John W. De Forest, *Honest John Vane* (1875, reprint; State College: Pennsylvania State University Press, 1960), 77–78.

42. De Forest, *Honest John Vane*, 131.

43. Alan Trachtenberg, *The Incorporation of America: Culture and Society in the Gilded Age* (New York: Hill and Wang, 1982), 3–10.

44. Remonstrance of the Cherokee, Creek, Choctaw, and Seminole Delegates, February 28, 1876, 44th Cong., 2d sess., Senate Committee on Territories, RG 46, Sen 44A – H24, NA; Memorial of Indian Delegates Petitioning for the Forfeiture of Certain Conditional Land – Grants, January 8, 1880, Hargrett Pamphlet Collection, GM; *Cherokee Advocate*, March 9, April 27, November 30, 1878; Reply of the Chickasaw, Choctaw, Seminole, Creek, and Cherokee Indians, [1886], folder 3786, roll 38, Cherokee Nation Papers, WHC.

45. Protest of the Cherokee Nation against a Territorial Government, January 30, 1871, Hargrett Pamphlet Collection, GM; Memorial of the Cherokee

Nation, February 2, 1875, 43d Cong., 2d sess., S. Doc. 66 (Serial 1630); Memorial of the Delegates of the Cherokee Nation, March 3, 1875, 43d Cong., 2d
sess., H. Doc. 99 (Serial 1655); Delegation Report, 1876, Cherokee National
Records, federal relations, roll 77, OHS; Memorial of the Cherokee Delegation,
[undated, ca. 1880], 46th Cong., 2d sess., House Committee on Indian Affairs, RG 233, HR 46A – H10.2, NA; *Cherokee Advocate*, March 11, 1876, March 9,
August 3, 1878, March 17, 1880, July 27, 1881. For the North Carolina Cherokee
issue, see Morris L. Wardell, *A Political History of the Cherokee Nation, 1838–
1907* (1938, revised; Norman: University of Oklahoma Press, 1977), 241–54. For
the issue of legal jurisdiction and courts in the Indian Territory, see Jeffrey
Burton, *Indian Territory and the United States*, especially 46–71, 123–70.

46. Milne, *The American Political Novel*, 35–36.

47. *Cherokee Advocate*, June 29, 1878.

48. *Cherokee Advocate*, August 3, 10, 1878, March 24, 1880; Letter of Cherokee
Delegates, *Cherokee Advocate*, July 30, August 6, 13, 1879.

49. Summers, *Era of Good Stealings*, 304–6.

50. *Cherokee Advocate*, February 9, 1878.

51. Miner, *Corporation and the Indian*, 118–42; William W. Savage, Jr., *The
Cherokee Strip Live Stock Association: Federal Regulation and the Cattleman's
Last Frontier* (Columbia: University of Missouri Press, 1973), 33–66.

52. There was a Cherokee precedent for this idea, although I do not know
whether Boudinot was aware of it. In 1845 William Holland Thomas organized the North Carolina Cherokee settlements of Cheoah and Quallatown
into a corporation called the Cherokee Company, chartered by the state. The
charter was granted under a state law meant to encourage the raising of
silkworms, but the point of the company was to protect the Cherokee lands.
In 1889 another act of incorporation created a legal entity called the Eastern
Band of Cherokee Indians. This act, with amendments, still functions as the
band's constitution. John Finger, *The Eastern Band of Cherokees, 1819–1900*
(Knoxville: University of Tennessee Press, 1984), 44–45, 73–74, 155–56.

53. *Cherokee Advocate*, March 7, 1877.

54. *Cherokee Advocate*, June 27, 1877.

55. *Cherokee Advocate*, June 27, 1877.

56. McLoughlin, *After the Trail of Tears*, 279–81.

57. *Cherokee Advocate*, June 10, 1876.

58. *Cherokee Advocate*, November 5, 1870, December 23, 1876, March 2, 1881.

59. *Cherokee Advocate*, June 27, 1877.

60. For example, Resolutions of the Board of Trade, Kansas City MO, January 20, 1879, 45th Cong., 3d sess., House Committee on Territories, RG 233, HR 45A – H23.5, Oklahoma Petition, Mitchellville IA, [1886], 49th Cong., 2d sess., House Committee on Territories, RG 233, HR 49A – H23.2, Petition, Eddyville NY, [1886], 49th Cong., 2d sess., House Committee on Territories, RG 233, HR 49A – H23.2, NA.

61. Memorial and Resolutions Adopted by the Convention for the Opening of the Indian Territory, February 8, 1888, 50th Cong., 2d sess., House Committee on Territories, RG 233, HR 50A – H28.2, NA, 5, 7, 9, 12.

62. Petition, Eddyville NY, [1886], 49th Cong., 2d sess., House Committee on Territories, RG 233, HR 49A – H23.2, NA. For the depiction of delegates as corrupt lobbyists, see "The Philips Steal," pamphlet by Elias C. Boudinot, April 17, 1884, folder 3820, clippings from the *Indian Chieftain*, [ca. 1885], folder 3788, roll 38, Cherokee Nation Papers, WHC. See also testimony by pro – territorial witnesses printed in Appendix, Report on the Indian Territory, February 11, 1879, 45th Cong., 3d sess., Senate Report 744, (Serial 1839); Report on the Leasing of Lands to Citizens of the United States, April 24, 1884, 48th Cong., 1st sess., H. Rep. 1345 (Serial 2257); Report of the Delegation, October 1885, folder 528, roll 5, Cherokee Nation Papers, WHC.

63. For Knights of Labor petitions, see especially the papers of the House Committee on Territories of the 49th and 50th Congresses. The petition quoted is Oklahoma Petition, Akron, Ohio, Knights of Labor, January 30, 1886, 49th Cong., 2d sess., House Committee on Territories, RG 233, HR 49A – H23.2, NA. The Cherokee delegation report for 1886 complained about the presence of lobbyists in Washington claiming membership in the Knights of Labor. Delegation Report, 1886, Cherokee National Records, federal relations, roll 79, OHS, 3. See also, *Washington Post*, February 25, 27, 28, 1889, for an exchange of arguments regarding the Cherokee cattle leases.

7. "THIS NEW PHASE OF THE INDIAN QUESTION"

1. Nell Irvin Painter, *Standing at Armageddon: The United States, 1877–1919* (New York: W. W. Norton, 1987), xxxvii; Henry George, *Progress and Poverty* (1879, reprint; New York: Robert Schalkenbach Foundation, 1981), 552.

2. Letter of W. P. Adair, Cherokee Delegate, Addressed to His People (pamphlet), September 20, 1870, folder 3792, roll 38, Cherokee Nation Papers, WHC, 8.

3. Francis Paul Prucha, *American Indian Policy in Crisis: Christian Reformers and the Indian, 1865–1900* (Norman: University of Oklahoma Press, 1976), 72–78.

4. Gae Whitney Canfield, *Sarah Winnemucca of the Northern Paiutes* (Norman: University of Oklahoma Press, 1983), 201–4.

5. Prucha, *American Indian Policy in Crisis*, 79–102; Robert M. Utley, *Frontier Regulars: The United States Army and the Indian, 1861–1891* (New York: MacMillan, 1973), 197–205, 219–62; Robert W. Mardock, *The Reformers and the American Indian* (Columbia: University of Missouri Press, 1971), 115–28. For a particularly strong statement of the Indian Bureau's opposition to transfer, see N. G. Taylor's 1868 report as commissioner of Indian affairs, November 23, 1868, 40th Cong., 3d sess., H. Doc. 1 (Serial 1366), 461–82. See also, George W. Manypenny, *Our Indian Wards* (1880, reprint; New York: Da Capo, 1972), 373–94.

6. *Cherokee Advocate*, July 22, 1876. For other examples of the *Advocate*'s reporting of the Sioux conflict, see August 26, September 2, 1876, February 3, March 28, June 6, September 19, October 24, 1877. Generally these reports took the form of reprinted items from other newspapers with commentary from the *Advocate*'s editor.

7. *Cherokee Advocate*, July 22, 1876.

8. *Cherokee Advocate*, August 19, 1876, October 17, 1877, April 13, 1878, August 13, 1879.

9. The Indians' most thorough discussion of transfer appeared in Protest of the Lawful Delegates of the Civilized Nations of Indians, March 27, 1876, 44th Cong., 2d sess., Senate Committee on Indian Affairs, RG 46, Sen 44A – H9, NA. See also Protest of the Delegates of the Cherokee, Creek, and Choctaw Nations, January 14, 1869, 40th Cong., 3d sess., S. Doc. 24, (Serial 1361); Delegation Report, 1876, Cherokee National Records, federal relations, roll 77, OHS; *Cherokee Advocate*, May 13, 1876.

10. Delegation Report, 1876, Cherokee National Records, federal relations, roll 77, OHS. The Cherokee delegates were Daniel H. Ross, W. P. Adair, Rufus Ross, and John L. Adair.

11. Delegation Report, 1876, Delegation Report, November 7, 1878, Cherokee National Records, federal relations, rolls 77 and 78, OHS; *Cherokee Advocate*, April 1, May 13, 1876. The newspaper citations refer to letters from the Cherokee delegation reporting to the Nation on matters in Washington.

These were an almost weekly feature of the *Advocate* while Congress was in session.

12. Acts Instructing the Delegation, December 4, 1873, December 7, 1877, December 8, 1894, November 27, 1895, Cherokee National Records, federal relations, rolls 77, 78, and 79, OHS; Acts Instructing the Delegation, December 5, 1882, December 5, 1884, December 12, 1885, December 20, 1886, folders 520, 523, 530, 538, roll 5, Cherokee Nation Papers, WHC.

13. Report of the Delegation, October, 1885, folder 528, roll 5, Cherokee Nation Papers, WHC.

14. Prucha, *American Indian Policy in Crisis*, 228–33; Angie Debo, *The Road to Disappearance: A History of the Creek Indians* (Norman: University of Oklahoma, 1941), 97–99.

15. Prucha, *American Indian Policy in Crisis*, 132–33, 113–28; Frederick E. Hoxie, *A Final Promise: The Campaign to Assimilate the Indians, 1880–1920* (Lincoln: University of Nebraska Press, 1984), 1–5.

16. Hoxie, *Final Promise*, 6–9.

17. Hoxie, *Final Promise*, 9–10.

18. Hoxie, *Final Promise*, 27–28; Prucha, *American Indian Policy in Crisis*, 158–60.

19. Francis Paul Prucha, ed., *Americanizing the American Indians: Writings of the "Friends of the Indian," 1880–1900* (Cambridge MA: Harvard University Press, 1973), 1–9.

20. Merrill E. Gates, "Land and Law as Agents in Educating Indians," in Prucha, *Americanizing the American Indians*, 49–52.

21. Report of the Commissioner of Indian Affairs, 1876, 44th Cong., 2d sess., H. Doc. 1 (Serial 1749), 389–91; Report of the Commissioner of Indian Affairs, 1883, 48th Cong., 1st sess., H. Doc. 1 (Serial 2191), 17–20; Grant Foreman, *A History of Oklahoma* (Norman: University of Oklahoma Press, 1942), 215–18. For Cherokee reactions to the boomer schemes and their defeat by the federal government, see *Cherokee Advocate*, May 28, April 30, 1879, January 5, February 18, August 11, September 1, October 13, 1880, January 12, 1881.

22. Memorial and Resolutions Adopted by the Convention for the Opening of the Indian Territory, February 8, 1888, House Committee on Territories, 50th Cong., 1st sess., RG 233, HR 50A – H28.2, NA, 4–6, 9; Henry L. Dawes, "The Indians of the Indian Territory," 1894, in Prucha, *Americanizing the American Indian*, 321–23.

23. Memorial and Resolutions . . . for the Opening of the Indian Territory, 2; Memorial of C. Brownell, July 9, 1888, 50th Cong., 1st sess., S. Doc. 153 (Serial 2517), 7; Dawes, "The Indians of the Indian Territory," in Prucha, *Americanizing the American Indian*, 321.

24. Prucha, *American Indian Policy in Crisis*, 241–52.

25. Prucha, *American Indian Policy in Crisis*, 387; *Cherokee Advocate*, December 9, 1881, April 2, 1886; Appeal of the Delegates of the Chickasaw, Creek, and Cherokee Nations, [1887] folder 3846, roll 38, Cherokee Nation Papers, whc; Objections of the Delegates of the Chickasaw, Cherokee, and Creek Nations to the Bill Entitled "An Act for the Allotment of Lands in Severalty to Indians," 1887, folder 3873, roll 38, Cherokee Nation Papers, whc.

26. William G. McLoughlin, *After the Trail of Tears: The Cherokees' Struggle for Sovereignty, 1839–1880* (Chapel Hill: University of North Carolina Press, 1992), 279–81, 307–12; *Cherokee Advocate*, August 24, 1872, May 23, May 30, 1874, January 13, October 24, 1877.

27. Thomas Burnell Colbert, "Visionary or Rogue? The Life and Legacy of Elias Cornelius Boudinot," *Chronicles of Oklahoma* 65 (Fall 1987): 271–72.

28. Spencer S. Stephens, The Indian Question, 1882, folder 3801, roll 38, Cherokee Nation Papers, whc.

29. Testimony of Gus Ivey, April 12, 1878, Testimony of Samuel Downing, April 19, 1878, 45th Cong., 3d sess., S. Rep. 744 (Serial 1839), 97–106, 133–38.

30. Remarks of W. P. Adair, January 31, 1876, House Committee on Territories, 44th Cong., 2d sess., rg 233, hr 44A – F36.6, na, 19; Remonstrance of the Cherokee, Creek, Choctaw, and Seminole Delegations, February 28, 1876, folder 3825, roll 38, Cherokee Nation Papers, whc, 6; Memorial of the Indian Delegates, [1876], folder 3825, roll 38, Cherokee Nation Papers, whc; Reply of the Chickasaw, Choctaw, Seminole, Creek, and Cherokee Indians, [1886], folder 3786, roll 38, Cherokee Nation Papers, whc; *Cherokee Advocate*, December 3, 1879, January 19, March 2, 1881.

31. Brief on Behalf of the Cherokee Nation, May 3, 1879, Hargrett Pamphlet Collection, gm, 12–13; Memorial of the Indian Delegates, February 16, 1880, 46th Cong., 2d sess., S. Doc. 41 (Serial 1890); *Cherokee Advocate*, December 3, 1879, March 2, 1881.

32. Memorial of the Indian Delegates, February 16, 1880, 46th Cong., 2d sess., S. Doc. 41 (Serial 1890), 7.

33. Appeal of the Delegates of the Chickasaw, Creek, and Cherokee Nations

to the President of the United States, [1887], folder 3846, roll 38, Cherokee Nation Papers, WHC, 5.

34. Circe Sturm, *Blood Politics: Race, Culture, and Identity in the Cherokee Nation of Oklahoma* (Berkeley and Los Angeles: University of California Press, 2002), 78–81.

35. Petition to William McKinley, [1897], letter no. 23600, RG 75, Bureau of Indian Affairs, letters received, NA; Keetoowah Resolutions, November 28, 1900, letter no. 60681, RG 75, Bureau of Indian Affairs, letters received, NA.

36. Sturm, *Blood Politics*, 78–81; M. Annette Jaimes, "Federal Indian Identification Policy," in *The State of Native America: Genocide, Colonization, and Resistance*, ed. M. Annette Jaimes, 123–32 (Boston: South End, 1992); Angie Debo, *And Still the Waters Run: The Betrayal of the Five Civilized Tribes* (Princeton NJ: Princeton University Press, 1940), 179–80.

37. Memorial to Congress, April 22, 1878, 45th Cong., 2d sess., House Committee on Territories, RG 233, HR 45A – H23.5, NA, 5.

38. *Cherokee Advocate* (delegate letter from Washington), April 28, 1880.

39. Francis Paul Prucha, *The Great Father* (Lincoln: University of Nebraska Press, 1984), 659; Prucha, *American Indian Policy in Crisis*, 230–31; Schurz, "Present Aspects of the Indian Problem," in Prucha, *Americanizing the American Indian*, 21; Debo, *Road to Disappearance*, 100–101.

40. *Cherokee Advocate*, October 16, 1885.

41. Angie Debo, *And Still the Waters Run*, 12–13. The 1890 census reported that whites outnumbered Indians two – to – one in the Five Tribes' country. The census takers, however, categorized individuals by physical appearance, so they almost certainly classed some bicultural mixed – race Indians as whites.

42. Charles Thompson to Carl Schurz, August 1, 1878, reprinted in *Cherokee Advocate*, August 17, 1878; Summary of the Census of the Cherokee Nation, 1881, Cherokee Nation Papers, folder 3824, roll 38, WHC; Joel B. Mayes to John Noble, May 17, 1889, letter no. 13196, Joel B. Mayes to Benjamin Harrison, August 27, 1889, letter no. 25286, RG 75, Bureau of Indian Affairs, letters received, NA; Appeal of the Delegates of the Five Civilized Nations, reprinted in *Cherokee Advocate*, February 27, 1895.

43. *Cherokee Advocate*, March 5, 1879.

44. D. W. Bushyhead, Annual Message, November 10, 1879, reprinted in *Cherokee Advocate*, November 26, 1879; W. P. Ross, Speech before the Committee on Territories, January 23, 1879, reprinted in *Cherokee Advocate*, March

5, 1879; Joel B. Mayes, Annual Message, letter no. 42152, RG 75, Bureau of Indian Affairs, letters received, NA, 12–13.

45. H. Craig Miner, "Dennis Bushyhead," in *American Indian Leaders: Studies in Diversity*, ed. R. David Edmunds (Lincoln: University of Nebraska Press, 1980), 192–205; John Bartlett Meserve, "Chief Dennis Wolfe Bushyhead," *Chronicles of Oklahoma* 13 (Autumn 1935): 349–59.

46. Eric Foner, *The Story of American Freedom* (New York: W. W. Norton, 1998), 115–37; Allan Trachtenberg, *The Incorporation of America: Culture and Society in the Gilded Age* (New York: Hill and Wang, 1982), 70–100; Painter, *Standing at Armageddon*, xxxvii–xliv, 24–35, 64–71.

47. Cherokee Memorial to Congress, in *Cherokee Advocate*, April 25, 1884.

48. Protest of the Representatives of the Indian Territory, in *Cherokee Advocate*, January 19, 1881.

49. Cherokee Memorial to Congress, in *Cherokee Advocate*, April 25, 1884; Cherokee Delegation to President Grover Cleveland, July 30, 1886, Cherokee National Records, federal relations, roll 79, OHS.

50. Cherokee Memorial to Congress, in *Cherokee Advocate*, April 25, 1884.

51. Protest of the Representatives of the Indian Territory, in *Cherokee Advocate*, January 19, 1881.

52. Joel B. Mayes, Annual Message, November 4, 1891, letter no. 42152, RG 75, Bureau of Indian Affairs, letters received, NA, 12.

53. D. W. Bushyhead, Summary of the Census of the Cherokee Nation, 1881, folder 3824, roll 38, Cherokee Nation Papers, WHC, 4.

54. *Cherokee Advocate*, January 23, 1889.

55. Remonstrance of the Cherokee, Creek, Choctaw, and Seminole Delegations, February 28, 1876, folder 3825, roll 38, Cherokee Nation Papers, WHC, 11.

56. Defense of the Cherokee Indians, reprinted in *Cherokee Advocate*, April 13, 1881.

57. *Cherokee Advocate*, January 23, 1889. In case the argument regarding American ideals was not enough to convince one that allotment was wrong, the *Advocate* also printed the text of the Cherokees' patent under the heading, "What do you say to the following; reader – –wherever and whoever you are?"

58. Cherokee Ultimatum, October 28, 1897, transcript in box III, folder 158, D. W. Bushyhead Collection, WHC.

59. George, *Progress and Poverty*, 388.

60. Speech transcribed in Terence Powderly, *Thirty Years of Labor, 1859–1889* (1890, reprint; New York: A. M. Kelley, 1967), 173–74. For a more extensive comparison of Indian and American discussions of land monopoly, see Alexandra Harmon, "American Indians and Land Monopoly in the Gilded Age," *Journal of American History* 90 (June 2003): 106–33. Harmon's essay (which appeared as I was finishing the last revisions for this book) and this chapter use some of the same Cherokee resources, although she and I come to somewhat different conclusions.

61. See, for example, Oklahoma Petition, Akron OH, Knights of Labor, January 30, 1886, 49th Cong., 2d sess., House Committee on Territories, RG233, HR 49A – H23.2, NA. The papers of the House Committee on Territories of the 49th and 50th Congresses contain a large number of similar petitions.

62. Remonstrance of the Cherokee, Creek, Choctaw, and Seminole Delegations, February 28, 1876, folder 3825, roll 38, Cherokee Nation Papers, WHC, 11; Knights of Labor Preamble, in Powderly, *Thirty Years of Labor*, 128–30. The first paragraph of the Preamble called for "all who believe in securing 'the greatest good for the greatest number' to aid and assist" the Knights of Labor.

63. Memorial of the Cherokee Nation, February 7, 1894, letter no. 15143, RG 75, Bureau of Indian Affairs, letters received, NA, 1; Foreman, *History of Oklahoma*, 238–43. Other negative Cherokee responses to creating a territory open to settlement on these lands include Joint Resolution of the Cherokee Legislature, December 3, 1886, Delegation Report, November 18, 1888, Cherokee National Records, federal relations, roll 79, OHS; Delegation Report, December 1889, folder 545, roll 5, Cherokee Nation Papers, WHC.

64. Memorial and Joint Resolution, November 29, 1893, Cherokee National Records, federal relations, roll 79, OHS, 2.

65. *Cherokee Advocate*, October 3, 1894; Painter, *Standing at Armageddon*, 110–40; Morton Keller, *Affairs of State: Public Life in Late Nineteenth Century America* (Cambridge MA: Harvard University Press, 1977), 565–87.

66. Act to Appoint a Commission, January 17, 1894, Cherokee National Records, federal relations, roll 79, OHS; To the President and Congress, February 21, 1894, Cherokee National Records, foreign relations, roll 81, OHS; Prucha, *American Indian Policy in Crisis*, 387–89; Morris L. Wardell, *A Political History of the Cherokee Nation, 1838–1907* (1938, reprint; Norman: University of Oklahoma Press, 1977), 313–15; Loren N. Brown, "The Establishment of the Dawes Commission for the Indian Territory," *Chronicles of Oklahoma* 18 (Spring 1940): 171–81.

67. Meredith Kidd to C. J. Harris, May 11, 1894, Cherokee National Records, federal relations, roll 79, OHS.

68. Hoke Smith to Henry Dawes, May 6, 1895, Cherokee National Records, federal relations, roll 79, OHS.

69. C. J. Harris to the Dawes Commission, August 25, 1894, in *Cherokee Advocate*, September 5, 1894.

70. National Council to the Dawes Commission, December 8, 1894, Cherokee National Records, federal relations, roll 79, OHS.

71. Report of the Commission to the Five Civilized Tribes, November 20, 1894, 14–20; Prucha, *American Indian Policy in Crisis*, 392–94; Dawes, "Indians of the Indian Territory," 317–27; Wardell, *Political History of the Cherokee Nation*, 315–16.

72. Remarks before the House Judiciary Committee, January 10, 1895, letter no. 9036, RG 75, Bureau of Indian Affairs, letters received, NA, 15; Report of the Delegation [December 1895], Cherokee National Records, federal relations, roll 79, OHS, 1–5; Wardell, *Political History of the Cherokee Nation*, 316–17.

73. Remarks before the House Judiciary Committee, January 10, 1895, letter no. 9036, RG 75, Bureau of Indian Affairs, letters received, NA, 2.

74. Remarks before the House Judiciary Committee, January 10, 1895, letter no. 9036, RG 75, Bureau of Indian Affairs, letters received, NA, 7–8, 20–21, 27–29; An Appeal by the Delegates of the Five Civilized Nations, reprinted in *Cherokee Advocate*, February 27, 1895.

75. Report of the Delegation [December 1895], Cherokee National Records, federal relations, roll 79, OHS, 6–9, 29–30. Angie Debo quoted this report at length at the end of the first chapter of *And Still the Waters Run*. For some reason, she left Walter A. Duncan off her list of 1895 delegates, although it seems likely that Duncan, who led the group and wrote most of its correspondence, composed this striking document. Angie Debo, *And Still the Waters Run*, 27–30.

76. Report of the Commission to the Five Civilized Tribes, November 18, 1895, 68–79; Cherokee Delegates to the House and Senate, February 12, 1895, RG 46, Senate Committee on Indian Affairs, Sen 53A – J14, NA; Mayes to Grover Cleveland, December 23, 1895, letter no. 10221, RG 75, Bureau of Indian Affairs, letters received, NA; Wardell, *Political History of the Cherokee Nation*, 317–18.

77. Cherokee Chief and Delegates to the President, February 2, 1895, letter no. 6276, RG 75, Bureau of Indian Affairs, letters received, NA.

78. Wardell, *Political History of the Cherokee Nation*, 318; Debo, *And Still the Waters Run*, 32.

79. Appeal of the Delegates of the Cherokee Nation, April 6, 1897, in Delegation Report, July 1897, series 1, box 2, folder 11, J. B. Milam Collection, University of Tulsa (Tulsa OK), 10–15; Cherokee Commissioners to the Dawes Commission, October 28, 1897, Memorial to the Senate and House of Representatives, [October or November 1897], RG 46, Senate Committee on Indian Affairs, Sen 55A – J14, NA.

80. Minutes of the Cherokee Commission, August 16–21, 1897, Cherokee National Records, federal relations, roll 79, OHS, 4, 7.

81. Minutes of the Cherokee Commission, August 16–21, 1897, Cherokee National Records, federal relations, roll 79, OHS; Keetoowah Petition, [1897], letter no. 23600, RG 75, Bureau of Indian Affairs, letters received, NA; Cherokee Commissioners to the Dawes Commission, October 28, 1897, RG 46, Senate Committee on Indian Affairs, Sen 55A – J14, NA.

82. Prucha, *American Indian Policy in Crisis*, 390–401; Hutchins and West to Mayes, July 11, 1898, Cherokee National Records, federal relations, roll 79, OHS.

83. Report of the Commission to the Five Civilized Tribes, September 1, 1899, 9.

84. Act Appointing a Commission, November 28, 1898, Minutes of the Joint Session United States Commission and Cherokee Commission, December, 1898–January, 1899, Cherokee National Records, federal relations, roll 79, OHS; Debo, *And Still the Waters Run*, 34–35; Wardell, *Political History of the Cherokee Nation*, 322–23.

85. Cherokee Agreement, Report of the Commission to the Five Civilized Tribes, September 1, 1899, 49–59.

86. Cherokee Agreement, Report of the Commission to the Five Civilized Tribes, September 1, 1900, 35–44; Keetoowah Resolutions, November 28, 1900, letter no. 60681, RG 75, Bureau of Indian Affairs, letters received, NA; Wardell, *Political History of the Cherokee Nation*, 323–25. Circe Sturm discusses the issue of black Cherokee identity. Sturm, *Blood Politics*, 186–89.

87. Cherokee Agreement, Report of the Commission to the Five Civilized Tribes, July 20, 1902, 101–9; Wardell, *Political History of the Cherokee Nation*, 326–27.

88. Janey B. Hendrix, "Redbird Smith and the Nighthawk Keetoowahs," *Journal of Cherokee Studies* 8 (Fall 1983): 73–81.

89. Foreman, *History of Oklahoma*, 310–316; Debo, *And Still the Waters Run*, 162–65; Amos Maxwell, "The Sequoyah Convention," *Chronicles of Oklahoma* 28 (Summer 1950): 161–92, (Fall 1950): 299–340.

90. Maxwell, "Sequoyah Convention," 330–33.

EPILOGUE

1. Angie Debo, *And Still the Waters Run: The Betrayal of the Five Civilized Tribes* (Princeton NJ: Princeton University Press, 1940), 91.

2. Debo, *And Still the Waters Run*, 6, 379; Theda Perdue and Michael Green, *The Columbia Guide to American Indians of the Southeast* (New York: Columbia University Press, 2001), 120.

3. Debo, *And Still the Waters Run*, 92–125.

4. Debo, *And Still the Waters Run*, 89–90, 179–80.

5. Debo, *And Still the Waters Run*, 181.

6. Debo, *And Still the Waters Run*, 182–97.

7. Debo, *And Still the Waters Run*, 230–57.

8. Debo, *And Still the Waters Run*, 373.

9. Debo, *And Still the Waters Run*, 64–65; Rennard and William M. Strickland, "Beyond the Trail of Tears: One Hundred Fifty Years of Cherokee Survival," in *Cherokee Removal: Before and After*, ed. William L. Anderson, 122–23 (Athens: University of Georgia Press, 1991).

10. Georgia Rae Leeds, *The United Keetoowah Band of Cherokee Indians in Oklahoma* (New York: Peter Lang, 1996), 10–13.

11. Debo, *And Still the Waters Run*, 368–39; Perdue and Green, *Columbia Guide*, 121.

12. Debo, *And Still the Waters Run*, 370–71; Leeds, *United Keetoowah Band*, 14.

13. Perdue and Green, *Columbia Guide*, 122; Leeds, *United Keetoowah Band*, 14–21.

14. Strickland and Strickland, "Beyond the Trail of Tears," 128; Circe Sturm, *Blood Politics: Race, Culture, and Identity in the Cherokee Nation of Oklahoma* (Berkeley and Los Angeles: University of California Press, 2002), 90–91.

15. Strickland and Strickland, "Beyond the Trail of Tears," 130.

16. Strickland and Strickland, "Beyond the Trail of Tears," 130; Sturm, *Blood Politics*, 91, 93.

17. Circe Sturm notes that the decision to distribute the claims money to

Cherokees by blood continued the nineteenth-century practice of restricting black Cherokee citizens' access to tribal resources. Sturm, *Blood Politics*, 92.

18. Strickland and Strickland, "Beyond the Trail of Tears," 128–30; Sturm, *Blood Politics*, 92–93.

19. Strickland and Strickland, "Beyond the Trail of Tears," 131; Sturm, *Blood Politics*, 94; Leeds, *United Keetoowah Band*, 71–74.

20. Circe Sturm's book has a brief description of the crisis of the late 1990s. Sturm, *Blood Politics*, 102–3. Detailed information can be found in the Cherokee Nation's official newspaper, *Cherokee Phoenix and Indian Advocate* (formerly *Cherokee Advocate*); the *Cherokee Observer*, an independent monthly; and the *Tulsa World*.

21. *Cherokee Phoenix and Indian Advocate*, Spring 2001; Winter, Spring, and Fall 2002; July and August 2003. Regarding the dates in this citation, the *Phoenix* was published quarterly until 2003, when it switched to monthly issues.

BIBLIOGRAPHY

PRIMARY SOURCES

Oklahoma Historical Society. Oklahoma City
    Cherokee National Records. Microfilm.
    Indian-Pioneer History Collection. Microfilm.
    International Council File. Section X. Indian Archives.
Western History Collection. University of Oklahoma, Norman
    Cherokee Nation Papers. Microfilm.
    W. P. Boudinot Collection.
    D. W. Bushyhead Collection.
    C. J. Harris Collection.
    J. B. Mayes Collection.
    Oochalata Collection.
    W. P. Ross Collection.
Gilcrease Museum. Tulsa OK
    Hargrett Pamphlet Collection.
    Grant Foreman Papers.
University of Tulsa. Tulsa OK
    J. B. Milam Papers.

NEWSPAPERS

Cherokee Advocate. Tahlequah, Cherokee Nation. 1845–50, 1873–98.
Indian Chieftain. Vinita, Cherokee Nation. 1882–1900.
Indian Journal. Muskogee, Creek Nation. 1876–98.

OTHER

Adair, W. P. "The Indian Territory in 1878." *Chronicles of Oklahoma* 4 (Fall 1926): 255–74.
Annual Reports of the Commission to the Five Civilized Tribes, 1894–1905.
Beeson, John. *A Plea for the Indians.* 1857. Reprint. Medford OR: Webb Research Group, 1994.

Colyer, Vincent. *Peace with the Apaches.* 1872. Reprint. Freeport NY: Books for Libraries Press, 1971.

Dale, Edward Everett, and Gaston Litton, eds. *Cherokee Cavaliers: Forty Years of Cherokee History as Told in the Correspondence of the Ridge-Watie-Boudinot Family.* 1939. Reprint. Norman: University of Oklahoma Press, 1995.

Foreman, Grant, ed. *A Traveler in Indian Territory: The Journal of Ethan Allen Hitchcock.* Norman: University of Oklahoma Press, 1930.

George, Henry. *Progress and Poverty.* 1879. Reprint. New York: Robert Schalkenbach Foundation, 1981.

Hays, Robert G., ed. *A Race at Bay: New York Times Editorials on "the Indian Problem," 1860–1900.* Carbondale: Southern Illinois University Press, 1997.

Jackson, Andrew. Annual Message. December 8, 1829. *Messages of General Andrew Jackson.* Concord NH, 1837: 59–61.

"Journal of the General Council of the Indian Territory." *Chronicles of Oklahoma* 3 (April 1925): 33–44.

Karcher, Carolyn, ed. *Lydia Maria Child: Hobomock and Other Writings on Indians.* New Brunswick NJ: Rutgers University Press, 1986.

Manypenny, George W. *Our Indian Wards.* 1880. Reprint. New York: Da Capo, 1972.

Moulton, Gary E., ed. *The Papers of Chief John Ross.* 2 vols. Norman: University of Oklahoma Press, 1985.

Perdue, Theda, ed. *Cherokee Editor: The Writings of Elias Boudinot.* Knoxville: University of Tennessee Press, 1993.

————, ed. *Nations Remembered: An Oral History of the Cherokees, Chickasaws, Choctaws, Creeks, and Seminoles in Oklahoma, 1865–1907.* Norman: University of Oklahoma Press, 1993.

Powderly, Terrence. *Thirty Years of Labor, 1859–1889.* 1890. Reprint. New York: A. M. Kelley, 1967.

Prucha, Francis Paul, ed. *Americanizing the American Indian: Writings by the "Friends of the Indian," 1880–1900.* Cambridge MA: Harvard University Press, 1973.

————, ed. *Cherokee Removal: The "William Penn" Essays and Other Writings by Jeremiah Evarts.* Knoxville: University of Tennessee Press, 1981.

Tatum, Lawrie. *Our Red Brothers and the Peace Policy of President Ulysses S. Grant.* 1899. Reprint. Lincoln: University of Nebraska Press, 1970.

Thoburn, Joseph B., ed. "The Cherokee Question." *Chronicles of Oklahoma* 2 (Summer 1924): 141–242.

U.S. Office of the Adjutant General. *Letters Received, 1871–1880.* Record Group 94. Microfilm 666. National Archives. Washington DC.

U.S. Bureau of Indian Affairs. *Letters Received.* Centennial Exhibition, 1875–1878. Cherokee Agency, 1859–1874. Union Agency, 1875–1880. Record Group 75. Microfilm 234. National Archives. Washington DC.

U.S. Bureau of Indian Affairs. *Letters Received, 1881–1906.* Record Group 75. National Archives. Washington DC.

U.S. Congress. House. *Cherokee Disturbances, 1845.* 29th Cong., 1st sess. H. Doc. 185. Serial 485.

———. *Correspondence on Outrages Committed Among Cherokees, 1845.* 29th Cong., 1st sess. H. Doc. 92. Serial 483.

———. *Files of the House Committee on Indian Affairs.* Record Group 233. 39th—55th Cong. National Archives. Washington DC.

———. *Files of the House Committee on Territories.* Record Group 233. 39th—55th Cong. National Archives. Washington DC.

———. *Memorial of Cherokee Delegates to the Senate and House of Representatives, February 27, 1829.* 20th Cong., 2d sess. H. Doc. 145. Serial 187.

———. *Memorial of Yearly Meetings of the Society of Friends, January 25, 1869.* 40th Cong., 3d sess. H. Doc. 29. Serial 1385.

———. *Memorial of the Delegates and Representatives of the Cherokee Nation, West, April 1, 1840.* 26th Cong., 1st sess. H. Doc. 162. Serial 366.

———. *Memorial of the Delegates of the Cherokee Nation, March 3, 1875.* 43d Cong., 2d sess. H. Doc. 99. Serial 1655.

———. *Memorial of the Principal Chief and Others of the Cherokee Nation, February 18, 1865.* 38th Cong., 2d sess. H. Doc. 52. Serial 1232.

———. *Memorial of the Treaty Party of Cherokee Indians, April 13, 1844.* 28th Cong., 1st sess. H. Doc. 234. Serial 443.

———. *Memorial on Behalf of the Indians by the United States Indian Commission, July 20, 1868.* 40th Cong., 2d sess. H. Doc. 165. Serial 1350.

———. *Official Proceedings of the Council with the Indians of the West and Southwest, September 8–21, 1865.* 39th Cong., 1st sess. H. Doc. 1. Serial 1248.

———. *Protest of the Creek and Cherokee Delegations, March 3, 1873.* 42d Cong., 3d sess. H. Doc. 110. Serial 1573.

————. *Protest of the General Indian Council of the Indian Territory, December 6, 1873.* 43d Cong., 1st sess. H. Doc. 88. Serial 1618.

————. *Report of the Indian Peace Commissioners, January 7, 1868.* 40th Cong., 2d sess. H. Doc. 97. Serial 1337.

————. *Report on the Leasing of Lands to Citizens of the United States, April 24, 1884.* 48th Cong., 2d sess. H. Rep. 1345. Serial 2257.

U.S. Congress. Senate. *Condition of the Indian Tribes: Report of the Joint Special Commission, January 26, 1867.* 39th Cong., 1st sess. S. Rep. 156. Serial 1279.

————. *Exhibiting Present State of Difficulties Existing and Arrangements Made, or Attempted, between Government and Cherokee People, 1840.* 26th Cong., 1st sess. S. Doc 347. Serial 359.

————. *Files of the Senate Committee on Indian Affairs.* Record Group 46. 39th—55th Cong. National Archives. Washington DC.

————. *Files of the Senate Committee on Territories.* Record Group 46. 39th—55th Cong. National Archives. Washington DC.

————. *Memorial of Indian Delegates, February 16, 1880.* 46th Cong., 2d sess. S. Doc. 41. Serial 1890.

————. *Memorial of Lewis Downing, March 23, 1869.* 41st Cong., 1st sess. S. Doc. 16. Serial 1399.

————. *Memorial of the Cherokee Delegates to the Senate and House of Representatives, May 17, 1834.* 23d Cong., 1st sess. S. Doc. 386. Serial 242.

————. *Memorial of the Cherokee Nation, February 2, 1875.* 43d Cong., 2d sess. S. Doc. 66. Serial 1630.

————. *Memorial of the Delegates of the Cherokee, Creek, and Choctaw Nations of Indians, May 23, 1870.* 41st Cong., 2d sess. S. Doc. 143. Serial 1408.

————. *Memorial of the Principal Chief and Delegates of the Cherokee Nation, March 14, 1870.* 41st Cong., 2d sess. S. Doc. 83. Serial 1408.

————. *Message of the Cherokee Delegates Transmitting the Address of the Grand International Council, June 14, 1870.* 41st Cong., 2d sess. S. Doc. 154. Serial 1408.

————. *Message of the President of the United States Communicating the Second Annual Report of the Board of Indian Commissioners, February 10, 1871.* 41st Cong., 3d sess. S. Doc. 39. Serial 1440.

————. *Message of the President of the United States on the Proceedings of a the Council of Indian Tribes Held at Okmulgee, January 30, 1871.* 41st Cong., 3d sess. S. Doc. 26. Serial 1440.

Bibliography

————. *Protest of the Delegates of the Cherokee, Creek, and Choctaw Nations, January 14, 1869.* 40th Cong., 3d sess. S. Doc. 24. Serial 1361.

————. *Report on the Indian Territory, February 11, 1879.* 45th Cong., 3d sess. S. Rep. 744. Serial 1839.

SECONDARY SOURCES

Abzug, Robert H. *Cosmos Crumbling: American Reform and the Religious Imagination.* New York: Oxford University Press, 1994.

Agnew, Brad. *Fort Gibson: Terminal on the Trail of Tears.* Norman: University of Oklahoma Press, 1980.

Agnew, Kelley. "Tragedy of the Goingsnake District: The Shoot-out at Zeke Proctor's Trial." *Chronicles of Oklahoma* 66 (Spring 1988): 90–99.

Anderson, William L., ed. *Cherokee Removal: Before and After.* Athens: University of Georgia Press, 1991.

Andrew, John A., III. *From Revivals to Removal: Jeremiah Evarts, the Cherokee Nation, and the Search for the Soul of America.* Athens: University of Georgia Press, 1992.

Andrews, Thomas F. "Freedmen in Indian Territory: A Post–Civil War Dilemma." *Journal of the West* 4 (July 1965): 367–76.

Ballman, Gail. "The Creek Treaty of 1866." *Chronicles of Oklahoma* 41 (Winter 1970–71): 184–96.

Bercovitch, Sacvan. *The American Jeremiad.* Madison: University of Wisconsin Press, 1978.

————. *The Rights of Assent: Transformations in the Symbolic Construction of America.* New York: Routledge, 1993.

Berkhofer, Robert F. *The White Man's Indian: Images of the Indian from Columbus to the Present.* New York: Knopf, 1978.

Beider, Robert E. *Science Encounters the Indian, 1820–1880: The Early Years of American Ethnology.* Norman: University of Oklahoma Press, 1986.

Bhabha, Homi K. *The Location of Culture.* London: Routledge, 1994.

Boemeling, Carol. "Cherokee Indian Agents, 1830–1874." *Chronicles of Oklahoma* 50 (Winter 1972–73): 437–57.

Bogue, Allan G. *From Prairie to Corn Belt: Farming on the Illinois and Iowa Prairies in the Nineteenth Century.* Chicago: University of Chicago Press, 1963.

Bolt, Christine. *American Indian Policy and American Reform*. London: Allen and Unwin, 1987.

Brown, Loren N. "The Dawes Commission." *Chronicles of Oklahoma* 9 (March 1931): 71–105.

———. "The Establishment of the Dawes Commission for the Indian Territory." *Chronicles of Oklahoma* 18 (March 1940): 171–81.

Burke, Joseph C. "The Cherokee Cases: A Study in Law, Politics, and Morality." *Stanford Law Review* 21 (February 1969): 500–31.

Burton, Jeffrey. *Indian Territory and the United States, 1866–1906: Courts, Government, and the Movement for Oklahoma Statehood*. Norman: University of Oklahoma Press, 1995.

Canfield, Gae Whitney. *Sarah Winnemucca of the Northern Paiutes*. Norman: University of Oklahoma, 1983.

Caywood, Elzie Ronald. "The Administration of William C. Rogers: Principal Chief of the Cherokee Nation, 1903–1907." *Chronicles of Oklahoma* 30 (Spring 1952): 29–37.

Champagne, Duane. *Social Order and Political Change: Constitutional Governments among the Cherokee, the Choctaw, the Chickasaw, and the Creek*. Stanford CA: Stanford University Press, 1992.

Chapman, Berlin B. "The Cherokee Commission, 1889–1893." *Indiana Magazine of History* 42 (June 1942): 177–90.

———. "Secret Instructions and Suggestions to the Cherokee Commission, 1889–1890." *Chronicles of Oklahoma* 26 (Winter 1948): 449–58.

Chaput, Donald. "Generals, Indian Agents, and Politicians: The Doolittle Survey of 1865." *Western Historical Quarterly* 3 (July 1972): 269–82.

Cochran, Thomas C., and William Miller. *The Age of Enterprise: A Social History of Industrial America*. 1942. Revised. New York: Harper and Row, 1961.

Colbert, Thomas Burnell. "Visionary or Rogue? The Life and Legacy of Elias Cornelius Boudinot." *Chronicles of Oklahoma* 65 (Fall 1987): 268–81.

Coleman, Michael C. *Presbyterian Missionary Attitudes toward American Indians, 1837–1893*. Jackson: University Press of Mississippi, 1985.

Conser, Walter H., Jr. "John Ross and the Cherokee Resistance Campaign, 1833–1838." *Journal of Southern History* 44 (May 1978): 191–212.

Danziger, Edmund J., Jr. *Indians and Bureaucrats: Administering the Reser-*

vation Policy During the Civil War. Urbana: University of Illinois Press, 1974.

———. "The Office of Indian Affairs and the Problem of Civil War Refugees in Kansas." *Kansas Historical Quarterly* 35 (Autumn 1969): 257–75.

Darling, Ernest F. "Lincoln's Message to the Indian Territory." *Chronicles of Oklahoma* 63 (Summer 1985): 186–91.

Davis, Kenneth Penn. "The Cherokee Removal, 1835–1838." *Tennessee Historical Quarterly* 32 (Winter 1975): 311–30.

Debo, Angie. *And Still the Waters Run.* Princeton NJ: Princeton University Press, 1940.

———. *The Road to Disappearance: A History of the Creek Indians.* Norman: University of Oklahoma Press, 1941.

Degler, Carl N. *The Age of the Economic Revolution, 1876–1900.* Glenview IL: Scott and Forseman, 1967.

Denson, Andrew. "Muskogee's Indian International Fairs: Tribal Autonomy and the Indian Image in the Late Nineteenth Century." *Western Historical Quarterly* 34 (Autumn 2003): 325–45.

———. "'Unite with Us to Rescue the Kiowa's': The Five Civilized Tribes and Warfare on the Southern Plains." *Chronicles of Oklahoma* 81 (Winter 2003–2004): 458–79.

Dippie, Brian. *The Vanishing American: White Attitudes and U.S. Indian Policy.* Middletown CT: Wesleyan University Press, 1982.

Doran, Michael F. "Population Statistics of Nineteenth Century Indian Territory." *Chronicles of Oklahoma* 53 (Winter 1975–76): 492–515.

Drinnon, Richard. *Facing West: The Metaphysics of Indian-Hating and Empire-Building.* Minneapolis: University of Minnesota Press, 1980.

Edmunds, R. David, ed. *American Indian Leaders: Studies in Diversity.* Lincoln: University of Nebraska Press, 1980.

Fischer, LeRoy H. "United States Indian Agents to the Five Civilized Tribes." *Chronicles of Oklahoma* 50 (Winter 1972–73): 410–14.

Foner, Eric. *Reconstruction: America's Unfinished Revolution.* New York: Harper and Row, 1988.

———. *The Story of American Freedom.* New York: W. W. Norton, 1998.

Foreman, Carolyn Thomas. "Joseph Absalom Scales." *Chronicles of Oklahoma* 28 (Winter 1950): 418–33.

———. "The Coodey Family of the Indian Territory." *Chronicles of Oklahoma* 25 (Fall 1947): 323–41.

Foreman, Grant. *The Five Civilized Tribes.* Norman: University of Oklahoma Press, 1934.

———. *A History of Oklahoma.* Norman: University of Oklahoma Press, 1942.

———. *Indian Removal.* Norman: University of Oklahoma Press, 1938.

———. "The Trial of Stand Watie." *Chronicles of Oklahoma* 12 (Fall 1934): 305–39.

Franks, Kenneth. "The Implementation of the Confederate Treaties with the Five Civilized Tribes." *Chronicles of Oklahoma* 51 (Spring 1973): 21–33.

———. *Stand Watie and the Agony of the Cherokee Nation.* Memphis TN: Memphis State University Press, 1979.

Fredrickson, George M. *The Arrogance of Race: Historical Perspectives on Slavery, Racism, and Social Inequality.* Middletown CT: Wesleyan University Press, 1988.

———. *The Inner Civil War: Northern Intellectuals and the Crisis of the Union.* New York: Harper and Row, 1965.

Gaines, W. Craig. *The Confederate Cherokees: John Drew's Regiment of Mounted Rifles.* Baton Rouge: Louisiana State University Press, 1989.

Garrison, Tim Allen. *The Legal Ideology of Removal: The Southern Judiciary and the Sovereignty of Native American Nations.* Athens: University of Georgia Press, 2002.

Gates, Warren J. "Modernizing as a Function of an Agricultural Fair: The Great Grangers' Picnic Exhibition of Williams Grove, Pennsylvania 1873–1916." *Agricultural History* 58 (Fall 1984): 262–79.

Gibson, Arrell Morgan. "An Indian Territory United Nations: The Creek Council of 1845." *Chronicles of Oklahoma* 39 (Winter 1961–62): 398–413.

Gittinger, Roy. *Formation of the State of Oklahoma, 1803–1906.* Norman: University of Oklahoma Press, 1939.

Goodrich, Carter. *Government Promotion of American Canals and Railroads, 1800–1899.* New York: Columbia University Press, 1960.

Hagan, William T. *United States-Comanche Relations: The Reservation Years.* New Haven CT: Yale University Press, 1976.

Harmon, Alexandra. "American Indians and Land Monopoly in the Gilded Age." *Journal of American History* 90 (June 2003): 106–33.

Harring, Sidney L. *Crow Dog's Case: American Indian Sovereignty, Tribal Law, and United States Law in the Nineteenth Century.* New York: Cambridge University Press, 1995.

Harris, Neil. *Cultural Excursions: Marketing Appetites and Cultural Tastes in Modern America.* Chicago: University of Chicago Press, 1990.

Heimann, Robert K. "The Cherokee Tobacco Case." *Chronicles of Oklahoma* 41 (Fall 1963): 299–322.

Hendrix, Janey B. "Redbird Smith and the Nighthawk Keetoowahs." *Journal of Cherokee Studies* 8 (Spring 1983): 22–29, (Fall 1983): 73–85.

Hinsley, Curtis M., Jr. *Savages and Scientists: The Smithsonian Institution and the Development of American Anthropology, 1846–1910.* Washington DC: Smithsonian Institution Press, 1981.

Horsman, Reginald. *Race and Manifest Destiny: The Origins of American Racial Anglo-Saxonism.* Cambridge MA: Harvard University Press, 1981.

Hoxie, Frederick E. *A Final Promise: The Campaign to Assimilate the Indians, 1880–1920.* Lincoln: University of Nebraska Press, 1984.

Hudson, Charles M. *The Southeastern Indians.* Knoxville: University of Tennessee Press, 1976.

Jaher, Frederic Cople, ed. *The Age of Industrialism in America: Essays in Social Structure and Cultural Values.* New York: Free Press, 1968.

Jaimes, M. Annette, ed. *The State of Native America: Genocide, Colonization, and Resistance.* Boston: South End, 1992.

Johnson, Walter A. "Brief History of the Missouri-Kansas-Texas Railroad Lines." *Chronicles of Oklahoma* 24 (Fall 1946): 340–58.

Josephy, Alvin. *The Civil War in the American West.* New York: Knopf, 1991.

Kammen, Michael. *A Season of Youth: The American Revolution and the Historical Imagination.* New York: Knopf, 1978.

Keith, Harold. "Problems of a Cherokee Principal Chief." *Chronicles of Oklahoma* 17 (Fall 1938): 296–308.

Keller, Morton. *Affairs of State: Public Life in Late Nineteenth Century America.* Cambridge MA: Harvard University Press, 1977.

Keller, Robert H., Jr. *American Protestantism and American Indian Policy, 1869–82.* Lincoln: University of Nebraska Press, 1983.

Kelman, Ari. "Deadly Currents: John Ross's Decision of 1861." *Chronicles of Oklahoma* 73 (Spring 1995): 80–103.

Kelton, Paul. "William Penn Adair: Cherokee Slaveholder and Indian Freedom Advocate." *Chronicles of Oklahoma* 77 (Spring 1999): 22–53.

Klein, Maury. *Unfinished Business: The Railroad in American Life*. Hanover NH: University Press of New England, 1994.

———. *Union Pacific: Birth of a Railroad, 1862–1893*. New York: Doubleday, 1987.

Kniffen, Fred. "The American Agricultural Fair: The Pattern." *Annals of the Association of American Geographers* 39 (1949): 264–82.

———. "The American Agricultural Fair: Time and Place." *Annals of the Association of American Geographers* 41 (1951): 42–57.

Kremm, Thomas W., and Diane Neal. "Civil War Controversy." *Chronicles of Oklahoma* 70 (Spring 1992): 26–45.

Krupat, Arnold. *Ethnocriticism: Ethnography, History, and Literature*. Berkeley and Los Angeles: University of California Press, 1992.

Leeds, Georgia Rae. *The United Keetoowah Band of Cherokee Indians in Oklahoma*. New York: Peter Lang, 1996.

Littlefield, Daniel F. *The Cherokee Freedmen: From Emancipation to American Citizenship*. Westport CT: Greenwood, 1978.

Litton, Gaston L. "The Principal Chiefs of the Cherokee Nation." *Chronicles of Oklahoma* 15 (Fall 1937): 253–70.

Maddox, Lucy. *Removals: Nineteenth-Century American Literature and the Politics of Indian Affairs*. New York: Oxford University Press, 1991.

Mahon, John, ed. *Indians of the Lower South: Past and Present*. Pensacola FL: Gulf Coast History and Humanities Conference, 1975.

Marbut, F. B. *News from the Capitol: The Story of Washington Reporting*. Carbondale: Southern Illinois University Press, 1971.

Mardock, Robert. *The Reformers and the Indian*. Columbia: University of Missouri Press, 1971.

Maxwell, Amos. "The Sequoyah Convention." *Chronicles of Oklahoma* 28 (Summer 1950): 161–92, (Fall 1950): 199–340.

May, Katja. *African Americans and Native Americans in the Creek and Cherokee Nations, 1830s to 1920s*. New York: Garland, 1996.

Mayall, Mildred P. *The Kiowas*. Norman: University of Oklahoma Press, 1971.

McLoughlin, William G. *After the Trail of Tears: The Cherokees' Struggle for Sovereignty, 1839–1880*. Chapel Hill: University of North Carolina Press, 1993.

———. *Champions of the Cherokees: Evan and John B. Jones*. Princeton NJ: Princeton University Press, 1990.

————. *The Cherokees and Christianity, 1794–1870: Essays on Acculturation and Cultural Persistence.* Athens: University of Georgia Press, 1994.

————. *Cherokees and Missionaries, 1789–1839.* New Haven CT: Yale University Press, 1984.

————. *Cherokee Renascence in the New Republic.* Princeton NJ: Princeton University Press, 1986.

McNeill, Kenneth. "Confederate Treaties with the Tribes of the Indian Territory." *Chronicles of Oklahoma* 42 (Winter 1964–65): 408–20.

Mercer, Lloyd J. *Railroads and Land Grant Policy: A Study in Government Intervention.* New York: Academic Press, 1982.

Meserve, John Bartlett. "Chief Colonel Johnson Harris." *Chronicles of Oklahoma* 17 (Spring 1938): 17–21.

————. "Chief Dennis Wolfe Bushyhead." *Chronicles of Oklahoma* 13 (Fall 1935): 349–59.

————. "Chief Lewis Downing and Chief Charles Thompson (Oochalata)." *Chronicles of Oklahoma* 16 (Fall 1938): 315–25.

————. "Chief Thomas Mitchell Buffington and Chief William Charles Rogers." *Chronicles of Oklahoma* 17 (Summer 1939): 135–46.

————. "The Mayes." *Chronicles of Oklahoma* 15 (March 1937): 56–65.

————. "William Potter Ross." *Chronicles of Oklahoma* 15 (Spring 1937): 21–29.

Milam, John B. "The Opening of the Cherokee Outlet." *Chronicles of Oklahoma* 9–10 (Fall, Winter, Spring 1931–32): 268–86, 454–75, 115–37.

Milne, Gordon. *The American Political Novel.* Norman: University of Oklahoma Press, 1966.

Milner, Clyde. *With Good Intentions: Quaker Work among the Pawnees, Otoes, and Omahas in the 1870s.* Lincoln: University of Nebraska Press, 1982.

Miner, H. Craig. *The Corporation and the Indian: Tribal Sovereignty and Industrial Civilization in the Indian Territory, 1865–1907.* 1976. Reprint. Norman: University of Oklahoma Press, 1988.

Moore, Cherie Adair. "William Penn Adair." *Chronicles of Oklahoma* 29 (Spring 1951): 32–41.

Morgan, H. Wayne, ed. *The Gilded Age: A Reappraisal.* Syracuse NY: Syracuse University Press, 1963.

Moses, L. G. *Wild West Shows and the Images of American Indians, 1883–1933.* Albuquerque: University of New Mexico Press, 1996.

Moulton, Gary E. *John Ross: Cherokee Chief*. Athens: University of Georgia Press, 1978.

———. "John Ross and W. P. Dole: A Case Study of Lincoln's Indian Policy." *Journal of the West* 12 (July 1973): 414–23.

Murray, David. *Forked Tongues: Speech, Writing, and Representation in American Indian Texts*. Bloomington: Indiana University Press, 1991.

Nelson, Dana. *The Word in Black and White: Reading "Race" in American Literature, 1638–1867*. New York: Oxford University Press, 1982.

Nichols, David. *Lincoln and the Indians: Civil War Policy and Politics*. Columbia: University of Missouri Press, 1978.

Noonan, John T., Jr. *Bribes*. New York: MacMillan, 1984.

Norgren, Jill. *The Cherokee Cases: The Confrontation of Law and Politics*. New York: McGraw-Hill, 1996.

Nye, Wilbur S. *Carbine and Lance: The Story of Old Fort Sill*. Norman: University of Oklahoma Press, 1942.

Painter, Nell Irvin. *Standing at Armageddon: The United States, 1877–1919*. New York: W. W. Norton, 1987.

Pearce, Roy Harvey. *Savagism and Civilization: A Study of the Indian and the American Mind*. Baltimore: Johns Hopkins Press, 1967.

Perdue, Theda. *Cherokee Women: Gender and Culture Change, 1700–1835*. Lincoln: University of Nebraska Press, 1998.

———. *"Mixed Blood" Indians: Racial Construction in the Early South*. Athens: University of Georgia Press, 2003.

Perdue, Theda, and Michael Green. *The Columbia Guide to American Indians of the Southeast*. New York: Columbia University Press, 2001.

Prosterman, Leslie. *Ordinary Life, Festival Days: Aesthetics in the Midwestern County Fair*. Washington DC: Smithsonian Institution Press, 1995.

Prucha, Francis Paul. *American Indian Policy in Crisis: Christian Reformers and the Indian, 1865–1900*. Norman: University of Oklahoma Press, 1976.

———. *American Indian Policy in the Formative Years: The Trade and Intercourse Acts*. Cambridge MA: Harvard University Press, 1962.

———. *American Indian Treaties: The History of a Political Anomaly*. Berkeley and Los Angeles: University of California Press, 1994.

———. "Andrew Jackson's Indian Policy: A Reassessment." *Journal of American History* 56 (December 1969): 527–39.

————. "The Board of Indian Commissioners and the Delegates of the Five Tribes." *Chronicles of Oklahoma* 56 (Fall 1978): 247–64.

————. *The Great Father*. Lincoln: University of Nebraska Press, 1984.

Rampp, Larry C., and Donald L. Rampp. *The Civil War in the Indian Territory*. Austin: University of Texas Press, 1975.

Ritchie, Donald A. *Press Gallery: Congress and the Washington Correspondents*. Cambridge MA: Harvard University Press, 1991.

Robinson, Ella. "Indian International Fair." *Chronicles of Oklahoma* 17 (Fall 1939): 413–16.

Royce, Charles G. *The Cherokee Nation of Indians*. Chicago: Aldine, 1975.

Rydell, Robert W. *All the World's a Fair: Visions of Empire at American International Expositions, 1876–1916*. Chicago: University of Chicago Press, 1984.

————. *The Books of the Fairs: Materials About World's Fairs, 1834–1916, in the Smithsonian Institution Libraries*. Chicago: American Library Association, 1992.

Satz, Ronald. *American Indian Policy in the Jacksonian Era*. Lincoln: University of Nebraska Press, 1975.

Savage, William W., Jr. *The Cherokee Strip Live Stock Association: Federal Regulation and the Cattleman's Last Frontier*. Columbia: University of Missouri Press, 1973.

Saxton, Alexander. *The Rise and Fall of the White Republic: Class Politics and Mass Culture in Nineteenth-Century America*. London: Verso, 1990.

Sharpe, Jenny. "Figures of Colonial Resistance." *Modern Fiction Studies* 35 (Spring 1989): 137–55.

Shea, William J., and Earl J. Hess. *Pea Ridge: Civil War Campaign in the West*. Chapel Hill: University of North Carolina Press, 1992.

Sheehan, Bernard W. *Seeds of Extinction: Jeffersonian Philanthropy and the American Indian*. Chapel Hill: University of North Carolina Press, 1973.

Slotkin, Richard. *The Fatal Environment: The Myth of the Frontier in the Age of Industrialization, 1800–1890*. New York: Atheneum, 1985.

Smedley, Audrey. *Race in North America: Origin and Evolution of a Worldview*. Boulder CO: Westview, 1993.

Sober, Nancy Hope. *The Intruders: Illegal Residents of the Cherokee Nation, 1866–1907*. Ponca City OK: Cherokee Books, 1991.

Somkin, Fred. *Unquiet Eagle: Memory and Desire in the Idea of American Freedom*. Ithaca NY: Cornell University Press, 1967.

Stanton, William. *The Leopard's Spots: Scientific Attitudes toward Race in America, 1815–1859*. Chicago: University of Chicago Press, 1960.

Starr, Emmet. *History of the Cherokee Indians and their Legends and Folk Lore*. Oklahoma City: Warden, 1921.

Strickland, Rennard. *Fire and the Spirits: Cherokee Law from Clan to Court*. Norman: University of Oklahoma Press, 1975.

Sturm, Circe. *Blood Politics: Race, Culture, and Identity in the Cherokee Nation of Oklahoma*. Berkeley and Los Angeles: University of California Press, 2002.

Summers, Mark W. *The Era of Good Stealings*. New York: Oxford University Press, 1993.

Takaki, Ronald. *Iron Cages: Race and Culture in Nineteenth-Century America*. New York: Knopf, 1979.

Thompson, Margaret Susan. *The "Spider Web:" Congress and Lobbying in the Age of Grant*. Ithaca NY: Cornell University Press, 1985.

Thornton, Russell. *The Cherokees: A Population History*. Lincoln: University of Nebraska Press, 1990.

Trachtenberg, Alan. *The Incorporation of America: Culture and Society in the Gilded Age*. New York: Hill and Wang, 1982.

Utley, Robert M. *Frontier Regulars: The United States Army and the Indian, 1866–1891*. New York: MacMillan, 1973.

Viola, Herman J. *Thomas L. McKenney: Architect of America's Early Indian Policy, 1816–1830*. Chicago: Sage Books, 1974.

Vipperman, Carl J. "Forcibly If We Must: The Georgia Case for the Cherokee Removal, 1802–1832." *Journal of Cherokee Studies* 3 (Spring 1978): 104–11.

Ward, Mary Jane. "Fight For Survival: The Indian Response to the Boomer Movement." *Chronicles of Oklahoma* 67 (Spring 1989): 30–49.

Wardell, Morris. *A Political History of the Cherokee Nation, 1838–1907*. 1938. Reprint. Norman: University of Oklahoma Press, 1977.

Ware, James W. "Indian Territory." *Journal of the West* 12 (July 1973): 490–98.

Watson, Harry L. *Liberty and Power: The Politics of Jacksonian America*. New York: Hill and Wang, 1990.

Weeks, Philip. "From War to Peace: Rutherford B. Hayes and the Administration of Indian Affairs, 1877–1881." *Old Northwest* 11 (Fall 1985): 149–72.

Bibliography

Wilkins, Thurman. *Cherokee Tragedy: The Ridge Family and the Decimation of a People*. 1970. Revised. Norman: University of Oklahoma Press, 1986.

Williams, Robert A., Jr. *Linking Arms Together: American Indian Visions of Law and Peace, 1600–1800*. New York: Routledge, 1999.

Wilson, T. Paul. "Delegates of the Five Civilized Tribes to the Confederate Congress." *Chronicles of Oklahoma* 53 (Fall 1975): 353–66. Young, Robert. *White Mythologies: Writing History and the West*. London: Routledge, 1990.

INDEX

In the *Indians of the Southeast* series

William Bartram on the Southeastern Indians
Edited and annotated by Gregory A. Waselkov and
Kathryn E. Holland Braund

Deerskins and Duffels
The Creek Indian Trade with Anglo-America, 1685–1815
By Kathryn E. Holland Braund

Searching for the Bright Path
The Mississippi Choctaws from Prehistory to Removal
By James Taylor Carson

Demanding the Cherokee Nation
Indian Autonomy and American Culture, 1830–1900
By Andrew Denson

Cherokee Americans
The Eastern Band of Cherokees in the Twentieth Century
By John R. Finger

Choctaw Genesis, 1500–1700
By Patricia Galloway

The Southeastern Ceremonial Complex
Artifacts and Analysis
The Cottonlandia Conference
Edited by Patricia Galloway
Exhibition Catalog by David H. Dye and Camille Wharey

The Invention of the Creek Nation, 1670–1763
By Steven C. Hahn

An Assumption of Sovereignty
Social and Political Transformation among
the Florida Seminoles, 1953–1979
By Harry A. Kersey Jr.

The Caddo Chiefdoms
Caddo Economics and Politics, 700–1835
By David La Vere

Choctaws in a Revolutionary Age, 1750–1830
By Greg O'Brien

Cherokee Women
Gender and Culture Change, 1700–1835
By Theda Perdue

The Brainerd Journal
A Mission to the Cherokees, 1817–1823
Edited and introduced by Joyce B. Phillips and Paul Gary Phillips

The Cherokees
A Population History
By Russell Thornton

Buffalo Tiger
A Life in the Everglades
By Buffalo Tiger and Harry A. Kersey Jr.

American Indians in the Lower Mississippi Valley
Social and Economic Histories
By Daniel H. Usner Jr.

Powhatan's Mantle
Indians in the Colonial Southeast
Edited by Peter H. Wood, Gregory A. Waselkov, and M. Thomas Hatley

Creeks and Seminoles
The Destruction and Regeneration of the Muscogulge People
By J. Leitch Wright Jr.